D1187720

Reforging a Forgotten History

Reforging a Forgotten History
Iraq and the Assyrians in the Twentieth Century

Sargon George Donabed

EDINBURGH
University Press

© Sargon George Donabed, 2015

Transferred to digital print 2015

Edinburgh University Press Ltd
The Tun – Holyrood Road
12 (2f) Jackson's Entry
Edinburgh EH8 8PJ
www.euppublishing.com

Typeset in 11/15 Adobe Garamond by
Servis Filmsetting Ltd, Stockport, Cheshire,
and printed and bound in Great Britain by
CPI Group (UK) Ltd, Croydon CR0 4YY

A CIP record for this book is available from the British Library

ISBN 978 0 7486 8602 5 (hardback)
ISBN 978 0 7486 8603 2 (webready PDF)
ISBN 978 0 7486 8605 6 (epub)

The right of Sargon George Donabed to be identified as author of
this work has been asserted in accordance with the Copyright, Designs
and Patents Act 1988 and the Copyright and Related Rights
Regulations 2003 (SI No. 2498).

Published with the support of the Edinburgh University Scholarly
Publishing Initiatives Fund.

Contents

Figures

Tables

Abbreviations

AAS	Assyrian Academic Society
ADM	Assyrian Democratic Movement
ADO	Assyrian Democratic Organization
AI	Amnesty International
AIDP	Association internationale de droit pénal
AIJ	International Alliance for Justice
AIR	Air Ministry Files, Public Record Office, London
AUA	Assyrian Universal Alliance
CO	Colonial Office Files, Public Record Office, London
FIDH	International Federation for Human Rights
FO	Foreign Office Files, Public Record Office, London
HRW	Human Rights Watch
ICP	Iraqi Communist Party
IMF	Iraq Memory Foundation
IPC	Iraqi Petroleum Company
KDP	Kurdistan Democratic Party
MARA	Modern Assyrian Research Archive
NARA	National Archives and Records Administration (USA)
NCRD	Nineveh Center for Research and Development
PUK	Patriotic Union of Kurdistan
RAF	Royal Air Force
TNA	The National Archives (UK)
UAR	United Arab Republic
UNGC	United Nations Genocide Convention
XXH	Kheit Kheit Allap I & II

Acknowledgements

I am indebted to a variety of people for their support and kindness. Firstly, without the diligence and guidance from the team at EUP – Nicola Ramsey, Ellie Bush, Eddie Clark, Rebecca Mackenzie and especially my copy editor, Jonathan Wadman – I don't know how this work could have found its culmination. Cheers to you all.

A special thanks to those who passed on personal experiences – specifically Elias Haroon, who was kind enough to allow me to articulate his story. Elias Haroon survived the massacre at Simele as a young child. During our interview session he remarked on my research protocols for the oral history portion. Assuring him that I would not use his name in the study if so desired, Elias responded, 'I will give you my name, and my father's name, as well as that of my grandfather. Anyone who does not is not truly a man.' After some months had passed following my initial ethnographic research, I recall receiving a phone call one afternoon. Elias asked me one simple question in his native tongue: 'Lad, when will your book come out?'

'Soon. It will take some time,' I responded.

Elias took a deep breath and began, 'Our story has to come out. It is important. People should know what happened to the Assyrians during Simele or in the villages years later. No one knows our story.'

I thanked him for his confidence in my work and for all of his information and material and assured him the book would indeed be printed. Despite this, till today I never truly grasped the importance of an academic work to real people. Of course I had lofty ideas that what I did mattered, but that was more a way to assuage any feelings of inadequacy. The truth was, it meant a great deal to Elias, as it revealed his life, his experience, indeed his significance. 'Someone has to tell our story, tell the world what happened to us. Just so they know, just so they know.' I hope I did them justice. Without them, this work would never exist.

To my family and friends, especially George and Elsie, Ninos, Shamiran, Heather Snow, Manuel and Anna Sousa and family, and the unsung heroes, Cheeks, Ghost, Monster† (we miss you, little one) and Tails, wherever he may be – this work was born of your constant support and empathy, including a persistent reminder that amid such undertakings there is neither substitute nor greater inspiration than joy come of gratitude for being a part of something larger than oneself.

Further, much appreciation for their invaluable aid is due to Peter Sluglett, Hannibal Travis, Mar Emmanuel Emmanuel, Mikhael Benjamin, David Malick, Hormuz Bobo, Afram Koumi, Nahrin Barkho, Fadi Dawood, Ferida Danyal, Father Gregory Christakos, Nicholas Al-Jeloo, Tomas Isik, Aryo Makko, Efrem Yildiz, Nineb Lamassu, Atour and Janey Golani, Michael Youash, Joseph Hermiz, Firas Jatou, Yourem Mako, Efrem Yildiz, Robert Karoukian, Ninos David, Alda Benjamen, Mark Tomass, Peter BetBasoo and Shamiran Zendo. Ann Hanson for her aid in indexing. Also to the Roger Williams University Foundation to Promote Scholarship and teaching for granting me time to write through course releases. While the following have passed on, this work would have been impossible without their efforts: Yacoub Khoshaba and his photographs of Barwar's destruction, Professor Father J. Brian Peckham (1934–2008) for his kindness and compassion as well as direction, Dr Hirmis Aboona (1940–2009) for his generosity and pioneering, and Dr Donny George Youkhanna (1950–2011) for his courage and resolve. Although we never met, a special heartfelt thanks to James Oliver Rigney Jr (Robert Jordan, 1948–2007), who created a world with friends who have been my companions for many years. His creativity remains an inspiring reminder of the power inherent in the fashioning of stories.

> The Wheel of Time turns, and Ages come and pass, leaving memories that become legend. Legend fades to myth, and even myth is long forgotten when the Age that gave it birth comes again. In one Age, called the Third Age by some, an Age yet to come, an Age long past, a wind rose in the Mountains of Mist. The wind was not the beginning. There are neither beginnings nor endings to the turning of the Wheel of Time. But it was *a* beginning.
>
> Robert Jordan, *Eye of the World* (1990)

For my parents, George and Elsie Donabed

In memory of Shamson Orahem Babella (1924–2012),
the most brilliant storyteller I had the honour of knowing.

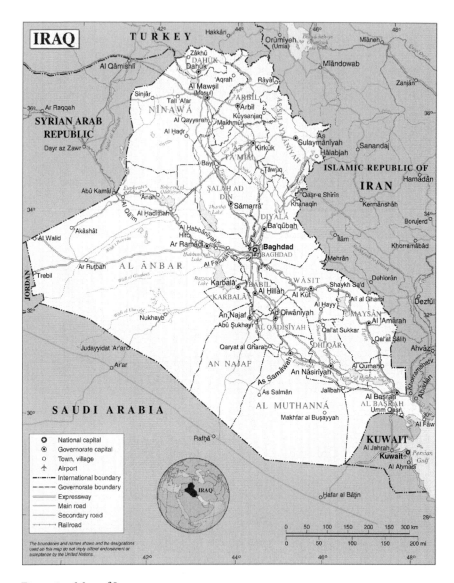

Figure 1   Map of Iraq

Introduction

Inspired by the suffering of Iraq's martyrs – Sunni and Shiite, Arab, Kurd, and Turkomen, and the remaining brethren in all communities – inspired by the injustice against the holy cities in the popular uprising and against the marshes and other places; recalling the agonies of the national oppression in the massacres of Halabja, Barzan, Anfal and against the Faili Kurds; inspired by the tragedies of the Turkomen in Bashir and the suffering of the people of the western region . . .[1]

Constitution of Iraq (2005)

Half of writing history is hiding the truth.

Captain Malcolm Reynolds, Serenity (2005)

An unnamed song is like an unnamed child, it has no identity.

Robyn Hitchcock, musician

Recent events in Iraq, especially those which surfaced between January and March of 2014 calling for an autonomous or independent state in the Nineveh province of the country, have brought the minority issue and the Assyrians closer to the spotlight. In theory, the province could become a bastion for the ethnic and religious minorities who have become the last living link to ancient Mesopotamia in a period where their numbers have drastically decreased due to displacement, war, immigration, economic hardship, and ethno-religious and political discrimination.[2] Demographic change would speak to that reality as the overall population of Christians, the overwhelming majority of whom are of Assyrian descent, decreased from 1.4 million in 1987 to approximately 750,000, or 3 per cent of the Iraqi population, by

2005, according to the United States Department of State. In the 1980s they made up roughly 30 per cent of the population of the northern regions of Iraq and there were approximately 700,000 more living in diaspora.[3] Between 2005 and 2014 many continued to find themselves part of a disproportionate number of internally displaced persons with little hope of an end to their plight.[4]

On 10 June 2014 the group known originally as the Islamic State of Iraq and the Levant/Syria (ISIL/ISIS) and later simply as IS, began to take control of Mosul, marking Christian houses with the Arabic letter N for Nazarene/Christian. Those who could not pay the Islamic tax or *jizya* were forced to convert or flee. By late July there were no Christians left in Mosul, the few families who remained forced to convert, and all of the churches and monasteries not destroyed had come under IS control. On the road to the elimination of anything deemed contrary to their particular view of Islam, IS destroyed shrines such as that of Nabi Yunis/the Prophet Jonah, which sat atop a church and earlier an ancient Assyrian temple, now part of the rubble. Between the destruction of the old Christian sites, ancient temples and artefacts, and conversion/forced expulsion, few remnants of Assyrian identity and life survive.[5]

By 8 August IS had captured the last Assyrian strongholds in the region, namely Qaraqosh/Baghdede, Alqosh, Tel Keppe and Karamles, forcing approximately 200,000 Christians and their families to flee to Iraqi Kurdistan. Many more fled outside the Middle East with aid from their kin in diaspora. IS then took the Sinjar Mountains, and in the process drove any Yezidis who had not been killed or captured and sold into slavery into the harsh terrain, where many died of thirst in the 45°C heat. Some were used as human shields against pêşmerge troops while taking Christian villages.[6] It was a human rights disaster. Further, even the military actions of the United States would have repercussions as depleted uranium from missiles and bombs has poisoned the earth and groundwater, making the region more and more of an enormous brownfield.[7] In reality there may soon be no Assyrians left in the region as remnants of ancient Mesopotamia, both animate and inanimate, have become existentially threatened in Iraq.

But these events, taken out of their historical context, may not make a great deal of sense to readers who have no knowledge of the Assyrians, whether in the context of their diaspora, Iraq or the Middle East in general.[8]

The Assyrians

Geographically, Assyrians are a transnational population indigenous to northern Mesopotamia (effectively ancient Assyria and its environs), part of today's northern Iraq, southeastern Turkey, northwestern Iran and northeastern Syria.[9] They speak Assyrian, sometimes referred to as a modern form of Mesopotamian Aramaic (also more commonly in scholarly parlance as Neo-Aramaic and Neo-Syriac), with a heavy Akkadian influence (both Akkadian and Aramaic were official languages in the ancient Neo-Assyrian Empire, which flourished from 934 BC to approximately 600 BC)[10] as well as utilising classical Syriac as an ecclesiastical tongue. Today many continue to affiliate with one of the following Christian religious communities: the Chaldean Catholic Church, the Assyrian Church of the East (referred to as Nestorian), the Syrian Orthodox Church (referred to as Jacobite and originally in English as Assyrian Apostolic)[11] and the Syrian Catholic Church.[12] In the past two millennia, the Assyrians have been more widely known by their ecclesiastical designations, increasingly balkanised, mostly due to their incorporation into Muslim-dominated states.[13]

Their language and material culture constitutes the oldest continuous tradition in Iraq. From ancient Arba'ilū to Arbela during the Christian period in the ecclesiastical province of Adiabene between the fifth and the fifteenth centuries, the presence and culture of the people of upper Mesopotamia endured. Adiabene itself included Mosul, Nineveh, Karkā d-Beth Slōkh (ancient Arrapḫa and today's Kirkuk), Beth Nuhadra (today's Dohuk) and beyond, but as part of the central authority of the so-called Nestorian Church or Assyrian Church of the East.[14]

Despite this history, Assyrians are both actively (directly) and passively (indirectly) unimagined from the Middle East, its culture and its history, even in periods where they play a pivotal role. In true Gramscian fashion, they are functionally of the subaltern. Few people know of these remnants of the ancient world and their history, particularly in a twenty-first-century context. Part of the lacunae stems from popular culture and knowledge accumulated from soundbites of modern media and scholarship, which have labelled

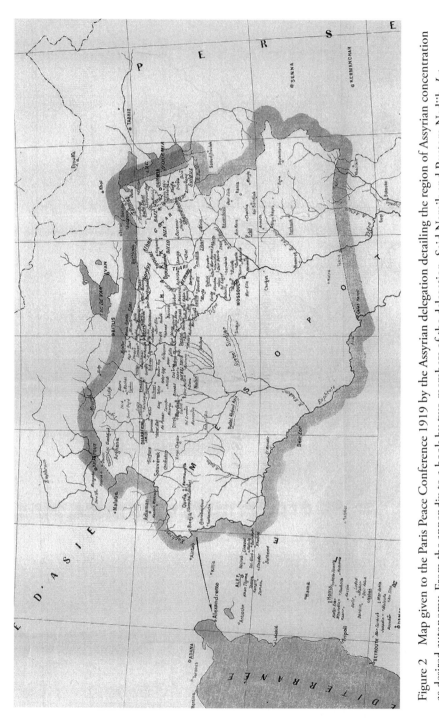

Figure 2   Map given to the Paris Peace Conference 1919 by the Assyrian delegation detailing the region of Assyrian concentration as desired autonomy. From the appendix to a book by two members of the delegation, Saïd Namik and Rustom Nedjib, *La Question assyro-chaldéenne devant la Conférence de la paix* (Paris, 1919). The term 'Assyro-chaldéenne' is a French-created noun that reflects the Franco-Catholic focus on the Catholic/Chaldean religious element of the Assyrians, which in turn harks back to the early Dominican missionary activity in Mesopotamia

and mislabelled these people with designations including Iraqi Christians, Kurdish Christians, Arab Christians, Syriac-speaking Christians, Aramaic-speaking Christians, Syrian Christians, Nestorians, Jacobites, Chaldeans, Persian Christians, Semitic Turks, Turkish Christians, and a host of other appellations. Besides displaying a lack of clarity and consistency, most of these terms are unapologetically unsuitable or with varying degrees of veracity have been imposed by others as more 'proper' historic identities. In some cases they have been actualised by the community itself, creating further confusion.[15]

This work is concerned with the Assyrians and their relationship to Iraq in the twentieth century.[16] Since the formation of the modern Middle East following the First World War they have been both a numerical and a political minority and thus have found little room for inclusion in the nation-states created after the war, in particular for the purposes of this study Iraq, with the exception of their commodification and commoditisation.[17] In previous literature, the Simele massacres of 1933, arguably the defining moment of Iraqi nationhood, are dismissed or glossed over with little attention paid to the personal experience of survivors.[18] The Anfal campaign (1988), made notorious by popular media outlets during the trial of Saddam Hussein, is framed solely as a Kurdish experience. The natural question becomes: were the Assyrians and other minorities simply bystanders – victims of collateral damage who played a passive role in the history of Iraq?

While views on ownership and possession (and by extension indigeneity) as expressions of power and agency have changed, a characteristic of the modern political climate as defined by still fairly feudal nation-states continues to be a numerically small, landless and dispossessed people, indigenous or not, as subordinate or at best ancillary to the past, present and future of the territory in question. The addition of an Assyrian narrative crafts an evocative history of Iraq and the Middle East in general. Stories which have been denigrated to footnotes in history books and the margins of memory are integral to producing and relating a more inclusive and representative accounting of events. Such stories represent living communities; each individual experience is both distinct and simultaneously reflective of the whole community and region.

History is a story, a memory of a memory and in some fashion a quest for immortality. The retelling of experience or narrative is an attempt to assure an instinctive human hope that something of worth will endure eternally. Yet, history is an equal process of forgetting, a counterpart to remembrance. As no story can ever be history in its totality but rather a perspective of the whole, *half of writing history* will always *hide truth* since certain perspectives inevitably subsume or consume others. The necessity of this investigation – its evidence, its analysis and the lacunae which it fills – begins with and is driven by a normative condition that there is meaning in all experience and, though limited by its perspective, integral to a more complete representation. It is an assumption that life and the experience thereof is always something of value, of worth. Thus it is this accepted pattern – stories of 'Sunni and Shiite, Arab, Kurd, and Turkomen', chronicles bereft of the Assyrians and their experience – which sparked this investigation, which seeks herein to reforge or reshape a history by bestowing a name to a character and a voice to a ballad, thereby restoring significance and meaning to an experience.

Language is a powerful tool. Terms and ideas have weight and further, they influence emotions and shape thoughts that in turn shape actions. Iraq, like all such labels, becomes what people define it to be; it becomes words on a page, words in the news, and while Iraq creates the news, media and books create Iraq and moreover how people view Iraq and how Iraq and the peoples of the region see themselves. Words can also derogate, denigrate and uncreate. As names sometimes epitomise and create people, individuals and communities (though they fall well short in an attempt to encompass their entireties in a simple word), so when such a name is overlooked, those it describes in essence lack form and being. The Assyrians lack identity as a part without its whole. So too without the Assyrians the historical record of Iraq is wanting. If the Assyrians are forgotten and fade, with them vanishes their perspective, the personification or avatar of the historical narrative, which this book reforges by acknowledging meaning as inherent to existence regardless of geopolitics. History or stories exist at all times and in all places. In the words of the Armenian–American writer William Saroyan from the short story *Seventy Thousand Assyrians*, 'I am thinking of Theodore Badal, himself seventy thousand Assyrians and seventy million Assyrians, himself Assyria, and man, standing in a barber shop, in San Francisco, in 1933, and being, still, himself, the whole race.' Hence this work lends new voices, like that of a Theodore Badal, to the record of the past, making them essential building blocks rather than the distant echoes to which they have been consigned.

Yet, in a more focused manner one must consider the query of historian Benjamin White: while these 'minorities are not marginal to the history of modern states, how has their history been marginalised?'[19] White offers reasons for how this is accomplished, pegging both majorities and minorities as culpable. In addition, something remains aloof that could ascertain not only the *how* but also the *why*. So this work addresses the following general questions:

1. Did/do Assyrians play an active role in the history of Iraq? If so, then
2. a. What are those ways in which the Assyrians contribute to (in this geopolitical case) Iraqi history?
   b. How and why is the Assyrian role in the (or a) narrative diminished or unnoticed both directly and indirectly and what purpose does that diminution serve?
   c. Is there a way to remedy it?

This inquiry begins from a purely inductive position leading back to the general deductive syllogistic method in order to problematise the lacunae of the Assyrians in Middle Eastern and Iraqi history, since it is the most undeviating tactic with measurable consequences, an Ockham's razor: major premise, minor premise and conclusion. The normative premise is that all peoples and communities are integral to the human history of the Middle East including Iraq; the Assyrians are a community of Iraq; the Assyrians are an integral part of Iraq.

On the other hand, how does one circumvent the perceived problem of exceptionality or uniqueness of experience? The continued debate over numerical and political minorities and indigenous peoples remains resolute in the belief that minority and indigenous histories are consistently exclusive and have no basis in the more official narratives including purportedly more inclusive ones. The phenomenon of the Assyrian–Iraqi case is, like any people/community, both exceptional and not. It is exceptional because it is not exceptional. In other words the non-exceptionality or lack of a marked history equal to all others and warranting equal exposure makes the case remarkable as it has thus far remained subordinate.

Initially, this study is at its core a microcosm for a macrocosm. If one accepts the premise, complete with the inherent impediments which may arise from it (a premise that remains appropriated by but little adhered to by researchers), that the best approach to understanding the past is a holistic one, inclusive of all its parts, and if the Assyrians have some relation to Iraq, then in order to more holistically or universally grasp Iraq and its modern history one must understand the Assyrians therein. This work weaves the Assyrians into the power relations of the formation and state-building processes of the Iraqi state in the twentieth century but also unpacks other narratives outside the traditional normative majoritist histories, all the while probing why some perspectives or histories are remembered, and others unheeded and unheard. Assyrian narratives of Iraqi history on their own illuminate a few major themes which mark them as an unequivocally recognised part of the historical milieu in the region. In order to make proper sense of the problem, initially, they must be understood as narratives within the discourse on Iraqi studies, creating the necessity of their inclusion as part and parcel of a more complete history.

Secondly, this work offers a technique for understanding the commodification and commoditisation of people, land and cultures, and thereby comprehending forms of extermination by examining the development of that commodification between the years 1933 and 1988. Furthermore, the book is a study of the deep correlation of place (or land) to identity and vice versa: how both identity and place (or land) and all their interactions influence the acceptance and availability of narratives/stories, which in turn influence perceptions of belonging and notions of home from internal and external viewpoints. Finally, if identity survives when place is destroyed, how does it shift, and further, is a new 'place', both figuratively and literally, found? The relationship of the Assyrians to the land and how that link is perceived is of great significance to this work.

This book also functions as a case in point of the unimagining of communities in the nation-building schema and the continued struggle for power, be it social, political, economic etc. From a more political angle, it delineates how emerging states respond to contentious pluralism or groups they perceive as a threat to their attempts at political, economic, social and territorial consolidation. Comparisons are drawn between the present narrative and that of other minorities and indigenous peoples and comparable events such as the Wounded Knee massacre of the Lakota by the United States 7th Cavalry regiment in 1890 and the treatment of Japanese Americans in the United States during the Second World War.

If we accept the premise of a holistic approach to history then the first act of the Iraqi regime's new military force against unarmed civilians, the Simele massacre, should be noted. Just two months later, in the winter of 1933, a young Raphael Lemkin, eventual creator of the United Nations Convention on the Prevention and Punishment of the Crime of Genocide (1948), was moved to begin his attempts at defining and codifying crimes of 'barbarity' and 'vandalism'.[20] Theoretically the same should be true of those hundreds of villages, churches, and schools destroyed alongside Kurdish ones in the 1960s–1980s. Yet, the Assyrian ones are curiously absent from the narrative, which begs the question: what does this gap in the literature tell us about how history is written, processed and remembered?

The most balanced approach appeared to be a direct objectivist/positivist one in order to frame the *why* and *how* of the Assyrian lacunae.[21] During the course of ferreting out what the focus of this work would become it was strikingly apparent that while sometimes the Assyrians were mentioned in modern secondary sources, it was more often than not as an afterthought, even though in Western colonial archival sources (British, French and US) from the early 1900s and from the 1930s in the wake of the Simele massacre there are numerous records. One can add to that an inability of scholars to read Assyrian memoirs in their original language, an ostensible lack of desire to search for them in the first place, as well as an apparent disdain for the ethnographic work perhaps ideally suited to this indigenous group.[22] Moreover, little that transpired in the history of Iraq, according to many chronologies, involved the Assyrians in a major role, including what some authors have termed the 'Simele incident'.[23] It was as if the story was veiled or obscured, either directly or indirectly. And if the Assyrians are a people who exist in Iraq and if the 'incident' of Simele was a defining moment of Iraqi nationhood, and if indeed the Assyrians fought alongside Kurds for their rights during the 1960s–1980s, losing hundreds of villages and finding refuge in the West (for many years being the largest expatriate Iraqi community), how could they *not* have played a major role in the history of the region?

But while this approach is important, it lacks ascendancy as objectivism assumes one tool to repair the damage. A further reading of civil rights writer and activist Audre Lorde makes it clear that objectivism, or the positivist discourse in the form of colonised academic research, is part of the reductionist problem as it calculates people and actions as scientists measure natural phenomena, diminishing them to numbers and on a page in a detached way, or at least assuming the guise of a dispassionate endeavour supported by science.[24] Positivism is a tool, neither one of my own devising nor one that is able (at least on its own) to solve the issue of inattention, for 'the master's tools will never dismantle the master's house. They may allow us to temporarily beat him at his own game, but they will never enable us to bring about genuine change.'[25] Nor is it suitable for it lacks substance and empathy for *the studied*. It may be able to argue the significance of the Assyrians in Iraq, but as time passed the theory would lose prominence, most likely overwhelmed by longstanding rubrics, once again unimagining the Assyrians.

Other tools situate the issue with greater accuracy. Unsurprisingly Edward Said's *Orientalism* creates a powerful dualistic worldview and explicates a variety of issues from a constructivist viewpoint. But here the Assyrians still do not figure: they are neither Arab nor principally Muslim. Yet Said's framework for the attitude of how people define themselves and others is pertinent. In essence Assyrians function as the Third World of the Third World and 'Assyrian issues are thus now no longer real history' and have been relegated to '4th world identity issues'.[26] While misunderstandings of the West have led to the Assyrian overshadowing in recent years, misunderstandings of the East have done likewise for a lengthier period; in other words, the Orient too otherises the Assyrians. Furthermore, the ever-sung archetype of a 'Sunni, Shia and Kurdish' Iraq endures because people believe what scholars and the media continue to report and compose as truth. The notion that scholars are experts and history is fact (or if recounted enough it becomes fact), granting both Western and non-Western scholars (who operate in a similar framework that benefits those in power) authority which intentionally and unintentionally marginalises Assyrians and others.

The post-structuralist and/or constructivist approach, while partially useful, has two major pitfalls or internal contradictions. While one would assume in such an approach Assyrianesque narratives would be viewed alongside thousands of others, they have not been, or at least not on an equal footing. Why? There are two reasons. Firstly, the inherent logical conclusion to constructivist discourse ends in nihilism. In effect the narratives have no meaning as every narrative can be deconstructed an infinite amount of times, which in turn deconstructs meaning. Secondly, in order for post-structuralists/constructivists to counter the objectivist colonial metanarrative of the state, they have utilised other majoritist perspectives. This approach leaves room for hierarchical structures which can impose, relegate and even overwhelm more modest community narratives. In Middle East studies, scholars simply reproduce the metanarrative in a different light which marginalises indigenous and minority groups to a citation in history. Academics do this because they have an inherently normative agenda, from either an oriental or an occidental perspective. In other words, the failure of Saidist orientalist discourse was and indeed is that it fails to see that majority groups and states in the Middle East otherised sub-groups long before the Western colonialist and imperialist enterprise.

The ontological postulation of this study believes that modern constructivist notions of created realities, and in this case created histories, make it impossible for the Assyrians to play a role in Iraq. Consensus deals with numbers, and the numbers of realities/narratives of Iraqi history which acknowledge the role of the Assyrians are few, partially because most of those who view the Assyrians as essential to Iraqi history are the Assyrians themselves and as an indigenous minority they 'have been excluded, marginalised and "Othered".'[27] How does one avoid reinforcing power structures and creating a monolithic explanation of the puzzle, or a metanarrative? Likewise, how can the Assyrian case gain ascendency, importance and meaning amid a myriad of narratives where they play a minor role simply due to the fact that power structures influence scholarship as well as politics, and individual narratives as well as the metanarrative? In addition by virtue of individuality, there are far fewer Assyrians writing their history, telling their account of events, which in a post-structuralist world means that the more individual narratives of majority groups (written by those groups or from the perspective of those groups) the less important the Assyrian narrative becomes. How then is the impasse skirted?

A New Approach to Meaning

This impasse generates the need for a new foundation that will not assimilate, violate or do violence to the Assyrian and other similar cases. Thus there is a distinct difference between this new worldview and the objectivist/positivist and constructivist ones. While I am concerned with the overall puzzle that is reality or history I am also concerned with a small piece which makes up the reality or history. Essentially there is the need for a pragmatic approach to why all the elements, the pieces (including the Assyrians) matter to the puzzle (the history of Iraq). This new ontological and epistemological approach, which could be applied to all such similar cases, could be a bridge across the vast chasm between the objectivists and constructivists. It is a balance of three postulations that simultaneously incorporate and counter both positivism and constructivist theories. The three axioms are: (1) Human reality is shaped largely by socially accepted 'knowledge' of that reality. (2) Intent therefore, is a powerful instrument that is employed both heedfully and unwittingly to either produce and/or extinguish significance. These two axioms, while constructivist in nature, have failed to incorporate or guarantee the inclusion of the Assyrians in Iraqi history on their own. But the final postulation, while initially appearing objectivist in its principle approach, has a built in failsafe. (3) Both relative axiomatic expressions (1) and (2) are beholden to an objective reality concomitantly defined by yet greater than and independent of their suppositions.

There exists a real normative project which posits the Assyrians as a people, as a culture, as individuals, matter, and that merely through their 'being' they are vital components to the puzzle and their deeds have meaning in the context of Iraqi history.[28] I began imagining existence as a borderless, omnidirectional, omni-coloured, ever-expanding, three-dimensional tapestry. Adding then the fourth dimension of *time*, as the study of history deals with everything that has happened, whether we view it as linear or cyclical, granting it another infinite quality – change. Finally there was an even more elusive immeasurable character of reality that I could not quantify and indeed found difficult to qualify. This becomes, in my opinion, *meaning*: an attribute which can only be partially described by human perception or language since it is by its very nature inadequate as humanity is but one element of reality. Furthermore I accept the axiom that while each element of reality is different, it is of equal significance. From a theological perspective, it is the *soul* or *spirit* of something. It is the difference between viewing all the threads which make up a hand-woven rug, and seeing the graceful pattern expressed on the obverse; the difference between having all the knowledge concerning a matter and the wisdom to understand it. To put it another way, history or the past is an infinitely faceted gem and while this book is a work of Middle East history, to put it in anthropological terms, it combines elements of *an* emic history of the Assyrians and Iraq with *an* etic history utilising a variety of other narratives and formulating them in a way which may reveal a more balanced representation of the past.[29] An emic meaning or account comes from a person within the culture. 'Etic', on the other hand, refers to the view of an observer with a goal of neutrality in language, judgement, assessment etc., eliminating the bias of the investigator. The two accounts are sometimes termed an insider and an outsider perspective respectively.

Again *an* in opposition to *the* must be stressed given my approach to the totality of history, especially in response to why the Assyrian model not only makes a difference but is fundamental to our understanding of (in this case) Iraqi history; while all of the stories or narratives are part of and necessary to the whole, it is unreasonable to expect a full understanding simply by considering the parts which make up the whole since there are innumerable stories – making *the* story, the metanarrative, which is not simply a combination of them but rather lies beyond them as well. And finally, each story lacks something of its own: its own meaning, its spirit or soul which is mysterious or unique despite its equality to all others.[30] This has been the continued problem of historians. In other words, the understanding of history can be segmented thus:

1. there is a totality to history, and
2. the parts comprise the whole, yet
3. one cannot understand the whole without all the parts, and

4. there is an infinite number of parts, which are borderless and ever expanding, creating space and new stories, thus

5. making the whole always transcendent of our complete understanding of it, yet

6. reminding us of the immeasurable meaning to each story which, though unique to each case, entwines all the pieces of the fabric of reality as an ever-shifting multi-hued infinite cloak.

I would like to propose the concept of *panenhistoricism* for this view. It is an ontological worldview that suggests each perspective (histories) or experience is reflective of the whole (history) and integral to it as well as the whole (history) being reflective of the parts (histories), while transcending them in its totality. It is a solution to the rational objectivist overpowering nature of the metanarrative and the post-structuralist/constructivist fear of the metanarrative of dominant groups since each story/thread is of equal yet intrinsic value to the lifecycle of events.[31] In essence it allows for an infinite number of universalities. Secondly, it also relegates the post-structuralist/constructivist cultural relativist (which necessarily links to moral relativism if one accepts ethics as a cultural creation) approach, which inevitably trends toward a deconstructing path to nihilism by reinserting individual meaning and value to each narrative in an authentic manner, and, furthermore, goes beyond simply enhancing the narrative to changing the fundamental nature and indeed importance of narratives. In other words it accepts the normative framework that while there may be individual experience and meaning assigned to existence, *meaning* and *existence*, while universally or in totality mysterious, are eternally present (or eternal presences). To borrow the interpretation of the 'Great Spirit or Great Mystery' from the Santee Dakota writer Ohiyesa (Charles Alexander Eastman):

> The original attitude of the American Indian toward the Eternal, the 'Great Mystery' that surrounds and embraces us, was as simple as it was exalted. To him it was the supreme conception, bringing with it the fullest measure of joy and satisfaction possible in this life. The worship of the 'Great Mystery' was silent, solitary, free from all self-seeking. It was silent, because all speech is of necessity feeble and imperfect; therefore the souls of my

ancestors ascended to God in wordless adoration. It was solitary, because they believed that He is nearer to us in solitude, and there were no priests authorized to come between a man and his Maker. None might exhort or confess or in any way meddle with the religious experience of another. Among us all men were created sons of God and stood erect, as conscious of their divinity. Our faith might not be formulated in creeds, nor forced upon any who were unwilling to receive it; hence there was no preaching, proselyting, nor persecution, neither were there any scoffers or atheists.[32]

If meaning then is accepted as immeasurable or unquantifiable and the understanding of it as imperfect, then how could such an element be contained? How does one define that which by its very nature escapes definition? One must become aware of and bequeath significance to its individual and interrelated parts, as only through their life and experience does a fuller understanding of the eternal mystery come about. Using J. R. R. Tolkien's Middle-Earth as the principal reality, independent scholar Patrick Curry observed the importance of Tolkien's myth for the modern world, especially in terms of the significance of individual natural place in an increasingly mechanised and homogenous world:

> Middle-Earth's places – each wood and indeed glade within it, streams no less than mighty rivers and individual mountains as much as their ranges, let alone villages towns and cities: each one unique, and all named not arbitrarily, but as they are natured – these are among its chief glories and embody its wisdom.[33]

Thus creation is a reflection of the creator. Applied to the historical case and indeed places of Iraq as each unique Assyrian experience of human, village, cultural site etc., with an appellation and character according to its nature, it offers wisdom in the form of a more complete and representative understanding of Iraqi history.

Moving Forward with Purpose

In order to support this panenhistorical view of the past, this study actively reinserts the Assyrians into the fabric of Iraq, in a sense granting them agency. This will be done by discussing the violent and non-violent suppression of

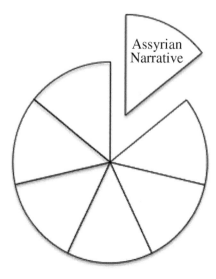

Figure 3   Granting agency: this chart represents an Assyrian narrative of their twentieth-century experience in Iraq. The first part of the process is to tell a story illustrating it as of equal value to the whole of the country's history

their identity including physical place in Iraqi nation-building from the 1930s to 1988. In essence it demonstrates that the Assyrians are critical (as Assyrians) to the history of the Middle East and specifically Iraq by raising a previously unrecognised matter: that the decay experienced by the Assyrians during the second half of the twentieth century can be argued as part and parcel of the unimagining of minorities and indigenous people in the struggle for economic, social and political power – often through violent coercion and policies of fear, which, when not recognised and confronted (in an ethical manner) by scholars, politicians, activists and others, continue until the community is treated (if it is considered at all) as negligibly significant collateral damage, partially dooming its future and in turn destroying part of the whole which makes up Iraq.[34] Despite this panenhistorical ontological approach to the past, this work is not meant to be comprehensive, as none are, but rather aims to be an integral thread in the expanding tapestry of the saga that is the Middle East and more specifically Iraqi history.

Scientists and philosophers often ponder the implications of and hierarchy between the indirect gradual disappearance of a species or a people or a culture due to war, disease, environmental degradation etc. and a direct active

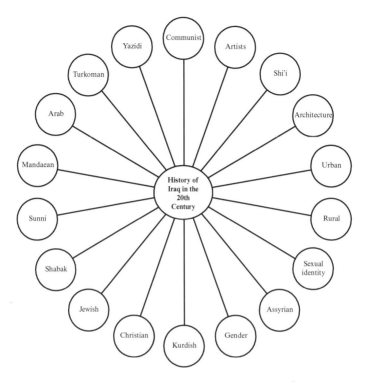

Figure 4   This chart illustrates various perspectives or identifiers that create lenses through which experience is filtered. These factors are infinite and further they are not monolithic categories as each contains distinct individual narratives reflective of its whole. Furthermore each perspective or category above could equally be swapped for the central theme or whole, depending on the overall context that one wishes to use as the foundation or framework

purging that utilises immediate physical power to accomplish said goal. In doing so they assign value and blame based on a culturally influenced ethical system. Yet to those affected, a convenient rational theory does little to stem loss. Likewise, few consider the mode of extinction as it occurs. Scientists, historians, scholars in general, a day late and a dollar short, spend copious hours in study formulating countless hypotheses as to how and why this eradication occurred. Scholarship is generally a passive field, thinking, postulating, wondering, deliberating long after the event has passed. Yet even in their passivity, historical narratives can be active forms of preservation and/or eradication. *Vocatus atque non vocatus, Deus aderit.* (Bidden or unbidden, God is present.)[35]

The history of the Assyrians, and this case study of Iraq, is a prime example. Some investigators are hesitant to side with those perceived simply as victims (rather than agents in their own right), to be seen as activists rather than objective researchers relating the facts. But if being victimised is part of the story, then it *must be conveyed as part of the story*, though not the whole story. The Assyrians also participated as actors in foundational events which would shape the twentieth century. The goal is for this work to be an epochal point for future exploration. Yet as more individuals tell their story and actively engage the academy there will certainly be a reaction, a backlash specifically geared towards deconstructing, questioning and mocking rather than *re*-fashioning or *re*-forging. This is not necessarily grafting a new tale, but rather *remembering* an old one while retelling it with greater empathy for things others may have considered circumstantial details. It involves shattering a story and using the fragments along with other pieces to forge it

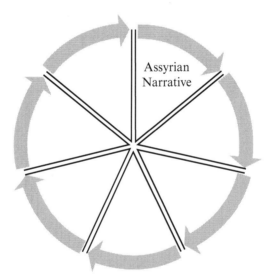

Figure 5   This diagram demonstrates the interdependency and interconnectivity of the narratives which is only possible if and when an Assyrian narrative is re-forged and secondly reinserted into the body of histories that contextualise Iraqi history. Also it solves the issue of relation based on Benjamin White's theory that within national or majority histories, minorities 'enter the picture only to the extent that their history touches on the majority' while at the same time safeguarding against self-marginalisation

anew. When this occurs, it will be evident that the thread of the Assyrians had become a prominent and integral part of the histories, a reminder of the necessary panenhistorical basis.

And so to commence this version of the saga with the final question '*Is there a way to remedy this to give real meaning* to a comparatively anonymous existence?', the answer is yes,[36] by reconstructing the history of Iraq as wanting, partial, incomplete, and the understanding of it as futile without the inclusion of Assyrians and their presence as indigenous to the region, as natives rather than foreigners. This is the first bulwark: in simple terms, reframing the Assyrians as an inseparable segment of the history of the region, state and nation of Iraq. Thus the antithesis or remedy to fragmentation is the interweaving of narratives or perspectives (while not losing their distinctiveness), making one impossible to tell without the other; to remember that history, and the history of twentieth-century Iraq, is a series of interrelated threads woven into a gradually ever-expanding and ever more detailed landscape.

Chapter Analysis

The first chapter discusses methodology while conceptualising the Assyrian question in the field of Middle Eastern history and contextualising it within various historiographical contexts. It details all the past and recent discussions on human rights with a focus on the development of hierarchies of suffering both as presented politically to the mainstream public and in academia. This will enhance the argument for the undeniability of the significance of the Assyrians.

Chapter 2 presents a basic history of the Assyrians and explains their demographic distribution before, during and after the First World War. It discusses their involvement in various world conferences as well as external conflicts and internal divergences. Further, it clarifies the lens through which the Assyrians were and indeed continue to be viewed in most histories of the region.

Chapter 3 addresses in detail the Simele massacres by weaving together three distinct stories of the events: British, Iraqi and Assyrian. Thus it is built on British archival material from 1933; Iraqi apologias from archival sources; the writings of Khaldun Husry, son of Arab nationalist Sāṭiʿ al-Ḥuṣrī; Assyrian eyewitness reports from oral sources; and material from the League of Nations archive. Furthermore, the American documents from the period were also inspected for perhaps a fourth narrative of events. This chapter exposes and explores reactions to Simele by Assyrians, Iraqis and the British and American governments. It frames Simele as the critical event that defined the emergent Iraqi nation-state. The chapter proceeds to briefly contextualise the Assyrian influence on other ideologies and mainstream politics.

Chapter 4 examines the period from end of the Second World War through the end of the monarchy to Abdul Karim Qasim (1958–63). It also discusses the armed autonomist movement, sometimes known as the Barzani uprising or Kurdish–Iraqi War, and the position of the Assyrians in it from 1961 to 1963 and the following years. This period witnessed massive upheavals in all aspects of Iraqi society during the clashes between government military and non-governmental opposition forces.

Chapter 5 focuses on the 1970s. It includes the renewal of internal fighting between the Iraqi government and opposition groups and further forced demographic shifting. It elucidates the destruction of villages in the mid-1970s and the border clearings of 1977–8, including the setting up of collective towns in the midst of a large ethnic cleansing campaign. The research examines the villages affected and their historical and cultural significance to the Assyrian population. The chapter also takes a critical look at governmental acculturation policies and their effect on individuals.[37]

Following the border clearings, Chapter 6 surveys the 1980s from the rise of Saddam Hussein and the Iran–Iraq War to the Anfal period and its aftermath. It begins with a review of Anfal-related material and literature. The empirical contribution of this chapter is a list of Assyrian villages destroyed during the 1980s. This list of villages and their historical significance was compiled with the aid of NGO documentation and corroborated by oral interviews parallel to those compiled in Chapters 4 and 5. The list is included in full detail in Appendix A.

The findings of the chapters are readdressed and analysed in their larger contexts in Chapter 7. This chapter also discusses the recognition of the Assyrian experience and the precedence it sets within a global context. Further, it confronts reasons for and dimensions of acculturation, comparing Eastern ethnic-based nations and Western civic democracies and their treatment of minorities and indigenous peoples. A brief conclusion brings the argument full circle with considerations for the future and new ways of viewing historical research outside age-old rubrics founded in propagandistic and negligent assumptions of human society. Lastly included are two extensive appendices: the first, as mentioned above, contains basic historical data concerning those villages that were affected during distinct intervals of the twentieth century, including cultural edifices, population and known geographic details, while the second contains important archival material.

Notes

1. Based on http://www.npr.org/documents/2005/aug/constitution_ap_8-29.pdf (accessed 20 August 2014).
2. Ali Mamouri, 'Assyrians discuss possible state in Iraq', Al-Monitor, 20 August 2013, http://www.al-monitor.com/pulse/originals/2013/08/assyrians-iraq-autonomous-state-dreams.html (accessed 7 July 2014); American Embassy in Baghdad to Secretary of State, 'Ninewa: diversity of views from Assyrian Christian Leaders in Al-Qosh', Confidential Baghdad 002139, http://wikileaks.ch/cable/2008/07/08BAGHDAD2139.html (accessed 7 July 2014). For reports concerning maltreatment of Assyrians in the Nineveh region as well as attempts at Kurdifying see Preti Taneja, *Assimilation, Exodus, Eradication: Iraq's Minority Communities since 2003* (London: Minority Rights Group International, 2007), 20.
3. United States Department of State, Bureau of Democracy, Human Rights, and Labor, 'International Religious Freedom Report 2005: Iraq', http://www.state.gov/j/drl/rls/irf/2005/51600.htm (accessed 7 July 2014). Due to the framework and function of Islamic and Christian politics in the Middle East (the Assyrians being a predominantly religiously Christian population), church/ecclesiastical leaders have generally held the majority control over their respective flocks and thus are inevitably those interviewed, surveyed and queried by news outlets, government personnel and scholars in their studies on the region and its people. In that vein this USDOS report sectarianises their population.
4. Mardean Isaac, 'The desperate plight of Iraq's Assyrians and other minorities,' *The Guardian*, 24 December 2011.
5. Numerous outlets have covered the situation. See Jack Healy, 'Exodus from north signals Iraqi Christians' slow decline', *New York Times*, 10 March 2012, http://www.nytimes.com/2012/03/11/world/middleeast/exodus-from-north-signals-iraqi-christians-decline.html?pagewanted=all&_r=0 (accessed 20 August 2014).

For more on the Jonah shrine and Assyrian temple see Eve Conant, 'Q&A: Why Sunni extremists are destroying ancient religious sites in Mosul', National Geographic Daily News, 2 August 2014, http://news.nationalgeographic. com/news/2014/08/140802-iraq-mosul-christian-muslim-islamic-state-syria-history/ (accessed 20 August 2014).

6. Margaret Talev and Tony Capaccio, 'US jets, drones hit militants in new round of strikes in Iraq', Bloomberg, 9 August 2014, http://www.bloomberg.com/news/2014-08-08/obama-pulled-back-into-iraq-conflict-amid-genocide-threat. html (accessed 20 August 2014).

7. There are numerous cases of humans and animals with severe birth defects and high rates of cancer due to depleted uranium. Some US veterans have also cited this as the cause for their inability to function in society. See Deborah Hastings, 'Sickened Iraq vets cite depleted uranium', Boston.com, 12 August 2006, http://www.boston.com/news/education/higher/articles/2006/08/12/is_an_armament_sickening_us_soldiers/?page=full (accessed 20 August 2014).

8. Assyrians accounted for more than 80 per cent of the Iraqi diaspora in the US through the 1960s.

9. The most common endonym or autonym used cross-denominationally by Assyrian commoners and elites alike in the twenty-first century is *Sūrōyō/ Sūrāyā* (western/eastern dialects) to refer to themselves and *Sūrayt/Sūreth* to denote their native tongue. Both are derived directly from the Neo-Assyrian word (going back to at least the seventh century BC) [Assūrāyu], which 'had a shorter variant [Sūrāyu] in the seventh century'. See Simo Parpola, 'National and Ethnic Identity in the Neo-Assyrian Empire and Assyrian Identity in the Post-Empire Times', *Journal of Assyrian Academic Studies* 18.2 (2004), 16–17.

10. See Geoffrey Khan, 'Remarks on the Historical Background of the Modern Assyrian Language,' *Journal of Assyrian Academic Studies* 21.1 (2007), 5–6. This is a more detailed account of modern Assyrian and its relation to Aramaic/Syriac and Akkadian. See also Simo Parpola, 'Assyrian Identity in Ancient Times and Today', 9, www.aina.org/articles/assyrianidentity.pdf (accessed 7 July 2014); Parpola, 'National and Ethnic Identity in the Neo-Assyrian Empire and Assyrian Identity in Post-Empire Times'.

11. See Naures Atto, *Hostages in the Homeland, Orphans in the Diaspora: Identity Discourses among the Assyrian/Syriac Elites in the European Diaspora* (Leiden: Leiden University Press 2011), 157. The book is a comprehensive study of identity issues among Jacobite Assyrians in the European context.

12. Prior to the rise of local nationalisms in the region, some Yezidis, like the Christian communities mentioned above, espoused Assyrian descent, and many nineteenth- and twentieth-century scholars believed that to be the case. See W. Francis Ainsworth, 'The Assyrian Origin of the Izedis or Yezidis – the So-called "Devil Worshippers",' *Transactions of the Ethnological Society of London*, vol. 1 (1861), 11–44. For further discussions on how the Yezidis self-identified as such, see Mark Sykes, *The Caliphs' Last Heritage: A Short History of the Turkish Empire* (London: Macmillan, 1915), 93, quoted in Christine Allison, *The Yezidi Oral Tradition in Iraqi Kurdistan* (Richmond: Curzon Press, 2001), 40; Isya Joseph, *Devil Worship: Sacred Books and Traditions of the Yezidiz* (Boston: Gorham Press, 1919), 92. Henry Layard also discussed the preservation of Assyrian myth and legend by the Yezidi and Christian religious communities: see Austen Henry Layard, *Nineveh and Its Remains: With an Account of a Visit to the Chaldæan Christians of Kurdistan, and the Yezidis, or Devil Worshippers; and an Enquiry into the Manners and Arts of the Ancient Assyrians* (London: John Murray, 1849), 190.

13. If one had to strictly define the Assyrians, perhaps the most inclusive and thorough recent definition comes from Agnes Korbani, *The Political Dictionary of the Modern Middle East* (Lanham, MD: University Press of America, 1995).

14. E. A. Wallis Budge (ed.), *The Book of Governors: The Historia Monastica of Thomas, Bishop of Marga, AD 840, vol. II: The English Translation* (London: Kegan Paul, Trench, Trübner, 1893), 316.

15. See Sargon Donabed, 'Rethinking Nationalism and an Appellative Conundrum: Historiography and Politics in Iraq', *National Identities* 14.4 (2012), 407–31 for a full discussion of this issue.

16. The terms 'Chaldean', 'Jacobite' and 'Nestorian' are used to refer to the ethnic Assyrian members of the Chaldean Catholic Church, Syrian Orthodox Church and Assyrian Church of the East respectively, as points of reference and for statistical purposes. While I acknowledge 'Nestorian' and 'Jacobite' to be largely pejorative today, I have used them in conjunction with current appellations, as many archival records erroneously use these labels. There is also a current trend that has aided the creation of distinct and often hostile ethnic groups from one people based on these ecclesiastical adherences. It may be applicable to use the neologism 'balkanisation' in terms of Assyrians being ethnically identified (and later in some cases identifying themselves) by their ecclesiastical background in a sectarian fashion. 'Sectarianisation' is an alternative term.

17. The Assyrians' importance as a fighting force in the First World War and the levies or as an actual physical buffer or wall are prime examples of this

phenomenon and will be discussed further. If 'numerical' is linked to quantity then 'political' must be linked to quality of both economic and social power, which are indeed precursors to and building blocks of political power. The issue of the commodification and commoditisation of people is taken even further by Gloria Jean Watkins (bell hooks) in the term 'cultural commodification'.

18. See, for example, the BBC's timeline of events in Iraqi history and even Iraqi Kurdistan history. Both are largely partial to current majority perspectives and make no mention of Simele as a specific event, nor are the Assyrians mentioned in general (http://www.bbc.com/news/world-middle-east-14546763; http://www.bbc.com/news/world-middle-east-15467672; accessed 7 July 2014).

19. Benjamin Thomas White, *The Emergence of Minorities in the Middle East: The Politics of Community in French Mandate Syria* (Edinburgh: Edinburgh University Press, 2011), 211.

20. Agnieszka Bieńczyk-Missala (ed.), *Rafał Lemkin: A Hero of Humankind* (Warsaw: Polski Instytut Spraw Międzynarodowych, 2010), 79.

21. Perhaps the best explanation of such an approach (at least for my formulations) was demonstrated in a fantasy series by Terry Goodkind entitled The Sword of Truth. By all accounts it seems evident that Goodkind's 'rules' were largely constructed around a portion of Ayn Rand's philosophy of objectivism. See Terry Goodkind's Sword of Truth series. While I employ a multitude of ideas and mechanisms to draw out and then analyse the elements of this work, I have incorporated works from seemingly distant fields such as fantasy literature (apparent here), religious studies and ecological philosophy, as they offer much insight for this case.

22. This also occurs in more popular works in a visual media age by scholars, journalists, activists etc. See Deborah Ellis, *Children of War: Voices of Iraqi Refugees* (Toronto: Groundwood, 2009) and Mark Kukis, *Voices from Iraq: A People's History 2003–2009* (New York: Columbia University Press, 2011) as examples where Assyrians find little or no inclusion.

23. Most fascinating is how this has become part of mainstream knowledge: see http://www.britannica.com/EBchecked/topic/39628/Assyrian-incident (accessed 7 July 2014). For chronologies see 'Iraq profile', BBC News Middle East, 24 June 2014, http://www.bbc.co.uk/news/world-middle-east-14546763 (accessed 7 July 2014); Charles Tripp, *A History of Iraq*, 2nd ed. (Cambridge: Cambridge University Press, 2002), x–xvi.

24. Linda Tuhiwai Smith, *Decolonizing Methodologies: Research and Indigenous Peoples*, 2nd ed. (London: Zed, 2012), 44–5.

25. Audre Lorde, *Sister Outsider: Essays and Speeches* (New York: Random House, 2012), 112.
26. Prof. Peter Gran, personal correspondence with author, 11 November 2013.
27. Smith, *Decolonizing Methodologies*, 35.
28. There is a common phrase in Assyrian to signify when a person or thing is missing from where it ought to be: '*shawpeh mabyuneleh*', literally 'its place (where it belongs) is showing'.
29. See Kenneth Lee Pike (ed.), *Language in Relation to a Unified Theory of Structure of Human Behavior*, 2nd ed. (The Hague: Mouton, 1967); Conrad Kottak, *Mirror for Humanity: A Concise Introduction to Cultural Anthropology*, 4th ed. (Boston: McGraw-Hill, 2006), 47.
30. I would like to explore this more in the future as it seems the spiritual views of the Lakota, Nakota and Dakota echo this concept, with their expression of Wakháŋ Tháŋka, sometimes translated as 'Great Spirit' or 'Great Mystery'.
31. See Jean-François Lyotard, *The Postmodern Condition: A Report on Knowledge*, tr. Geoff Bennington and Brian Massumi (Minneapolis: University of Minnesota Press, [1984] 1997), xxiv–xxv.
32. Kent Nerburn (ed.), *The Soul of an Indian and Other Writings from Ohiyesa (Charles Alexander Eastman)* (Novato, CA: New World Library, 2001), 5–6.
33. Sue Clifford and Angela King, 'Losing Your Place', in *Local Distinctiveness: Place, Particularity and Identity*, quoted in Patrick Curry, *Defending Middle-Earth: Tolkien, Myth and Modernity* (Boston: Houghton Mifflin, 2004), 145.
34. On 24 September 2008, Iraq's Council of Representatives voted to eliminate Article 50 of the Provincial Law. This article, which had passed into legislation only two months earlier, on 22 July, guaranteed almost fifty reserved seats (as in a quota system) in provincial councils for minorities: see 'UNPO calls for return of Article 50', Unrepresented Nations and Peoples Organization, 12 October 2008, http://www.unpo.org/article/8775 (accessed 8 July 2014). The repeal of the act was marked by the ethnic cleansing of Christians in Mosul in October: see Bradley S. Klapper, '3,000 Christians Flee "Killing Campaign" in Mosul, Iraq' Huffington Post, 11 October 2008, http://www.huffingtonpost.com/2008/10/11/3000-christians-flee-kill_n_133912.html (accessed 8 July 2014).
35. A proverb of Erasmus, later copied by Jung. It serves as an appropriate reminder of the omnipresence of meaning, discerned or not, accepted or not, that pervades all things.
36. Smith, *Decolonizing Methodologies*, 144–62.

37. This problem continues in the Assyrian diaspora today. See the Arab American Institute's demographics page, http://www.aaiusa.org/pages/demographics/ (accessed 8 July 2014), which lists Assyrians as constituting 5 per cent of the Arab-American population.

I

Integrating the Assyrian Question

Injustice anywhere is a threat to justice everywhere.

Martin Luther King Jr

To return to the tripartite inquiries of the introduction in reverse, a solution to remedy the situation is now loosely established and will become more apparent in the succeeding chapters. The second major query mentioned comprises two parts: (a) What are the ways in which the Assyrians contribute to (in this geopolitical case) Iraqi history? (b) How and why is the Assyrian role in the (or a) narrative diminished or unnoticed both directly and indirectly and what purpose does it serve? As the major queries outlined, my own epistemology and methods are influenced by a *panenhistorical* approach to the past, meaning an inherent interconnectivity of all things which make up the experience of the past. Touching on this theme, it would do the reader well to recall the words of Martin Luther King Jr in his letter from a Birmingham jail: 'Injustice anywhere is a threat to justice everywhere. We are caught in an inescapable network of mutuality, tied in a single garment of destiny. Whatever affects one directly, affects all indirectly.' In a very real way, this testifies to the importance of the Assyrian case for Iraq and the Middle East, as a microcosm reflective of a macrocosm.

Returning yet again to the introduction, part of remedying the problem of unacknowledgement is tying their (the Assyrians') past, present and future in with that of all of Iraq and its communities. The question becomes: on whom does the onus fall to create and sustain this effort? The Assyrians themselves are laden with the burden of responsibility for recounting their own history, otherwise they will continue to be omitted or relegated to a tertiary role of consequence in modern dialogues regarding Iraq. They have only recently become more involved in writing their own history, and that of their experience in Iraq, and offering it to a wider audience. There are numerous reasons for this, including the circumstance that academic pursuits are of minimal importance to peoples still living in a transient survival mode. It stands to reason that being a stateless, oppressed, underrepresented and sometimes unrecognised people can lead to further disassociation from such pursuits. To illustrate this I retreat to Dr King and utilise his paradigm that allows us to understand how oppressed or marginalised people/communities respond to oppression. I will endeavour to place each element of the paradigm in the context of the Iraqi Assyrian case.[1]

> *Acquiescence*: the oppressed resign themselves to their doom. They tacitly adjust themselves to oppression and thereby become conditioned to it.

Acquiescence is embedded in the Assyrian community in different forms, an example being accepted 'isations or ications' of new identities, especially sectarian ones (solely based on religious ties), which sometimes vie for supremacy and total consumption of identity rather than being a complimenting layer.

> *Physical violence and corroding hatred*: Violence often brings about momentary results. Nations have frequently won their independence in battle. But in spite of temporary victories, violence never brings permanent peace. It solves no social problem; it merely creates new and more complicated ones.

Some resort to violent confrontation with their oppressors. As an example, both the Armenian and the Palestinian causes elicit(ed) a great deal of political, scholarly and mass media-oriented attention and coverage, due (at least in part) to violent actions against Turks and Israelis respectively. Ingrained hatred has the knack of being fostered in succeeding generations and staying forgiveness, comprising both group and individual emancipation. Additionally, there is a possibility of such animosity then transferring to the oppressor group and blinding them to their own subjugation of others. Justice untempered by mercy depreciates into self-righteousness. The conversion of oppressed to oppressor is a common phenomenon of human civilisation.[2] While the Assyrians fought in the armed anti-government struggle of the 1960s and more recently formed a militia under the umbrella of the Assyrian Democratic Movement (ADM) in 1979, they have not resorted to violence for violence sake; in other words they have at most been willing to defend using force only when physically attacked.

> *Non-violent Resistance.* Like the synthesis in Hegelian philosophy, the principle of non-violent resistance seeks to reconcile the truths of two opposites, acquiescence and violence, while avoiding the extremes and immoralities of both. The non-violent resister agrees with the person who acquiesces that one should not be physically aggressive toward his opponent; but he balances the equation by agreeing with the person of violence that evil must be resisted. He avoids the non-resistance of the former and the violent resistance of the latter. With non-violent resistance, no individual or group need submit to any wrong, nor need anyone resort to violence in order to right a wrong. Non-violent resistance is not aimed against oppressors, but against oppression.

Of the three elements, King believed that only the option of *non-violent resistance* (in its various emanations) offered a path to freedom and liberation from past wounds. A pitfall of the Assyrians remains the acrimony caused by years of acquiescence. Dividing already numerically and politically limited groups halves their strength, making non-violent protest complex to say the least. However, this can be and in some cases has been remedied with a more ethical concern among researchers towards the Assyrian experience. For Assyrians, recounting experiences of Iraq, allowing them to tell their own stories, is not only a form of catharsis parallel to ethical practices of research, but more basically, it enriches the mosaic of Iraq. Additionally, it relates camaraderie in Iraq with other communities at an individual human level, reminding the reader of shared experiences and further that political systems are not the people and have seldom been truly representative of the people. This allows for a more bottom-up history of Iraq, rather than the usual state-, party- or military-oriented narrative so commonly recounted. Yet, despite all of this, there remains an innate aversion to works by Assyrians, making alleviating the condition challenging.[3]

A Historiography of Historiography and a Theoretical Framework

Different parts of the picture highlight the same frame

Jurassic 5, 'Work It Out'

Deeply embedded in this work is a methodological lens that will be useful for similar cases of historical alienation and disenfranchisement. To that end, this work builds partly on theories of history and religious studies/theology to create a panenhistorical worldview that is inclusive by its very nature. By contrast, as historian Chris Lorenz explains, the way history has been practised in a bipartite structure has involved 'scientific' historians affirming an epistemological claim with a practical end in mind:

> The epistemological claim related to the status of history writing as a *Wissenschaft*, that is, a methodical truth-seeking discipline: academic history, above all else, claimed to do away with all myths about the past and to replace them with The Truth – or, at least, some truths.
>
> Next to this epistemological claim, however, academic history always claimed to fulfill a practical function, namely, to provide a certain degree of guidance in practical life . . . For most professional historians over much of the nineteenth and twentieth centuries this practical orientation was about creating some kind of identification with the state, most often the nation-state. This was no accident since the professionalisation of academic history was very much a state affair; most professional historians were literally fed by the state. Not without justification, then, have historians been called 'priests of the state'.[4]

Bearing this in mind, the very nature of the academic discipline of history is embedded in state structures and apparatuses which, in some fashion, claim an irrevocable link to historical fact and Truth. The panenhistorical paradigm refashions or reforges that by allowing for many truths *sans* hierarchical structures to generate a more thorough depiction of the Truth while at the same time acknowledging this very pursuit as beyond human capacity.[5] Lorenz, harkening back to the early nineteenth-century Prussian philosopher and empiricist historian Wilhelm von Humboldt, remarks:

Humboldt's equally famous treatise *On the Historian's Task* (1821) empha-
sises the 'theoretical', non-empirical aspect of scientific history even more
clearly than Ranke: 'The historian's task is to present what actually happened. [. . .] An event, however, is only partially visible in the world of the
senses; the rest has to be added by intuition, inference, and guesswork.' The
facts are just the 'raw material, but not history itself. [. . .] The truth of any
event is predicated on the addition – mentioned above – of that invisible
part of every fact, and it is this part, therefore, which the historian has to
add. Regarded in this way, he does become active, even creative [. . .].'[6]

The panenhistoricist would further argue that while history is in the imagining of the raw data or facts into a story, perspective playing a large role in
interpretation, raw material or fact is also neither true nor false but also
embedded in perception. One historian's fact is another's fancy.

To return to Iraq, the last twenty years have seen an increase in research
on the Iraqi state that has taken place from a variety of perspectives. Much
of this, especially in relation to Iraqi Assyrians, is deconstructed and
reviewed in an article entitled 'Rethinking Nationalism and an Appellative
Conundrum'.[7] The article included celebrated historians of Iraq from Hanna
Batatu and Peter Sluglett to Charles Tripp, Sami Zubaida and others. The
findings of the research into the historiography supported the theory that
even the most recent publications, while purporting to be inclusive by the
simple fact that more information is readily available to the modern historian, use the same dogmatic lens and interpretation that confine Assyrians to
little beyond sectarian divisions – far more so than the Assyrians themselves
did, specifically referring to early in the twentieth century before widespread
Arabisation, in what is sometimes dubbed their nationalist discourse.

Some historians espouse a left-leaning, anti-nationalist, anti-colonialist
perspective on the Middle East, and more recently minorities and issues
surrounding the buzzword term 'agency' have become part and parcel of
the discourse. Despite this and by the very nature of the apparatuses that
fund academia, most continue to engage in national histories or utilise the
language of the nation-state.[8] Iraq is a prime example. In 1991, historians
Peter Sluglett and Marion Farouk-Sluglett illustrated the problematic nature
of Iraqi studies and historiography:

1. The notion of the heterogeneity of Iraqi society is another theme
    that needs further definition and refinement. The facts are that the
    population of Iraq, now about 18 million, is divided on both ethnic
    and sectarian lines. Of course, neither the communities nor the sects
    constitute homogeneous or monolithic single entities. As far as it is
    possible to make any general calculations (since only primary religious
    affiliation, that is 'Christian' or 'Muslim' is recorded in Iraqi censuses),
    some 72 percent are Arabs, about 22 percent Kurds, and the remainder
    Turcomans, Armenians, and others. Muslims make up 95 percent;
    the remainder are Christians and members of various heterodox sects.
    Almost all Kurds (apart from the Yazidis), and all but a tiny minority
    of Arabs (who are Christians), are Muslims; to that extent, therefore,
    there is a degree of homogeneity arising from the fact that some 70
    percent of the population is both Muslim and Arab . . .

2. Among the more tragic aspects of the brutal and despotic regimes
    under which the population of Iraq has suffered for so long is that
    many of its most talented citizens have been forced into exile and that
    the best of its scholars can only express themselves freely outside Iraq.

3. More insidious is that, until recently, much that has purported to be
    scholarly writing on Iraq, including books that still find their way into
    university reading lists, consists either of uncritical apologia for present
    or past regimes or records the 'official version' of events, presented by
    the researcher as if it were historical fact.[9]

To summarise and explain, the Slugletts' second notion above accurately
acknowledges a harsh reality of despotic governments whereby due to the
brutality of past regimes it has been difficult for any Iraqis to convey their
perspective or to craft their own narratives of historical events. On the other
hand, notions one and three create a plethora of issues in which they appear
to contradict each other. Notion three negates the second half of notion one.
To clarify, a quintessential drawback to contend with is state or majority apo-
logia. In fact while this has shifted (at least in outward appearance in recent
years) the history of the region is still neatly packaged in state records. Census
accounts for example are one of many nation-political and institutional apparatuses which are conceived and utilised in a way to reflect the aspirations

of the state. On the other hand, notion one repudiates that: Iraqi society is discernibly heterogeneous and the communities from which it is built are far from homogenous, being (quite panenhistorically speaking) something more than simply the sum of their parts. Yet, while this is the case, there is a remarkable range of homogeneity as 70 per cent of the population is Arab and Muslim according to state census accounts. On a return to academic history's birth from within the nation-state, it appears blindingly obvious yet unquestioned that census accounts are in fact trappings of the national agenda of the state, thus begging the retort, what is more apologetic than archival sources?

What is additionally overlooked is state apologias may also mirror a Western perspective. This stems in part from a sometimes conscious and at other times unconscious assumption that archival accounts (especially British, French etc.) are etic and more culturally neutral than authoritarian government archives, certainly more so than personal emic tales and accounts of events, and further, that oral accounts are coloured by bias whereas Eastern and emphatically Western archival records are less corruptible and more salient. In essence utilising materials, names, vocabulary, including writing under a proper name and surname or government agency, creates a sense of verisimilitude, granting the narrative greater authenticity, and decreasing attachments and venality.

Included in this viewpoint is a predisposition for scholars to maintain the status quo. Giles Mohan and Gordon Wilson have called into question similar propensities in the field of development studies, which they so appropriately term 'regimes of truth and currencies of expertise' for research methods, topics and findings that at least uphold or endorse and at most edify the proclivity for particular hegemonic discourses.[10] Such scholarship, which by its very research furthers the hegemonic understanding of history even in its sympathies, is discussed in a critique of modern civilisation and the pervasiveness of 'pop' monoculture (perhaps in this case academic monoculture is more appropriate) in the following quote by Sue Clifford and Angela King:

> The bigger the scale the more reduced the sensitivity and the easier it becomes to steamroller strategies for the 'greater good' which prescribe the same solutions to subtly different circumstances encouraging convergence and homogeneity . . . thereby missing the whole point.

... The forces of homogenization rob us of visible and invisible things
which have meaning to us, they devalue our longitudinal wisdom and erase
the fragments from which to piece together the stories of nature and history
through which our humanity is fed. They stunt our sensibilities and starve
our imagination.[11]

Thus to return to the importance of individual or 'smaller-scale' narratives
reflective of Patrick Curry's named places and Martin Luther King Jr's
reminder of the interconnectedness of justice, let us view some native sources.

Reflections on native sources

With this knowledge and recalling King's idea of resistance, a look back into
the histories of Iraq and its societies, past and present, shows an Assyrian
narrative in diverse forms. If and how they were used becomes the question.
To illuminate this a closer look at a native account of the Assyrians in Iraq
and specifically the Simele massacres written by Iraqi author Yusuf Malek is
a logical point of departure.

Yusuf Malek was born 1899 in the Chaldean or Catholic stronghold of
Tel Keppe (Telkaif) in Iraq.[12] He was educated at Latin College in Baghdad
and later at the American College in Basra.[13] Captured by the Turkish military during the First World War, Malek later escaped and took work with the
Iraqi civil service from June 1917 to September 1930. In 1920, he was special
assistant to the governor of Samarra, and finally he held the office of secretary
for the administration inspector in the Nineveh (Mosul) region. He left Iraq
for Beirut in April 1931 and, along the way, remained in Aleppo for a general
conference of Assyrians and Kurds. Malek regularly challenged the British
high commissioner in Iraq for his treatment of Assyrians in official positions,
which led the high commissioner to complain to the French authorities in
Lebanon. Malek made regular attempts to return to Iraq but was continually
denied re-admittance by the Iraqi government at the behest of the British
consul general of Beirut, Sir Harold Satow.[14]

Two days after the initial massacres in Simele, the French authorities in
Beirut asked Malek to leave Lebanon, where he published a regular newspaper, *Atra* ('Country'). He later joined the exiled Patriarch of the Church of
the East in Cyprus, Mar Eshai Shimun, in order to take the Assyrian cause

to the international community. Following the horrendous events of Simele in August 1933, the two Assyrians left Cyprus for Geneva, to petition the League of Nations in September and October of that year. Malek wrote his *magnum opus*, *The British Betrayal of the Assyrians*, in 1935, in protest at what he perceived as continuous maltreatment of the Assyrians by the British administration in Iraq, especially in response to the Simele massacres.[15] While it appears from the title that the author laid the bulk of the blame for the Assyrian predicament and the devastation dealt to them in 1933 at the feet of the British colonial power, the book retains a native perspective of one who laboured alongside the British and later critiqued their motives and integrity. In fact Malek charged the following fifteen officials, eight Iraqi and seven British, as responsible for the massacres either through direct action or indifference:

> Rashid Ali al-Gaylani, Prime Minister
> Hikmat Sulayman, Minister of the Interior
> Yasin al-Hashimi, Minister of Finance
> Nuri al-Said, Minister of Foreign Affairs
> Muhammed Amin Zaki, Minister of Justice
> Jalal Baban, Minister of Defence
> Rustam Haidar, Minister of Communications and Works, assistant to T. E. Lawrence
> Sayyid Abdul Mahdi, Minister of Education
> Sir Francis Humphrys, British ambassador to Iraq
> Captain V. Holt, oriental secretary to the British embassy, Baghdad
> Sir Kinahan Cornwallis, chief administrative inspector
> Major C. J. Edmonds, first assistant advisor to Cornwallis
> Major W. C. F. A. Wilson, administrative inspector, Mosul
> Colonel R. S. Stafford, administrative inspector, Mosul
> Major Douglas B. Thompson – English expert on the Assyrian settlement

As a counterbalance to these accusations, four sections of the book were either written by or republished with permission by British authors: the Introduction (William Ainger Wigram, Anglican priest); Chapter 5, on the Baqubah and Mindan refugee camps (Colonel F. Cunliff-Owen); Chapter 13, regarding the Assyrians in 1918–19 (Colonel J. J. McCarthy); and Chapter 29, entitled 'The Crisis in Iraq' (Lieutenant Colonel A. T. Wilson). The book includes an extensive appendix containing copies of correspondence from Assyrian, Iraqi and British officials as well as a partial list of villages destroyed and names of Assyrians executed during the events.[16]

While not disputing the existence of bias, *The British Betrayal* retains an inclusive narrative filtered through the perspective of a native Iraqi who worked in the region as an interpreter for the British and their Indian regiments and was with them during the failed assault known as the Battle of Ctesiphon in 1915. He was later part of the siege of Kut al-Amara, which lasted from the end of that year until the spring of 1916. Following the surrender of the starving British garrison to Ottoman forces on 29 April, Malek along with the other prisoners was sent on foot to Aleppo to be pressed into work. He escaped within two months and, as mentioned above, was later employed by the British in the Iraq civil service.

Though Malek was an Iraqi who lived and worked in the region under the British and who had close ties to the Patriarch of the Church of the East, his work is perceived as a 'polemic' utilising 'fantastical accounts' and is simply 'not a trustworthy source'.[17] Incongruously in the Iraqi nationalist argument that 'in the case of the Assyrian Affair of 1933 history has been decidedly the propaganda of the victims', Khaldun Husry, son of staunch Arab nationalist Sāṭiʿ al-Ḥuṣrī, found himself published in in the *International Journal of Middle East Studies* (IJMES) in 1974, which afforded his article a sense of integrity unavailable to Malek.[18] The work, which extensively employs British FO archival documents, is certainly polemical. Analytically, the argumentation focuses on exonerating the Iraqi government, of which Malek was a part, of any wrongdoing. Husry employs basic logical reasoning to promote his perspective of the case, sometimes questioning British accounts as circumstantial while at other times utilising archival sources as if they were infallible.[19]

One of the sources Husry employs is Lieutenant Colonel Ronald Sempill Stafford (1890–1972), British administrative inspector for Mosul. Regarded by some as an Assyrian apologist, in actuality he considered the Assyrians to be 'savage and uncivilized', exemplifying the emblematic disdainful colonial attitude for the colonised regardless of religious adherence.[20] This attitude transferred to and was adopted by the British protégés, the new Iraqi administration (including Khaldun Husry and his father) and King Faisal, who himself regarded the Assyrians contemptuously as 'boorish and child-like'.[21] Yet it is Husry and his perspective that have become the foundation for all things Simele, and while problematic, some experiential information should be scrutinised in greater detail.

> The writer met Bakr Sidqi for the first time a few days after his return from Mosul. When he patted me on the shoulder and asked me what I wanted to be when I finished school I said: an army officer. (So popular was the army then that probably no boy of the writer's age could think at the time of taking any other profession.)[22]

Husry was an eyewitness to the celebrations for the returning Iraqi troops and remembers his feelings (and that of a large portion of the country) well. This one statement tells of nascent Iraqi Arab nationalism tied to a strong military, setting its prominence in Iraqi politics in the future. Yet, there remains the paradox of the Assyrian perspective as nothing beyond 'a tired account of an oppressed minority'.[23]

In framing the criticism of the production of discursive knowledge relating to the events of 1933 a disparity exists. Whereas the discourse on British colonial and imperial history in Iraq has correctly deconstructed and scrutinised its effects on the socio-cultural, economic and political transformation of Iraqi society, a similar account of British treatment of Assyrians in Iraq by Assyrians writing during this critical period is often dismissed as invalid, ethnocentric, and thus not worthy of consideration, essentially creating a form of domination and repression/oppression in academic discourse.

There are at least three other Assyrian sources which are intrinsically vital to the early historiographical record of Iraq: Malik Yaqo d'Malik Ismael's *Aturayé w-tre plashe tībilayé* ('Assyrians and the Two World Wars', 1964), 'Abdyešu' Barzana's *Šinnē d-'asqūtā: Qrābā d-Dayrabūn w-Gunḥā d-Simele* ('Years of Hardship: The Battle of Dayrabūn and Massacre of Simele', 2003), and *Assyrian Struggle for National Survival in the 20th and 21st Centuries* (2012), written by Malik Loko Shlimon d'bit Badawi. Malik Ismael and Loko Shlimon's works come from the perspective of tribal leaders and levy officers.

Both were intensely involved in the settlement of the Hakkâri Assyrians and were among those who decided to leave for Syria. Their works give interesting eyewitness accounts of the events leading up to the Simele massacre, as well as examining the internal politics of the Assyrians, especially within the patriarchal family, which included Mar Eshai Shimun, the Patriarch himself, his aunt, the Lady Surma, and his father, Rab Tremma (later promoted to Rab Khayla or General) Dawid. Shlimon's work is of great relevance as it contains original letters from the 1920s and 1930s that communicate a different and additionally complex story of the internal politics of the Assyrian community. Finally Barzana's text is an eyewitness account of a fifteen-year-old boy who participated in the skirmish between the Iraqi army and the Assyrians on 4 August 1933 at Dayrabūn, a village near where the borders of Iraq, Syria and Turkey meet.

A chapter in a book entitled *Writing the Modern History of Iraq: Historiographical and Political Challenges*, published in 2012 and based on a conference held in Geneva in 2008, zeroes in on the fear of the sectarian master narrative. In the chapter, twelve 'methodological suggestions for dealing with reporting with a sectarian bias on the post-2003 situation in Iraq' are listed, one of which is:

> Question the representativeness of individuals who speak in the name of sectarianism. For example, who is an Assyrian in Iraq? What about those Christians who prefer to describe themselves as Chaldeans and see themselves as Iraqis rather than as an ethnic minority in search of a homeland? Historically, the most ardent 'Assyrianists' among the Iraqi Christians are also the smallest and by far the most recent addition to the Christian Community – the Nestorians, previous inhabitants of the Hakkari mountains who were settled in Iraq after the First World War.[24]

The suggestion achieves two things: first, it reminds the reader of issues of context due to the absence of historical processes, an absence which can consequently create what it purports to safeguard against, namely sectarianism; and second, it illustrate some of the continuing generalisations or stereotypes of who Assyrians are and whence they came. There has been a general postulation become fact that the Assyrians are in some form alien to the region, perhaps partly because they are predominantly distributed between four contiguous Middle Eastern states and thus constitute a transnational community. I propose the following alleged truisms, popularly and often academically accepted, concerning the Assyrians:

1. Assyrians are Nestorians from the Hakkâri mountains in Turkey.
2. Only Nestorians (who are not native to Iraq) are Assyrians.
3. They are better referred to under more neutral and less political terms like Iraqi Christians (or by ecclesiastical grouping).
4. Their own experiences and self-histories are 'fantastical' tales, 'nationalist polemics' and cannot be objective.
5. Simele was an isolated event in Iraqi history.

The minority is unimagined by the majority narrative(s) since the majority narrative(s) require hegemony to retain power. This is furthered in all aspects of the nation's culture from school curriculums to media to politics and everything in between. This issue can be termed *subordinating narrativisation*.

A partial remedy to this problem is the introduction of historical Assyrian material culture (discussed in the subsequent chapters) as well as innovative perspectives which challenge previous assumptions of 'alienness'. In the case of the description of Assyrians as the 'most recent edition' to Iraq or as refugees from Turkey following the First World War, N. E. Bou-Nacklie clarifies similar characterisations in Syria in a table concerning ethnic groups recruited by the French to participate in a local security force. The group 'Christians' is divided into 'Local' and 'Foreign' by the French. In a footnote Bou-Nacklie states:

> There were admittedly groups of Assyrians and Armenians in the region long before Islam; they are referred to as foreign because most of the recruits from these two groups – from Turkey and Iran – came from the embittered, impoverished, and unemployed Armenians and Assyrian refugees who flocked to the Troupe recruitment centers.[25]

Such sentiments are echoed by Tareq and Jacqueline Ismael, who note that 'Assyrians have ancient roots in the Iraq but their population had increased markedly since the beginning of WWI'.[26] Essentially, one must recognise that the settlements of this community, like all others, fluctuated and transformed over both time and an expansive territory undelineated by modern borders. The political placement of such borders did not create a new reality, but rather simply how the reality was viewed. In other words utilising a historical soundbite (migration during the First World War) as the basis for a presumed truism (Assyrians are foreign to Iraq) by upholding it as the initial event of its kind (as if the region post-WWI was as now) is detached from the reality of history as a series of continuous interconnected processes. Much of this stems from an inability to note that Assyrians in early twentieth-century Iraq could be categorised as geographically distinct yet interrelated groups:

1. Those who at the time of the division of the Ottoman Empire resided in what would become Iraq, including urban Assyrians who were largely Arabised from Chaldean (Catholic) and Jacobite-rite (Orthodox) religious communities, and rural Assyrians to the far north who were largely unassimilated, retaining native languages and culture, of Chaldean and Church of the East (Nestorian) religious denominations (see Figure 6).
2. Those Assyrians of Hakkâri and Urmia, numbering Chaldean, Nestorian and Protestant denominations, forced into Iraq during the fighting of the First World War.

In order to arrive at a more genuine panenhistorical understanding (steering clear of the subordination trap) illustrated via objectivist discourse, this work adopts as its core the necessity of telling and retelling unidentified, dismissed or rejected narratives within a given historical period without declaring each as objective truth ('master narrative') but rather as a continuous contribution to the whole as an ever-expanding puzzle with no discernible borders. The more observable the pieces are, the greater the chance for an improved understanding of the intricacies while recognising the infinite nature of the puzzle, allowing it to remain just out of reach and making new studies and perspectives perpetually essential. Problematising and resolving the accepted truisms and assumptions will situate Assyrians in the midst of all other narratives that engage Iraqi history in a proper panenhistorical web.

Finally, aligning with Benjamin White's understanding that if within majority histories or writing national histories, minorities 'enter the picture

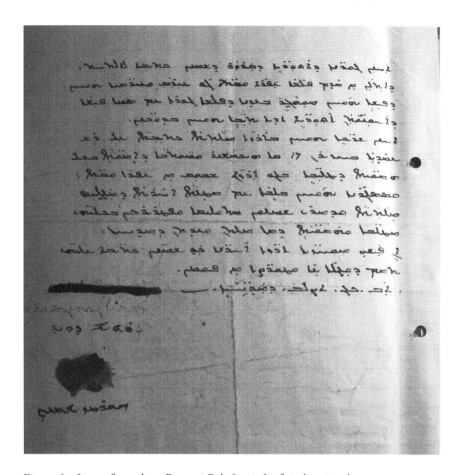

Figure 6   Letter from three Barwari Bala Iraqi chiefs indicating they were landowners and had dwelt in the region long before the war, yet became refugees along with the rest of their brethren from Hakkâri and Urmia. The chiefs also make evident their support of Mar Eshai Shimun, Patriarch of the Church of the East, in his temporal endeavours

only to the extent that their history touches on the majority', then a solution to the inattention is to give Assyrian narratives agency to forge an account of Iraqi history, making them necessary to the account and all subsequent narratives.[27] Thus the Assyrian perspectives that had previously been inadequately studied will be reinserted and analysed as part of the larger history. If Sami Zubaida's article title 'The Fragments Imagine the Nation' is to be accepted, then it must be actualised. The Assyrians must be part of imagining or reimagining Iraq. This book is just that: an aspiration to enhance the vibrancy of the story by incorporating various perspectives and personal experience.

Key Sources: Mapping Iraqi Assyrians and Sectarianisation

To illuminate the issue of identity fragmentation and its connectedness to place, which contributed to a lacunae of references to the people in question, the Western Christian missionary enterprise must be examined to determine its role in triggering and instigating additional perplexities. Almost all nineteenth-century information on the Assyrians that is studied or reproduced is based on sources by Western travelogues. The Assyrians had long contact with the Church of England under the auspices of the Archbishop of Canterbury. While most of the explorers were missionaries, many if not all were also politically motivated, demonstrating deep religion–state connections in what many would have thought of as a post-Enlightenment 'secular' western Europe. They included Edward Lewes Cutts, George Percy Badger and archaeologists such as Sir Austin Henry Layard. In many ways they served as a bastion of the British crown/church fearful of growing French Catholic influence; an unremitting competition beginning in 1534.

From the mid-1850s to 1971, the Ordo Praedicatorum, also known as the Roman Catholic Dominican Order, had been converting large numbers of predominantly Nestorian Assyrians to Catholicism, further fragmenting the community. Yet some knowledge and perhaps wisdom may be drawn from an otherwise questionable endeavour. It is undeniable that Christian ecclesiastical communities were actively engaged in data collection. A prime example of this is the Dominican father and scholar Jean-Maurice Fiey, who between 1940 and 1960 compiled a three-volume ecclesiastic geography of northern Iraq, which he later entitled *Assyrie chrétienne* ('Christian Assyria'), published between 1963 and 1965. Fiey's work prompted a fellow Dominican, Fr Josephe Omez, to cartographically detail the settlement of Christian villages in the region during this period. When the map was completed it was entitled 'Les Chrétiens en Iraq, régions de Mossoul, Alcoche, Zakho, Amadia, Aqra, seules les localités où se trouvent des Chrétiens figurent sur cette carte (situation en 1961)'[28] and records more than 230 villages in northern Iraq, not including areas to the east such as Arbil and Kirkuk, both with significant Assyrian communities.[29] The work, while fairly extensive, was incomplete for these eastern regions, as 1961 saw the first of three waves of large-scale demographic shifting of Assyrians in Iraq during the second half of the twentieth century, which began alongside the armed autonomist movement (also referred to as the Kurdish uprising, the Kurdish–Iraqi War, or the Barzani uprising).

The labour of Omez was based on his own personal observations, Fiey's work and many Syriac manuscripts that detailed the past significance and location of cultural sites, many of which have since been destroyed or fallen into ruin from disuse. Furthermore, the Dominican map and its key, which mention the ecclesiastical ties of each village – including Chaldeans, Syrians, Nestorians, Jacobites, Gregorians, Armenians, Protestants and Seventh-day Adventists, Greek Catholics, the Orthodox, and Latin-rite Christians – helped to identity religious affiliation, necessary for detailing changes in affiliation over the years. The first four sects constitute the majority of Assyrians,

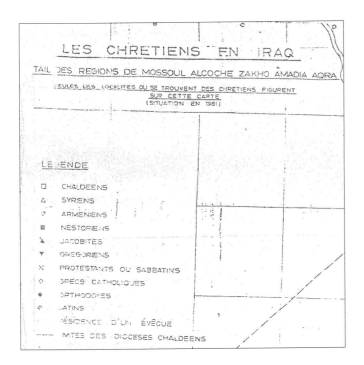

Figure 7   The original legend to Father Josephe Omez's map

while the latter six are more recent additions to Iraq and exist mostly in urban areas.[30]

The previously unpublished Dominican map along with the historical empirical evidence gathered sheds light on the Assyrian indigeneity to Iraq, distinct from the colonial-invented notions of invaders or mercenaries deposited in Iraq by the British following the First World War. The empirical portion of the study is built on the following research: the nineteenth- and early twentieth-century histories of the villages are based on Fiey's work, which is in turn grounded in early studies such as that done by Badger.[31] All population statistics from 1850 are based on Badger as well, though his numbers should be understood in light of his own reduction of all population numbers by one-third, as he felt the Patriarch Mar Shimun and Archdeacon Qasha Auraha had exaggerated them.[32] The figure of one-third is completely arbitrary and problematic, and while Badger cites personal observation as his justification for adjustment, his explorations were brief at best and never thorough as he himself did not travel to each village mentioned. Furthermore it must be noted that Badger's studies were carried out immediately following the massacres of Assyrians in Bohtan and Hakkâri by Bedr Khan Beg (1840–3), again calling into question the accuracy of the statistics. I have therefore added the original figures to show the range between those of Badger and the official church figures.

The statistics from 1913 arise from Chaldean priest Joseph Tfinkdji's research but are subject to scrutiny since the numbers are solely indicative of the Chaldean religious community. The numbers by Tfinkdji are also rounded estimates. Population figures from 1957 are based on the 1957 Iraqi census, which was also used by researcher Majed Eshoo.[33] Eshoo (a pen name) is also the main source for the situation during the 1961–3 civil wars in Iraq. Eshoo likely utilised this pseudonym as a means of protection from possible retribution; after having spoken with various Assyrians in Iraq, it appears that Eshoo's work drew the suspicion of some Iraq officials.[34] His compilation is indebted to the ADM's research and collections, as well as other Assyrian groups and local NGOs, including the Nineveh Center for Research and Development (NCRD), which has corroborated much of Eshoo's research and begun a collection of Anfal-related material. These studies are incorporated into a January 2003 report co-published by the International Federation for Human Rights and the International Alliance for Justice, entitled *Iraq: Continuous and Silent Ethnic Cleansing – Displaced Persons in Iraqi Kurdistan and Iraqi Refugees in Iran*.

The significance and steadfastness of Eshoo's work is comparable to that of Shorsh Haji Resool's research on Kurdish villages and the Anfal campaign. In the case of studying minorities, since much of the research on them is more often done by the minority themselves, objectivity is often legitimately questioned but also illegitimately dismissed. With regard to the legitimate concern over Assyrian objectivity, the Assyrian researchers, for whatever reason, have not had the advantage of added support from NGOs such as Human Rights Watch (HRW) that have worked alongside Kurdish researchers since 1991. This study has elected to use these compilations under scrutiny and to further substantiate their evidence through oral interviews.

As a brief aside, it is logical to expect some sensationalism in the Assyrian-compiled data, as the events were traumatic for the individuals involved. However, this should not negate the data's utility and importance. As Assyrians are neglected from generalist histories, ethnographic/oral history (the people themselves as living repositories of history) becomes a crucial tool for both the researcher and the researched in order to provide some agency within experienced events. It is fascinating that while all archives are written by humans and subject to the exact same deficiency of human error, many written by those who did not witness the events which they depict still appear as more objective in the literature. The reality remains that living human beings and their experience are an equally valid historical source and thus should be used, especially in cases of explicit governmental propaganda and/or a lack of written sources due to political, social or economic maladies and misfortunes, from destruction of material culture to fear tactics to problems with illiteracy and, as was the case with some indigenous cultures, lack of a written language.

It is worth recalling that if indigenous populations or minorities did not produce their own research, much of today's academic research by scholars would not have begun. History is generally written by the victor, and even in a world of progress and technology, indigenous populations have often been scorned. One should not forget the example of Carthage and her culture, which, despite its grand history, comes to us through the writings of her enemies and conquerors, the Romans, who had in fact obliterated most of the Carthaginian records.

The more recent statistics are based on my field research, the HRW findings, the Assyrian Academic Society's (AAS) previously unpublished 'Field Mission Iraq 2004, Report and Database' (primarily an ethnographic study of the region), the work of the NCRD, based in Qaraqosh, Iraq, and finally my oral interviews. Fieldwork in Iraq today must be scrutinised, as after 1991 and 2003 Iraq has seen large-scale demographic shifts and even some village rebuilding.[35] In addition, the fluidity of the destruction makes it difficult to pinpoint the exact date of devastation and, in some cases, the actual location of every village, school and monument destroyed.[36] Many of the archival documents consulted in this investigation come from the League of Nations Archives in Geneva, the (British) National Archives (TNA) in Kew, west London, and the (US) National Archives and Records Administration (NARA), located in College Park, Maryland. The Boston Athenaeum and the Congregational Library in Boston were also consulted. Few academics working on this period consult NARA as they were a minor player in the events in mandate and post-mandate Iraq, in essence once again assuming TNA to be more relevant and thereby constructing a hierarchy of sources. In the case of Simele, most studies rely solely on British Foreign Office documents or Air Ministry files and do not consult the Assyrian records, letters etc., making the event one-sided and lacking in depth. I elected to use many of the US documents, as the United States seems to have had a less involved role due to the fact that it still maintained a relative degree of isolation and unlike the British had fewer stakes in Iraq prior to the Second World War; the primary US foreign interest at the time concerned Latin America. Therefore, the archives of the AAS, the Ashurbanipal (Assyrian Universal Alliance Foundation) Library in Chicago, the Modern Assyrian Research Archive in Frölunda, Sweden, and the files of the NCRD. Numerous personal archives including the collection, housed in Michigan, of Afram Rayis, former secretary general of the Assyrian Universal Alliance (AUA), which includes the *Assyrian Sentinel*, the organ of the AUA was also consulted.

With reference to Iraqi government documents seized after the fall of the Ba'th regime, the papers will also help to illustrate the government policies aimed against the Assyrians, Kurds and others. Following the first Gulf War, many documents were found by the Kurdish political parties the Kurdistan Democratic Party and the Patriotic Union of Kurdistan, as well as some Assyrian parties such as the ADM. With the aid of the US Foreign Relations Committee and Middle East Watch they were brought to the United States in 1993 for scanning and processing and housed in Colorado. In 2007, the originals were sent back to Iraq, though not to the central government.[37] These documents are also subject to review and reliability questioning.[38] The Iraq Memory Foundation (IMF, the successor to the Iraq Research and Documentation Project) went to Iraq following the second Gulf War and captured numerous documents from Baghdad that they brought back to their headquarters in Washington, DC, and later stored at the Hoover Institution. In January 2008 these were also scrutinised.[39] The sub-sections analysed included the Ba'th Regional Command Collection and the North Iraq Data Set. Furthermore I was able to obtain both originals and copies of documents from Assyrian political and civil society organisations in Iraq, some of which corresponded to those housed at Stanford. The most important set of these is perhaps the Secret Documents of the Iraqi Government, as collected by the ADM.

This research is also interdependently interlaced by interviews conducted with more than 100 Assyrians from 2004 to 2013, many immigrants from Iraq following the US-led Gulf War in 1991, concerning their lives as Assyrians under successive Iraqi regimes. The interviewees were chosen based on their place of residence in Iraq (villages) and from a range of Assyrian ecclesiastical communities. The bibliography lists Assyrians who represent the villages discussed in the body of this study for the period of 1933 to 1991, though some also dwelled in the major cities of Baghdad, Mosul, Dohuk and elsewhere. The questions and approach used in the interview process were evaluated and approved by the Office of Research Ethics at the University of Toronto and all subsequent ethnographic work followed the same trajectory.

There is an added importance to the inclusion of personal oral interviews with individuals from 1933 to the Anfal campaign. These interviews refute or corroborate the data of archival materials and secondary sources, as well as provide an alternative view of events. Furthermore, as expressed by Linda Tuhiwai Smith (pertinent in the Assyrian case), since indigenous peoples struggled under colonialism against a Western view of their history, this allows for the Assyrians to retell part of their history from their own perspective, which in some ways circumvents both Western and Eastern views of Assyrian history.[40] As such it is the onset of remedying an ethical dilemma created by the now unequivocal assumption that the Assyrians are inconsequential to the history of Iraq and the modern Middle East. Yet in order to illustrate these problems and misconceptions, and attempt to remedy the Assyrian lacuna, a very unpretentious and rudimentary argument based in syllogisms must be made, a marriage of two seemingly incompatible views as the former argues the malleable and capricious nature of history where the latter discusses straightforward cause and effect. Both deal with *how* the past is remembered but also *why* it is remembered.

One particular drawback to oral memory is its inconsistency, especially with, in the case of Simele, a gap of more than eighty years. This concern cannot be avoided in any historical study. Also there exists a supposition that the more the accounts substantiate one another the more valid or true they become. This too is a problematic theory as again it implies more in the sense of 'majority equals truth', or at least alludes to things having greater accuracy, which is not necessarily the case. Furthermore, while historians are overly concerned with the reliability of human memory, they should be equally wary of official documentation. Most written knowledge begins as oral knowledge, which, too, is subject to personal interpretation and political bias. It is equally arguable and evident that the same historic event has multiple and often-conflicting written accounts and further, that those sources accumulated and displayed in archives and museums are filtered through a very tangible national lens.

The photographs included in this study are necessary for assessing the extent of the destruction in the various Assyrian villages. Since the villages have either been obliterated completely or, in some cases, recently rebuilt, these visual aids both verify the destruction and allow the reader to better perceive the damage to this community's culture and obtain a sense of the magnitude of the historic importance of these sites. These visual aids will supplement the village descriptions and histories in the body of this research.[41] In addition the breadth of this research is limited by the same sources it is indebted to. In most cases, all the research conducted, including by human rights NGOs, is subject to the influence of modern politics, just as all pre-modern records are equally subject to political bias. Knowing this, it is understandable that most knowledge regarding events in Iraq contains various political, ethnic and religious biases, especially since the state- and nation-building process is still under way in both central Iraq and Iraqi Kurdistan. This being the case, the question remains, where does our Iraqi-Assyrian narrative begin?

Notes

1. The three responses of oppressed peoples to oppression are based on and quoted directly from Martin Luther King Jr, *Stride toward Freedom: The Montgomery Story* (Boston: Beacon Press, [1958] 2010), 206–10.
2. In the case of Kurds oppressed by the Iraqi regime then oppressing Assyrians and others see 'Political Oppression and Targeting in the KRG: A Personal Story of Terror and Tragedy', *ISDP Issue Focus*, October 2007, http://www.iraqdemocracyproject.org/issuefocus_political.html (accessed 8 July 2014); 'KRG Continues to Fail Vulnerable Minorities in Iraq', *ISDP Policy Alert*, 5 December 2011, http://www.iraqdemocracyproject.org/policy_alert_16.html (accessed 8 July 2014).
3. This aversion is reflected in studies on other minorities and indigenous communities around the globe.
4. Chris Lorenz, 'Drawing the Line: "Scientific" History between Myth-making and Myth-breaking', in Stefan Berger, Linas Eriksonas and Andrew Mycock (eds), *Narrating the Nation: Representations in History, Media and the Arts*, (New York: Berghahn, 2008), 36.
5. The question for some becomes: if it is by its very nature unknowable, then why the pursuit? The answer is discussed in greater detail below.
6. Lorenz, 'Drawing the Line', 48.
7. Sargon Donabed, 'Rethinking Nationalism and an Appellative Conundrum: Historiography and Politics in Iraq', *National Identities* 14.4 (2012): 407–31.
8. Many funding sources for academia are government based, such as the National Endowment for the Humanities and the National Science Foundation.
9. Marion Farouk-Sluglett and Peter Sluglett, 'The Historiography of Modern Iraq', *American Historical Review* 96.5 (1991), 1408, 1412–13.

10. Giles Mohan and Gordon Wilson, 'The Antagonistic Relevance of Development Studies', *Progress in Development Studies* 5.4 (2005), 266.

11. Sue Clifford and Angela King, 'Losing Your Place', in *Local Distinctiveness: Place, Particularity and Identity*, quoted in Patrick Curry, *Defending Middle-Earth: Tolkien, Myth and Modernity* (Boston: Houghton Mifflin, 2004), 145.

12. Malek also published further works in English, French and Arabic, including *Les Conséquences tragiques du mandat en Iraq* ('The Tragic Consequences of the Mandate in Iraq') in 1932, *Simmel, the Cemetery of Betrayed Giants* in 1938, *Kurdistan, Aw Bilād al-Akrād* ('Kurdistan, or the Land of the Kurds') in 1945, and a weekly political newspaper, *Al-Hurriya* ('Freedom'), from 1957 until his death two years later.

13. See the back cover of Malek's *The British Betrayal of the Assyrians* (Chicago: Assyrian National Federation/Assyrian National League of America, 1935).

14. Ibid., ii.

15. *Assyrian Star*, March–August 1996. See also *Zinda Magazine*, 13 October 1997.

16. Malek, *The British Betrayal of the Assyrians*, 333–9. This list is corroborated by or based on 'Report of Mar Shimun, Catholicos Patriarch of the Assyrians, Oct. 8, 1933', *Protection of Minorities in Iraq*, League of Nations, Geneva, 31 October 1933.

17. Author's personal correspondence with an unnamed academic.

18. Khaldun S. Husry, 'The Assyrian Affair of 1933 (I)', *International Journal of Middle East Studies* 5.2 (1974), 161.

19. Khaldun S. Husry, 'The Assyrian Affair of 1933 (II)', *International Journal of Middle East Studies* 5.3 (1974), 346.

20. R. S. Stafford, *The Tragedy of the Assyrians* (London: George Allen & Unwin, 1935), 12.

21. Orit Bashkin, *The Other Iraq: Pluralism and Culture in Hashemite Iraq* (Stanford, CA: Stanford University Press, 2009), 198. In many cases, this attitude is reflective of early portrayals of Native Americans as savage and uncivilised, which in later years developed into a more romanticised (and perhaps slightly less degrading) view of the 'noble savage', something British attitudes to Assyrians seemed to portray as well. It should become blatantly evident after reading the majority of this work that the Arab ruling elite had far more in common with and would reap far more rewards from British intervention than their co-religionist Assyrians would.

22. Husry, 'The Assyrian Affair of 1933 (II)', 354–5.

23. Author's personal correspondence with an unnamed academic.

24. Reidar Visser, 'The Sectarian Master Narrative in Iraqi Historiography', in Jordi Tejel, Peter Sluglett, Riccardo Bocco and Hamit Bozarslan (eds), *Writing the Modern History of Iraq: Historiographical and Political Challenges* (Hackensack, NJ: World Scientific, 2012), 56–57.

25. N. E. Bou-Nacklie, 'Les Troupes Speciales: Religious and Ethnic Recruitment, 1916–46,' *International Journal of Middle East Studies* 25.4 (1993), 650. The quote also cites Albert Hourani, *A Vision of History* (Beirut: Khayats, 1961), 101–3.

26. Tareq Y. Ismael and Jacqueline S. Ismael, *Government and Politics of the Contemporary Middle East: Continuity and Change* (Abingdon: Routledge, 2011), 192.

27. Benjamin Thomas White, *The Emergence of Minorities in the Middle East: The Politics of Community in French Mandate Syria*, (Edinburgh: Edinburgh University Press, 2011), 211.

28. I am very grateful to Fr Yousif Thomas OP of Baghdad, who kindly provided me with the unpublished map through Professor Amir Harrak. Despite the comprehensiveness of Omez's work and my own work's indebtedness to it, there are a few limiting gaps. Due to the condition of the map, some villages remain unreadable. I have attempted to clarify as many as possible, yet some remain unrecognisable. Further, it must be mentioned that since Omez utilised his own French spellings, I have adjusted the village names to be more consistent with Assyrian pronunciation and etymology, where appropriate. Nevertheless, a combination of this map and United Nations Humanitarian Affairs reference maps on Iraq has allowed for a more accurate demarcating of Assyrian villages, which, when possible, includes longitudinal and latitudinal coordinates. See Appendix B.

29. Some 37,720 people were forcibly displaced from Kirkuk between 1970 and 1990, while more than 182,000 went missing; see *Iraq: Continuous and Silent Ethnic Cleansing – Displaced Persons in Iraqi Kurdistan and Iraqi Refugees in Iran* (Paris: FIDH/International Alliance for Justice, 2003), 7.

30. See Hormizd Rassam, 'Biblical Nationalities Past and Present', *Transactions of the Society of Biblical Archaeology, vol. 8* (London: Society of Biblical Archaeology, 1885), 370. Rassam, a native Assyrian (of the Chaldean Church) archaeologist, mentions that with the exception of some Armenian families in Baghdad and Diyarbekir, the rest of the Christians of the region of Iraq and the old vilayet (province) of Mosul are 'Chaldean Nestorians, Chaldean Catholics, Syrian Jacobites, and Syrian Catholics'.

31. See J.-M. Fiey, *Assyrie Chrétienne*, 3 vols (Beirut: Imprimerie Catholique, 1963); George Percy Badger, *The Nestorians and Their Rituals*, 2 vols (London: Darf, [1852] 1987).

32. Badger, *The Nestorians and Their Rituals*, vol. 1, 392.

33. Majed Eshoo, 'The Fate of Assyrian Villages Annexed to Today's Dohuk Governorate in Iraq and the Conditions in These Villages Following the Establishment of the Iraqi State in 1921', tr. Mary Challita (2004), Assyrian General Conference website, http://www.assyriangc.com/magazine/eng1.pdf (accessed 9 July 2014).

34. Eshoo's writings have been republished by various Assyrian news agencies and political groups, including the Assyrian National Assembly (ANA – an Iraqi Assyrian political group). His writings (and those of the ANA) have singled out certain persons of rank in the Kurdistan Regional Government for crimes against local Assyrians, perhaps adding to possible disfavour and the need for the past and continued use of a pseudonym.

35. See Hannibal Travis, 'After Regime Change: United States Law and Policy Regarding Iraqi Refugees, 2003–2008', *Wayne Law Review* 55.2, 1009–61.

36. For the use of diacritics in the names of villages, I have tried to remain close to the local Assyrian and Kurdish pronunciation and Syriac manuscript renditions, but this has been difficult for the mapping section as the British and French renditions of Assyrian village names are sometimes grossly inaccurate in comparison with the native spelling and/or pronunciation.

37. See 'Perspectives', Trudy Huskamp Peterson, Certified Archivist, http://trudypeterson.com/perspectives (accessed 9 July 2014).

38. Concerning these Iraqi documents, it is possible that some may be forgeries, due to the chaos in Iraq following the 2003 invasion, where much Ba'th stationery was stolen. Since it is impossible to detect this with accuracy, I have been as cautious as possible in my approach and mentioned discrepancies where apparent.

39. See http://www.iraqmemory.org/en/index.asp (accessed 9 July 2014). Special thanks are due to Professor Kanan Makiya for his aid and permission to browse the IMF documents long before they were removed from the online archive. The removal of such material from Iraq under intellectual property rights and its return to Kurdish political parties rather than to the Iraqi National Library and Archives is another issue which has been addressed by some academics but requires further unpacking and discussion.

40. Smith, *Decolonizing Methodologies*, 33.

41. I was unable to obtain high-quality scans of many of the villages and their

cultural sites, but they can be viewed online at sites such as http://www.barwar.net, a major portal to individual village sites including http://www.assyrian-dooreh.com (both accessed 9 July 2014).

2

Framing the Assyrian Narrative: Late Nineteenth and Early Twentieth Century

> It was an ill day for his tribe when he led them to fight in a war for the liberty of small nations. Now we have to meet death at long last, so let us prepare to face the enemy whom we know, that we may the more readily forget the desertion of those whom we once thought to be our friends.[1]

Yaqo Ismael translating for his father, Malik Ismael,
of Upper Tiyari, 1932

Assyrian Demography: Between Deteriorating Empires and Colonial Expansion

Contextualising the Assyrians, starting in the late nineteenth century in the region of Iraq, begins by distinguishing them socially and geographically (which sometimes includes dialect and ecclesiastical adherence) into two major categories. While the two groups had a notion of shared ancestry there were some distinctions that waxed and waned throughout the centuries.[2]

The first group comprised those centred in and around the cities of Mosul, Arbil, Kirkuk, Zakho and Dohuk in modern-day Iraq, most of whom were converted from the Church of the East/Nestorianism (though bastions of Nestorians remained in and around the Barwar and Sapna regions and elsewhere) or Orthodoxy (referred to predominantly as Jacobite) to Catholicism primarily via Dominican missions. Many were urban dwellers, some having lost their native Assyrian-Aramaic language to Arabic and were thus Arabised. Others who had retained their mother tongue lived in large semi-rural regions.[3]

The second category of Assyrians hailed from the region of Hakkâri in today's southeastern Turkey and Urmia in northwestern Iran. They fled during the Great War into what would become Iraq. They were typically rural, predominantly of Nestorian ecclesiastical background in Hakkâri with some Uniate Catholics, while the Urmia Assyrians numbered many Protestants, Catholics and Russian Orthodox. The Hakkâri segment also made up the bulk of the Iraqi Levies in the latter years of their institution, alongside Assyrians of Barwar and Sapna.

In both cases, the Assyrians were native to the region of northern Mesopotamia, which would later find itself divided by Western political entities during colonial expansion. Not unlike the scramble for Africa following the Berlin Conference in 1884, Assyrians, like many native African peoples, found themselves fragmented by arbitrarily created boundaries that would become the basis for internal and external components of otherisation.

In many ways, the mid-nineteenth century is a prudent starting point for this study of the Assyrians and the state as it elucidates the transition period of the Middle East from Ottoman Empire to nation-states. During this period, many rural Assyrians living in today's southeast Turkey had been living for centuries in close proximity to their Kurdish neighbours in similar tribal and social formations, and in relative autonomy, free from most state influence. This relative independence would come to an end with the rise of a prominent and powerful Kurdish chieftain, Bedr Khan Beg. Bedr Khan's campaigns were initially directed against Ottoman rule, and in many cases Assyrians and Kurds fought together to 'defend their autonomous status'.[4] Yet, once the Ottomans ceased their attacks on Bedr Khan in 1842, he directed his attention towards the Assyrians – the culmination of an attempt at power consolidation. During his rise to power, Bedr Khan massacred approximately 10,000 people among the Assyrian tribes of the Bohtan and Hakkâri regions in one campaign in 1842.[5] The Ottomans capitalised on the ambitiousness of Bedr Khan, and once the independent Assyrian tribes had been subdued, the Ottomans planned to eliminate the bastion of Kurdish power.[6]

Modern Roots of Interreligious Animosity[7]

While Assyrian woes seemed to be felt by co-religionists half a world away, missionaries seemed less interested in preservation of Assyrians and their way of life, and more interested in their conversion to the 'true faith'. Such evangelising activity especially among the Nestorians and Orthodox of Urmia

(Reza'iyeh, Iran), provided opportunities for conversion and forced moderni-
sation (ripe with a Christian martyr complex) in the guise of humanitarian aid:

> In their eagerness to foster a culture of missionary service among Nestorians,
> the Americans encouraged their students to identify with a vision of the
> future in which Christians who suffered persecution became leading agents
> in Christ's triumph of the world. This vision nurtured expectations of mar-
> tyrdom and happened to coincide with the violence that the Nestorians
> were actually suffering at the hands of Muslims, partly as a result of mis-
> sionary involvement in Nestorian affairs. Missionaries took the massacre of
> mountain Nestorians by Kurds in 1843 as an opportunity to foster conver-
> sion experiences in the refugees who poured into Urmiyah, and Asahel
> Grant wrote positively about the effect of survivors' sufferings on their
> religious lives: 'A new hope seemed to kindle in their bosoms,' he wrote
> after the massacres, 'they eagerly drank the encouragement I presented.'[8]

Many acrimonious divisions within the Assyrian community can be traced to
such missionary aid following the massacres. The assistance of Asahel Grant
further fostered anti-Christian sentiments among the Assyrians' Muslim
neighbours. It also added to interdenominational intolerance, which, in
the case of Eastern Christianity, certainly needed no supplementary fuel.[9]
Finally, the American missions had 'stirred up and created much hostility
between the various tribes, on the one hand, and the *maliks* and the patriarch,
on the other', thus dividing the previously independent and reasonably unified Nestorian Assyrian community as well as, in some cases, contributing to
a general Assyrian culture of apathy.[10]

George Percy Badger, a nineteenth-century English scholar of the Church
of the East, spent a year during 1842–3 among Nestorian Assyrians, travers-
ing the region more to create opposition to Grant and the Protestants (whom
he loathed) as well as the persistent Catholic enterprise, than as a missionary
priest. The idea of favouritism granted to the Assyrians by virtue of their
Christian religion was not necessarily accurate. Edward Lewes Cutts, who
followed Grant to the region, as part of the Archbishop of Canterbury's mission, remarks in his travelogue that while he served in some capacity during a
eucharistic service, he did not fully commune with the celebrants as they and
the church remained anathematised by heresy.[11]

The Dominican (Catholic) interest and aid for Christians was certainly focused on the Chaldean sect (including increasing their numbers through proselytisation) by virtue of it being Catholic, though they, as well as the Protestants, actively fed off the dying legacy of the Church of the East as it had no wellspring of restoration or protection. During this post-Bedr Khan period, the Assyrian Church of the East's foothold in the plains of Nineveh, in particular at Rabban Hormizd in Alqosh, was finally shattered by the Dominican missions, who were converting the bulk of the region to Catholicism propelled by a desire for a French/Catholic beachhead in the region, aided by a red herring in the guise of benevolence and coupled with the Church of the East's poor socio-economic status.[12] The coercive conversion to Catholicism of those Hakkâri Nestorians seeking refuge in the Mosul region in exchange for basic sustenance, and the lack of support and aid for those Nestorian and Jacobite Assyrians unwilling to convert, is testament to the beginnings of conflict and hierarchy within the community based on sectarian divisions.

The Roman Catholic Church was the most authoritative of the three Western missions vying for supremacy in the region. Its presence served two purposes: first, to convert the Assyrians by any means, including bribery and preferential treatment for converts, as seen in the relatively poor treatment of the local Nestorians and Jacobites;[13] and second, the Catholic missionaries endeavoured to further French imperial interests in the region in order to offset growing British authority. It is conceivable that the less-than-cordial reaction of the Patriarch of the Church of the East (Nestorians), Mar Shimun XVII Abraham, to a bribe and promise to make him head of all Christians of the East sparked French-led Catholic annoyance:[14]

> Tell your master that I shall never become a Catholic; and should you even induce my whole people, to the last man, to do so, I would sooner become a Dervish, or a Koordish Moollah, than degrade myself by an alliance with the people.[15]

This patriarchal impudence, coupled with the already ingrained revulsion for the 'heresy' of the Nestorians (and Jacobites), further fuelled the missionaries to actively convert the entire region, or see the end of an ancient heresy. The French used this opportunity under the guise of the Catholic Church to increase their control over the region as well, leaving the natives to reap the problematic consequences of these communal divisions inculcated by various colonial powers.[16]

The depth of this French-Catholic connection was formidable. As early as the 1830s, the three main Christian merchant families of Iraq, the Rassams, the Halabis and the Sayighs, were tightly bound to French trade in the region, which multiplied their assets 'bolstered by their conversion and sponsorship of Catholicism in Mosul under the Dominicans'.[17] Furthermore, the most prominent among the merchant families adopted Catholicism 'as a marker of affluence', emboldening young Catholic peasants of Mosul's plains to unyoke themselves from the Diyarbekir and Alqosh dioceses by supporting an independent patriarchal see in the city of Mosul itself.[18] While the original reason for conversion may have been personal profit, the socio-economically based enmity which it produced became ingrained within sectarian divisions in that its influence desired to 'divert dues paid by Christians [Assyrians] as taxes to the Nestorian [Assyrian Church of the East] diocese'.[19] So the Assyrians found themselves in the midst of a sectarian power struggle for the Middle East between the French/Dominican Catholics, the English/ Anglicans (Badger, Rev. Wigram, Layard) and the Americans/Presbyterians (Grant, Cumberland, Shedd). This missionary activity, including conversion and evangelisation missions in the mid- to late-nineteenth century, though non-violent, further contributed to increased Muslim persecution as well as intra-Assyrian social and religious antagonism.[20]

In the realm of figures, exact population statistics, especially those of the Ottoman Empire concerning the Assyrians, are difficult to legitimise.[21] One reason stems from the fact that large numbers of Assyrians had lost their native tongue. In the case of Armenian-speaking Assyrians, for instance (especially in the regions of Harput, Malatiya and Adana), more than 175,000 were slain and listed as Armenian atrocities during the First World War.[22] This is partly since, in the example of the Jacobite Church 'they remained attached to the Armenian patriarchate for civil affairs' under Ottoman rule.[23] According to the 1849 census the population of Mosul totalled 2,050 Muslim families, 200 Jewish families and 1,100 Christian families.[24] Moreover, 'Amēdīyāh had more than 2,000 Assyrian Christian and Jewish families in the 1840s. A decade later, there were barely 300 remaining in those communities combined, due to continued oppression

Table 1 Assyrian population statistics in Van and Hakkâri (includes Bitlis and Erzeroum but excludes Sa'irt)[25]

Source	Year	Ecclesiastical affiliation	Assyrian population	Total population
J. G. Taylor (consul of Erzeroum)	1869	Nestorians	110,000	1,130,400
Vital Cuinet[26] (French geographer)	1870	Nestorians	97,000 (52,000 semi-autonomous)	–
Berlin Project	1878	Nestorians	14,000	1,700,000
Official to Sir Charles Dilke	1880	Nestorians	84,995	1,220,038
Armenian Patriarch	1880	Nestorians	85,000	758,000
Vice Consul Clayton	1880	Nestorians	53,940	–
Official figures (Baker Pasha)	1880	Nestorians	61,778	1,208,540
Official figures	1880	Nestorians	29,350 (males)	156,692 (males)

by what Badger termed 'Muhammadan despotism'.[27] Demographic estimates of Assyrians vary for numerous reasons including limited accessibility to their mountain steadings. General numbers for the Assyrians from the region of Hakkâri who fled into Iraq during the period of the Great War, as mentioned in the beginning of the chapter, are given in Table 1, specific tribes are mentioned in Tables 2 and 3. In the case of the Tkhuma tribe, their numbers had been greatly reduced following the slaughter in the wake of the rise of Bedr Khan in 1842. Peculiarly, despite this and other Kurdish–Assyrian intercommunal calamities, there is much evidence of an uneasy yet functional coexistence at the tribal level.[28]

But how did the largely rural Hakkâri Assyrians become entwined with the British authorities and how did this affect their identification both internally within the larger Assyrian community (including among urban Chaldeans and Syrian Orthodox/Catholics) and externally, by the British, Iraqi Arabs, Kurds and others? The majority of the citations of 'Assyrian' in British archival documentation refer to those highlanders of Hakkâri in present-day Turkey who lived as independent tribes prior to the First World War. The British interest in the martial spirit of the highlanders of Hakkâri

Table 2 Assyrian population statistics of '*Ashiret* (independent) Nestorians in 1869[29]

'Ashiret	Houses	Total population
Tiyari	2,500	15,000
Diz	2,400	14,400
Jilu	2,000	12,000
Baz	1,700	10,200
Tkhuma	1,500	9,000
Walto	650	3,900
Other		12,000
Total		**76,500**

Table 3 Assyrian population statistics of *Rayat* (subject) Nestorians in 1869[30]

Rayat	Houses	Total population
Mar Bishu	1,200	7,200
Albaq (Elbek)	720	4,320
Van District	700	4,200
Gawar	600	3,600
Leyone	600	3,600
Mahmoodieh	500	3,000
Norduz	500	3,000
Gawar Pinyānish	300	1,800
Pinyānish	300	1,800
Oromaree	200	1,200
Shemdino	45	370
Deyree	60	360
Doskee	20	120
Kharawatta	7	40
Total		**34,610**

was methodically beneficial, especially the skills of the independent tribes of Tiyari, Tkhuma, Jilu, Diz and Baz, leading to their commodification in the period prior to the First World War:

> The Ashiret can furnish 13,000 able-bodied men, all armed with good muskets . . . The knowledge of their strength, their poverty, and the non-fulfillment of lavish promises made to them by the Turks subsequent to Bedr Khan Beg's massacre of the Nestorians, together with constant skirmishes with the Moslem Koords, keep up that martial spirit, unfavourable

to entire submission, inclining them in consequence to warlike rather than peaceful pursuits.[31]

The British military would use this intelligence to their advantage in the near future as they armed these Assyrians, who would also become problematically referred to as 'British protégés' in the Middle East, due to their Christian religious affiliation. By the turn of the century those Assyrians of the regions of Urmia and Hakkâri, not counting the Tigris region, amounted to more than 450 villages and between 18,000 and 20,000 families, totalling 126,000–140,000 people in 1902–3.[32] Hannibal Travis, Associate Professor of Law at Florida International University, estimates that using the Armenian patriarchal assumption of a 25 per cent population growth ever 20 years, this was but part of a much larger population of 600,000–800,000 that would fluctuate dramatically.[33] The data suggests that at the onset of war there were an estimated 80,000 Assyrians in the Tigris valley from Mosul to the villages of the Bohtan region, 35,000 in seventy villages in Urmia and Salamas, and 100,000 in Hakkâri.[34]

The First World War

In most cases, the First World War was the epitome of violence in an age of nationalist and colonial fervour.[35] It embodied the final efforts of dying empires to retain some semblance of power in the midst of the failing the old world order and the rise of the new nation-state, which would forever change the political power structure. Late 1914 saw an initial build-up of Turkish military forces in Assyrian regions of the sanjak of Hakkari. Between Turkey's entrance into the First World War in November and March 1915, both Russian and Turkish leaders courted the Assyrians. A prolonged battle at Sarikamish, which lasted from 22 December 1914 until 17 January 1915, featured a number of major mêlées. Elsewhere the Wali of Julamerk, fearful that the Assyrians might side with the Russians, preemptively struck at them in the region of Albaq.[36] This required the Assyrians to become mobile. January saw a major engagement as Enver Pasha brought two corps to cut the Russian lines south of Kars in northwest Turkey, eventually capturing the city as well as Sarikamish and the majority of the railway. The Russians would pull back to Djoulfa as the Assyrians and Armenians under commander

Raphael Khan protected the besieged villages of the plains while an evacuation of inhabitants began in earnest.[37]

By March 1915, more than 100 Assyrian villages were destroyed while 12,000 refugees fled to the Caucasus and more than 27,000 men, women and children were butchered in the Urmia region alone. In the village of Ada, some 300 Assyrians were locked inside a church and burned alive.[38] Meanwhile, in an act of extermination in Gulpashan, the last of the villages to be destroyed by March 1915, Kurdish forces urged on by Ottoman promises massacred the entire male population of the village and carried away its young women.[39] Later that spring Turkish authorities arrested Hormuzd, a brother of Patriarch Mar Benyamin Shimun who had been living and studying in Istanbul, and moved him to Mosul as ransom until the patriarch had declared war against Russia.[40] The mountaineer Eastern Assyrians[41] were forced into the fray after these attacks and the slow surrounding of their Hakkâri homes by Kurdish Ottoman troops. They moved from their homes to higher elevations in the fastness of the mountains. As the siege wore on, food became scarce, most surviving on the fruit of the mulberry tree alone. This continued through August. Realising the gravity of the situation, in mid-July Mar Shimun called a war council where he and the tribal chieftains decided to approach the Russians for support in escaping the current siege and slow wasting of their people. Promises of support furthered the Assyrians' desire to connect with Allied forces; they hoped the Allies would plead with the Russians for assistance. As their trek continued, in late September of 1915, the men of Tkhuma who remained defended their land with homemade ammunition and fought for two days (27–28 September) until their villages of Gundiktha and Mazra among others were destroyed.[42] A day later bands of Kurds looking for the Patriarch, who had been in Tal overseeing the burial of his brother Eshaya, killed upwards of 500 and took captive around 200 women and children along with livestock and household goods.[43]

In October 1915 a contingent of the Hakkâri tribes finally made the long trek to Russian-controlled Persia just west of Lake Urmia, which already held a bastion of their lowland brethren.[44] There they formed battalions to stem the Ottoman Turkish and Kurdish advance, which had begun its plundering across Assyrian lands. In 1916, acting on governmental authority, companies of Turks and Kurds massacred villages in the Bohtan region where those women who were not killed ended their own lives rather than suffer the alternative of being carried off into captivity.[45]

Autumn 1917 was a time of great transformation in the war. In Russia the Bolshevik revolution had arisen, causing chaos on the battlefront for soldiers deciding to whom allegiance was owed. Northwest Persia, and the region of Urmia in particular, originally under heavy Russian influence, paid a particularly high price. Anarchy governed the day as the Bolsheviks ordered the return of Russian troops in the Caucasus front in November. The American missionaries hinted at incidents of Muslim-on-Christian violence as retribution for acts committed by the failing Russian forces. Ironically, the Russian trade of weapons and ammunition to local Kurds and Persians would become problematic for the already tenuous relationship with Assyrians and other Christians.[46]

As the Russians withdrew from the battlefront, the Allies approached the Assyrians for aid in holding the eastern front alongside Georgian and Armenian companies. The retreating Russians had left some machine guns, as well as ammunition which was supplemented by 20,000 French Lebel rifles and dispersed throughout the troops commanded by General Petros Elia of Baz on one flank, and Malik Khoshaba of Lower Tiyari on the other.[47] According to eyewitness Mary Shedd, on 22 February 1918 the Persians attacked the Christian part of Urmia. In her letters, she recognised the military tactics of Malik Khoshaba, recently converted to American Protestantism, and Petros Elia that were able to drive the Persians back till the Assyrians controlled the greater part of the city.[48] Until March 1918 and the Brest-Litovsk Treaty that ended Russian participation in the war, the Assyrian militia with 25,000 soldiers was able to hold the Urmia region in six major engagements against legions made up of German, Kurdish and Turkish troops.[49] On the third day of that formative month, along with 150 men acting as vanguard, Mar Benyamin Shimun was assassinated in Salamas by Agha Simko Ismail Shikak under a flag of parley as he turned to leave in his carriage.[50]

In April, a Turkish force began advancing against the Assyrian positions in the east. Assyrian troops were able to turn the Turks back at Ushnu, creating a seemingly striking victory. They were not able to celebrate for

long as their brethren, some 4,000 strong who had settled at Khoy, 50 kilometres north of Salamas, were unexpectedly attacked and massacred by
Simko Ismail and his men, who had escaped Assyrian retribution.[51] By July
1918, the Ottoman advance into Assyrian territory instigated the major
flight. American Protestant missionaries William Ambrose Shedd and Mary
Lewis Shedd, then proselytising among the Assyrians, observed a variety of
calamities and heroism during their time in residence. Such events were
consistent throughout the run of the war. Relentless combat, killing, death,
forced expulsion, and loss of home and hearth exemplified the period. The
Assyrians of Urmia refer to this time as *Raqa raqa* or more simply 'the Flight'
or 'the Escape' as a mass exodus of 30,000 men, women and children from
among themselves and their Hakkâri brethren traversed the region, travelling
more than 600 kilometres to Baqubah, a refugee camp 30 miles northeast of
Baghdad.[52] Records count almost a third dying along the way, some of exposure, others murdered by bandits on the road. Most men were killed outright.
Younger women were carried off as brides if they were lucky, raped and left
for dead if not, while the elderly were killed and burned to extract gold they
had allegedly swallowed. Those with child were slaughtered in a manner that
pushed the boundaries of savagery as the unborn were cut from mother's
wombs, killing both mother and child.[53] Those who were lucky enough to
make it to the camp were fatigued and destitute.

Early in its history, Brigadier General H. H. Austin became the com-
mandant of the camp, one of the few places of refuge. In his memoirs Austin
relates numerous observations of the framework, activities and personnel
of Baqubah. Those musings indicate that there were few Catholics in the
camp, which was reflective of a larger community issue. Austin offers an
anecdote about the intra-community obstacles faced by those Assyrians who
had fought in the war, and those who had remained neutral. He observes that
when the British took control of the region, those of Chaldean ecclesiastical
bearing tried to take credit for the opposition of their brethren against the
Turks and Kurds. Anecdotally he refers to an Assyrian mountaineer who had
made the trek from Urmia to Mosul in stealth (telling the tale of his travels to
Austin months later) receiving poor treatment at the hands of the Chaldeans
(Catholics) he encountered 'though they were of his own race and blood'.[54]
Such tension became more palpable in later years as identity fragmentation

was added to geographical and ecclesiastical divisions amidst overt and subtle policies of assimilation. This was coupled with geopolitics and became even more evident as the Assyrians were courted yet again by the French.[55]

Besides the tribal chieftains and religious hierarchy, the Assyrians had numerous individuals who wielded power within the community as well as without. One charismatic leader, Malik Kambar Warda of Jilu, appeared in 1918 with a new plan as an alternative to the British plan for the Assyrians. Kambar was a Catholic (Chaldean) to whom France had promised the establishment of a self-ruling protectorate in the Syrian Jazira region. France commenced communications with Kambar through the Chaldean Church, the normal conduit between Rome and France and the Assyrians.[56] After the flight of refugees from Urmia to Georgia and Armenia in January 1918, Kambar had settled in Georgia with 170 people from his tribe. Here, he commenced relations with Georgian officials as the spokesman for the refugees. In Tbilisi 7,000 Assyrian refugees also met Dr Fraidon (Aturaya) Bet-Avraham, a philosopher and theorist behind modern Assyrianism, who at that time was a physician in the Russian army.[57]

It is not clear exactly when, but at the behest of local leaders, Kambar and his family travelled to Istanbul early in 1920 and there met Fr Paul Barro and Mgr Petros Ubaid of the Chaldean Church. Later, General Henri Joseph Eugène Gouraud of the French Fourth Army invited Malik Kambar to Beirut, where he arrived on 7 July 1920. At that time Gouraud divulged to Kambar that France had decided to allot Djeziret Ben Omar, Urfa (Edessa) and Mardin to the Assyrians if he were to return to the Caucasus and raise a militia.[58] The French and Assyrian leaders, especially those Chaldean-rite individuals like Petros Elia, had begun talks that would entice the Assyrians to the northwest and Syria, away from British influence. This became a tangible fear for British authorities. In some cases the French movement in Mosul itself was done under the guise of Dominican camaraderie, all of which was an attempt to further draw the Assyrians into a military role to be used at France's behest.[59]

The concerns of the British were valid as the Assyrians both courted and were courted by the French. Kambar had a significant military in the jazirah and the British feared mounting French influence over the battle-hardened Assyrians.

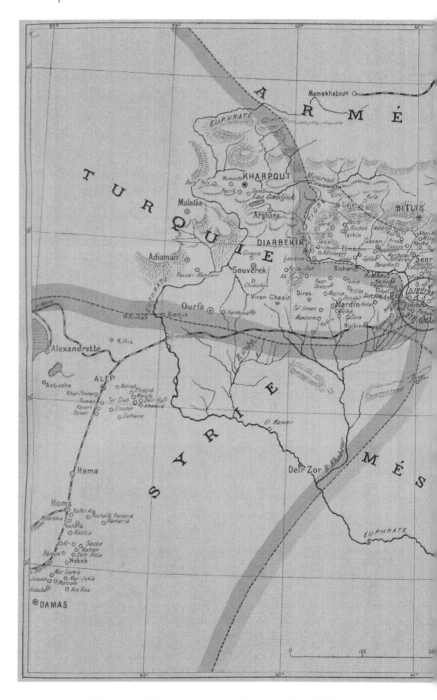

Figure 8 General Petros Elia's map of Assyrian territory from confidential letter
No. 2990 to Sir Percy Cox, High Commissioner, Mesopotamia, 28 December 1920,
FO 839/23

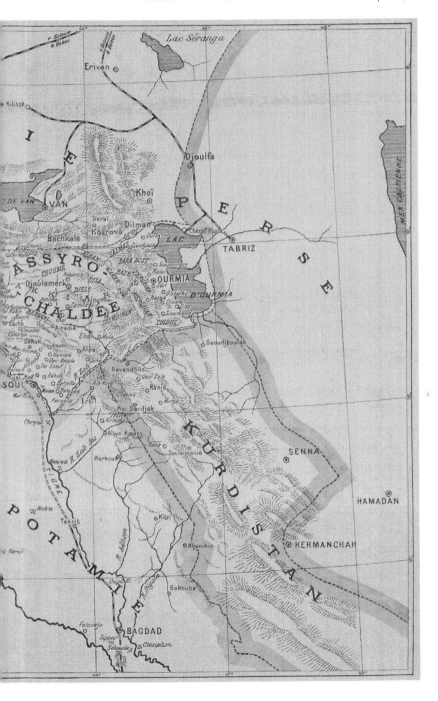

From Versailles 1919 to Lausanne 1923[60]

In the diplomatic arena, conceivably emboldened by the principles set forth in Woodrow Wilson's Fourteen Points of 1918, especially those concerning the rights to self-determination and autonomy, delegations were formed. Crossing ecclesiastical lines the Transcaucasian delegation included Shlimon Ganja, Lazar George, Abraham Yohannan PhD[61] and Lazar Yacoboff of Iran.[62] From the United States, Captain Dr Abraham K. Yoosuf, of Worcester, Massachusetts (Jacobite) and Rev. Joel Werda, president of the Assyrian Associations of America (Protestant) represented the Assyrians of America alongside Bishop Severius Afram Barsoum, of the Assyrian Apostolic Church of Antioch (Jacobite).[63]

Abraham K. Yoosuf (1866–1924), an army paramedic, was born in Harput (Kharput), Elazig, in 1866. He graduated from Central Turkey College in Aintab in 1886.[64] In 1889, Yoosuf moved to the United States and in 1895 graduated from Baltimore Medical College. He founded the Assyrian Benevolent Association in 1897. As a response to what he felt was continuous persecution against Christians in the Ottoman state, Yoosuf published *The Religion of Muhammad and Christian Sufferings*, wherein he spoke on the religious reasons for intolerance in the East and specifically on the Armenian question in Turkey.[65] He then conducted postgraduate work in London and Vienna in 1912 before returning to Turkey at the onset of the Balkan Wars, where he volunteered as a surgeon for the Red Crescent Society and was decorated for his medical prowess by Sultan Abdel Hamid.[66] Yoosuf returned to the United States and soon offered his medical services again during the First World War among the American forces, where he attained the rank of major. He eventually settled in Worcester, Massachusetts. Following the war and the massacres committed against the Assyrians, Yoosuf, along with his friend Joel (Yoel) Werda, attended the Paris Peace Conference in 1919. Speaking on Turkish reforms and the division of the Ottoman Empire, Yoosuf remarked, 'Reforms under the Turkish rule must be dismissed as hopeless. The history for the past hundred years has been a history of reform written in the blood of Assyrians.'[67] After what he and fellow Assyrians felt was a conference on unfulfilled promises, he returned to the United States. Yoosuf published various academic articles in the field of medicine and wrote prolifically for various

Assyrian publications, including the *Assyrian Progress* and the *New Assyria*, both published in the United States.[68]

Yoosuf was one of many Jacobite Assyrians to attend and support the delegation to the conference. Perhaps the best-known advocate of this delegation was Bishop Severius Afram Barsoum (1887–1957), born in Mosul. He was instrumental in requesting for an Assyrian homeland.[69] The written manifesto of the desires of some attendees was later formulated as *The Claims of the Assyrians as Presented to the Paris Peace Conference of 1919*, which defined the Assyrian people as including Nestorians, Chaldeans, Jacobites, a Maronite element, Persian Assyrians, Assyrians in Russia, and a Muslim Assyrian group that included Shakkaks[70] and Yezidis.[71] The Assyro-Chaldean delegation to the Paris Peace Conference in 1919 provided the following figures including a total worldwide population (excluding India) of 1,015,000 (see Table 4):[72]

The massacres of Assyrians and others in the waning Ottoman Empire and Persia during the First World War, which saw the deaths of possibly two-thirds of the entire Assyrian population,[73] were the inaugural enterprise of the Kemalist nation-building project.[74] Though the Assyrians were not completely eradicated, the data suggests at least one-third perished during the massacres while forced expulsion caused a major demographic shift that would frame Assyrian relations with what would become the new state of Iraq. Furthermore the assumption of the delegations to the conference in 1919 that their Allied leanings would grant them a hearing met with impediments.

Table 4 Assyrian population figures of the Middle East presented to the Paris Peace Conference 1919

Region	Number of Assyro-Chaldeans
Hakkâri	165,000
Diyarbekir	117,000
Mosul	122,000
Urmia and Salamas	78,000
Saʻirt (Seert)	61,000
Urfa and Aleppo	16,000
Deyr-Zor	4,000
Total	**563,000**

The Assyrian delegation from Iraq under Lady Surma d'Mar Shimun, sister of the late Benyamin Shimun, the Church of the East patriarch assassinated by Agha Ismail Simko, and aunt to the then current Patriarch Eshai, was met in London by British officials but prevented from journeying to Paris and petitioning its case.[75] S. Antoine Namik, R. Louis Nedjib, and Dr Jean Zebouni also attended and were greeted as part of the Assyro-Chaldean representation.[76]

As the Treaty of Versailles never settled the issue of the Ottoman Empire for the Allies, two other conferences including negotiations and treaties occurred. Eventually signed on 10 August 1920 following negotiations that began in April, the Treaty of Sèvres became the newly formulated peace treaty between the Ottomans and the Allied forces. In a letter to the conference Bishop Barsoum on April 1920 furthered the Assyrian desire for a homeland by introducing himself thus:

> Nous avons l'honneur d'exposer à la Conférence de la Paix que S.B. notre Patriarche nous a chargé de venir lui porter l'écho des malheurs et des voeux de notre nation syrienne, ancienne descendante de la race assyrienne, qui reside en general en Mésopotamie et en Arménie. [We have the honour to bring before the Peace Conference information entrusted to us by His Beatitude our patriarch, information concerning the sufferings and the wishes of our Syrian nation, descendants of the ancient Assyrian race, who chiefly reside in Mesopotamia and Armenia.][77]

Despite pleading and attempts at inclusion, Assyrian voices were largely ignored. Article 62 of the treaty stated, 'The scheme shall contain full safeguards for the protection of the Assyro-Chaldeans and other racial or religious minorities within these areas . . .'[78] For the Assyrian representatives, this was both too general as well as inherently problematic as it and they were confined under the larger section on Kurdistan. Ultimately, the Treaty of Sèvres failed as the relationship between Sultan Mehmed VI in Constantinople and Mustafa Kemal (Atatürk) and the nationalists of Anadolu ve Rumeli Müdafaa-i Hukuk Cemiyeti was completely sundered by the creation of the Grand National Assembly (GNA) in Ankara at the end of April 1920. The Kemalists were outraged at Sèvres and due to their overwhelming popularity, effectively made the treaty null and void.

Battles waged across Turkey for the next two years. In November 1922 another chance for restitutions came through the Treaty of Lausanne, but again the Assyrians were not allowed a seat at the talks. The pact was finally signed 24 July 1923 by İsmet İnönü of the GNA, in effect eliminating the power of the sultanate. Despite a lack of Assyrian participation, General Petros Elia began lobbying the Turkish government in earnest for the right of the mountaineer Assyrians to return to their indigenous lands in the Hakkâri region.[79] This was seen as a whimsical fancy and dismissed by the new government initially. But individuals and organisations continued their petitioning efforts. In most cases, the Assyrians took what jobs they were allotted, and in many cases such positions further commodified their soldiering prowess.

While France unofficially held much of modern Syria and Lebanon (from the San Remo conference in 1920) and Britain much of modern Iraq, French-mandate Syria was not considered internationally ratified until 29 September 1923. Soon thereafter, France dissolved Malik Kambar Warda's Assyro-Chaldean battalion and amalgamated it with the French Foreign Legion. When this occurred, Kambar moved to Lebanon to join the more diplomatic efforts of Yusuf Malek and others including Petros Elia, now abroad in France.

The Period of the Iraqi Levies and the Assyrian Settlement[80]

If a sword had memory, it might be grateful to the forge fire, but never fond of it.

Robert Jordan, *Winter's Heart*

Administratively, the new Iraq was divided into liwas or provinces, formerly vilayets under the Ottomans. Liwas were divided into *aqḍiyah* (singular *qadaa*) or districts and further into *nawāḥī* (singular *nāḥiyah*) or sub-districts. The chief administrative official of a liwa is a *mutasarrif*, of a *qadaa* a *qaim-aqam* and of a *nāḥiyah* a *mudir*. While the British governed the region with a local (predominantly Sunni Arab) leadership, it became apparent something supplementary would be needed.

Following the First World War, most of the highlanders of Hakkâri were forced out of their homes and established themselves among their kin across the newly created border. Whether of their own volition or not, these dispossessed Assyrians were a vital component in protecting British interests including the territorial integrity of both Turkey and Iraq, especially after the extension of the Soviet rule over Caucasia in 1921. While many saw them as but chess pieces to be utilised, several governmental officials felt compelled to honour previous promises. Since there was no political boon in aiding this numerical minority, it remains probable that dissidents among the British officers speaking out against the poor treatment of the Assyrians were fulfilling an unheeded sense of military honour and loyalty:

> The Assyrians deserve well of us. They have had less than justice at our hands. They can expect it from no other Government, and care for their interests is, in my humble view, one of our major obligations in Iraq.[81]

Whether or not the British were sympathetic to the Assyrians at an individual level was superseded by larger political and military expediency. The former desire to create both a Kurdistan and an Assyria in the region was discussed by both the British Foreign Office and A. T. Wilson, the acting British civil commissioner in Iraq, from 1918 to 1920.[82] The imperial historian Arnold Toynbee, a participant in British colonial decision-making, proposed another autonomous enclave for the Assyrians of Tur Abdin (inaccurately referred to as Jebel Tur in archival sources) within the Mosul vilayet, to effectively make two regions.[83] Neither of these aspirations came to fruition. When another problem presented itself, it became apparent that perhaps both could be satisfied with one solution. Realising that they required a local security force in the region of Iraq, the British adopted the same strategy they maintained in India. A militia was recruited from among the local population and subjected to training and deployment under a British officer, centring on military execution and loyalty.[84] This ensured the protection of His Majesty's interests, including oil reserves and airbases, in the newly established Iraq while lessening expenses.[85]

In 1915 Major John Inglis Eadie of the Indian Army 'recruited forty Mounted Arabs from the tribes round Nasiriyah, on the Euphrates, for duty under the Intelligence Department'.[86] After various name changes, this growing force became known as the Iraqi Levies. Originally consisting solely of Arabs during recruitment in 1915, the levies are sometimes thought of as a colonial police force for British authority.[87] By 1919 a large number of Kurds had been added to the fighting forces, leading to their official renaming on 12 August as the Arab and Kurdish Levies.[88] Only after small Assyrian battalions had fought the Barwari, Goyan and Guli Kurdish tribes in ʿAmēdīyāh on 8 August 1919 and shown fighting prowess did they catch the attention of the British.[89] Major recruitment of Assyrians began during this time.

Over the years, the Assyrians found themselves skirmishing with their neighbours with various intentions. September 1919 saw them successfully defend the Assyrian repatriation camp at Mindan, 30 miles northeast of Mosul, against Kurdish forces. As a counterstroke, they effectively contained the rebellious activities of Sheikh Mahmud Barzinji in 1919, who proclaimed himself king of an independent Kurdish state, and later in July 1920, when Arab forces attacked the Baqubah refugee camp, the Assyrian forces led a successful defence and counterattack, though vastly outnumbered.[90]

Though some repatriation of Assyrians had commenced to an area north of Rowanduz, by 11 June 1920 there were a reported 26,000 Assyrians and 14,000 Armenians in the Baqubah refugee camp.[91] The refugees faced threats from Arab attacks in the midst of region-wide uprisings as mentioned above. Five months later, a report stated that the Assyrians had been moved and concentrated in Mosul despite the uneasiness surrounding the revolts. Intriguingly it is at this very same time that the French took an interest in the Assyrians and their predicament.[92] In 1921, while the new Iraqi army was being created, Arabs were advised to transfer from the levies to the newly fashioned armed forces. It was clear that this was an opportune moment to recruit the services of the Assyrians to assist in the majority of levy duties.[93] Sensing that the Assyrians would not be well received in the new Iraqi army nor in Iraq itself, the British presented recruitment as a way for them to retain their martial spirit, further otherising them from the newly created Iraqi polity. Other Iraqi communities including the Sunni intelligentsia fostered and promoted rumours that the British harboured co-religionist sympathies for the Assyrians, which began to filter down through the general population, widening the gap between Assyrians and other communities of Iraq.[94]

The initial British recruitment began at the Mindan camp. 'All they wanted was that the British should send them back to their country [Hakkâri], which they had lost through joining the Allies.'[95] After constant urging by the British officers and Rev. W. A. Wigram, whom these Assyrians had held in high esteem, some fifty men conceded and were unceremoniously guided into the British ranks. Though initially relenting, these fifty men attempted once again to withdraw but were blocked. Two leading British officers took the new troops and some of their family members in two groups, the first heading towards Nabi Yunis and the second towards 'Aqra. Among those first levy officers were *Rab-Khamshi* Yusuf Yokhana I,[96] and later Daniel Ismael, the son of Malik Ismael, leader of the Assyrians of Upper Tiyari.[97] This distancing from their cultural and communal relations invigorated a sense of cultural survival among the resettled Assyrians, a sense embedded in folklore and ancient cultural characteristics that had been preserved for centuries in their mountainous enclaves.

The Assyrians' role in the levy consisted of spearheading attacks, defending military camps and, in some cases, suppressing rebellions and uprisings.[98] This followed a more recent failed coup by the Iraqi army under General Abdul-Jabar Barzinji (later friend to Mustafa Barzani). Yet although the Assyrians, like the Kurds, Arabs and Turkomans, worked with the British to secure the newly formed Iraqi state, and in many cases were instrumental in suppressing various sectarian revolts and movements, they were singled out in the following years for the brunt of anti-British and anti-Western sentiment.[99]

Conflicting ideologies

Any partiality shown to the Assyrians by the British would be calculable or measurable in various capacities. A detailed look at the new education system by Stephen Hemsley Longrigg (1893–1979), British officer and petroleum company executive, relates that by the end of 1919, seventy-five primary schools had been opened throughout Iraq. Fifty-six employed Arabic as the primary language, eleven Turkish, seven Kurdish and one Persian.[100] In reference to those private institutions, Longrigg states only that the Jewish and Christian schools, as well as foreign mission schools, were 'fostered by support and subsidy'.[101] Additionally any independence such schools enjoyed was quelled quickly. For example, those religious schools in and around Mosul divided by ecclesiastical sect (Chaldean, Syrian Orthodox, Syrian Catholic) were taken over by the Ministry of Education in 1920, allegedly with the consent of the religious heads. The language of instruction became (if it was not already) Arabic, and there was no doubt that under the newly minted system, devised by the noted Arab nationalist Sāṭiʿ al-Ḥuṣrī, the indoctrination of an Arab ideology was gradually and deliberately formalised in the education system.[102]

The same can be said of printing presses in Baghdad, Basra, Najaf, Sulaymaniyah, Mosul and Kirkuk during the same period.[103] Neither the language of the Assyrians nor they themselves were represented. The *modus operandi* of both of these social and educational institutions by the British further ostracised the Assyrians from the general Iraqi populace, hindering their integration into Iraq's cultural mosaic. Those familiar with Arabic became influenced and later assimilated by the Iraqi political machine through the printing press and by the late 1930s through radio, while some (mostly Hakkâri Assyrians) were labelled at times as a tiny foreign Christian community distinct from their brethren across the border.

Concurrently alongside Arab nationalism, the early 1920s saw the development and propagation of nationalist ideas and tendencies among the Assyrians and Kurds, albeit still in a fledgling phase, with far less promotional power than al-Ḥuṣrī.[104] Initially, the Assyrian nationalist network consisted of transnational and non-sectarian elites living in a variety of countries. In some cases those persons worked in conjunction with each other, in other cases they worked contrary to one another.[105] In the midst of broken promises, the desire for an Assyrian homeland created what may be called a more fervent pan-Assyrian nationalist sentiment. As early as April 1917, poet and writer Dr Fraidon (Aturaya) Bet-Avraham (1891–1926) had completed the integrally Marxist yet nationalist Urmia Manifesto, calling for a united free Assyria from Tur Abdin and Nisibis to Hakkâri, Mosul and Urmia with economic and military ties to Russia.[106] Alongside Benyamin Arsanis, Baba Bet Parhad and others, Bet-Avraham created the Assyrian Socialist Party the same year.[107]

Beginning with Soviet expansion into Central Asia and the Caucasus in 1921, Western powers embarked upon a policy of supporting highly centralised nationalist and militarist regimes in Iran, Iraq, Syria and Turkey. Likewise, in the midst of competing ideologies, communism found fertile ground within various Middle Eastern minority communities. This great game would shape the fate of the Assyrians and others who would become pawns in a Cold War battlefield. Yet the Assyrians were not without some influence, though perhaps at an individual level, notably with the birth of

Pyotr (Petros) Vasili. Vasili, raised and educated in Tbilisi, Georgia, was the child of an Assyrian immigrant from the ʿAmēdīyāh region in Iraq, and strongly influenced by the labour movements of the new twentieth century. In the early 1920s he immigrated back from Tbilisi to his father's home-land, where while living and working as a tailor he began to build a strong ideological following throughout the country. Celebrated for 'teaching his competitors more modern methods of tailoring', in reality he was laying the foundation for the Iraqi Communist Party (ICP).[108] From its establishment in 1934 (having conceivably gained impetus from the massacre at Simele the previous year) until the 1970s, the ICP played a fundamental role in shaping the political landscape of Iraq.

On the educational flank, the refugees, who in the minds of Arab nationalist intellectuals and British alike were perceived as 'alien,' integrated and contributed to a territory on the verge of change. Notwithstanding the nationalisation of schools begun in 1920, an Assyrian school (Madrashtā Ātūraytā) and printing press were founded in Mosul in 1921 and overseen by Qasha Joseph (Yosip) de Kelaita until 1945. By 1922 there were around 130 students enrolled in the coeducational facility, which required pupils to study Assyrian, Arabic and English as well as mathematics, history, science, religion and music, with scouting added by 1923. An attempt at secularisation of the school was made by some prominent teachers including Benyamin Arsanis, but was ultimately rebuffed by church officials.[109]

General Settlement Plans

Prior to the creation of the modern Middle East, the Iraq, Syria and Turkey of contemporary maps were still part of an Ottoman empire with ever-shift-ing borders. Many communities including Armenians, Assyrians, Kurds and Yezidis had lived in this region for centuries, travelling frequently within it with little governmental interference. The later division of the region into modern states served to alienate largely homogeneous populations from each other at the stroke of a pen. Thus, the Assyrians became divided between four modern nation-states, which, from their perspective, certainly reflected artificial demarcations. These new borders created a greater sense of territo-rial nationalism and territorial fear. Iraqi fears of a possible threat posed by the still-armed and well-trained alien Assyrians provided the blueprint for plans to urbanise them. These plans were optimal in both pacifying and later Arabising the Assyrian community in Iraq. Assyrians resisting Arabisation and assimilationist policies were continually alienated as foreigners: part of that alien element from beyond Iraq, and ill suited to integration therein. Despite this, many attempts were made with colonial assistance to settle certain segments of their population in Iraq.

The settlement of the Urmia and Hakkâri Assyrian refugees in Iraq is best divided into three major periods: 1920–5, 1925–32 and 1932–3.[110] The Assyrians little desired to leave the fastness of their mountain homes and be integrated into larger nation-states as they feared repercussions from their Muslim neighbours, a fear attributed by many to a sense of co-religionist sympathy afforded them by the British. Initially, the British had discussed the idea of allocating part of the Hakkâri range to Iraq, which would allow the Assyrians to be settled in their former homes as a homogeneous group with autonomy, and some Assyrians attempted unsuccessfully to return to this former territory in 1922–3. The League of Nations would also fail them in this instance, negotiating a return to Turkey while seemingly oblivious of their expulsion that very same year.[111]

Despite their military aid, having successfully repelled the Turkish invasion of Mosul, the reality remained that the possible settlement of Assyrians was objectionable to local Mosulis. In a telegram of May 1923, handwritten in English and entitled 'Petition to King, Prime Minister and Rashid Beg', 147 notables of Mosul requested the removal of the Assyrians of Tiyari living in the Mosul region. The notables made it clear that if the Crown were unwilling or unable to commit to action, then they should be notified so that they might take matters into their own hands.[112] Their action was partially motivated by the rise of pan-Arabism influenced by Sāṭiʿ al-Ḥuṣrī as it had been his focus as director of education in Iraq, and would in turn influence an entire generation.[113]

Ultimately the Iraqi government agreed to a settlement plan on 30 April 1924 which was explained in detail at the Constantinople Conference, held on 19 May. Sir Percy Cox, high commissioner of Iraq, stated:

> His Majesty's Government has decided to endeavour to secure a good treaty frontier, which will at the same time admit of the establishment

of the Assyrians in a compact community within the limits of the territory in respect of which His Majesty's Government holds a Mandate
under the authority of the League of Nations, if not in every case in their
ancestral habitation, at all events in suitable adjacent districts. This policy
for the settlement of the Assyrians has the full sympathy and support of
the Iraqi Government, which is prepared for its part, to give the necessary
co-operation for giving effect thereto.[114]

While it appeared at first that the British had found a place for the Assyrians
in the new Iraq, the conference agreement never came to fruition as Turkey
evicted the Assyrians from their homes in Hakkâri in the autumn of 1924.
Having no alternative, some retained the hope that the British would find
them a place in Iraq, which they did as part of the Iraqi Levies, thus retaining
a sense of obligation to aid in the settlement of these former Hakkâri mountaineers in Iraq. During the settlement process some British representatives
attempted without success to persuade Iraqi officials to integrate the Assyrians
into the workforce, especially the tribal chiefs or maliks. 'It was unfortunate
that red tape, suspicion, and a general dislike of Assyrians stood in the way, as
nothing could have been more successful in inducing the Assyrians to accept
their lot.'[115] Thus, for a time, the Assyrians were left in a precarious position,
surrounded by competitors and countries seemingly unconcerned of their
welfare, especially as it produced little political or economic benefit. The
Assyrians became an encumbrance – a burden easier set aside or disposed of,
leaving them at the mercy of geopolitical manoeuvrings and schemes.

Foreshadowing ten years into the future and the continued disillusion-
ment concerning lack of rights in 1933, it was evident that some Assyrians
such as Malik Ismael of Upper Tiyari would not be amiable to the settlement
arrangements.[116] It was obvious even then that Ismael and his son Yaqo along
with the bulk of those under their care wanted to emigrate long before the
infamous border crossing of 4 August 1933. Why ten years, a battle and a
massacre needed to ensue for the authorities to take note can be chalked up
to blatant negligence or conspiratorial designs.

In the years following the Great War, the numbers of Assyrians had
halved once again.[117] Having no recourse as they found themselves strangers
and unwanted in the Mosul region, the second settlement schema, 1925–32,

saw a number of Hakkâri tribesmen attempt to resettle in the Hakkâri region only to be repelled by the Turkish forces during the beginning of what was termed the Z Plan.

The Z Plan, implemented by the Iraqi authorities with direction from the British, was used to spread the Hakkâri Assyrians throughout northern Iraq. Following the failure of the reparations scheme developed by Assyrian commander Petros Elia and the British, 7,450 Assyrians were settled in the regions of Dohuk, Zakho, and 'Aqra between 1924 and 1928.[118] As Sir Francis Humphrys, the British high commissioner in Baghdad, stated, 'The Assyrians provide an excellent buffer vis-à-vis the Kurds' for the Iraqi state.[119] That was indeed the only recorded motive the Iraqi government voiced for keeping the Hakkâri Assyrians in Iraq proper. As the regions considered hospitable were promoted, many succumbed to infectious diseases such as malaria, which ran rampant through the settlements. These settlements, resembling ramshackle refugee camps, became so disease ridden and famished that at times the death toll was estimated at above 95 percent in particular areas.[120] Because of the poor conditions of their settlement, many desired to return to their Hakkâri villages. Meanwhile, the Turkish consul general in Baghdad stated on 25 June 1928, 'The Turkish amnesty law did not cover the Assyrians, who would not be permitted in any circumstances to enter Turkey; and . . . any Assyrian who attempted to enter Turkey would be punished.'[121] Thus, the Hakkâri contingent had no way home and began to suffer from the condition of dispossession.

Finally, the third period, 1932–3, saw a settlement attempt based on a League of Nations resolution. No plan came to culmination, leaving them targets once again. Despite their military role in the First World War (at least that of the independent Hakkâri tribes), the events of the conflict would cripple this people for decades to follow. The Western romanticisation of their downfall was expressed by the historian D. K. Fieldhouse as an unfortunate yet otherwise acceptable event:

> Such was the beginning of the end of an ancient, brave, and warlike race of mountaineers. They lingered for another twelve to fifteen years and more will be heard of them later; but the fact [that] they had joined the victorious Allies and lost everything as a result was the primary cause of all their

subsequent troubles, and historians will no doubt have great difficulty in excusing the Allies – particularly the British – for the way this small and gallant nation was let down.[122]

Despite external politics, the Assyrians were not without their own internal issues, and not unaware of their own shortcomings, as this song demonstrates:

Khā millat surtā d-Suryāyé,	A small nation of Assyrians,
Pīsh-lā zlīmtā b-Yūropnāyé.	Persecuted by Europeans.
Jwanqoh pīshé akh gīwāyé,	Her youths have become as beggars,
'Aynéh 'al zūzé d-Inglisnāyé.	Their eyes fixed upon English money
Gūrānan pīshé 'uldīyé,	Our leaders were fooled,
Zubné millattan b-rūpīyé.	They sold our nation for pennies (rupees).
Kul khā ṭawūyā bar qnayteh,	Everyone seeking after his own welfare,
d-Garwis-leh shimmā d-bayteh.	To further his family name.
Rābā shinné min qamaytā,	Many years ago,
Ātūr ki-khakmā-wā kullāh brītā.	Assyria ruled the entire world.
Zhāré 'allo,	The poor thing,
Hadiyā b-kirrī dwīqtā baytā.	Now she rents a home.
Kmā d-līt-lan khubbā w-khūyādā,	As long as we lack love and unity,
Gāw dāh ahwal b-hāwakh qyādā.	We will continue to burn in this situation.
Har akh d-hāw nāshā sayyadā	Just like the fisherman
d-Dāré gardūh w-līt-lā paydā.[123]	Who casts his net to no avail!

They grieved their leaders' decision to place hope in European powers and many became resigned to their fate, not unaware of their own naïveté. This, coupled with distrust fostered by power politics and endless religious and tribal divisions and disunity, created large-scale apathy and dissention within an already dispossessed population. Despite various tribulations, the previously displaced community began to build itself a home where it was able, as illustrated in Kirkuk, where the transient Hakkâri and Urmia Assyrians erected a school in 1928 under the direction of Rev. Isaac Rehana until he was deported to Cyprus in 1933 for political reasons.[124] A vibrant ecclesiastical community which had thrived from the fourteenth to the nineteenth century had returned in the midst of urbanisation and settlement schemes to an ancestral region. Communal action was varied and not as monolithic as previously assumed even within the three sub-groups and their social and political strata.

Notes

1. A. M. Hamilton, *Road through Kurdistan: The Narrative of an Engineer in Iraq*, new ed. (London: Faber & Faber, 1958), 217.
2. These markers are more for the researcher than for the Assyrians themselves. No doubt there are an incalculable number of exceptions to such 'rules' but for the purpose of keeping the work based on notions of Western research, I have elected to aid the reader in understanding the variant groupings.
3. See Hanna Batatu, *The Old Social Classes and the Revolutionary Movements in Iraq* (London: Saqi, [1978] 2004). Though Batatu offers no explanation for the term, it is likely he assumed those 'Arabised' to have been from urban regions, to have lost their native tongue, and perhaps no longer to hold any major sense of distinctness from their Muslim neighbours other than their Christian faith.
4. Hirmis Aboona, *Assyrians, Kurds, and Ottomans: Intercommunal Relations on the Periphery of the Ottoman Empire* (Amherst, NY: Cambria Press, 2008), 190.
5. Hannibal Travis, '"Native Christians Massacred": The Ottoman Genocide of the Assyrians during World War I', *Genocide Studies and Prevention* 1.3 (2006), 329. Also see Aboona, *Assyrians, Kurds, and Ottomans*, 196–208.
6. Aboona, *Assyrians, Kurds, and Ottomans*, 191.
7. Portions of this section have been published in Sargon Donabed, 'Rethinking Nationalism and an Appellative Conundrum: Historiography and Politics in Iraq', *National Identities* 14.4 (2012), 407–31.
8. Amanda Porterfield, *Mary Lyon and the Mount Holyoke Missionaries* (New York: Oxford University Press, 1997), 75.
9. Eden Naby, 'The Assyrians of Iran: Reunification of a "Millat", 1906–1914,' *International Journal of Middle East Studies* 8.2 (1977), 239.
10. Aboona, *Assyrians, Kurds, and Ottomans*, 206. Most other works focus on the damaging effect the missions had on Assyrian–Kurdish, Assyrian–Arab

or Assyrian–Turkish relations while neglecting the more negative consequence within the Assyrian community itself. For a case on the conversion
of indigenous groups to Catholicism, see Peter Iadicola and Anson Shupe,
Violence, Inequality, and Human Freedom, 2nd ed. (Lanham, MD: Rowman &
Littlefield, 2003), 197.

11. Edward Lewes Cutts, *Christians under the Crescent in Asia* (London: Society for
Promoting Christian Knowledge / New York: Pott, Young, 1877), 221.

12. Aboona, *Assyrians, Kurds, and Ottomans*, 279.

13. Horatio Southgate, *Narrative of a Visit to the Syrian Church of Mesopotamia*
(New York: Dana, 1844), 237–8; George Percy Badger, *The Nestorians and
Their Rituals* (London: Darf, [1852] 1987), vol. 1, 170.

14. Justin Perkins, *A Residence of Eight Years in Persia among the Nestorian
Christians; with Notices of the Muhammedans* (Andover, MA: Allen, Morrill &
Wardwell, 1843), 278.

15. American Sunday-School Union, Committee of Publication, *The Nestorians of
Persia: A History of the Origin and Progress of That People, and of Missionary Labours
among Them* (Philadelphia: American Sunday-School Union, 1848), 125.

16. Aboona, *Assyrians, Kurds, and Ottomans*, 72–4.

17. Dina Rizk Khoury, *State and Provincial Society in the Ottoman Empire: Mosul
1540–1834*, (Cambridge: Cambridge University Press, 1997), 147.

18. Ibid, 148.

19. Ibid.

20. Most of the literature on the American Protestant missions in north Iraq is
housed at the Presbyterian Historical Society in Philadelphia. Some of it is
reproduced in Kamal Salibi and Yusuf K. Khoury (eds), *The Missionary Herald:
Reports from Northern Iraq 1833–1870* (Amman: Royal Institute for Inter-faith
Studies, 1995).

21. Indeed this is the case for all communities during this period. There is no
reason to assume the Ottoman or Armenian statistics, for that matter, are any
more correct or valid than the Assyrian ones.

22. *The Claims of the Assyrians before the Conference of the Preliminaries of Peace
at Paris* (Paris: Rosen, 1919), also seen in Joel E. Werda, *The Flickering Light
of Asia or the Assyrian Nation and Church* (Joel E. Werda, 1924), 199–200.
See also David Gaunt, 'Failed Identity and the Assyrian Genocide', in Omer
Bartov and Eric D. Weitz (eds), *Shatterzone of Empires: Coexistence and Violence
in the German, Habsburg, Russian, and Ottoman Borderlands* (Bloomington:
Indiana University Press, 2013), 318.

23. Roderic H. Davison, *Nineteenth-century Ottoman Diplomacy and Reforms* (Istanbul: Isis Press, 1999), 395.

24. Badger, *The Nestorians and Their Rituals*, vol. 1, 82.

25. Major Trotter to Mr Goschen, Inclosure 3, Table II A, FO 424/107, pp 177–9, no. 104/3; Table III, FO 424/107, p. 180, no. 104/3.

26. Vital Cuinet, La Turquie d'Asie: géograph*ie administrative, statistique, descriptive et raisonée de chaque province de l'Asie-Mineure (Paris: Leroux, 1890–95), vol. 2,* 526–7; Martin van Bruinessen, Agha, Shaikh and State: The Social and Political Structures of Kurdistan (London: Zed, 1992), 197. In the sense of being autonomous, these Assyrians were not subject to any Kurdish amirs or aghas. The autonomous Assyrian regions are as follows: Baz, Diz, Jelu, Tkhuma and Tyari. There are no precise population statistics of the Hakkâri Nestorians because the relative inaccessibility of certain villages of the mountainous region probably made an accurate tally highly difficult in the 1870s.

27. Ibid., 202.

28. As testament to this, in 1928, Sheikh Ahmed of Barzan, his brother Mustafa Barzani and their relatives were taken by Malik Barkhu to Tkhuma in the Hakkâri range to find refuge from Turkish forces. See David Barsum Perey JSD, *Whither Christian Missions? Reflections on the Works of a Missionary and on the Assyrian Case*, rev. ed. (Paterson, NJ: Kimball Press, 1946), 24; Theodore d'Mar Shimun, *The History of the Patriarchal Succession of the d'Mar Shimun Family*, 2nd ed. (Turlock, CA: Mar Shimun Memorial Foundation, 2008), 124. This anecdote, though a footnote in the struggles and wars of the early twentieth century, speaks to tentative receptivity, based in natural localism transitioning through the generations, of the Kurds and Assyrians towards one another.

29. Based on Consul Taylor to the Earl of Clarendon, in 'Report on the Social and Political Condition of the Consulate for Koordistan', 19 March 1869, Inclosure no. 25, *Reports by Her Majesty's Diplomatic and Consular Agents in Turkey Respecting the Condition of the Christian Subjects of the Porte 1868–75* (London, 1877).

30. Ibid.

31. Consul Taylor to the Earl of Clarendon.

32. This is my conservative estimate (at seven persons per household) based on oral interviews, the figures of Commander (Agha) Petros Elia in General Petros Elia to Mr Forbes Adam, 26 November 1922, FO839/23, Assyrian maps of the region at the turn of the century, and William A Shedd, 'The Syrians of Persia

and Eastern Turkey', *Bulletin of the American Geographical Society* 35.1 (1903), 7. There are many inaccuracies in Shedd's work and it is simply not precise enough. The phrase 'Tigris valley' could reflect anything from Mosul to Sa'irt. Shedd estimated five persons per family in the Urmia region through Baradost and seven for all other regions. It appears he simply based his estimates on the 1870s records and included 338 villages and 13,335 families, totalling 80,645 people. Including the Tigris valley the sum increased to over 110,000 people in 1903. See Arianne Ishaya, 'Settling into Diaspora: A History of Urmia Assyrians in the United States', *Journal of Assyrian Academic Studies* 20.1 (2006), 4, quoting V. Minorsky, 'Urmiya: A District & Town in the Persian Province of Adharbaijan', in *Encyclopedia of Islam*, 1st ed. (1934).

33. Hannibal Travis, *Genocide in the Middle East: The Ottoman Empire, Iraq, and Sudan*, (Durham, NC: Carolina Academic Press, 2010), 273. Travis notes that by comparison the total Iraqi population increased by 75 per cent, from 4.8 million to 8 million, between 1947 and 1965. See Helen Chapin Metz (ed.), *Iraq: A Country Study*, 4th ed. (Washington, DC: Library of Congress, 1990), 79.

34. William Walker Rockwell, *The Pitiful Plight of the Assyrian Christians in Persia and Kurdistan* (New York: American Committee for Armenian and Syrian Relief, 1916), 11–12. Also Joseph Naayem, *Shall This Nation Die?* (New York: Chaldean Rescue, 1921), 261–5 mentions 100,000 for a mountaineer population and 60,000 for Urmia and the surrounding plains.

35. The destruction of the Assyrians during the First World War is dealt with in detail by Hannibal Travis, Anahit Khosoreva, David Gaunt and others. For Assyrian eyewitness sources see Naayem, *Shall This Nation Die?*; Abraham Yohannan, *The Death of a Nation; or, the Ever Persecuted Nestorians or Assyrian Christians*, (New York: G. P. Putnam's Sons, 1916); Abel Messiah Nu'man Qarabashi, *Dmo Zliho (Bloodshed/Vergossenes Blut:: The Sorrowful Massacres and Tragedies of the Years 1915–1918* (Jönköping, Sweden: Ashurbanipals Bokförlag, 1997).

36. Brigadier-General J. G. Browne, 'The Assyrians: A Debt of Honour', *Geographical Magazine* 4.6 (1936), 431.

37. Naayem, *Shall This Nation Die?*, 268–9.

38. Ibid., 272.

39. 'US flag saves Christians in Turkish raid,' *San Antonio Light*, 25 March 1915. This is echoed by the eyewitness account of a Chaldean priest, Paul Bedjan, to 'Syrian Orthodox' bishop Afram Barsoum. See Khalid Dinno and

Amir Harrak, 'Six Letters from Paul Bedjan to Aphram Barsoum, the Syriac Orthodox Patriarch of Syria and Lebanon', *Journal of the Canadian Society for Syriac Studies* 9 (2009), 55–73, especially 55, 56, 65.

40. Rockwell, *The Pitiful Plight of the Assyrian Christians in Persia and Kurdistan*, 31.

41. In geographical opposition to the Western Assyrians of the Tur Abdin, Mardin, Diarbekir, Malatya, Adana, Harput, Sivas etc. Among the Assyrians today sometimes the terms *madinkhaya/madinhoyo* (easterner) and *ma'erwaya/ma'erwoyo* (westerner) are used to distinguish geography, dialect and church affiliation.

42. Rockwell, *The Pitiful Plight of the Assyrian Christians in Persia and Kurdistan*, 38.

43. Ibid., 39.

44. Daniel Silverfarb, *Britain's Informal Empire in the Middle East: The Case Study of Iraq 1929–1941* (New York: Oxford University Press, 1986), 34.

45. William Walker Rockwell, *The Pitiful Plight of the Assyrian Christians in Persia and Kurdistan*, 14–15.

46. Mary Lewis Shedd, *The Measure of a Man: The Life of William Ambrose Shedd, Missionary to Persia* (New York: George H. Doran, 1922), 218.

47. Naayem, *Shall This Nation Die?*, 281. As reported by several witnesses to the negotiations, the Assyrians, should they be victorious, were promised money, equipment, arms, reinforcements to substitute for weary volunteer soldiers, and autonomy.

48. Shedd, *The Measure of a Man*, 231. Petros Elia (1880–1932), often referred to using the honorific Agha, was born in the Hakkâri region of Baz and was a convert to Catholicism. He worked in the Turkish consulate in Urmia, as he was fluent in eight languages, and became consul in 1909. He was a weathered military leader of the Hakkâri Assyrians, which consisted entirely of voluntary recruits from the regions of Tur Abdin and Syria. Following the end of the war, he laboured to find a suitable home for the Assyrians from 1919 until 1923, when he was exiled by British–Iraqi authorities to France for a period (Christoph Baumer, *The Church of the East: An Illustrated History of Assyrian Christianity* (London: I. B. Tauris, 2006), 261). In 1932, Elia died in his home in Toulouse, France, as he worked on his memoirs ('Friend of Allies dies', *Canberra Times*, 11 April 1932).

49. Naayem, *Shall This Nation Die?*, 265.

50. Ibid., 286; John Joseph, *The Modern Assyrians of the Middle East: Encounters with Western Christian Missions, Archaeologists, and Colonial Powers* (Leiden: Brill, 2000), 147.

51. Memorandum by the Secretary of State for India, 'The Assyrian and Armenian Refugees in Mesopotamia', 4 November 1920, CAB 24/114/74.

52. For a full discussion of the Baqubah camp see Fadi Dawood, 'Minorities and Makings of the Modern Iraqi State: Refugees and Warriors – The Case of Assyrians 1920–1933', PhD thesis, School of Oriental and African Studies, University of London, 2014.

53. Secretary of State for Foreign Affairs to Earl Curzon of Kedleston, 4 March 1919, FO 608/97, Note 169, forwarding memorandum from Dr E. W. McDowell, political officer in Mosul, entitled 'Atrocities Committed by the Turks in the Mosul Vilayet Enclosing a Memorandum of Atrocities', 25 December 1918.

54. H. H. Austin, *The Baqubah Refugee Camp: An Account of Work on Behalf of the Persecuted Assyrian Christians* (London: Faith House Press, 1920), 99–100.

55. It was evident as early as 1916 from the Sykes–Picot agreement that France and Great Britain had desires to continue their spheres of influence in the Middle East. Though the agreement was loosely held together early on, it congealed over the succeeding treaties and was cemented with the creation of the respective mandate authorities by the League of Nations.

56. This becomes quite obvious after an in-depth scrutiny of Fr M. Kyriakos and Dr V. Yonann, 'Devant la Conference de la paix', *Action assyro-chaldéenne* 1 (1920). The periodical, published out of the residence of the Patriarchal Vicariate of the Chaldean Church in Beirut, is entirely in French and contains letters and commentaries from a variety of dignitaries.

57. Sam Parhad, *Beyond the Call of Duty: The Biography of Malik Kambar of Jeelu* (Chicago: Metropolitan Press, 1986), 21.

58. Ibid., 25–7; *Declaration du Général Gouraud, Haut commissaire français en Syrie & Cilicie*, Dossier 5: Étude sur la question assyro-chaldéenne et formation d'un bataillon, 12 July 1920. This is evidenced by the map (Figure 8) as well as Secret Dispatch No. 676 from Special Service Office, Mosul, to divisional advisor, Mosul, 19 June 1922; Secret Telegram No. 686 (Y1115) from Special, Mosul to General, Baghdad, 29 June 1922; Secret Dispatch No. I/2138 from General Headquarters, British Forces in Iraq, to secretary to the high commissioner, Baghdad, 9 July 1922, regarding French desire to control upper Khabur and Balikah valleys, AIR 23/449.

59. Confidential Dispatch No. So1738 from secretary to high commissioner for Iraq to General Headquarters, and advisor to the Ministry of Defence, 25

August 1922, enclosing letter No. 5780/C/21 from divisional advisor, Mosul to advisor to the Ministry of Interior, 15 August 1922, regarding reports concerning French officers' involvement with Arab Shaeikhs and Yezidi Aghas, AIR 23/449.

60. For a full analysis of the Assyrian delegation at the Peace Conference 1919 see Claire Weibel Yacoub, *Le Rêve brisé des Assyro-Chaldéens: l'introuvable autonomie* (Paris: Cerf, 2011).

61. Yohannan was an ordained Episcopal priest, having attended the General Theological Seminary in New York, as well as a lecturer in Oriental languages at Columbia University. His PhD was in Semitic and Indo-European languages.

62. *A Catalogue of Paris Peace Conference Delegation Propaganda in the Hoover War Library*, Hoover War Library, Biographical Series I (Stanford, CA: Stanford University Press, 1926), 7, 80.

63. This event among growing Syrian and Arab nationalism coupled with the Simele massacres would lead Barsoum, enthroned as Patriarch of Antioch in Syria on 30 January 1933, to alter of the name of the church to 'Syrian', beginning a process of de-Assyrification of the Jacobites.

64. Harold Perch, 'Biography of Abraham K. Yousef', in *Fiftieth Anniversary of St Mary's Assyrian Apostolic Church* (Worcester, MA: St Mary's Assyrian Apostolic Church, 1974).

65. A. K. Yoosuf, *The Religion of Mohammed and Christian Sufferings* (Worcester, MA, 1905).

66. See 'Real terrors of war', *Lowell Sun*, 10 September 1914; Sargon Donabed, *Remnants of Heroes: The Assyrian Experience* (Chicago: Assyrian Academic Society Press, 2003), 93.

67. 'Capt. Yoosuf pleads Assyrian cause', *Lowell Sun*, 7 September 1919.

68. For a full history of Yoosuf's accomplishments in New England see Albert Nelson Marquis, *Who's Who in New England*, 2nd ed. (Chicago: A. N. Marquis, 1916), 1189.

69. See Sargon George Donabed and Shamiran Mako, 'Ethno-cultural and Religious Identity of Syrian Orthodox Christians', *Chronos* 19 (2009), 106; Donabed, *Remnants of Heroes*, 97.

70. *The Claims of the Assyrians as Presented to the Paris Peace Conference of 1919*; Donabed and Donabed, *Assyrians of Eastern Massachusetts* (Charleston, SC: Arcadia, 2006), 81. 'Shakkak' (also 'Shikak') most probably refers to a Kurdish-speaking tribe situated to the west of Urmia and Salamas. Their leader, Ismail

Simko, was the assassin of the Nestorian Patriarch Mar Benyamin Shimun and 150 of his bodyguards in March 1918. The reason for their inclusion may stem from some Assyrian records, which refer to the Kurdish-speaking Shikaks using the honorific 'uncle' for the Nestorian Patriarch. See Werda, *The Flickering Light of Asia*, 201.

71. *Claims of the Assyrians as Presented to the Paris Peace Conference of 1919*, in Werda, *The Flickering Light of Asia*, 199–202. It is also true that the Assyrian desire for an autonomous region and/or to remain in the regions of Mesopotamia which would be under British or American mandate had its basis in fear of persecution by their Muslim neighbours. See the section concerning Mesopotamia in the King–Crane Commission Report, 28 August 1919. The commission was an official investigation during 1919 by the United States government into the circumstances and conditions existing in certain parts of the former Ottoman Empire.

72. This refers to the population in 1918 but neglects those Assyrian regions under the jurisdiction of the Armenian patriarchate (i.e. Harput, Erzerum, Van, Bitlis and Sivas), where the patriarchate estimated an Assyrian population of 123,000. See David Gaunt, *Massacres, Resistance, Protectors: Muslim–Christian Relations in Eastern Anatolia during World War I* (Piscataway, NJ: Gorgias Press, 2006), 405–6. James Tashjian, *Turkey: Author of Genocide – The Centenary Record of Turkey 1822–1922* (Boston: Commemorative Committee on the 50th Anniversary of the Turkish Massacres of the Armenians, 1965), 23–4 refers to 500,000 Assyrians of all Christian denominations living in Turkey. This is without regard to those under the Armenian patriarchate. See 'La Question assyro-chaldéenne', *Action assyro-chaldéenne* 1 (1920), 11.

73. David Gaunt cites preliminary numbers at around 200,000 persons (Gaunt, *Massacres, Resistance, Protectors*). 'La Question Assyro-chaldéenne' cites 250,000 dead from a then current population of 1,520,000, which included the 'community of India' (p. 11). See also Travis, '"Native Christians Massacred"', 350 n2. Tashjian, *Turkey: Author of Genocide* cites 424,000 Assyrians killed under the failing Ottoman state since 1895 (p. 24).

74. In a 16 December 2007 press release, the International Association of Genocide Scholars voted to recognise what they termed genocides inflicted on Assyrian and Greek populations of the Ottoman Empire and succeeding states between 1914 and 1923.

75. Gaunt, 'Failed Identity and the Assyrian Genocide', 329.

76. Peace Conference diary entry, 17 April 1919, Cary T. Grayson Papers, Woodrow Wilson Presidential Library. See also 'La Délégation assyro-chaldéenne', *Action assyro-chaldéenne* 1 (1920).

77. Archevêché Syrien de Syrie, Memorandum 128, Archevêque Severius Barsoum, Paris, 2 April 1920, and secret letter No. AJ76 from Severius Barsum to Mr Lloyd George, Prime Minister, March 1920, CAB 29/30.

78. The full treaty can be viewed at http://wwi.lib.byu.edu/index.php/Section_I,_Articles_1_-_260 (accessed 10 July 2014).

79. İsmet İnönü, 'Hey'et-i Vekîle Riyâsetine', tr. Racho Donef, *Turkish Historical Society*, 15 January 1923. See also Eastern Conference Lausanne, Autonomy for Assyrian Christians, FO 839/23.

80. See Betty Cunliffe-Owen, *Thro' the Gates of Memory: From the Bosphorus to Baghdad* (London: Hutchinson, 1924) for a very candid and orientalist account of events following the First World War concerning the Assyrians in Iraq and the Urmia region of Iran.

81. Arnold T. Wilson, 'The Middle East', *Journal of the British Institute of International Affairs* 5.2 (1926), 96–110.

82. Wilson took over while Sir Percy Cox was temporarily in Iran.

83. John Fisher, *Curzon and British Imperialism in the Middle East 1916–19* (London: Frank Cass, 1999), 251–2.

84. In the 1920s the French recruited a similar force made up largely of non-dominant communities in mandate Syria, referred to as Troupes spéciales du Levant.

85. Between 1920 and 1930 all 102,000 British and Indian troops were gradually withdrawn from Iraq. See Briton Cooper Busch, *Britain, India, and the Arabs 1914–1921* (Berkeley: University of California Press, 1971), 448; Silverfarb, *Britain's Informal Empire in the Middle East*, 48.

86. J. Gilbert Browne, *The Iraq Levies 1915–1932* (London: Royal United Service Institution, 1932), 1.

87. Ibid.

88. Ibid., 4, 14. Thus, the initial postulation of most previous scholarship concerning the Assyrians as holding a favoured position within the British military is incorrect. Contrary to this proposal, the Assyrians were quite late in joining the Iraqi Levies. For the makeup in 1920 see the Arab and Kurdish Levy and Gendarmerie Proclamation, 1920, AIR 5/295.

89. Browne, *The Iraq Levies*, 7.

90. Ibid.

91. Memorandum by the Secretary of State for War, 'Refugee Camp in Baqubah in Mesopotamia', 13 June 1920, CAB 24/107/62.

92. Memorandum by the Secretary of State for India, 'The Assyrian and Armenian Refugees in Mesopotamia', 4 November 1920, CAB 24/114/74.

93. Browne, *The Iraq Levies*, 14.

94. This is true of inter- as well as intra-community relationships as many of the Nestorians (Assyrian Church of the East) as well as Chaldeans and Jacobites dwelling in Mosul and to the north further distanced themselves from each other in a gradual self-sectarianisation process. Refer to Austin's comments above for earlier intra-community animosity.

95. Browne, *The Iraq Levies*, 15.

96. *Rab* is reflective of an ancient Assyrian title for soldiers of rank. In this instance, *rab-khamshi* denotes that Yokhana was the commander of fifty men. There were also higher- and lower-ranked officers, denoted by the number of men under their command, including for instance, *rab-isra*, *rab-imma* and *rab-trimma*, or commander of 10, 100 and 200 respectively. The highest rank of general was referred to as *rab-khayla*.

97. Browne, *The Iraq Levies*, 15.

98. Such a role was exemplified during the rebellion of Sheikh Ahmed of Barzan, the older brother of Mustafa Barzani (leader of the KDP), in 1931. See Browne, *The Iraq Levies*, 73.

99. Surprisingly, whether due to their small numbers or to their hope that the British, French or others would make good with their word to grant them an autonomous region, Assyrians had not participated in any rebellion up to this point in Iraqi history.

100. Stephen Longrigg, *Iraq 1900–1950: A Political, Social, and Economic History* (Beirut: Librairie du Liban), 110.

101. Ibid.

102. Observations of His Majesty's Government on the Petition Dated the 23rd of September 1930 from Captain A. Hormuzd Rassam, Relating to the Position of Non-Moslems in 'Iraq and Also on Captain Rassam's Letter of the 9th of December 1930 to the Chairman of the Permanent Mandates Commission, CO 730/163/1. See a full discussion of this in Phebe Marr, 'The Development of a Nationalist Ideology in Iraq 1920–1941', *Muslim World* 75.2 (1985).

103. Longrigg, *Iraq 1900–1950*, 110.

104. 'Nationalist' and 'nationalism' are problematic terms due to the negative ideas associated with them today, as are the terms 'intellectual' and 'elite'. None is

properly defined and thus I am hesitant to use them. Moreover, there were those writers and actors among the Assyrians who advocated for a free and independent homeland, and those who did not concern themselves with the issue.

105. This is clearly evident in the interactions between the Assyrian delegates to the Paris Peace Conference of 1919, as illustrated and discussed in the personal notes of Abraham K. Yoosuf, now housed in the MARA collection, as well as in the writings of Malik Kambar Warda of Jilu as seen in *Khuyada Umtanaya* (founded in 1928) and *Action assyro-chaldéenne*, both published in Beirut.

106. See Fred Aprim, 'Assyrians in the World War I Treaties: Paris, Sèvres, and Lausanne', *Assyrian Star* 58.1 (2006); Sergei G. Osipov, 'Fraidon Atturaya in the Focus of the Soviet Press', *Melta* 10 (2000).

107. Despite his Russian leanings, he was imprisoned and died in jail at the age of thirty-five.

108. Batatu, *The Old Social Classes and the Revolutionary Movements In Iraq*, 404.

109. See the Assyrian School of Mosul Project, which contains photographs and information concerning the school and its history (http://www.aina.org/mosulschool/school.htm (accessed 11 July 2014)).

110. Yusuf Malek, *The Assyrian Tragedy* (Annemasse, Switzerland: Granchamp, 1934), 36. The third period will be discussed in the following chapter.

111. Stafford, *The Tragedy of the Assyrians*, 87.

112. Secretariat of HE the High Commissioner of Iraq, Baghdad to advisor to the Minister of the Interior, Baghdad, Memorandum, 14 June 1923, AIR23/449.

113. Joseph Sassoon, *Saddam Hussein's Ba'th Party: Inside an Authoritarian Regime* (Cambridge: Cambridge University Press, 2012), 17.

114. Stafford, *The Tragedy of the Assyrians*, 83–4.

115. Ibid., 61.

116. Secretariat of HE the High Commissioner of Iraq, Baghdad to Air Headquarters, Baghdad, Memorandum, 26 September 1923, AIR23/449. The callousness with which the Assyrians are addressed is palpable as the death of Shamasha Nanu or Ashitha is referred to in the appendix to the memo as a 'thorn removed'. Furthermore, it seemed that the government (British–Iraqi) recognised that they had ignored Assyrian leadership structures when they bypassed the maliks to appoint government liaisons.

117. Ibid.

118. *Military Report on Iraq (Area 9) Central Kurdistan*, Air Ministry, 1929, 196–8.

119. Paul Knabenshue, US ambassador to Iraq, to Secretary of State, 'Assyrian Problem – British Policy', 28 August 1933, 890g.4016 Assyrians/86.

120. Yusuf Malek, *The Assyrian Tragedy*, 18–20.

121. League of Nations Secretariat, *League of Nations Questions* (1935), 12.

122. David K. Fieldhouse (ed.), *Kurds, Arabs and Britons: The Memoir of Wallace Lyon in Iraq 1918–44* (London: I. B. Tauris, 2002), 83.

123. As sung by Shamshon Orahem Babella to the author in California during an informal recorded interview in the summer of 2006. Babella was born in the Urmia region in Iran and lived much of his life in Iraq in the refugee settlement of Gaylani Camp Babella and his family were among those forced to leave Iraq under Ba'th pressure for being 'Iranian' by birth in the early 1980s. The song was sung by him during a conversation about the Assyrian situation in Iraq following British withdrawal. The song seems to be solely oral in character, and other Assyrians of the same generation, including some of those interviewed for this book, were familiar with it. Thanks to Nicholas Al-Jeloo for his comments and creation of a superb transliteration system.

124. The Assyrians of Kirkuk website contains information about the history of Assyrians in the region post-WWI including names of graduates and volunteer organisations, as well as numerous photographs. See http://www.assyriansofkirkuk.com.

3

Iraq: Building a 'Nation'-State

We preferred our own way of living. We were no expense to the government. All we wanted was peace and to be left alone.

Crazy Horse, Oglala Lakota, 1877

Between 1914 and 1933 the Middle East transformed rapidly. Nationalism became a new cash crop, a commodity more profitable than oil. Where this created new possibilities and prospects in the region, it also gave birth to tales of broken promises and future despondency. Forced from semi-autonomy into the First World War, the Assyrians watched as their patriarch Mar Benyamin Shimun XXI was murdered by Agha Simko Ismail in 1918 under a flag of parley, only to find themselves alongside the very same Kurds, completely homeless following the war. Soon after the Assyrians in Iraq became detached from their brethren, divided via borders of newly conceived states by the very powers they had endeavoured to aid in the Great War. But it was the events of the late 1920s and early 1930s that would in many ways cement the community's socio-economic, ethno-cultural and religious trajectory to the present. According to Yusuf Malek, (then working for the secretary to the administration inspector in Mosul), as early as 1929 circulars from the Iraqi ministries were disseminated throughout the Kurdish regions of northern Iraq, pressing for a massacre of the Assyrians.[1] As the attempt initially gained little support, officials began to play on religious animosities and a more assertive call for a general massacre of Christians was announced. This call appealed to fundamentalist religious convictions, bridging the gap between Kurd and Arab.[2] In this instance, it was the British forces in the streets of Mosul that prevented an immediate massacre.

During the late 1920s, Assyrians had been targeted by central-government manoeuvrings. Seventy-six individuals were marked for political assassination during this time.[3] In 1930, five Assyrians were found murdered near Rawanduz, and more near Mosul, with no criminal investigation into the killings.[4] The machinations of Baghdad were obvious in its attempts to pit the Kurds and Assyrians against each other, while at the same time uniting Iraqis in their hatred of 'outsiders' and 'tools' of Western occupation. During the same year, relations between Britain and Iraq became closer still with the new Anglo-Iraqi Treaty. The treaty, not very dissimilar to the original of 1922 paid particular attention to continued relations between the two countries following significant oil discoveries in 1927. In light of these discoveries, the stability of the Iraqi regime became of paramount importance. They were prepared to admit the Iraqi state into the League of Nations provided Iraq signed a treaty of alliance safeguarding Britain's oil rights.

The Patriarch and Temporal Authority

By 1931 the Permanent Mandates Commission of the League of Nations approved Iraq's admission as an independent sovereign state into the League of Nations, with the recommendation that it guarantee certain rights to its minorities.[5] In light of this news, Assyrians under the leadership of Mar Eshai Shimun, cognisant of the imminent termination of the mandate, held a general conference in Mosul pressing their case at the upcoming Geneva meeting. During his visit with the mountaineers in Mosul in 1931, Sir Francis Humphrys, UK high commissioner to Iraq, promised his full support at Geneva only to verbally assail Mar Eshai Shimun and his leadership at the meeting.[6] In general, British officers thought very little of Humphrys and believed he was ill prepared for the task of leadership. Captain Gerald de Gaurey was among those colonial officials who believed that Humphrys had little skill, was quite egotistical, driven by ambition, and only held his position through his friendship with King George V.[7]

Roger Cumberland, an American missionary, noticed a shift in the Assyrian political stance on the return of Captain Anthony Hormuzd Rassam, (grandson of the vice consul of the British in Mosul and the first Middle Eastern archaeologist, Hormud Rassam), and Captain Matthew Cope from England in 1929.[8] The major concern of the Iraqi government

seemed to be the ambitions of Mar Shimun to retain his temporal authority over the mountaineers. Prior to 1930 there seemed little evidence that
the patriarchal family which included Mar Shimun's aunt Surma, would
become inflexible in their political ambitions. Rassam and Cope brought
with them some secret political intelligence which they utilised to stir
Assyrian desires towards independence and autonomy.[9] Cumberland
reported that in a speech about Easter in 1931, the Lady Surma allegedly
proclaimed, 'We will be kings or we will be killed.'[10] Despite the obvious
disagreement over patriarchal family's temporal authority it is pertinent to
recall British/Iraqi usage of the power wielded by that family to their own
advantage. In the early 1920s, while chaos and a general uncertainty gripped
the Assyrian population, the British continued their recruitment of young
men en masse to the Iraq levy battalions through such means:

> I found that the present system of recruiting through the Patriarchal
> family, Maliks, and villages is extremely satisfactory. The influence of the
> Patriarchal family throughout all the districts appear[s] to be enormous.
> At each village the inhabitants crowded round David de Mar Shimun,
> the Patriarch's father, to kiss his hand while men and women would leave
> their work in the fields on hearing that he was going by and rush up to do
> the same.[11]

Thus it should not have been a shock to find the patriarchal family both wield-
ing temporal authority and desiring some sense of its continuation. While
Humphrys harboured ill feelings toward Mar Eshai Shimun, he did present
some of the petitions to the League of Nations as provided to him by the
Assyrians. One petition was sent by Captain Rassam and included the concerns
of the Yezidi and Jewish communities. Another asked for special consideration
to migrate to French-controlled Syria, or out of the Middle East.

Letter to the Mandates Commission
By The Mar Shimun et al

Mosul, October 23rd, 1931
To: His Excellency
The Chairman, Mandates Commission
League of Nations, Geneva

Reference the attached document. I beg to convey to Your Excellency the following:

The Assyrian Nation which is temporarily living in Iraq, having placed before their eyes the dark future, and the miserable conditions which are undoubtedly awaiting them in Iraq, after the lifting of the mandate, have unanimously held a Conference with me in Mosul on the 20th October 1931. At this Conference were present the temporal and spiritual leaders of the Assyrian Nation in its entirety as it will be observed from the document quoted above bearing the leaders' signatures. The future conditions were fully discussed and these center around two points. (Can we or can we Not live in Iraq?) At the conclusion of lengthy deliberations, it was unanimously decided by all those present that it is quite impossible for us to live in Iraq. The leaders' Will was entrusted with me vide the document signed by them to explore all means that I deem possible to find a way for the emigration of the Assyrians from Iraq. Under the circumstances, I, together with the under mentioned signatories being the responsible leaders of the Assyrian Nation submit before Your Commission our Nation's humble request, which in past centuries numbered millions but reduced to a very small number due to repeated persecutions and massacres that faced us, we have been able to preserve our Language and Faith up to the present time. The Not distant past relating to the conditions of Our Nation has been fully made known to you by the medium of the official workers for our Nation. This being so, it is unnecessary for us to enlarge upon each item, BUT WE ARE POSITIVELY SURE THAT IF WE REMAIN IN IRAQ, we shall be exterminated in the course of few years.

WE THEREFORE IMPLORE YOUR MERCY TO TAKE CARE OF US, and arrange our emigration to one of the countries under the rule of one of the Western Nations whom you may deem fit. And should this be impossible, we beg you to request the French Government to accept us in Syria and give us shelter under her responsibility FOR WE CAN NO LONGER LIVE IN IRAQ and WE SHALL LEAVE.

Sd. Eshai Shimun
By the Grace of God,
Catholics Patriarch of the East

Other Signatories:
(Mar) Yosep Khnanishu, Metropolitan
(Mar) Zaya Sargis, by Grace Bishop
Khoshaba M. Yosep (Lower Tiyari)
Zaya M. Shamizdin
Malik Andrious, Jelu
Malik Marogil
Malik Khnanu, Tkhuma
Malik Khammo, Baz
Malik Ismael, Upper Tiyari

Copy to:
H.E. High Commissioner for Iraq
H.E. Minister for Foreign Affairs, London[12]

While the letter included all the major signatures of the maliks and chiefs, even those who would by 1933 become part of the 'anti-patriarchal faction', Humphrys dismissed these requests. In his argumentation he suggested to the committee that the petitions held no authority (especially Rassam's) despite being authorised by Mar Eshai Shimun.

At least three more petitions were sent by Assyrian groups to the League in 1931 and 1932. The requests and pleas to honour their promises fell on deaf ears, and the desire to continue to exploit Assyrian levy officers as guards for the airbases of Habbaniyya and Shu'aiba with no further obligations paved the way for the atrocities that would occur two years later.[13]

The handover of Iraq was now imminent. In May 1932 Mar Eshai Shimun again called a meeting of the heads of all the Assyrian tribal factions in communion with the Church of the East.[14] On 1 June the British were faced with the unthinkable: all Assyrian levy officers had signed a document voluntarily terminating their positions with effect from 1 July.[15] This was a major blow to the British, who relied on the Assyrians for internal Iraqi missions and peacekeeping. Mar Shimun called a secondary meeting on 16 June. As a result of both of these meetings, he was elected as the Assyrians' representative in any and all negotiations with secondary parties. The now fully sovereign Kingdom of Iraq was admitted to the League of Nations

unanimously on 3 October 1932, yet Britain retained many previous relations, especially those with the Iraqi Sunni elite and of course her treaty
guaranteeing oil rights.[16] Following the handover, in a final effort to bar-
gain with the League, Mar Eshai Shimun left for the Geneva conference in
December 1932.

The final decision of the League of Nations conference was released on
15 December 1932. The release made evident the failure of Assyrian aspirations as brought forth by Mar Eshai Shimun. The Patriarch left Geneva on
19 December and by the start of 1933 he had arrived in Damascus. There
he met with writer Yusuf Malek, informing him of what had transpired
at the convention.[17] It appeared that the Assyrian refugees of Hakkâri had
little hope of seeing promises fulfilled. Upon his arrival in Baghdad, Mar
Shimun was requested to report immediately to the police barracks as the
Iraqis wished to be assured of his obedience. On 5 January Mar Shimun was
invited to dinner at Sir Francis Humphrys's house, where he was pleaded
with to restrain the Assyrian levies from any reaction and to promise their
continued obedience to the British and the state. Seeing no other acceptable
options, Mar Eshai, exhausted and defeated, made his way back to Mosul
and called a final meeting on 16 January. Here he publicly explained the
outcome of the Geneva meeting and its possible effect to every malik and
rayis (headman) in attendance.

Discouraged by Britain's failure to make due on its promises, in January
1933 Rab Tremma Yaqo, the son of the elderly Malik Ismael of Upper Tiyari,
resigned from the Iraqi Levies. Yaqo had served with them for the three previous years at Diana, near Rawanduz, working with a New Zealand-born
British civil engineer, Archibald Hamilton, to create a new motor road from
Arbil through the gorge of Rawanduz into Iran.[18] When Yaqo had resigned
his levy commission both he and his father made their way to Simele, a large
village about 14 kilometres west of Dohuk. While some of the Assyrians in
Simele belonged to the tribe of Upper Tiyari, like Yaqo, the majority were
originally from the Baz region of Hakkâri. The bulk of the settled families of
Upper Tiyari occupied villages on the main road that stretched from Dohuk
to 'Amēdīyāh.

In a March 1933 letter to strategic ministries, King Faisal seemed
aware of the lack of national unity in Iraq. He remarked that 'an Iraqi

people does not yet exist' and rather what made up the country was 'throngs of human beings lacking any national consciousness or sense of unity . . . inclined toward anarchy and always prepared to rise up against any government whatsoever'.[19] Amid a rising tension which became palpable and at times physically threatening as the year wore on, Faisal's sentiments echoed in the halls of Iraq's elite ministries and the ears of ex-Sharifian officers, who led the 'Arab revolt' during the Ottoman period. The Assyrians were or had become a disease in the eyes of many in the Arab nationalist party Hizb al-Ikha al-Watani, founded by Ali al-Gaylani, an Arab nationalist and future Prime Minister of Iraq.[20] Whereas this generated complications, it also brought possible solutions for remedying the issue of Iraq's national unity. Officials surmised that a fabricated enemy of alien origin, speaking a barbaric tongue and adhering to an antiquated religion they held in common with the foreign British, could stem Kurdish and Shia insurgent tendencies and turn their focus to an enemy common to all.[21]

Thus a situation was fostered where a clash with the Assyrians became inevitable. On 31 March, Yaqo Ismael met with Mekki Beg al-Sherbiti, *qaimaqam* of Dohuk, and spoke at length of the desires of the Assyrian community, especially in regard to possible emigration. According to Yaqo's own memoirs, Mekki Beg responded positively, stating that those who wished to emigrate would be given leave to do so, while those who desired to integrate into Iraq would also be accommodated. From there Yaqo left to speak to the various villages of the new possibilities.[22] Concurrently, during May and June 1933 the government campaigned to urge Iraqis to donate funds for military supplies that would be used to quell the Assyrian unrest. At approximately the same time, Major Arnold Wilson recommended the summoning of the Patriarch Mar Eshai Shimun to Baghdad to be detained there. 'All necessary steps should be taken to oblige the Patriarchal family to accept the Dashtazi region [for settlement].'[23] On 22 May Mar Shimun indulged the request to meet with Hikmat Sulayman and a newly appointed settlement expert, Major Thompson, in Baghdad to discuss the Dashtazi settlement project. He addressed Assyrian autonomy with Hikmat Sulayman in May and early June. Following a breakdown of the talks, Baghdad decided it would be necessary to retain the cleric in custody, infuriating the Assyrian population worldwide as they feared a repeat of the assassination of Mar Benyamin Shimun.

Major Thompson, however, went directly to the Mosul region. There he spoke with forty Assyrians concerning the settlement. Thirty-six of them informed him that they agreed with the position of Mar Eshai Shimun. 'The remaining four said they would agree to whatever settlement the government proposed.'[24] At the time, Thompson recorded more than 400 families distributed over thirty-one villages between the Barwari Bala and Nerwa/Rekan regions who were under patriarchal authority, with a population of almost 3,000. Added to that were more than 3,500 families formerly of Hakkâri, around 24,500 people, giving a total of more than 27,500 Assyrians in Iraq under Mar Shimun's authority.[25]

Yaqo Ismael and others had felt betrayed by the British for whom they worked even prior to the beginning of the mandate. It was said the Assyrians were the only people in the new Iraq that had not rebelled or taken up arms against the authorities. Yet despite this and following numerous failed meetings, the detention of Mar Eshai Shimun in Baghdad, a campaign of slander and bribery, and no end to the settlement talks, Yaqo and Malik Loko of the Tkhuma tribe began a tour of the 'Amēdīyāh and Sapna regions to persuade Assyrians to not accept Iraqi nationality and any new settlement arrangement as it was unrealistic for the amount of people who needed residences. While the British, especially Lieutenant Colonel Ronald Sempill Stafford, administrative inspector for Mosul, felt this was antagonistic as well as a monumental error in judgement, Yaqo had earlier, when under the supervision of Archibald Hamilton building the new 'Hamilton Road', been notified point blank by a British officer, Captain Baker, of the major plan of settlement which would effectively disarm the mountaineer Assyrians, disband them and move them to regions in Iraq south of the river Zab. He then relayed this message to his ageing and ailing father, Malik Ismael, as Hamilton relates:

> Yacu spoke a few sentences to the old man, who had sat during our conversation still as some sculptured figure hewn from rock. He looked round upon us as Yacu ceased speaking and gave his reply in a voice that betrayed emotion. A grim, formidable warrior in his time, this head of the Fighting

Tiyaris, as they proudly called themselves. Even now as he spoke to his son he was calm and dignified, but no longer was there any hope to give life to his lined face.[26]

Yet the Iraqi government's response was an increase in military force.

> I must admit that it was with very considerable misgivings that, when consulted by Baghdad, I agreed to the employment of the Army. The Army officers were known to hate the Assyrians and in particular Bekir Sidqi, who was in command in the north, had openly stated what he would do to them if the opportunity occurred. The transfer of this officer had again and again been recommended by the British advisory officials, and, indeed, King Feisal in May promised that it would be immediately carried out. But he nevertheless remained at Mosul, with what tragic results . . .[27]

The Assyrians feared there was little chance for them in the new Iraq, and the failure of Mar Eshai Shimun at the League of Nations solidified that truth for Yaqo. Iraqi deputies made speeches in parliament on 29 June 1933, inciting hatred toward the Assyrians, which were disseminated and published in *al-Istiqlal* newspaper among others.[28] For the Assyrians, the future appeared bleak. Eventually, Yaqo, not desiring a conflict, returned from the mountains in late June or early July at the behest of Colonel Stafford, who had promised that any grievances would be discussed at Mosul.[29] There was no end to the anti-Assyrian fervour, for 'between July 1, and July 14, over eighty leading articles were written in the Iraqi press by all classes of the population, all demanding the final extermination of the Assyrians'.[30]

Factions

Mosul native Mekki Beg al-Sherbiti, *qaimaqam* of Dohuk, was a staunch Iraqi nationalist. Al-Sherbiti believed Mar Shimun, Yaqo and the Assyrians as a whole to be a major threat to the country. He had been instrumental in the defection of a number of Assyrian leaders.[31] Malik Yosip Khoshaba of Lower Tiyari was perhaps the greatest feather in the cap for the Iraqi regime. Khoshaba, a hero of the First World War, through lofty promises and bribery according to some and rational practicality according to others was cajoled into becoming a voice against autonomy. Mar Eshai Shimun, Yusuf Malek and others believed that Khoshaba was assured of being made *sheikh* of all Assyrians and his children were to be granted official titles in the military and government.[32] Indeed there seemed to be a mutual dislike between Khoshaba and Mar Eshai Shimun, which most probably stemmed from ecclesiastical divergences that came to the forefront in the First World War as Khoshaba became strongly aligned with the American Protestants and one of their 'mountain preachers' while Mar Shimun's leanings oriented towards the Church of England.[33] The Iraqi government furthered division and animosity between the Assyrian leaders by appointing Khoshaba president of the Assyrian Advisory Committee while the patriarch was detained in Baghdad.[34] Along with Khoshaba, Mar Zaya Sargis, Bishop of Jilu, was similarly influenced into a pro-government position with promises of houses, an unsettled land claim to be settled satisfactorily, and favourable positions in the government for family members.[35] Others would join this faction and thus the divide grew.

Two major groups emerged among the Assyrians that would eventually be apportioned simply as the patriarchal faction and the non-patriarchal faction. In fact, Iraqi and British officials utilised the terms to undermine the solidarity of the Assyrian tribes. The Iraqi Minister of the Interior called a meeting of the Assyrian leadership for 10–11 July, to be held in Mosul in the office of the acting *mutasarrif*, Khalil Azmi, along with Colonel Stafford and Major Thompson. There, the growing divide became terribly clear, and with Mar Eshai Shimun under house arrest at the YMCA in Baghdad, the rift would widen further.[36]

At the time, Yusuf Malek and others suspected that government officials would use the meeting to increase tensions with the hope that the Assyrians would in effect neutralise themselves:

> The meetings were arranged by the Government with the ulterior purpose of causing friction among the Assyrians by employing paid servants to cause quarrels at the meetings and to create disrespect for the leaders. This group was given the privilege of arming with daggers and revolvers and was spurred on by the officials to use abusive language to antagonize the leaders; but the latter, being apprised by experience dealt with the situation calmly and wisely. Thus the trouble at which the Government aimed was averted.[37]

Table 5 Pro- and anti-patriarchal tribal factions

Patriarchal faction

Mar Yosip Khnanisho, Metropolitan
Yaqo d'Malik Ismael, Upper Tiyari
Malik Loko Shlimon, Tkhuma
Qasha Gewargis, Tkhuma
Malik Andrewos, Jilu
Malik Hurmizd Younan, Mar Zaya
Shamasha Kanno?, Jilu
Malik Dawid, Tkhuma
Zadoq Nwiya, Ashitha, Lower Tiyari
Sayfo Keena, Bnay l'Gippa, Lower Tiyari
Rayis Booko, Ashitha, Lower Tiyari
Shamasha Yosip Eliya, Walto(b), Upper Tiyari
Rayis Odisho Khbash, Rumtha
Malik Qambar, Jilu
Rayis Yawp Sawkho, Chamba, Upper Tiyari
Rayis Younan, Halmon
Rayis Warda Oshana of Rarwa, Upper Tiyari
Shlimun Zomaya, Gundiktha, Tkhuma
Kuma Mkhamodo?, Baz
Hurmizd Talia, Baz
Telow Dawid, Baz

Non-patriarchal faction[38]

Mar Zaya Sargis, Bishop of Jilu
Malik Khoshaba Yosip, Lower Tiyari
Zaya d'Shamisdin, Lower Tiyari
Malik Khammo, Baz
Chikko Giwo of the house of Dadosh, Upper Tiyari
Odisho Dadesho, Walto, Upper Tiyari
Khayo(b) Odisho, Ashitha, Lower Tiyari
Gabriel Shimun, Baz
Shimun Barkhisho, Bnay Maya (Mata), Jilu
Odisho Qambar Lawando, Bnay l'Gippa, Lower Tiyari

Malik Loko, present at the meeting, agreed with Malek:

> The declared reason for the meeting was to get the two Assyrian par-
> ties reconciled with one another and to provide an opportunity . . . to
> explain to the Assyrians the Government's settlement policy . . . But the

real reason for the meeting was . . . to set a trap to create conflict between the Assyrian leaders.[39]

Loko's sentiments of the event echoed Malek's, and it became obvious that the Assyrians would have to speak to the government officials separately. Four of the patriarchal faction remained. Though the Assyrians narrowly averted disaster at the meeting, the situation was anything but pacified. The settlement policy in the Dashtazi region was unacceptable to the Assyrians (especially those not influenced by government enticement), and yet it was their only recourse. Those who abstained from the agreement to settle 15,000 persons in a region suited only for 200 families were told to leave the country at any time.[40] Two of the four patriarchal faction members, Malik Andrewos of Jilu and Mar Yosip Khnanisho, were given leave to exit as they felt they had little to offer. Only Yaqo Ismael and Loko Shlimon remained and when confronted with the ultimatum of going to Baghdad and convincing Mar Shimun to sign or leave, both refused. They feared detainment in Baghdad and had heard on good authority that this was the ultimate subtlety of the British–Iraqi regime. The *qaimaqam* of 'Amēdīyāh, Majid Baik, responded in repugnance to the British officers and acting *mutasarrif*. According to Loko he retorted:

> Your policy is weak and with this policy you will bring ruin to Iraq . . .
> Give us the order and we will carry the stick. Any Assyrian who does not
> listen, we will break his head, tie his hands and send him to the south of
> Iraq until he dies there . . . We are Kurds, and we and the Assyrians know
> each other well.[41]

In no uncertain terms, Loko and Yaqo were told to relocate to the capital, and while both knew that they must acquiesce, they had no intention of moving to Baghdad. In response to the situation, on the night of 14–15 July an armed group of Assyrians under the leadership of Yaqo and Loko of Tkhuma and four others left Mosul for Bosriya and then the village of 'Ain Diwar, on the border with Syria, which they reached on the 18th. They surrendered their arms to the French authorities and entered Syria, requesting settlement rights in the Khabur basin.[42] There, the French professed no understanding of the Assyrian issue.[43] Worried that their people in Iraq would follow, the leaders sent an immediate letter urging them to remain where they were. The letter was either misunderstood or disregarded as on 20 July, approximately a thousand men, all armed, having left their families in Iraq arrived in Feshkhābur.[44] Iraqi officials learned of the crossing only when the Assyrians sent a letter to the Minister of the Interior and former member of the Committee of Union and Progress (Young Turks), Hikmat Sulayman, which read as follows: [45]

July 23, 1933
Near Khanik

Minister of Interior, Baghdad
Excellency,

As a result of the Mosul meeting, the Iraqi Government policy was explained to us both regarding the settlement and the Patriarch.

The Mutasarrif openly said 'those unsatisfied with this policy are free to emigrate from Iraq'. Accordingly we have come to the frontier and we request the Iraqi Government not to block the road to those who want to join us.

We have no intention to fight unless forced.
Signed
Yaqo d'Malik Ismael (Upper Tiyari)
Malik Baito (Tkhuma)
Malik Loko Shlimun (Tkhuma)
Malik Warda (Diz)
Rayis Esha (Nochiyya)
Rayis Ishaq (Nochiyya)
Malik Maroguil (Sara)
Tooma d'Makhura (Baz)
Yushia Esho (Drinayi)
Malik Salim (Barwar)
Shamasha Ismail (Liwan)
Rayis Mikhail (Sara)
Esho d'Kelaita (Timar d'Wan)

The battle at Feshkhābur and Dayrabūn and the Iraqi government reaction

The regime feared the 'general atmosphere of government defiance was unsettling the Kurds' and even the Shias to the south.[46] Yet the Assyrians continued with attempts at moving across the border. On 25 and 26 July 190 men attempted to cross the border. Some were disarmed and arrested and others disarmed and let go, while a large portion made it across successfully with no incident on either side.[47] Over the course of 30 and 31 July the Assyrians became aware that they would be allowed settlement on the condition of disarmament. Most agreed, though some remained in Iraq, awaiting their families before proceeding. In Syria, French authorities reneged on their earlier promise and turned the Assyrians back due to a League decree concerning the illegality of the effort, with promises that they would be allowed to re-enter Iraq without incident.[48] Iraqi forces determined either to disarm or eliminate them began firing with machine guns on those who had crossed to the east side of the Tigris as well as those who remained on the west bank in Syria. Five thousand Iraqi soldiers and police including support aircraft were brought to bear against fewer than 800 Assyrians during the confrontation.[49] At the end of the skirmish by the count of Malik Loko Shlimon, thirteen Assyrians were dead and eleven wounded among dozens of Iraqi army casualties.[50]

Iraqi army battalions combed the area around Jebel Bekhair in the Zakho region between 5 and 9 August looking for Assyrians who had returned from Syria.[51] On 6 August some 392 Assyrians were reported to have gone back into Syria, where they were permanently detained and moved to the interior of the country, and on the evening of the 7th, French authorities gave leave for 1,500 people to be settled in the Syrian region.[52] While the Iraqis cried outrage at the French for allowing armed Assyrians to return to Iraq, the French response was simple: the British authorities in Iraq had granted the rifles to them and there was no evidence of any unlawful action taken with said arms.[53]

When news of the debacle at Feshkhābur and Dayrabūn reached Baghdad, fear was replaced by rage. Animosity against Assyrians throughout the country became an active physical threat:

> Even in the highest circles there was talk of the 'rid me of this turbulent priest' order. 'Let all the Assyrian men be killed,' they cried, 'but spare the

women and children as the eyes of the world are on us. Let the Arabs and Kurds be raised against the Assyrians. Let trouble be stirred up in Syria against the treacherous French.'[54]

Thus began a propaganda campaign. In August more than 230 anti-Assyrian articles were published.[55] The Ministry of Education solicited funds from students and teachers to purchase a tank, while their Arab nationalist neighbours in Syria proposed to send funds for a plane or tank to be used in the anti-Assyrian operations and to be named *Southern Syria*.[56] The propaganda machine reported that armed Assyrians returning from Syria had mutilated the bodies of Iraqi soldiers, despite other reports that the French had disarmed the Assyrians.[57] An investigation was launched and according to British reports, the army's political officer was interviewed:

> The political officer with the Army, who is present at Mosul, now gives the account that the Assyrians burnt all the piquet equipment and that he himself would go no further than to say the bodies were burnt inadvertently in the burning of the tent etc. As to the beheading, all he knows for a fact is that the unarmed(?) driver of the lorry had his throat cut.[58]

The reports indicated that the Iraqi political officer saw no evidence of methodical injury. Yet it is evident from the final line that regardless of the inquiry and evidence which would lessen the growing anti-Assyrian zealotry, despite the Army official's account, 'the story which is believed' and propagated became fact. True to his observation, the misinformation about Assyrians mutilating bodies gave rise to a call by the Ikha al-Watani (National Brotherhood) party in Mosul to eliminate all 'foreign elements' from Iraq, and it seemed Faisal had the intention to teach the Assyrians a lesson.[59]

On 7 August, three days after the fighting began, Air Vice Marshal C. S. Burnett, the British air officer commanding in Iraq, responded to an Iraqi request for assistance by providing 100 bombs for use in military operations against Assyrians.[60] While Burnett may have been initially reluctant, Article 5 of the Anglo-Iraqi Treaty of 1930 dictated that 'His Britannic Majesty must grant whenever possible ammunition arms equipment etc. for the forces of His Majesty the King of Iraq'.[61] He may have found numerous ways to circumvent the matter, but he conceded fairly quickly that it remained the only action to be taken. His sentiments were echoed by Prime Minister Ramsay MacDonald not long after.[62]

It is unclear why the Iraqi army moved to surround Simele as most of the men who had left for Syria were either hiding in the mountains, dead or actually in Syria, while Simele housed predominantly women and children as well as men who had not participated in the battles on the border and in fact had sided with the non-patriarchal faction led by Malik Khoshaba. By 8 August, army personnel from Zakho entered Simele and collected all the ammunition belonging to Assyrians in the village.[63] On the following day the weaponless men sought refuge in the local police headquarters, where they waited for the *qaimaqam* of Dohuk. Upon arrival the *qaimaqam* collected all the weapons and ammunition of the local Assyrians and sent it to Dohuk. Soon after he sent for a local priest, Qasha Sada, Badal of Kharab Kulki and Rayis Talo of Baz, who were rounded up with eleven other men and sent by armoured car to Dohuk, meeting their end in the vicinity of the village of Aloka, where they were shot.[64] Eyewitnesses reported of Sada that 'his male organ having been cut was placed in his mouth, his head had been severed from his body'.[65] This occurred consistently over the next few days: Assyrians were rounded up and shot in the road.

On the same day the Iraqi air force bombed the village of Ziwa and killed a woman, under the false pretence that Assyrians had been in the village. After further investigation, local residents stated that no Assyrians had been in the vicinity. The immediate British response to the grow-ing fear and destruction was indifference: 'Four squadrons of British Air Force, whose intervention has been confined, of recent months, to drop-ping leaflets on Assyrians telling them to surrender. [The Assyrians] did so and were massacred a day or two later in cold blood.'[66] On the 10th the round-up continued and Assyrians were taken again from the village and shot on the road. The army was in Simele, the last known residence of Yaqo Ismael, the leader of the troublesome element. While his wife was in residence, the vast majority of the Assyrians in Simele were in fact of the Baz tribe, and evidently not a party to the plans of the patriarchal faction led by Yaqo.[67]

The tide of hate arose across the country. Between 9 and 14 August Arab employees of the Iraq Petroleum Company (IPC) in Baiji, a refinery town more than 120 miles north of Baghdad on the way to Mosul, attacked local Assyrian workers in a fit of mob zealotry. As night fell on the infamous day of 11 August, Assyrians were attacked by what appeared to be both local tribesmen and IPC workers, who wounded fourteen and killed one. A few days later the IPC's Arab employees went on strike until the majority of Assyrian workers were let go.[68]

The Massacre at Simele

During those weeks preceding the massacre, Assyrians from south of Simele had begun moving into the village since suffering continuous raiding from nearby tribes. On Friday 11 August two lorry-loads of police from Dohuk visited Simele armed with machine guns.[69] On the same morning, following the entrance of the police, between 300 and 500 Assyrians came into the village. When they arrived they were asked to surrender their arms to the Iraqi military, who 'then proceeded to massacre them with machine gun and rifle fire. Aside from one wounded man, there were no survivors'; all the adult males in the village that day were killed.[70]

> A cold-blooded and methodical massacre of all the men in the village then followed, a massacre for which in the black treachery in which it was conceived and the callousness with which it was carried out, was as foul a crime as any in the blood-stained annals of the Middle East. The Assyrians had no fight left in them partly because of the state of mind to which the events of the past week had reduced them, largely because they were disarmed. Had they been armed it seems certain that Ismail Abawi Tohalla and his bravos would have hesitated to take them on in a fair fight. Having disarmed them, they proceeded with the massacre according to plan. This took some time. Not that there was any hurry, for the troops had the whole day ahead of them. Their opponents were helpless and there was no chance of any interference from any quarter whatsoever. Machine gunners set up their guns outside the windows of the houses in which the Assyrians had taken refuge, and having trained them on the terror-stricken wretches in the crowded rooms, fired among them until not a man was left standing in the shambles. In some other instances the blood lust of the troops took a slightly more

active form, and men were dragged out and shot or bludgeoned to death and their bodies thrown on a pile of dead.[71]

This was not the only incident, and the killing, raping and pillaging did not cease for a full month. Eyewitnesses recounted the abhorrent barbarity of the slaughter that affected both men and women. Women had their bellies slashed and their wombs ripped out and placed upon their heads for amusement. Girls were taken into captivity by the army, and were never seen again.[72] In one house, eighty-two men of the Baz tribe and their families who had surrendered were massacred. Even Goriel (Gabriel) Shimun of Baz, known to be friendly towards the Iraqi government, was shot while hoisting a white flag of parley.[73] Some children survived through the quick thinking of the womenfolk:

> My friends and I saw a plane fly into Simele and start firing on us. Assyrians gathered in houses. [Since the men were being slaughtered,] the women began making the young boys (including me) look like girls so they would not be killed. The third day after the killing began, they (some wearing Iraqi uniforms, some not) rounded up some Assyrians and said, 'Either become Muslim or we will kill you.'[74]

Initially this spared the boys and young men who were being killed on site. Soon this tactic too would fail as reports began to surface that even nine-year-old girls were being raped and burnt alive.[75] Most children were stabbed to death as they threw themselves over the naked and headless corpses of their mothers.

While the massacre had begun in Simele village, Assyrians were rounded up elsewhere, including the steps of the American mission house at Dohuk. On the same day, 11 August, two men of the Diz tribe were tied, handcuffed and escorted by five policemen towards a governmental building where they were shot in cold blood. A day later another Diz man, bleeding from a gunshot wound, was left by the local police to die by a stream 150 yards from the government building. The local priest, Qasha Shmiwal, was beaten, arrested and taken away by the *qaimaqam* and his men. He was later stripped, taken to a location out of sight and shot.[76]

According to reports, on 12 August eleven Assyrians were killed, seventeen wounded and seventeen more captured by a patrol.[77] On the 13th in the village of Badi more than forty Arab and Kurdish policemen took four men out of a house and shot them immediately. The elderly men were forced to walk to the nearby mosque and obliged to become Muslim. After the first refused and was killed, the remaining men silently accepted, whereupon they were instructed by the local mullah in the teachings of Islam and its expectations. This campaign against the men continued in Badi for five days and included the looting of households and finally the arrest and appropriation of most of the remaining young women to a nearby village; they were never heard from again.[78] Any fleeing Assyrians were shot on sight. The military had incited Kurdish irregulars to attack Assyrian regions, and in Dohuk and Zakho, more than 100 peasants, including priests on three occasions, were taken out of their houses by the Iraqi army and 'shot in batches'.[79]

> Here and there in the mountains they came up with fugitive Assyrians. And every Assyrian they caught they shot out of hand. Clearly by now the Army had decided that the Assyrians, as far as possible, were to be exterminated. No pretence was made that these operations had any purely military objective, for the Army Intelligence officers did not even take the trouble to cross-question the captured Assyrians, who were simply shot as they were rounded up . . . it was evident by now that the Army Command was quite certain in its own mind that, in its decision to wipe out the Assyrians, it would . . . be backed not only by Arab public opinion, but by the Baghdad Government.[80]

In his account of the events, Gerald de Gaury, British military officer to Saudi Arabia, lamented:

> Whoever fired the first shot in a brush on the Syrian frontier on the fourth of August, there could be no justification for the shooting down of Assyrians in villages far away . . . The people killed were entirely innocent. It was enough for them to be Assyrians to be shot.[81]

Beyond the death toll were many atrocities including women and children raped and abducted as booty, as well as hundreds of villages looted, razed and destroyed (see Table 6).[82]

Table 6 Villages destroyed, razed, looted and/or forcibly abandoned during the Simele massacres (*Region* is divided into governorate, district and sub-district – in some cases two of the three or all three are identical)[95]

	Village	Population/tribe	Families/houses	Region
1	Gere-Bahen			
2	Garmawa	Baz		Dohuk
3	Iazkin			Dohuk
4	Karrana	110 Baz	25 houses	Dohuk
5	Khabartu (Kabartu, Kabirtu)	Baz		Dohuk
6	Kola Hassan			Dohuk
7	Kore-Gavana	Upper Tiyari		Dohuk
8	Ruhaidi	Baz		Dohuk
9	Shindokha			Dohuk
10	Tutika			Dohuk
11	Aṭush			Dohuk ʿAmēdīyāh
12	Berbangi			Dohuk ʿAmēdīyāh
13	Cham Ashaki			Dohuk ʿAmēdīyāh
14	Deralok	130 Baz		Dohuk ʿAmēdīyāh
15	Gund Kosa	150 Lower Tiyari	28 families (in 1938)	Dohuk ʿAmēdīyāh
16	Musalakia			Dohuk ʿAmēdīyāh
17	Safra Zor	35		Dohuk ʿAmēdīyāh
18	Sawura (Sawra)			Dohuk ʿAmēdīyāh
19	Challik (Chelok, Chalke, Chelki)	210 Lower Tiyari		Dohuk ʿAmēdīyāh Barwari Bala
20	Kani Balav (Kanya Balave, Kani Balaf)	110 Lower Tiyari		Dohuk ʿAmēdīyāh Barwari Bala
21	Pirozan (Beluzan)	Tkhuma (200?)		Dohuk ʿAmēdīyāh Barwari Bala
22	Barzanke			Dohuk ʿAmēdīyāh Sarsang
23	Cham ʿAshrat	Upper Tiyari (70?)		Dohuk ʿAmēdīyāh Sarsang
24	Dohoke (Dahoki)	Tkhuma		Dohuk ʿAmēdīyāh Sarsang
25	Masiki (Musa Laka)	Baz (55?)		Dohuk ʿAmēdīyāh Sarsang
26	Qadish (Akdish)	(150?)		Dohuk ʿAmēdīyāh Sarsang
27	Sikrīne	Tkhuma (65?)		Dohuk ʿAmēdīyāh Sarsang

	Village	Population/tribe	Families/houses	Region
28	Suse (Cham Sus)	Lower Tiyari 200		Dohuk 'Amēdīyāh Sarsang
29	Tahlawa	Lower Tiyari (75?)		Dohuk 'Amēdīyāh Sarsang
30	Bazhora	Lower Tiyari		Dohuk 'Aqra Girdasin
31	Jalan-Arabok	Lower Tiyari		Dohuk 'Aqra Girdasin
32	Khalikan	Lower Tiyari	12 families (in 1938)	Dohuk 'Aqra Girdasin
33	Guske	Upper Tiyari		Dohuk 'Aqra Nahla
34	Kashkawa	134	35 families (in 1938)	Dohuk 'Aqra Nahla
35	Kortka (Kurtkan)	Lower Tiyari		Dohuk 'Aqra Nahla
36	Shirti (Sherita)	Lower Tiyari		Dohuk 'Aqra Nahla
37	Ala Kina			Dohuk Doski
38	Alqoshta (Alkishke)	Baz		Dohuk Doski
39	Cham Kare	Lower Tiyari		Dohuk Doski
40	Derke			Dohuk Doski
41	Gundikta (Gundik Nabi)			Dohuk Doski
42	Gund-Naze	Lower Tiyari		Dohuk Doski
43	Kavla-Sin (Kola-Sine, Kafla Sin, Kavla Hasan)	Upper Tiyari 80		Dohuk Doski
44	Korbel (Kar Bile, Karbil)			Dohuk Doski
45	Majal Makhte	Upper Tiyari (190?)		Dohuk Doski
46	Nawdara (Navdara)			Dohuk Doski
47	Aloka (upper)	Upper Tiyari (30?)		Dohuk Sheikhan Atrush
48	Badrdin (Badr al-Din)	Upper Tiyari		Dohuk Sheikhan Atrush
49	Bestawa (Bastava)			Dohuk Sheikhan Atrush
50	Nourdinawa (Nurdinawa)			Dohuk Sheikhan Atrush
51	Badariyah	100 Tkhuma		Dohuk Sheikhan Qasrok
52	Bajilla	Tkhuma		Dohuk Sheikhan Qasrok

Table 6 (continued)

	Village	Population/tribe	Families/houses	Region
53	Kifre	Tkhuma		Dohuk Sheikhan Qasrok
54	Malla- Birwan (Mulla Barwan)	35 Jilu		Dohuk Sheikhan Qasrok
55	'Ain Dulbe (Dulip, Deleb, Idlib)			Dohuk Simele
56	Badaliya	Baz		Dohuk Simele
57	Bakhitme			Dohuk Simele
58	Be Torshi (Batirshi, Batarshah)	Tkhuma/Upper Tiyari		Dohuk Simele
59	Cham Jihane (Jajamani)	Tkhuma/Upper Tiyari		Dohuk Simele
60	Cham-Gaur/Gawir	Lower Tiyari		Dohuk Simele
61	Dari			Dohuk Simele
62	Gera-Gora (Gre-Gure)			Dohuk Simele
63	Giril (Karpil, Garfil)	Tkhuma/Upper Tiyari		Dohuk Simele
64	Gutba (Qutba)			Dohuk Simele
65	Hajisni	Upper Tiyari		Dohuk Simele
66	Hejerke (Hizeerke)	Baz (85?)		Dohuk Simele
67	Kharab Kulke	Baz		Dohuk Simele
68	Kolabni (Kulabne)	Baz		Dohuk Simele
69	Kwashe (Kowashe)	Upper Tiyari		Dohuk Simele
70	Lazga (Lazaka, Lazkin)			Dohuk Simele
71	Mansuriya (Misurik)	Lower Tiyari		Dohuk Simele
72	Marona			Dohuk Simele
73	Mavan (Mawana)	Baz		Dohuk Simele
74	Muqble			Dohuk Simele
75	Qasr Yazdin	Baz		Dohuk Simele
76	Sayyid Zahir (Sezari)	Baz		Dohuk Simele
77	Ser Shari (Sar Shur)	Tkhuma/Upper Tiyari		Dohuk Simele
78	Simele	Baz		Dohuk Simele
79	Tel Zayt (Tal Zer)	Tkhuma/Upper Tiyari		Dohuk Simele
80	Der Jindi/Jundi			Dohuk Simele Fayda

	Village	Population/tribe	Families/houses	Region
81	Dosteka (Dostka)	Tkhuma		Dohuk Simele Fayda
82	Kani-Gulan			Dohuk Simele Fayda
83	Karaiphan (Cariphan, Kraipahin)	Shamizdin	11 families (in 1938)	Dohuk Simele Fayda
84	Khirsheniya	Marbishu/Jilu (15?)		Dohuk Simele Fayda
85	Qalaʿ d'Badri	Baz		Dohuk Simele Fayda
86	Reqawa (Rekawa)	Jilu, some Baz/ Marbishu	3 families (in 1938)	Dohuk Simele Fayda
87	Salaḥiya	Tkhuma		Dohuk Simele Fayda
88	Sheikhidra (Sheikh-Khidr)	Marbishu		Dohuk Simele Fayda
89	Sina			Dohuk Simele Fayda
90	Tel Hish (Tel Khish, Khishaf)	Tkhuma/Gawar/ Mar-Bishu		Dohuk Simele Fayda
91	Zeniyat	Baz		Dohuk Simele Fayda
92	Zorawa			Dohuk Simele Fayda
93	Bamir (Ba-Mere)	Bohtan		Dohuk Simele Slevani
94	Basitke (lower)	Tkhuma		Dohuk Simele Slevani
95	Basitke (upper)	Tkhuma		Dohuk Simele Slevani
96	Kar-Sin (Gar-Shin)	Tkhuma		Dohuk Simele Slevani
97	Spindarok	Lower Tiyari		Dohuk Zakho Guli
98	Babilo (Babalu)	Baz	18 families (in 1938)	Dohuk Zawita
99	Badi (Bade)			Dohuk Zawita
100	Bagiri (Bakir) Lower	Baz/Upper Tiyari 150		Dohuk Zawita
101	Bagiri (Bakir) Upper	Lower Tiyari		Dohuk Zawita

Table 6 (continued)

	Village	Population/tribe	Families/houses	Region
102	Baroski (Baroshke)	Upper and Lower Tiyari		Dohuk Zawita
103	Biswaya (Be Sawa)	Marbishu		Dohuk Zawita
104	'Ain Sifni	Baz		Ninawa Sheikhan
105	Basifni	Jilu		Ninawa Sheikhan
106	Naristik			Ninawa Sheikhan
107	Bativer (Be-Tafre, Ba-Tipre)	Upper Tiyari		Ninawa Sheikhan Atrush
108	Begahe (Begah)	Upper Tiyari		Ninawa Sheikhan Atrush
109	Benarink (Be-Naringe)	Upper Tiyari		Ninawa Sheikhan Atrush
110	Dizze			Ninawa Sheikhan Atrush
111	'Ain Baqri	Jilu		Ninawa Tell-Kayf Alqosh
112	'Ain Helwa	100 Bohtan	27 families (in 1938)	Ninawa Tell-Kayf Alqosh
113	Baqqaq	Baz		Ninawa Tell-Kayf Alqosh
114	Dikan (Dahkan, Dakhan)	32	5 houses	Ninawa Tell-Kayf Alqosh
115	Jarahiya	11 Jilu		Ninawa Tell-Kayf Alqosh
116	Karanjawa (Karanjak)	35		Ninawa Tell-Kayf Alqosh
117	Makana (Machna)	Jilu		Ninawa Tell-Kayf Alqosh
118	Pirozawa (Porusawa, Birozawa)	65 Baz		Ninawa Tell-Kayf Alqosh
119	Qasrune	38 Bohtan	7 families (in 1938)	Ninawa Tell-Kayf Alqosh
120	Taftiya(n) (Totiyan)	120		Ninawa Tell-Kayf Alqosh
121	Nāṣerīyā	41 Jilu	18 families (only 2 remained in 1938)	Sheikhan

The narrative of Jatou

The extermination plan did not end with the civilians at Simele. The government and military desired to make an example of the Hakkâri tribesmen for their settled brethren sympathetic to their cause. After the initial exterminations took place, a call from Baghdad was made to Jatou of Dohuk, a police station chief in 'Aqra.[83] Directives from Baghdad ordered Jatou to round up three truck-loads of Assyrians and bring them to Simele, presumably for execution. Jatou, himself an Assyrian, struggled with the order for a sleepless night as he relived the deaths of his sister and mother, who had been killed in the massacres not twenty years earlier in the failing Ottoman empire and the creation of the Young Turk regime. But by daybreak, he had come to a decision and executed the preliminary part of his orders.

As the native Assyrians (here many were of Chaldean ecclesiastical background) observed from rooftops, the former Hakkâri Assyrians were loaded onto the trucks. As they drove off, sighs were expelled and fears voiced as onlookers lamented, 'Shmutlokhun khasan' ('You have broken our strength [literally 'back']').[84] Jatou then drove his wards in the direction of Simele. At a major junction along the way he decided to turn off towards the town of Ma'althaya and continue to the Jacobite monastery of Mar Mattai, situated in a remote mountain pass 100 kilometres south of Simele. There he unloaded and spoke to a resident monk, threatening to return without notice to check on the welfare of his wards. The fugitives remained in the monastery for three months, after which time they began to trickle back towards their homes following a lull in the persecution and discrimination that had begun in August 1933. Thus some were saved, but the damage had been done. The message of what could happen to any man, woman or child identified as Assyrian created dread in their more integrated or assimilated brethren.

Rhetoric from the regime

As King Faisal was abroad, his regent, Prince Ghazi, gave permission to the leader of the governmental forces, Colonel Baqr Sidqi, to eliminate any and all Assyrians.[85] Sidqi, of Kurdish descent, was among many to utilise a growing tide of anti-Western, anti-Christian (Assyrian) rhetoric to further his consolidation of power. Sidqi used the murders of these thousands of Assyrian 'separatists', as they became popularly termed by the national media, to catapult his career as a military hero.[86] The government's rejoinder to the massacres was abject denial:

> The Iraq Government denies the massacre, claiming that it was punitive action against rebels. Obviously Government officials, the police and the army will not testify to it, and there seem to be no male survivors. Also intimidation would doubtless play a part in the prevention of testimony.[87]

When Faisal returned to comment on the issue, he stated, 'It is a disgrace to talk about massacres. Not one woman was molested.'[88] Eyewitness testimony, however, painted a very different picture:

> After killing all the men, the soldiers stripped the dead, taking their things of value, and went after the women. The Arabs and the Kurds looted the village. The better-looking women were mishandled, stripped, and let go. The wife of Yako, the supposed leader of the Assyrians, who left for Syria, was repeatedly violated, stripped, and let go, and so were her two daughters.[89]

The Minister of the Interior, Hikmet Beg Suleiman, had left Baghdad to see the destruction with his own eyes. His reaction was recorded by Colonel R. S. Stafford:

> I was sitting in my office on the morning of August 15th when Hikmet Beg returned. He came straight into my room in a state of collapse, for he had just come from Simmel, and even he, cynical Turk as he was, had been overcome by the horrors which he had seen. On the previous day I had received reports that there were large numbers of Assyrian women and children in Simmel living in a state of starvation, but not a word had been said in these reports about the massacre which was the cause of this destitution . . . When I visited Simmel myself with Major Thomson on August 17th few traces could be seen of what had occurred, but the sight of the women and children is one which I shall never forget – and I spent more than three years in the trenches in France![90]

To add further injury, on 16 August the Iraqi government passed an emergency law for the deportation of the entire family of the Church of the

Figure 9   Batarshah, approximately 15 miles northwest of Simele, reportedly attacked by Arab and Kurdish irregulars, 18 September 1933. The circular pits are traits of bombings (The Service of Air Vice-Marshal Gerard Combe in the Royal Air Force, 1923–1946, HU 89458, Imperial War Museum)

Figure 10   Dakhan or Dikan village following desertion of at least five families. Simele surveillance photo, AIR 2/883/002

Figure 11   Unnamed Assyrian village destroyed in 1933. Simele surveillance photo, AIR 2/883/010. Many thanks to Fadi Dawood for his extensive research in unearthing these photographs

East patriarch, including his father David and his brother Theodore. On the morning of 18 August, Mar Eshai Shimun along with his two relatives was carried by British aeroplane 'to Cyprus via Palestine accompanied by two Assyrian officers, Rab Imma Malik Hormiz of Tkhuma and Rab Khamshi officer Yaku Eliya'.[91] As for the mass destruction, there was a cursory official inquiry into the massacres, but no one was held responsible for the brutality reported. In stark contrast, in the wake of the crimes perpetrated against mostly unarmed civilians, Colonel Sidqi was promoted and received a victory parade upon his return to Baghdad.

The American minister resident/consul general in Iraq, Paul Knabenshue, reported in two dispatches at the end of August that parades for Iraqi troops in both Baghdad and Mosul were met by cheering men, women and children. Shops were closed and a holiday ensued amid palpable jubilation as the victorious troops were strewn with flowers and rosewater.[92]

> One section of the victorious Iraq army returning from the front is now quartered at Mosul, and another section is arriving at Baghdad to-day. Mosul gave an enthusiastic welcome to its allotment. Triumphal arches were erected, decorated with watermelons shaped as [Assyrian] skulls into which daggers were thrust and with red streamers suspended, intended, it is assumed, to represent blood.[93]
>
> Only one unfortunate incident marked the otherwise peaceful demonstration during the day. Most of the Baghdad Assyrian population, cognizant of the potential danger to themselves, remained quietly secluded in their houses. One recently discharged Assyrian Levies' Officer, however, was on his way to the railway station to meet his wife and family when the crowd suddenly espied and maliciously murdered him.[94]

The aftermath

Not only the massacres but also the repercussions from them exponentially altered as a whole. In Iraq as in Geneva, the Assyrians, both patriarchal and non-patriarchal factions, felt the chill of betrayal. The British voiced their fear for the safety of the Assyrians only to stall the inquiry commissioner, a representative of the League of Nations, in his attempts to enter Iraq in the immediate aftermath of Simele.

Since they had created this state of affairs, the British authorities were naturally disinclined to change it. Even after the end of the mandate, the embassy was more concerned to cover up for the Iraqi government than to deplore their sins of commission: after the Assyrian massacre in the summer of 1933, Sir Francis Humphrys recommended that Britain should do her utmost to forestall the dispatch of a League of Nations Commission of Enquiry.[96]

Perhaps a comment by William Yale sums up the colonial and Middle Eastern perceptions concerning the Assyrians and their harsh predicament: 'These valiant and stubborn people had come to the end of their long tempestuous history, victims of hatreds engendered by the clash between Western imperialism and the rising nationalism of Near Eastern peoples.'[97]

International Recognition?

Though influential writers and researchers lamented the Assyrian predicament, some strove to remedy the situation directly. In the most renowned case, the Simele massacres (alongside those of the Ottoman Empire) were not only invoked but became viable paradigms that influenced a young Raphael Lemkin in the development of a framework concerning the legal concept of mass murder. In October 1933, Lemkin left for Madrid to present a paper on terrorism to the Association internationale de droit pénal (AIDP). He had been moved to action by the horrific massacres and violent destruction in the wake of the tragedy in and around Simele on 11 August 1933 and during the following weeks.[98] Lemkin hoped that this event would garner sympathy for his proposals to the AIDP and League of Nations for outlawing crimes against humanity.[99] Lemkin proposed to outlaw barbarity, 'the extermination of ethnic, social, and religious groups by pogroms, massacres, or economic discrimination', and vandalism, 'the destruction of cultural or artistic works which embod[y] the genius of a specific people'.[100] Regrettably, his proposal was never voted on and upon his return to Poland he fell under pressure from the Polish Foreign Minister for comments made in Madrid to resign from his position as a public prosecutor. It was evident that promoting minority rights and challenging the status quo was not well thought of, and while Lemkin's professional life suffered, he continued to be propelled by the events of the First World War and Simele, as well as the treatment of European Jewry in the following decades, leading to the proposal and ratification of the Convention on the Prevention and Punishment of the Crime of Genocide (UNGC) by the newly formed United Nations in 1948. Lamentably for the victims of Simele and the First World War, the UNGC was not applied to prior events, as it lacked retroactivity.

Road to the Republic

The events of Simele served as a blueprint for succeeding governments' treatment of minorities, while catapulting the army into the centre of Iraqi politics. From 1933 until 1940, under the reign of Prince Ghazi, a series of military coups attempted to take control over the country until the crown prince's death in 1939. Meanwhile the Assyrians who had fled Iraq to Syria on that auspicious day in August in 1933 were now living new lives along the river Khabur. They settled in sixteen villages (see Table 7), four of which – Tel Chama, Tel Umrane and Tel Ajaj (of the Tkhuma tribe) and Tel Asafir (Diz) – were subsequently divided into fourteen new villages to give a grand total of twenty-six.[101]

Back on the other side of the border, not two years after Ghazi's death, on 1 April 1941, while Iraq was under the regency of Prince 'Abdallah (ruling for the underage Faisal II), the anti-British Prime Minister, Rashid 'Ali al-Gaylani, staged a successful coup. The new order under al-Gaylani was exceedingly Arab nationalist and at the least ideologically influenced if not supported by the fascist regime of Nazi Germany. In June 1941, after the Anglo-Iraqi War had ended, the Pan-Arab agenda under al-Gaylani's leadership became frighteningly apparent when Yunis Sab'awi, an associate of al-Gaylani's government and a member of the far-right and pan-Arab al-Muthanna Club, led a mob attack on the Baghdad Jewish community (who like the Assyrians were painted as supporters of the West), an assault sometimes referred to as the *farhud*.[102] The event, in blueprint rather than scope, exhibited uncanny and 'disturbing parallels' to Simele as yet another Iraqi community would suffer in the midst of political and security instabilities and arrogance.[103] The man at the centre of much of the ideology was Colonel Salah al-Din al-Sabbagh, who unlike Colonel Baqr Sidqi and others who

Table 7 Assyrian settlement along the Khabur, 31 August 1938

Village	Population	Tribe
Tel Tammar	1,542	Tiyari
Tel Umrane	1,077	Tkhuma
Tel Chama	1,054	Tkhuma
Tel Maghas	965	Sara
Tel Um Rafa	603	Tiyari
Tel Shamiran	574	Mar Bishu
Tel Nasri	501	Tiyari
Tel Jama	487	Halamon
Tel Tal'a	427	Sara
Tel/Wadi Massas	392	Barwar
Tel Asafir	361	Diz
Tel Hafyan	318	Quchanis
Tel Ajaj	146	Tkhuma
Tel Kaifji	141	Liwan
Tel Baz	137	Baz
Tel Um Kaif	113	Timar d'Van
Total	**8,838**	

utilised such movements for political gain, candidly believed in the discourse of the Pan-Arab movement.[104]

Al-Gaylani sundered the Anglo-Iraqi Agreement of 1930 with the besieging of the RAF force at Habbaniya, about 90 kilometres west of Baghdad, on 30 April 1941. In response to the coup, the British once again acted to restore the monarchy. The Iraqi levies of the RAF at Habbaniya still contained forty Assyrian officers and hundreds of others of various ranks who helped defend their position at the camp against foot soldiers as well as aerial attacks by German warplanes, effectively dissipating any momentum Gaylani had formed. Sending in larger forces, specifically the Indian 20th infantry brigade through Basra and reinforcements from the Transjordan, the British eventually quelled the rebellion by pursuing the Iraqi army to Fallujah and finally to Baghdad. A week later the monarchy was reinstated.

In the following years, integration into Iraq became the new concern of most Assyrians no longer a part of the levies force. Most settled/urban Assyrians managed to integrate with relative ease into the new culturally Arab-dominated Iraq with the exception of those farther north in the Dohuk and Zakho regions, where Arab influence was negligible.[105] In the example of the Mosul region, most urban dwellers identified solely with their religious community. Indeed, Assyrian-Aramaic had been lost among the majority of city dwellers of the region (those of the outlying villages excluded), though the form of Arabic spoken in Mosul (as well as the Syrian Jezirah) retained a strong Aramaic and Akkadian influence.[106] Undoubtedly, those tribes of the Hakkâri region lacked this assimilationist deportment and rather retained aspects of a fiercely sovereign tribal warrior culture, something akin to their Kurdish neighbours. Such an attitude and mindset would be the prime reason behind their initial and continued service in elite battalions in the Royal Air Force.

An added issue was a deliberate policy to contain any spread of (as well as Kurdish and Turkoman) nationalist sentiments and secondly, in the case of the Assyrians, the denial of nativeness. This became more apparent as the Iraqi monarchy attempted to consolidate control once again after the humiliation of the Gaylani coup, especially in the form of print capital as what was disseminated to the world about Iraq and its people. In an official governmental publication from 1946 entitled *Kingdom of Iraq*, Assyrians are mentioned briefly under the umbrella term 'Christians' and as Nestorians, 'who have the purely political denomination "Assyrians"' and were brought 'back to Iraq' in 1917 thanks to the 'fortunes of war'.[107]

The Assyrians found themselves bereft of positions and titles in post-1941 Iraq. They counted neither among the 'senior officials, magistrates, judges, army officers, or ministers' nor among the deputies in parliament, while other communities benefited tremendously.[108] Under these conditions, lacking both internal strength in numbers and political clout and external (foreign) support, the Assyrian cultural and national movement developed more slowly and with more difficulty than those of their Arab and Kurdish neighbours. This was especially true following the detrimental fragmentation of its religious communities, through foreign and domestic influence, and as a repercussion from the Simele massacre.

Consequently, early attempts at creating Assyrian cultural and political groups to aid in the establishment of Assyrian ethno-religious, cultural and political rights in Iraq were few. Some underground groups were established during this period, the most renowned of which was Khubbā w-Khuyada Ātūrayā (Assyrian Love and Unity). A previous organisation with the same initials, Kheit Kheit Allap (XXH), was founded in 1942 as an underground organisation among RAF personnel (as Assyrian activities deemed national-ist were forbidden by both the RAF and the Iraqi government) by a carpen-ter, Mushe Khoshaba, in Habbaniya. *Ousta* Mushe, as he was commonly known, was born in Solduz, Persia in 1876 and fought with General Petros Elia in the First World War.[109] As for Khubbā w-Khuyada Ātūrayā, its struc-ture was highly systematised with oaths of allegiance, secret ceremonies of initiation, codenames and passwords.[110] The movement found compatriots and supporters within the IPC in Kirkuk, Basra and Mosul, in Urmia in Iran and in Syria, as well as reaching across ecclesiastical lines to include the Church of the East, Chaldeans, Protestants, and others. XXH lasted until the end of the decade, when it disbanded in the midst of the chaos that ensued following the dismantling of the remaining levy battalions and their abandonment by the British military.[111]

By contrast, the Iraqi Communist Party (ICP) became a refuge for politi-cally and numerically smaller peoples with financial backing from a large external player. It grew intensely in popularity among the minorities in Iraq, especially the secular elites and academics. With Soviet expansion into central Asia and the Caucasus in 1921, Western powers had begun a policy of sup-porting the highly centralised, nationalist and militarist regimes in Iran, Iraq, Syria and Turkey. Assyrians through the ICP played a fundamental role in shaping the political history of Iraq. In 1941 Yusuf Salman Yusuf, known by the cadre name Fahd ('Panther'), became secretary of the party and set about restructuring the organisation and expanding membership among the working classes.[112] Yusuf integrated a greater population into the Communist Party, and between 1941 and 1949 under the restored monarchy, Assyrians made up a sizeable percentage of the party.[113]

The power of the King was failing, and a young Faisal II (not coming into his majority until May of 1953) could not control the ambitions of his regent, General Nur al-Din Mahmud, who had declared martial law in November 1952 after widespread discord and protests by the ICP. Such discord resulted in eighteen executions, the banning of various parties, and more than 300 arrests.[114]

Meanwhile the European continent faced the gradual development of ultra-nationalism, embroiling it in the tumultuous period of the Second World War. During this time, in some small yet significant way, the Assyrians continued to influence Raphael Lemkin. In the preface of his 1943 book *Axis Rule in Occupied Europe: Laws of Occupation, Analysis of Government, Proposals for Redress* Lemkin coined the term *genocide* (from the Greek *genos*, meaning 'race' or 'tribe,' and the Latin ending *-cide*, denoting 'killing'). He used the term synonymously with *ethnocide* (or cultural genocide/destruction), which he defined as a combination of the crimes of barbarism and vandalism, as brought forth to the AIDP in Madrid in late 1933.[115] Lemkin likened the brutal Nazi policies and massacres of the Jews during the Second World War and the Holocaust to the massacres of the Armenians (including the Greeks and Assyrians) in the waning Ottoman period during the nation-building process under the Young Turks.[116] Thus, two major events – the massacres of Simele and those within Eastern Anatolia – that Lemkin utilised to shed light on human rights violations on the international stage (especially in regard to the rise of the Nazi Party in Germany and the subsequent treatment of European Jewry) specifically involved the Assyrians. After numerous failed attempts, Lemkin would use those past atrocities as examples and momentum in the midst of the horrors of the Second World War to ignite support for the UNGC, which would go on to be ratified by the United Nations on 9 December 1948.[117]

Notes

1. Most of this is mentioned in oral accounts. See the story of Ezra Warda (Effendi) of Baz and his interception of the government telegram calling for an Assyrian massacre in 'Abdyešu' Barzana, *Šinnē d-'Asqūtā: Qrābā d-Dayrabūn w-Gunḥā d-Simele* ['Years of Hardship: The Battle of Dayrabūn and the Simele Massacre'] (Chicago: Assyrian Academic Society, 2003), 212–20.
2. Ibid.
3. Ibid., 324–5.
4. *Report by the UK to the League of Nations on the Administration of 'Iraq for the Year 1930*, Colonial No. 62 (London: 1931), 29.
5. Charles Tripp, *A History of Iraq*, 2nd ed. (Cambridge: Cambridge University Press, 2002), 74.

6. Yusuf Malek, *The British Betrayal of the Assyrians* (Chicago: Assyrian National Federation/Assyrian National League of America, 1935), 196–7.

7. Alexander Sloan, ambassador to Iraq, American Consular Services, American Consulate General, Jerusalem, Palestine, to Wallace Murray, Near Eastern Affairs, Department of State, 31 August 1933, 890g.4016 Assyrians/93.

8. Paul Knabenshue, US ambassador to Iraq, to Wallace Murray, containing letter from Mr Cumberland to Secretary of State, 13 September 1933, 890g.4016 Assyrians/110.

9. Theodore d'Mar Shimun, *The History of the Patriarchal Succession of the d'Mar Shimun Family*, 2nd ed. (Turlock, CA: Mar Shimun Memorial Foundation, 2008), 102–3.

10. Paul Knabenshue, US ambassador to Iraq, to Wallace Murray, containing letter from Mr Cumberland to Secretary of State, 13 September 1933, 890g.4016 Assyrians/110.

11. Memorandum from Air Headquarters, Iraq to secretary to high commissioner, Baghdad, 2 October 1923, enclosing secret report from Major J. M. S. Renton, Headquarters, Iraq Levies, Mosul to officer commanding, Iraq Levies, Mosul, 12 September 1923, AIR 23/449.

12. Malek, *The British Betrayal of the Assyrians*, 222–3. Use of capitals is true to Malek's version.

13. Tripp, *A History of Iraq*, 75. See also Rev. W. A. Wigram DD, *Our Smallest Ally: A Brief Account of the Assyrian Nation in the Great War* (London: Society for Promoting Christian Knowledge / New York: Macmillan, 1920); Humphrys as quoted in Malek, *The British Betrayal of the Assyrians*, 196.

14. D'Mar Shimun, *The History of the Patriarchal Succession of the D'Mar Shimun Family*, 105.

15. R. S. Stafford, *The Tragedy of the Assyrians* (London: George Allen & Unwin, 1935), 114.

16. Ibid., 78.

17. Malek, *The British Betrayal of the Assyrians*, 213.

18. See A. M. Hamilton, *Road through Kurdistan: The Narrative of an Engineer in Iraq*, new ed. (London: Faber & Faber, 1958). Hamilton speaks frequently of Yaqo and the attitude of the Assyrians during the creation of the road.

19. See Ofra Bengio, 'Faysal's Vision of Iraq: A Retrospect', in Asher Susser and Aryeh Shmuelevitz (eds), *The Hashemites in the Modern Arab World: Essays in Honour of the Late Professor Uriel Dann* (London: Frank Cass, 1995), 143–9.

An Arabic version exists in ʿAbd al-Razzaq al-Hasani, *Ta'rikh al-Wizarat al-ʿIraqiyya*, Vol. 3.

20. League of Nations, *Official Journal* 14 (December 1933), 1808.

21. Daniel Silverfarb, *Britain's Informal Empire in the Middle East: The Case Study of Iraq 1929–1941* (New York: Oxford University Press, 1986), 42.

22. Malik Yaqo Ismael, *Aturayé w-tre plashe tibilayé* ['Assyrians and the Two World Wars'] (Tehran: Assyrian Writers Board, 1964), 214–15.

23. Malek, *The British Betrayal of the Assyrians*, 238; 'Letter and Report from Major Thompson, Expert for the Settlement of the Assyrians in Iraq, to the Iraqi Government, Mosul, September 28, 1933', *League of Nations Official Journal* 14 (1933), 1831. The report was completed prior to the Simele massacres.

24. Malek, *The British Betrayal of the Assyrians* 240.

25. 'Letter and Report from Major Thompson', 1841. Thompson estimated five souls per family, rather lower than the reality of closer to seven. Thompson calls those of Hakkâri ex-Ottoman subjects, which is misleading as everyone in Iraq was an ex-Ottoman subject. Furthermore, Thompson seemingly is only concerned with those Assyrians under Mar Shimun's authority and therefore neglects Catholics and Jacobites.

26. Hamilton, *Road through Kurdistan*, 217.

27. Stafford, *The Tragedy of the Assyrians*, 137–8.

28. Ibid., 121.

29. Ibid., 139.

30. Malek, *The British Betrayal of the Assyrians*, 250. See also Silverfarb, *Britain's Informal Empire in the Middle East*, 42.

31. Stafford, *The Tragedy of the Assyrians*, 139.

32. Malek, *The British Betrayal of the Assyrians*, 221.

33. Mary Lewis Shedd, *The Measure of a Man: The Life of William Ambrose Shedd, Missionary to Persia* (New York: George H. Doran, 1922), 231.

34. Stafford, *The Tragedy of the Assyrians*, 122–3.

35. Malek, *The British Betrayal of the Assyrians*, 221.

36. Ismael, *Aturayé w-tre plashe tibilayé*, 223.

37. Malek, *The British Betrayal of the Assyrians*, 252.

38. The non-patriarchal faction grew in number to forty-five, claiming to represent approximately 2,160 families numbering around 15,000 people. They signed a document sent to the League of Nations stating that the Mar Shimun did not speak for all the Assyrians in Iraq. See *Textes des petitions et observations y relatives des puissances mandataires examinees au cours de la 22ème session de la*

commission permanente des mandats tenue a Genève du 3 novembre au 6 décembre 1932, League of Nations Archives, c.p.m. 1298.

39. Malik Loko Shlimon d'Bit Badawi, *Assyrian Struggle for National Survival in the 20th and 21st Centuries* (2012), 330, 333.

40. Malek, *The British Betrayal of the Assyrians*, 252.

41. Shlimon d'Bit Badawi, *Assyrian Struggle for National Survival in the 20th and 21st Centuries*, 331.

42. H. S. Goold, American Consulate General, Beirut, Syria to Secretary of State, 'Irruption of Assyrians', 9 August 1933, 890g.4016 Assyrians/61.

43. Shlimon d'Bit Badawi, *Assyrian Struggle for National Survival in the 20th and 21st Centuries*, 337.

44. There seems to be some discrepancy regarding the correct day. Loko mentions the 21st whereas Barzana, who was among those who arrived that day, recalls the 20th (Shlimon d'Bit Badawi, *Assyrian Struggle for National Survival in the 20th and 21st Centuries* 338–9; Barzana, *Šinnē d-'asqūtā*, 119–20. Here again it is worth remembering the constant confusion over the actual position of the border. Neither side seemed to know this and regularly debated about jurisdiction. See Secret Memorandum from Special Service Officer, Mosul to Air Staff (Intelligence), Air Headquarters, 23 July 1933, AIR 23/655.

45. Malek, *The British Betrayal of the Assyrians*, 254–5, also in Malik Loko Shlimon (d'bit Badawi), *Assyrian Struggle for National Survival in the 20th and 21st Centuries*, (2012), 340 as well as an original copy referred to as appendix 5.

46. Royal Government of Iraq, *Correspondence Relating to Assyrian Settlement from 13th July, 1932 to 5th August, 1933* (Baghdad: Government Press, 1933), 2.

47. Secret Memorandum from Special Service Officer, Mosul to Air Staff (Intelligence), Air Headquarters, 23 July 1933, AIR 23/655.

48. Shlimon d'Bit Badawi, *Assyrian Struggle for National Survival in the 20th and 21st Centuries*, 345.

49. Ibid., 347.

50. Ibid., 358–9.

51. Parallel to the unfolding tribulations and the in light of recent events, the British authorities created a list of undesirables who were slated for arrest and deportation to Baghdad, including Lady Surma, Dawid d'Mar Shimun, Zaya (Mar Shimun's uncle), Alexander (Mar Shimun's uncle), Dadda (agent of Mar Shimun), Malik Andrius, Malik Sawa of Tal, Father Ishaq and Father Hanna (possibly Church of the East priests), Shamasha Elia of Baz, Esho of Tkhuma, Adam Zir of Jilu, Attu son of Shlimun son of Malik Ismael, Malikisdek son

of Shlimun son of Malik Ismael, Yuhanna Qass Iskharia (a teacher), Matti of Quchanis, Yonathan Merkhail, Iskharia Patti, Father Paulos Bedari (a Chaldean priest), Father Akhikar Kalaita (a Chaldean priest) and Theodore (Mar Shimun's brother). Secret Memorandum, serial no. 125, from Special Service Officer, Mosul to Air Staff (Intelligence), Air Headquarters, 5 August 1933, AIR 23/655. Eventually only a handful were arrested and detained.

52. Goold to Secretary of State, 'Irruption of Assyrians'; Malek, *The British Betrayal of the Assyrians*, 254. See also Joseph Yacoub, *The Assyrian Question* (Chicago: Alpha Graphic, 1986), 14–15. For more on the Nestorian settlements along the Khabur in Syria, see *Settlement of the Assyrians of Iraq: Report of the Committee of the Council on the Settlement of the Assyrians of Iraq in the Region of the Ghab (French Mandated Territories of the Levant)*, League of Nations Publications, Series I: Political, vol. 1935.VII.12.3. See also Shlimon d'Bit Badawi, *Assyrian Struggle for National Survival in the 20th and 21st Centuries*, 356–7.

53. Goold to Secretary of State, 'Irruption of Assyrians'.

54. Stafford, *The Tragedy of the Assyrians*, 162.

55. Malek, *The British Betrayal of the Assyrians*, 267; Silverfarb, *Britain's Informal Empire in the Middle East*, 42.

56. General Conditions/5, Knabenshue, Baghdad, 3 May 1933, USDOS 890g.00; General Conditions/6, Knabenshue, Baghdad, 24 May 1933, USDOS 890g.00.

57. Stafford, *The Tragedy of the Assyrians*, 162; Report by Air Commodore A. D. Cunningham, 5 August 1933, AIR 23/655. The report was based on his recent visit to Mosul and stated that the stories were exaggerated and propagandistic.

58. See Secret Memorandum serial no. 126 from Special Service Officer, Mosul to Air Staff (Intelligence), Air Headquarters, 6 August 1933, AIR 23/655.

59. Report by Air Vice Marshal C. S. Burkett, Air Headquarters, Iran Command, of interview with King Faisal and Mr Ogilvie-Forbes at the Palace, 6 August 1933, AIR 23/655. The report contains the elements of Faisal's comments concerning the events at Feshkhābur and Dayrabūn.

60. Burnett to Air Ministry, 8 August 1933, FO 371/16884.

61. Silverfarb, *Britain's Informal Empire in the Middle East*, 43.

62. Sir Robert Vansittart to MacDonald, 7 August 1933, FO 371/16884, including a note from MacDonald dated 8 August 1933. This matter is covered extensively in Silverfarb, *Britain's Informal Empire in the Middle East*, 43–5.

63. Shlimon d'Bit Badawi, *Assyrian Struggle for National Survival in the 20th and 21st Centuries*, 364.

64. 'Statement Made by Yushiya Dinka, of Malik Ismail, Upper Tiyari, Exhibit E to Supplementary Petition, Dated September 24 1933, from the Mar Shimun, "Catholicos" Patriarch of the Assyrians to the League of Nations', *League of Nations Official Journal* 14 (1933), 1827.

65. 'Statement Made by Miryam, Wife of David Jindo, A Corporal in the Iraq Levies, Exhibit D to Supplementary Petition, Dated September 24 1933, from the Mar Shimun, "Catholicos" Patriarch of the Assyrians to the League of Nations', *League of Nations Official Journal* 14 (1933), 1826.

66. Malek, *The British Betrayal of the Assyrians* 262, 305.

67. Secret Memorandum No. 1/M/33 serial no. 114 from Special Service Officer, Mosul to Air Staff (Intelligence), Air Headquarters, 25 July 1933, giving a list of the Assyrian tribal leaders reported to be with the immigrants, none of whom were from the Baz tribe. AIR 23/655.

68. 'Attack on the Assyrian Employed by the Iraq Petroleum Company, Exhibit F to Supplementary Petition, Dated September 24 1933, from the Mar Shimun, "Catholicos" Patriarch of the Assyrians to the League of Nations', *League of Nations Official Journal* 14 (1933), 1828.

69. Extract from dispatch no. S11126 from Air Officer Commanding to Air Commodore Cunningham, 22 August 1933, enclosing translation from Arabic of proclamation by the acting *mutasarrif* of Mosul published in *Al Tariq*, 20 August 1933, AIR 23/656

70. United States Department of State, Diplomatic (no. 164), P. Knabenshue, Subject: 'Assyrians – Massacres in Northern Iraq', Baghdad, 21 August 1933; secret memorandum, serial no. 143, Special Service Officer, Mosul to Air Staff (Intelligence), Air Headquarters, 18 August 1933, AIR 23/656.

71. Stafford, *The Tragedy of the Assyrians*, 174.

72. Malek, *The British Betrayal of the Assyrians*, 281.

73. 'Statement Made by Miryam, Wife of David Jindo, a Corporal in the Iraq Levies, Exhibit D to Supplementary Petition, Dated September 24 1933, from the Mar Shimun, "Catholicos" Patriarch of the Assyrians to the League of Nations', *League of Nations Official Journal* 14 (1933), 1826. See also secret dispatch no. 30s/ADC/MSL from Air Commander Cunningham, Headquarters, no. 30 (B) Squadron, Royal Air Force, Mosul to Air Vice Marshal C. S. Burnett, Air Headquarters, Iraq Command, Hinaidi, 18 August 1933, enclosing secret statement from R. K. Odishu made to Major Merry, undated, AIR 23/656.

74. Elias Haroon Bazi (Hejerke-Simele), interview with author, 24 February 2008, Toronto. Elias Bazi lost his father and suffered personal injury, including being shot in the arm, and continues to feel discomfort and pain from shrapnel still lodged above his lip. See also Interview with Elias Haroon, Lamassu Nineb. (Eastern Assyrian Language). [Toronto, Canada, 2011]. Modern Assyrian Research Archive. This is echoed by 'Statement Made by Miryam, Wife of David Jindo'.

75. Malek, *The British Betrayal of the Assyrians*, 269.

76. 'Statement Made by Rabi Armunta, an Assyrian Woman, Exhibit C, to Supplementary Petition, Dated September 24 1933, from the Mar Shimun, "Catholicos" Patriarch of the Assyrians to the League of Nations', *League of Nations Official Journal* 14 (1933), 1825; 'Statement Made by Yushiya Dinka, of Malik Ismail, Upper Tiyari, Exhibit E to Supplementary Petition, Dated September 24 1933, from the Mar Shimun, "Catholicos" Patriarch of the Assyrians to the League of Nations', *League of Nations Official Journal* 14 (1933), 1827.

77. See secret report by Major C. J. Edmonds, Ministry of the Interior, Baghdad to Mr. G. A. D. Ogilvie-Forbes, British Embassy, Baghdad, 24 August 1933, AIR 23/656, which attempted to address a full account of the massacres.

78. 'Statement Made by Victoria Yokhannan, a Young Girl of 12 Years of Age of the Tribe of Diz, Exhibit B, to Supplementary Petition, dated 24 September 1933, from the Mar Shimun, "Catholicos" Patriarch of the Assyrians to the League of Nations', *League of Nations Official Journal* 14 (1933), 1825.

79. R. S. Stafford, 'Iraq and the Problem of the Assyrians', *International Affairs* 13.2 (1934), 176.

80. Stafford, *The Tragedy of the Assyrians*, 168.

81. Gerald de Gaury, *Three Kings in Baghdad: The Tragedy of Iraq's Monarchy* (London: I. B. Tauris, [1961] 2008), 89.

82. Estimates range from 2,000 to 6,000 for the number of persons killed. See USDOS, letter to Wallace Murray, American Consular Services, Near Eastern Affairs, American Consulate General, Jerusalem, Palestine, 31 August 1933. The figure usually mentioned of 300–305, used by Husry and others, is based on Stafford and only for 11 August in the village of Simele. Stafford himself only came to the scene some days later, and it was surmised at the time that most of the bodies had already been buried by the military to cover the massacre. The attacking of random villages was also reported in the *Iraq Times* on 19 August.

83. Jatou acquired an infamous reputation among local Kurdish tribesmen and bandits as a feared bounty hunter.

84. Firas Jatou (grandson of Jatou), interview with author, San Jose, CA, 5 July 2012.

85. Sidqi was well known for his anti-Assyrian sentiments. The British authorities had warned the Iraqi government of this and suggested his removal from the post as commander of the northern forces. The suggestion was agreed to but never carried out. See secret dispatch from Air Headquarters, Iraq Command Hinaidi to Mr. G. A. D. Ogilvie Forbes, British embassy, Baghdad, 25 July 1933, AIR23/655, p. 418.

86. Through the Simele massacres Sidqi gained enough prestige and power to challenge the Iraqi establishment in a failed coup attempt in 1936.

87. Paul Knabenshue, US ambassador to Iraq, to Secretary of State, 'Assyrian Problem – British Policy', 28 August 1933, 890g.4016 Assyrians/86.

88. 'No massacres: Feisal emphatic', *Brisbane Courier-Mail*, 6 September 1933.

89. Barclay Acheson, executive secretary, Near East Foundation to Hon. Wallace S. Murray, chief, Division of Near Eastern Affairs, 13 September 1933, 890g.4016 Assyrians/90.

90. Stafford, *The Tragedy of the Assyrians*, 170–1, 177–8.

91. Malek, *The British Betrayal of the Assyrians*, 272.

92. Paul Knabenshue, US ambassador to Iraq, to Secretary of State, 'Iraq's Victorious Army Returns to Baghdad', 30 August 1933, 890g.4016 Assyrians/89.

93. Paul Knabenshue, US ambassador to Iraq, to Secretary of State, 'Suppression of Assyrian Revolt', (no. 165), 23 August 1933, 890g.4016 Assyrians/82.

94. Knabenshue to Secretary of State, 'Iraq's Victorious Army Returns to Baghdad'.

95. Based on numerous sources including Malek, The *British Betrayal of the Assyrians, 338–9; 'Report of Mar Shimun, Catholicos Patriarch of the Assyrians, Oct. 8, 1933',* Protection of Minorities in Iraq, League of *Nations, Geneva, 31 October 1933; Settlement of the Assyrians of Iraq, League of Nations, Geneva, 18 January 1934, 0.69.1934.VII, enclosure II–IV,* 8–11; 'Sketch Map of Villages in Which Assyrians Were Settled 1920–1933', in Stafford, Tragedy of the Assyrians; Air Ministry and Foreign Office documents and pictures; and eyewitness testimony. In villages where a population returned, numbers *are given if reported.*

96. Peter Sluglett, *Britain in Iraq: Contriving King and Country 1914–1932* (New York: Colombia University Press, 2007), 212.

97. William Yale, *The Near East: A Modern History* (Ann Arbor: University of Michigan Press, 1958), 326.

98. Agnieszka Bieńczyk-Missala (ed.), *Rafał Lemkin: A Hero of Humankind* (Warsaw: Polski Instytut Spraw Międzynarodowych, 2010), 79; Tanya Elder, 'What You See before Your Eyes: Documenting Raphael Lemkin's Life by Exploring His Archival Papers 1900–1959', in Dominik J. Schaller and Jürgen Zimmerer (eds), *The Origins of Genocide: Raphael Lemkin as a Historian of Mass Violence* (Abingdon: Routledge, 2009), 31.

99. United States Department of State, Diplomatic, P. Knabenshue, Subject: 'Assyrians – Massacres in Northern Iraq', Baghdad, 21 August 1933.

100. John Cooper, *Raphael Lemkin and the Struggle for the Genocide Convention* (Basingstoke: Palgrave Macmillan, 2008), 18–19.

101. 'Assyrian villages on the Khabur: results of latest census', *Athra*, 5 January 1939.

102. *Farhud* is an Arabic word meaning 'pogrom' or 'violent riot.'

103. Eric Davis, *Memories of State: Politics, History, and Collective Identity in Modern Iraq* (Berkeley: University of California Press, 2005), 70.

104. Ibid., 71.

105. David Wilmshurst, *The Ecclesiastical Organization of the Church of the East 1318–1913* (Leuven: Peeters, 2000), 126, states that on the eve of the First World War there were 4,000 Nestorians and 12,000 Chaldeans in the 'Amēdīyāh, Barwar and 'Aqra regions. These numbers were extremely minimised as in all cases of Christian populations in the densely Muslim East. Smaller statistics guaranteed less attention from what were perceived as possibly hostile Muslim groups. Despite this discrepancy, it is certain there existed a significant number of Assyrians in the extreme north of what later became Iraq prior to the settlement of the Hakkâri mountaineers.

106. For more on the influence of Akkadian on the modern Arabic dialect of Mosul, see Amir Harrak, 'Middle Assyrian bīt ḫašīmi', *Zeitschrift für Assyriologie und Vorderasiatische Archäologie* 79.1 (1989), 67.

107. A Committee of Officials, *An Introduction of the Past and Present of the Kingdom of Iraq* (Baltimore, MD: Lord Baltimore Press, 1946), 29. Coming 'back' suggests returning to a place lived previously, and thus in this case while attempting to deny the Assyrians nativeness, the Iraqi authorities in fact established it.

108. Hamilton, *Road through Kurdistan*, 216.

109. Michael K. Pius, 'Koubba Khouyada Aturaya was Born in Desert', *Nineveh* 22.3 (1999), 17.

110. Ibid., 15.

111. Pius alleges that according to his interviewees Mushe was expelled in 1947 or 1948 but the organisation lasted until 1952 or 1955. See ibid., 16.

112. Robert Brenton Betts, *Christians in the Arab East: A Political Study* (Athens: Lycabettus Press, 1975), 177.

113. See Walter Laqueur, *Communism and Nationalism in the Middle East* (London: Routledge & Kegan Paul, 1956), for a description of minorities in the communist parties of in the Middle East. Despite their involvement, most works mention Assyrians briefly if at all, or generically as 'Christians'. In this book the Kurds occupy eleven pages and the Armenians two; the Assyrians are mentioned just once in passing. Despite his elite status, Fahd or Yusuf Salman Yusuf is only mentioned briefly under 'The Christian Orthodox Churches'. Pyotr (Petros) Vasili, the initial proponent of communism in Iraq, is not mentioned at all.

114. Phebe Marr, *A Modern History of Iraq* (Boulder, CO: Westview, 1985), 112–13.

115. Lawrence J. LeBlanc, *The United States and the Genocide Convention* (Durham, NC: Duke University Press, 1991), 18.

116. Ibid., 250.

117. 'Guide to the Raphael Lemkin (1900–1959) Collection, 1763–2002 (Bulk 1941–1951), American Jewish Historical Society, 2014, http://digifindingaids. cjh.org/?pID=109202 (accessed 14 July 2014).

4

The Birth of the Republic and
an Autonomist Struggle

The roots of violence: wealth without work, pleasure without conscience, knowledge without character, commerce without morality, science without humanity, worship without sacrifice, politics without principles.

Mahatma Gandhi

In 1955, with the years following the end of the Second World War providing a cushion, the Western powers signed the Baghdad Pact, bringing about the Central Treaty Organisation, in an attempt to keep Soviet influence in the Middle East at bay. Despite the fear of rising communism, the British began a slow withdrawal of troops and military institutions from Iraq. Prior to the dissolution of the levies in May 1955 (though the RAF remained until 1959), its soldiers worked predominately as guards, with an overall composition of approximately 1,200 Assyrians, 400 Kurds and 400 Arabs.[1] This external force was a constant threat to the ruling Iraqi elite, which perceived the highly trained and well-armed levies a threat to its sovereignty – a sovereignty dependent on the national unity of an otherwise pluralist society. Though their service in the levies was concluding, the troops were militarily recognised with medals of gallantry and valour for almost forty years of service. On 2 May 1955, the British finally transferred the last two airbases, Habbaniya and Shuaiba (Shaiba), to the Iraqi government.

City life had also begun to shift. Refugees who had settled in Baghdad formed Nādi al-Riyadhi al-Āthūrī (Assyrian Sports Club) as well as Nādi al-Thaqāfi al-Āthūrī (Assyrian Cultural Club) in March 1955.[2] The sports club became the focus of athletics not only for Assyrians but also for the entire country. It was here that the national footballers Emmanuel 'Ammo' Baba Dawud (who played from 1957 until 1967 and later coached the Iraqi

Figure 12   Assyrian Sports Club, Christmas/New Year 1967–8 (Men)

national team off and on from the late 1970s to the 1990s), Edison David (1955–65) and Douglas Aziz (1967–79) found their beginnings.[3] The same is true for basketball, volleyball, tennis and other sports[4] (see figures 12 and 13).

The 1958 Coup and Renewed Internal Strife

By February 1957 in the realm of politics, an opposition front had been established consisting of the National Democratic Party, Hizb al-Istiqlal al-Iraqi (the Iraqi Independence Party), the Iraqi Communist Party (ICP) and the Ba'th Party, which had approximately 300 members in Iraq in 1955.[5] It

Figure 13   Assyrian Sports Club, Christmas/New Year 1967–8 (Women)

became apparent that the opposition had no true power with which to contest the regime. Instead, it operated as a clandestine organisation of military officers who brought about the July 1958 coup.

On 14 July 1958, the downfall of the Iraqi monarchy (and the subsequent execution of King Faisal II, former regent Abdullah, and Prime Minister Nuri al-Said) and the formation of the Republic of Iraq under Free Officers General Abd al-Karim Qasim and his second, 'Abd as-Salam 'Arif gave new hope to a frustrated population. Renewed promises of minority rights gave Iraq's population reason for celebration. The new republic recognised Kurdish national rights and allowed Kurdish nationalists to organise openly after many years in hiding. In April 1959, the Kurdistan Democratic Party (KDP) was given permission to publish the daily newspaper *Xebat* ('Struggle'), and in the same month Mustafa Barzani, along with 850 other Kurds, returned from exile in the USSR aboard Soviet ships.[6] The Iraqi regime created representation of the republic including the Arab sword and the Kurdish dagger 'as a symbol of their formation of the Iraqi people since the ancient times and that they are partners in this nation' and further made the acceptance of the KDP, ICP and others official with the passing of the Associations Law on 6 January 1960, which allowed previously banned political parties (in this case anything non-governmental from as early as 1954) to practise openly.[7]

Such concessions were viewed as inadequate from the perspective of the Kurdish leadership and soon relations between the KDP and the new Iraqi regime deteriorated. Yet, while outwardly the KDP retained its anti-Qasim stance, some members within the party had agreed with 'the ICP's general view that Qasim should be supported because of his general commitment to anti-imperialism and his refusal to join the UAR [United Arab Republic].'[8] During this period of general discord, tensions flared up between the Barzani-led KDP and Qasim's regime over what political concessions Iraqi Kurds would be granted.

On 5 November 1960, Barzani left once again for the Soviet Union to garner more support, with the aim of forcing Qasim's government towards concessions. The year 1960 also witnessed a minor insurrection by the sheikh of the Surchi Kurdish tribe near Rawanduz in reaction to the Iraqi Agrarian Reform Law, which, interestingly, was quelled by local police, the ICP and a contingent of Barzani followers.[9] Such ever-changing loyalties and divisions within the autonomist movement would fluctuate throughout the 1960s. Monolithic rubrics concerned with ethnic-based alliances and enmities do not allow for a clear interpretation of communal relations during the 1960s, although the mutual distrust between Kurds and Assyrians for example had not disappeared. These tense relations were exploited by the Iraqi regime and other interested parties. The Kurds, like the Assyrians, were divided in their internal loyalties, and the constant struggles between the Surchi, Herki, Barzani, Bradost,[10] Lolani and Zebari tribes attest to such division. Due to longstanding tribal feuds, the Iraqi government was able to coax the Bradosts and Zebaris to fight on behalf of the government forces. Known disdainfully as *jaḥsh* ('foal/young donkey'), generally as *chatta* ('militia') or boastfully as *fursan* ('knights [of Saladin]') among the resistance forces, these fighters were despised for their pro-government actions.[11] Around 100 Kurdish chiefs were Iraqi government loyalists during this period.[12] These pro-government forces were initially indoctrinated to fight against their Kurdish kin by seeing them as 'traitors' of Islam.[13] Yet despite this, on many occasions, as illustrated by the demographic shift following this period and through first-hand accounts, the pro-government tribes targeted Assyrian villages more often than villages of Kurdish tribes. It is evident that the pro-government militia operated most frequently against the Assyrians rather than the more numerous Kurds.[14]

Yet, despite such internal divisions among both Assyrians and Kurds, the pro-government Zebari and Bradost Kurds managed to appropriate what the Assyrians began losing demographically, preventing the only other major ethnic group, the Arabs, from settling in the region.[15] By the time Barzani returned from the USSR in January 1961, fighting had erupted between the Barzanis and the neighbouring Bradosts and Zebaris. In the summer of 1961, further fighting broke out between the Barzanis and their traditional Kurdish rivals, the Herkis and the Surchis, who had been supported by the Iraqi government.[16] In September of the same year, Barzani forces occupied Zakho, causing the government to retaliate with air attacks on Barzan. Soon after the initial skirmishes, the Qasim-led government began its redress of the Kurdish question as military actions commenced against dissidents in the north. In many cases, the Iraqi military employed Zebari and Bradost Kurds as militias against the opposition, both Assyrian and Kurdish. The Zebari and Bradost irregulars forced many Assyrians, including those who had not found cause with 'Barzani's revolt', to flee their villages, while Zebari tribesmen ransacked, appropriated and resettled them.[17]

The Kurdish armed resistance for autonomy and recognition gained momentum, although the outbreak of military actions initially went unrecognised by the international community.[18] The fighting that had begun in 1961 in the northwest between the Barzanis and their tribal allies, and the Zebari tribe and their allies, initially resulted in victory for the Barzanis, routing their enemies far into Turkish territory. During this time, some Assyrians north of Mosul who found common cause with the Barzanis earned the respect of their Kurdish allies.[19] Qasim was not their enemy, and initially the Assyrians remained sidelined within the struggle, until Mustafa Barzani began a tour of the northern region attempting to recruit Assyrians to his cause prior to the outbreak of the war.[20] The strongest in the Barwar region, Barzani's message to the Assyrians was straightforward: join the movement or yield weapons for the struggle.[21] The Assyrians found themselves at a critical juncture: desiring freedom and self-governance, yet fearful of both the Iraqi regime and its Kurdish opponents.

The two options Barzani presented to the Assyrians had various implications: (1) they could support the Kurdish movement, which already had received backing from outside sources, and struggle alongside the Kurds for Assyrian rights, or (2) they could flee south to the major cities and assume the mantle of urbanisation and, thus, Arabisation. Furthermore, their villages had begun to see bombers, some attacked outright by government forces.[22] As a result of both options, a major demographic shifting of the Assyrians in north Iraq was under way, and regardless of choice, the final fibres of autonomy and connection to their ancestral lands would soon fray.

As a minority (ethnic, linguistic and religious) within a minority (non-Arab peoples of Iraq), the Assyrians lacked independent parties to protect their rights, since they had been subservient to British power under the levies. With the dissolution of the levies, they looked toward the formation of cultural and political parties that would protect their interests. Auspiciously for the Assyrians, April 1961 saw the birth of Kheit Kheit Allap II under the name Khuyada w-Kheirūta Ātūraytā (Assyrian Unity and Freedom). Their mission was to 'spread among our youth and students raising awareness about our rights and educating them about our history'.[23] Since the formation of such a party was outlawed, Baghdad and Kirkuk were dangerous places to be active. Though it succeeded among students and elites, the movement also took root among villagers in the Assyrian north. This progress would lead some Assyrians in the remote northern regions to side with the anti-government forces.

Elsewhere, the Assyrians found a home in places to the far south. The Qasim regime had allotted lands to be used for religious and cultural edifices and in 1960, the Assyrian community consecrated the church of Mart Maryam in the al-Joumhouria district of Basra. Furthermore thanks to the aptly termed society law, allowing for the formation of civic organisations upon the approval of the Ministry of Guidance and the Interior, Assyrians were able to create two distinct social associations: one charitable and linked to the church, known as the Assyrian Mercy Society, and another, the Rafidain Club in the district of al-Tuwaisa (later known simply as the Assyrian Club) for social events and athletics.[24] Slowly a disenfranchised and dispossessed community began to find purchase in the cities in the south as well as in their rural villages in the north.

Given the complexities surrounding communal relations during this period, it would be premature to assume that the autonomist movement back in the north was a specifically ethno-national Kurdish struggle; rather it was something larger. The Assyrians identified it as *pêşmerge* and defined the term, which was foreign to their native tongue, as simply 'guerrillas' or 'opposition fighters'.[25] This was illustrated by the 5,000-strong attack by Kurds and Assyrians on the Lolani and Zebari Kurdish tribes that were unwilling to accept Barzani's leadership of the armed resistance.[26] Despite some sections of the Assyrian population joining the resistance movement, other regions preferred non-alignment. In 'Amēdīyāh, for example, the Assyrian districts, which initially preferred to remain neutral during the infighting, 'passed from Barzani to Zebari hands in autumn 1961, and the pro-government forces pillaged and destroyed numerous villages'.[27] In the winter of 1961, Kurdish forces loyal to Barzani and those working for the Iraqi government remained in a stalemate. When Barzani's forces returned in December, they accused the Assyrians of treachery. Despite ardent Assyrian protests, the Barzani administration took over the town in December 1961 under the command of Mustafa Barzani, who 'had little time for his temporary Assyrian allies'.[28] In the village of Annūnē (Kani Masi), Barzani's men took revenge by killing every male aged over fifteen whom they could capture, including a bishop, two priests and more than fifteen men. Part of this retaliation stemmed from Annūnē's traditional support of the government as it was an administrative centre.[29] According to US Department of State reports Mustafa Barzani agreed to talks with Iraqi government officials in late December 1961. Prior to Barzani's intended arrival, which was briefly delayed, the Iraqi Air Force bombarded the meeting site, killing some of his supporters and further raising his ire. Soon afterwards Kurdish forces attacked several bastions of the Iraqi army, and during these engagements utilised less savoury techniques of torture and mutilation on the wounded and other prisoners. Arab officials fled to Baghdad for their lives as none felt safe in predominantly Kurdish regions.[30]

Those Assyrians who managed to escape the civil war fled to Turkey and eventually made their way to Baghdad.[31] By early January 1962, approximately 4,500 Assyrians had fled their homes for other parts of Iraq.[32] Though the Assyrians were left with few options, some held strong to their previous autonomy and independence, further strengthened by the *bazikke* tribal system,[33] which strengthened inter-tribal relations during times of war. Yet they were relegated to a marginal role in the sight of the American government and other Western powers despite the paradox of their relation to the civil war. According to a report from the American embassy in Baghdad:

> Although Christians are only of marginal importance in Iraq, it might be worthwhile to review briefly their role in the Kurdish revolt. Allowing for traditional Assyrian tendencies to play on the sympathies of their European Christian brethren and ignoring their reports of the number of the Assyrian dead and the size of Mulla Mustafa's forces, the situation in the Christian area seems to have been roughly as follows: When the revolt started, the Christians, who would have preferred to remain neutral, were surrounded by the Kurds and were forced to assist them; apparently some of the men actually joined the Kurdish insurgents. At this time Mulla Mustafa was solicitous of the Christian welfare and there were no accounts of any oppressive action. The government bombed the Assyrian villages, along with Kurdish Muslim ones; the Assyrians were angered and took a somewhat more active part in the Kurdish revolt. Their villages were then retaken by the government forces, or rather by Kurds cooperating with Baghdad who engaged in considerable looting and some murder. The Christians tried to propriate the government and to assure it that their loyalties were with Baghdad. When winter came, Mulla Mustafa returned to the villages, unopposed by the government or nearly so, and took vengeance upon the Christians for their 'treason' to his cause. Many of these villages are still cut off from the outside world and the Christians in Baghdad, while not believing that their women and children have been molested by the Kurds, do fear that their relatives still in the north are dying of hunger and exposure.[34]

The embassy's report is further confirmed by oral history and ethnography. Evidently, Assyrians were set on by both sides. Kurds who aligned with the Iraqi regime against the armed resistance were often 'chatta by day but pêşmerge by night' according to oral sources, something substantiated by the USDOS report.[35] Pro-government Kurds would resettle the appropriated villages and while some Assyrian villages were routed by the government in other regions, the Kurds would resettle both Assyrian villages and their own ethnic Kurdish ones. This was surely an unintended side-effect of the Iraqi governmental actions including the bombing of Assyrian villages, but one which ensured that, regardless of the victor, the Assyrians were the major political and demographic losers of the early 1960s.

Others, ever distrustful of the Iraqi government, united with the Kurdish struggle, hoping that through resistance they too would be granted equal rights within Iraq.[36] They were joined by additional opposition groups, including – unofficially – members of the ICP, which had a large minority contingent.[37] General numbers given for the paramilitary fighters vary. Some estimate 20,000 troops and 40,000 reserve fighters, although whether these were entirely made up of ethnic Kurds is uncertain.[38] Since the Assyrians were not unified in their stance, being neither entirely for nor against the autonomist movement, they faced repercussions on all sides. A product of this was the razing and plundering of the episcopal see of 'Amēdīyāh in 1963 by Zebari Kurds, another retaliatory massacre.[39] Between the hammer and the anvil, many felt little choice in becoming embattled during the civil war, regardless of support. While some of various denominations living north of Mosul were sympathetic to the Barzani-led opposition for the reasons outlined, it had been assumed that those of the Mosul region remained on good terms with the Iraqi government and, thus, generally neutral during the armed resistance. Alqosh, however, long a bastion of the ICP under the leadership of native Toma Tomas, was sometimes in support of the opposition and at others neutral, depending on ICP leanings.[40] Regardless of the tactical shifts, the town was subject to raids and massacres both by Kurdish forces loyal to Barzani and by the government militia forces, as power and politics fluctuated.[41]

Alongside Tomas, formed secondary individuals opposition groups loyal first to the Assyrian cause, meaning protection of villages from both the

Kurdish forces and the Baghdad regime. Kheit Kheit Allap was among those that weighed in on the endeavour, and interestingly, most members did so from cities such as Baghdad, Mosul and Kirkuk. Kheit Kheit Allap II was able, ideologically, to recruit Hurmiz Malik Chikko along with fifty of his followers to join the armed uprising in the north.[42] Chikko accepted on the condition of monetary support, which he hoped would allow the Assyrian resistance to be independent of the Kurdish parties, having his men receive financial assistance directly rather than through the KDP.[43] Chikko and his men fought the regime for some time alongside the Kurds, earning him notoriety within government circles for his battle prowess. Therefore, while he garnered fame among the Assyrian peasants, Ba'thists, much less forgiving of what they considered non-Arab transgressions since the death of Qasim in February 1963, followed Chikko closely.

Chikko increased his activities over the next two years until Ba'thists, along with foreign aid, cornered the military commander. He and six of his soldiers were surrounded by Syrian military and killed in the battle of Aloka on 2 December 1963.[44] Some Assyrians were among those Syrian military forces sent to stop Chikko. Most interviewees believe that the Syrian government was well aware of the irony in the plan to send fellow Assyrians from Syria to impede Chikko (without knowledge of who the target was), and did so at the behest of the Iraqi regime to strike at the heart of any further native resistance. According to accounts, when the Assyrians within the Syrian battalion realised whom they had helped murder, they were unable to hold their weapons, fell to their knees, and wept for their fallen brother and for their participation in the foul act.[45]

Chikko was greatly admired by his allies. Mustafa Barzani once stated, 'Should I have to put up a statue in Kurdistan, I would make one for the martyr (Hurmiz Malik Chiko).' Following his death, Barzani requested the directors of Kheit Kheit Allap II to appoint a replacement. The leadership then spoke with Talia Shino, a former Iraqi Levies officer, who accepted under the condition that his kin be cared for and protected.[46] But the damage had been done. Soon after, as one founder recounts, 'I and four of my comrades, members of the politburo, were arrested by Iraqi government agents in September 1965, and the organisation ceased to exist.'[47] The group members were subject to both physical and psychological torture during their imprisonment. Talia Shino himself was killed immediately following the destruction and dissolution of Kheit Kheit Allap II, in early 1966.[48]

The political proximity of certain Assyrian tribes to the Barzani Kurds is noteworthy. A popular view held by many Assyrians suggests that the Barzanis were in fact former Nestorians who had converted to Islam in the nineteenth century.[49] Since the Assyrians and the Kurds have inhabited roughly the same geographic area for centuries, certain ties and similarities in culture are visible, especially between the Assyrians and the Kurds of the Hakkâri region, which include a distinct tribal society that retained a strong degree of independence during Ottoman rule. These tribal affiliations later shifted to nationalist aspirations and sometimes to shared concerns within the communist movement in Iraq. Tribal politics among Kurds and Assyrians were not completely eliminated at this time, but rather adjusted to include a sense of secularism, though still very much tied to tribal and religious structures. The involvement of actors such as Chikko and Ethniel Shleimon of Dūre, the first martyr of the civil war (see Figure 14), in the uprising provokes questions about its designation as a Kurdish movement.[50]

After the overthrow of the Qasim regime on 9 February 1963, 'Abd as-Salam 'Arif took his position as President of Iraq. This period saw Iran begin a campaign to weaken Iraq internally by aiding Kurds in their battle against the state. It was also the zenith of the Cold War in the Middle East. In the midst of the chaos following Qasim's death and Cold War politics, certain events of the civil war were marked by international powers. In July 1963, the USSR accused Iraq of attempting to eliminate the Kurds and questioned the country's military actions as genocide under international law.[51] It is evident that at the time in question, the USSR had begun to support the Kurds not out of any sense of duty to them specifically but rather to indirectly aid the ICP, which had become another component in the autonomous uprising. The international community largely ignored this claim. Kurdish attempts to garner international recognition of the Iraqi government's military actions against the autonomist resistance were heard only by the Soviets and the socialist state of Mongolia.[52] The petition by these countries to the United Nations was dismissed, as the state of Iraq had again been acquitted of any crimes.

In 1964, a schism within the Assyrian Church of the East occurred and a new patriarch was installed in Baghdad for what was then named

Figure 14   Shrine to Ethniel Shleimon of Dūre, Barwar, honoured as the first martyr of the civil war in 1961. The shrine stands today in 'Amēdiyāh

the Ancient Church of the East. This move aimed to distinguish it from the Church of the East under the exiled patriarch Mar Eshai Shimun, a constant vocal opponent of the Iraqi state. This division, though on the surface based on liturgical calendar issues, was assumed to be an attempt by the post-Qasim regime to control a rogue element of the Assyrians, mostly those of the Tiyari and Tkhuma tribes. The Iraqi regime had no immediate control over Mar Shimun, who had been stirring up nationalist sentiment among Assyrians in the West, particularly in the United States. If a political manoeuvre, the installation of a new patriarch and the inevitable crevasse it created was tactically brilliant, giving the Iraq regime almost total control over all segments of Iraqi Assyrians through their highly influential religious leaders.

In 1964 as Mossad, the Israeli intelligence agency, hoping to quell Arab expansion, began supporting the Kurdish movement in earnest. Later that year, ideological and political conflicts within the KDP, between Mustafa Barzani and the party's political bureau, led *Xebat* editor Ibrahim Ahmed and Jalal Talabani, the future leader of the Patriotic Union of Kurdistan, to split from the party in July. In the early autumn, Barzani wrote numerous letters to both the Iraqi President, 'Abd as-Salam 'Arif, and President Gamal Abdel Nasser of the UAR stating the demands of the Kurds for self-governance. By November Barzani and his allies had created an eleven-member cabinet which included Talabani as well as a parliament, six members of which were appointed specifically by Barzani. Among these six appointees was Paul Bedari, a Catholic priest to represent the many Assyrian supporters of the anti-government movement.[53] Simultaneously, the Israeli Defence Minister, Shimon Peres, met with Kumran Ali Bedr-Khan (of the Bedr-Khan family of the Bohtan), who spied for the Israelis in the 1940s and 1950s, and began discussions that led to 'the first training course for pêşmerge officers', a three-month course first offered in August 1965.[54] With such support for the autonomist resistance, many Assyrians (particularly those formerly of Hakkâri) further aligned themselves with Kurdish parties, though not necessarily ideology of a greater Kurdistan. Debates on whether the Assyrians fought *for* the Kurdish cause or *alongside* the Kurds for their own freedom yield shaky distinctions. Moreover, most scholarship states prematurely that Assyrians fought *for* the 'Kurdish cause', and

Assyrian fighter Margaret George of Dūre village in Barwar is often cited as a *pêşmerge* fighter.[55] Indeed, Assyrian leaders were invited to attend the same council as Kurdish leaders, led by Barzani, in the 1960s. A few, like Franso Toma Hariri, who had been a major personage in the Barzani household for years becoming Mustafa Barzani's chief bodyguard, worked unabashedly for the KDP.[56] Furthermore, many Assyrians waged war alongside Kurdish *pêşmerge* in Assyrian-led and -soldiered battalions. Some directed their own battalions, which contained as many as 2,000 fighters.[57] Whether or not these activities gave the central government the motivation, the Assyrians soon became part of official documentation including the 1965 census forms (see Figure 15).

Elsewhere, the diaspora had increased in influence. On 10 April 1968, the Assyrian Universal Alliance (AUA) was created and held its first congress in Pau, France to devise a more cohesive Assyrian front. The organisation was described as 'as a world-wide organization seeking to represent a powerful voice for the Assyrians, committing itself to upholding the Assyrian culture around the world, whilst working to secure the human and national rights of the Assyrian people in their homeland and elsewhere'.[58] Of special interest here is the formation of the AUA from among various cultural groups, including the Assyrian Youth and Cultural Society in Iran, during a time of Ba'thification in Iraq. It was hoped that the AUA would become a voice for the unrepresented Assyrians in the Middle East, and especially Iraq, after Kheit Kheit Allap II had been effectively neutralised in early 1966 making apparent the need for external representation in order to survive and accost their grievances.

In the cities, cultural activities continued. Assyrian organisations thrived in two major urban centres, namely Baghdad and Kirkuk. While many families enjoyed relative peace and safety, members of suspect organisations came under fire. On 17 July 1968, a Ba'thist coup overthrew the third President of Iraq, 'Abd al-Rahman 'Arif, who had taken over following his brother's death in a helicopter crash. The new regime took control under Ahmed Hassan al-Bakr, with Saddam Hussein becoming deputy chairman of the new Revolutionary Command Council. As if in answer to growing fears regarding the new government's policies toward non-compliants, the Ba'th orchestrated the capture and subsequent imprisonment and torture of members of the Assyrian Charity Society in Kirkuk that same year.[59]

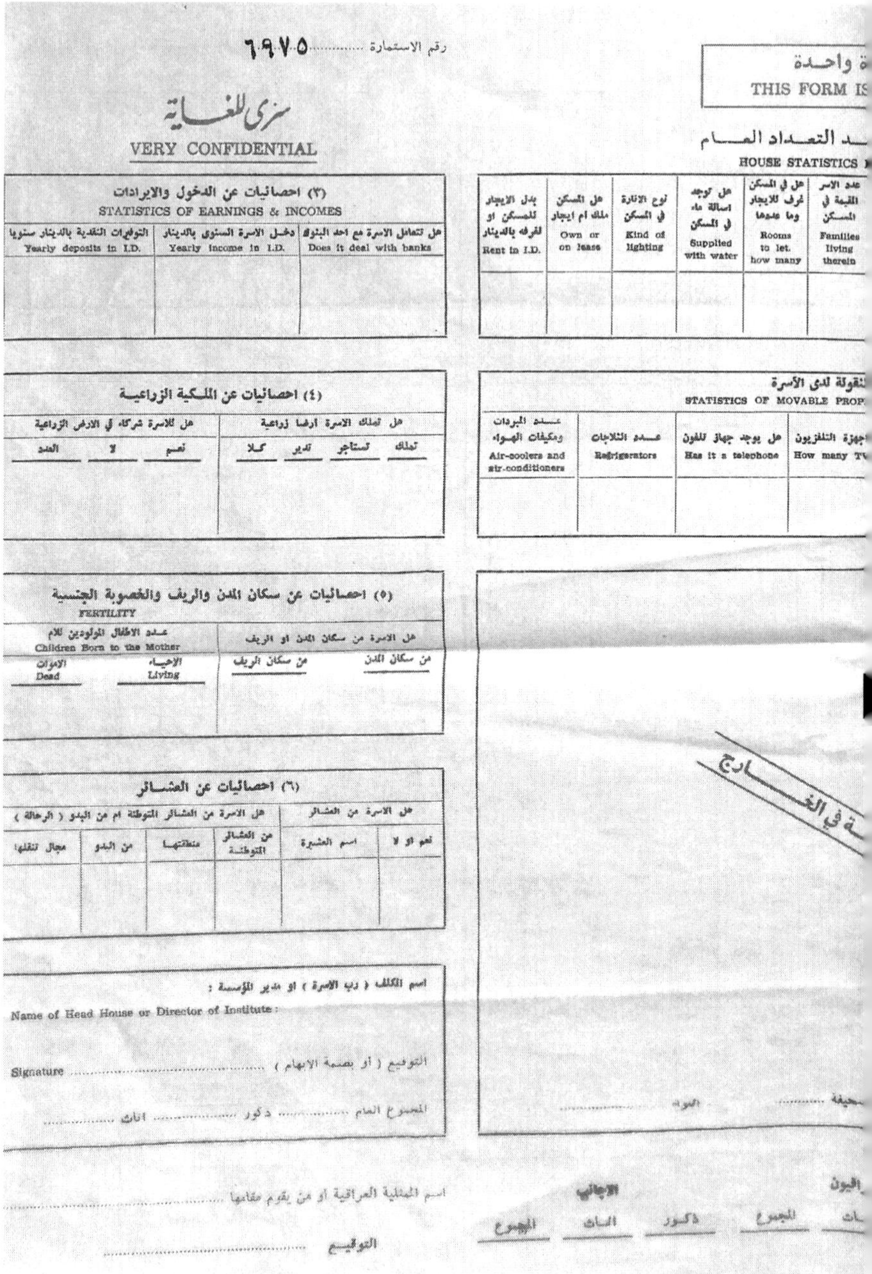

رقم الاستمارة ٦٩٧٥

سري للغاية
VERY CONFIDENTIAL

THIS FORM IS

HOUSE STATISTICS

(٣) احصائيات عن الدخول والايرادات
STATISTICS OF EARNINGS & INCOMES

التوفيرات النقدية بالدينار سنويا Yearly deposits in I.D.	دخل الاسرة السنوي بالدينار Yearly income in I.D.	هل تتعامل الاسرة مع احد البنوك Does it deal with banks

بدل الايجار او كراء للمسكن او لفرفه بالدينار Rent in I.D.	نوع الاثارة ملك ام ايجار في المسكن Own or on lease	نوع الانارة في المسكن Kind of lighting	هل توجد اسالة ماء في المسكن Supplied with water	هل في المسكن غرف للايجار وما عددها Rooms to let, how many	عدد الاسر او العوائل في المسكن Families living therein

(٤) احصائيات عن الملكية الزراعية

هل للاسرة شركاء في الارض الزراعية	هل تملك الاسرة ارضا زراعية
العدد / نعم	تملك / تستاجر / تدير / كلا

STATISTICS OF MOVABLE PROP.

عدد البرودات ومكيفات الهواء Air-coolers and air-conditioners	عدد الثلاجات Refrigerators	هل يوجد جهاز تلفون Has it a telephone	اجهزة التلفزيون How many TV

(٥) احصائيات عن سكان المدن والريف والخصوبة الجنسية
FERTILITY

عدد الاطفال المولودين للام Children Born to the Mother		هل الاسرة من سكان المدن او الريف	
الاموات Dead	الاحياء Living	من سكان الريف	من سكان المدن

(٦) احصائيات عن العشائر

مجال تنقلها	من البدو	منطقتها	من العشائر المتوطنة	هل الاسرة من العشائر المتوطنة ام من البدو (الرحالة)	اسم العشيرة	هل الاسرة من العشائر	نعم او لا

اسم المكلف (رب الاسرة) او مدير المؤسسة :
Name of Head House or Director of Institute :

التوقيع (أو بصمة الابهام)
Signature

المجموع العام .... ذكور .... اناث

اسم الهيئة العراقية او من يقوم مقامها

التوقيع

Figure 15   A portion of the 1965 Iraqi census (Afram Rayis private archive)

الوجه الاول من الاستمارة ــ (الصفحة الاحصائية)

الجُمْهُورِيَّةُ الْعِرَاقِيَّة

وزارة الداخلية

MINISTRY OF INTERIOR

مديرية تسجيل الاحوال المدنية العـامة

DIRECTORATE GENERAL OF CIVIL STATUS REGISTRATION

التَّعْدَادُ العَامُ لِسَنَةِ ١٩٦٥

Questionnaire for 1965 General Census

تعليمات للقائمين بالتعداد العام :

١ ــ اكتب المعلومات المطلوبة بوضوح وبخط جميل وبخط دقة متناهية بالحبر او بالحبر الجاف (الـكوبية) •

٢ ــ على قدر تعلق الامـر بالتعداد العام فقد اطنق علي كل مركز لواء اسم (مدينة) وعلى كل مركز قضاء او مركز ناحية اسم (قصبة) وفيما عدا ذلك فهو قرية او ريف •

٣ ــ دون اولا ارقام ما يتعلق بالاحصائيات المبينة في الوجه الاول من الاستمارة (الصفحة الاحصائية) كل في حقله بكل ضبط •

٤ ــ الاستمارة هي لأسرة واحدة عراقية كلياً او اجنبية كلياً او خليط من هنه وتلك كان يكون مع الأسرة العراقية بعض الأجانب او مع الأجنبية بعض العراقيين يسجل كل منهم في الحقل الخاص من الصفحة الثانية •

٥ ــ احرص على معرفة جنسية المواطن (تابعيته) ودون القيد في قسمه الخاص في الصحيفة القيدية •

٦ ــ حرر الايضاحات المطلوبة في قيد العراقي بموجب دفتر نفوس السنة ١٩٥٧ او دفتر نفوس سابق واذا لم يوجد محسما يطلب عليك صاحب القيد • واذا كان رب الأسـرة محسما وربغب في ابيصوم بمعـرفة بتحرير الايضاحات المتعلقة بعيده وقيود اسرار اسرته عنه ذلك ولا يجـوز لك ان تسمع من اجابة الطـب •

٧ ــ اجعل اهتمامك الكبير منصبا على ذكر رقم كل من الصحيفة وأنسجل واللواء التي دون فيهما قيد العراقي المسجل في السنة ١٩٥٧ •

٨ ــ صرح بقوميه (عنصريه) كل فرد من العراقيين حسب الأصل الذي ينحدر منه ان كان من العرب او الأكراد او التركمان او الأرمن او الايرانيين او الاشوريين او اليهود او غير ذلك •

٩ ــ اكتب نتائج التعداد التمهيدي في الحقـل الخاص فـي هـذه الصفحة عند الانتهاء من عملك حالاً •

امين الهلالي
مدير تسجيل الاحوال المدنية العام

الاستمارة لا
OR ONE FAMILY

(١) احصائيات عن المسكـ
NG THE GENERAL CENSUS

عدد غرف المسكن No. of rooms	مساحة البناء Area of building	نوع المسكن Type of house	رقم المسكن House No.		اسم الدولة Country	اسم المدينة او القصبة Town
			للبلدية Municipal	للتعداد العام Census		

(٢) احصائيات عن المتلكـ
AVAILABLE IN THE HOUSE AT PRESENT

عدد أجهزة الراديو How many radio sets	الطيور والدواجن Poultry & Birds		عدد الأنواع الحيوانات الأهلية Animals	
	العدد No.	النوع Kind	العدد No.	النوع Kind

خاص للتاشيرات في مقر التعداد العام
(لا يكتب هنا شيء•)

المعرافين والجاليات العرـ

رحلت قيود هذه الاستمارة (او بعضها) الى السجل ....

نتائج التعداد التمهيدي

عدد الافراد المدونين في الوجه الثاني من الاستمارة :

ذكور

The late 1960s saw an increase in fighting between the Iraqi government and those agents of resistance. It was here the power of diaspora politics was needed. On 29 May 1969, talks between the US government and Assyrian and Kurdish representatives took place in Washington, DC. There, the Assyrians and Kurds, working in tandem, hoped to garner American military and/or monetary support for their opposition struggle. One representative stated the following: 'Mr Andrews [Sam Andrews, secretary of the Assyrian American National Federation] said that the Assyrians are fighting the Iraqis alongside the Kurds. There is apparently complete confidence between the Kurds and the Assyrians and some integration of their fighting forces.'[60]

A letter sent by Mustafa Barzani himself addressing US Secretary of State William Rogers outlines the joint Kurdish and Assyrian resistance during the autonomist armed resistance as late as 1969. According to Barzani:

> In addition to the threat which this war has aimed at the existence and legitimate aspirations of our people, Kurds and Assyrians, it has brought disaster and affliction upon all its victims, deprived the people of Kurdistan, particularly the Assyrians and the Kurds, of education and health [needs], and rendered tens of thousands of them refugees.[61]

It is likely that Assyrian involvement in the armed resistance would guarantee future governmentire. Following that logic, it is not surprising that in the same year as the US–Assyrian–Kurdish meetings, the Iraqi government targeted the villagers of Ṣoriya in a massacre on 16 September 1969.

The Ṣoriya Massacre of 1969

The village of Ṣoriya is located on the banks of the Tigris and administratively assigned to the sub-district of Bateel in Dohuk. According to the 1957 census, Ṣoriya had a population of 102 people, and in 1969, the village had forty families.[62] At approximately 9.30 on the morning of Tuesday 16 September 1969, the village witnessed a massacre at the hands of Lieutenant Abdul Karim al-Jahayshee from Mosul in response to a pêşmerge-planted mine was detonated under a military car four kilometres away from the village.[63] As for the actual events of the massacre, the story of two survivors, Adam and Noah Yonan, lays bare the vivid events. Noah Yonan recounts:

I was ten years old and I fell on the ground. A woman fell over me and her blood covered me. Other children, too, were covered in blood and thought dead. At the same time, the Iraqi Army soldiers in our village began spreading out, shooting into houses and burning the houses . . . While we were running, wounded people escaping with us died of their gunshot wounds, bleeding to death. We were all running to the village of Bakhlogia, four kilometers away, to hide. We got to Bakhlogia, but the villagers couldn't give us refuge; it was too dangerous. So, we ran to another Christian village, Avzarook.[64]

It appeared the military intended to find guerrillas hidden within the village. Though the precise motivation behind the massacre of Ṣoriya remains unknown, the results are certain. The callous measures taken by the Iraqi army left forty-seven dead, including Rev. Ḥannā, the local priest, and twenty-two wounded (see Table 8).[65]

This operation at Ṣoriya was an echo of Simele: from the government and military announcements forbidding hospitals and medical facilities in the Mosul and Dohuk regions from giving aid to survivors, to the promotion of Abdul Karim al-Jahayshee.[66] Praise for the military actions of al-Jahayshee and the honours presented to Baqr Sidqi proved that these people were at the mercy of a violent nationalist regime not so unlike its colonial predecessor.

Demographic Situation

The period of internal fighting between the Iraqi government and anti-government groups including Kurdish, communist and Assyrian forces reshaped the region of northern Iraq. The demography of this region, once part of ancient Assyria, which offers some semblance of a homeland continuously inhabited for more than 4,000 years, saw major transformation following the armed struggles between the Iraqi government forces and autonomist sympathisers.[67] Around seventy towns and villages were destroyed and/or forcibly abandoned by their Assyrian inhabitants, as were more than 76 religious structures and other material items of cultural significance (see Table 9).

As many villagers had fled the region to bordering nations, two amnesties were issued three years apart, one specifically for Kurds in 1963, and one for all citizens in 1966.[68] The initial amnesty was issued by the newly formed 'Abd as-Salam 'Arif regime after the death of Qasim, and the second

Table 8 List of people killed in the Ṣoriya massacre on 16 September 1969

	Name	Sex	Age	Comments
1	Khamo Marogeh Shimun	M		Mayor. Shot immediately by Abdul Karim Jahayshee
2	Kathryn Sargis Shimun	F		Wife of Khamo Marogeh Shimun
3	Laila Khamo Shimun	F		Almost succeeded in killing Jahayshee
4	Mansour Isḥaq	M		
5	Kathryn Shimun Isḥaq	F		Wife of Mansour Isḥaq. Killed along with three-month-old child
6	Misso Marogeh Shimun	F		
7	Hermiz Marogeh Shimun	M		
8	Goro Hermiz Shimun	F		Wife of Hermiz Marogeh Shimun
9	Antar Hermiz Shimun	M	5	
10	Othman Suleiman	M		
11	Amina Rajab Suleiman	F		Wife of Othman Suleiman. Killed along with child
12	Nahida Othman Suleiman	F		
13	Sabiha Othman Suleiman	F		
14	Meho Hasan	M		
15	Miran Meho Hasan	F		
16	Ghariba Meho Hasan	F		
17	Mounir Yousif	M		
18	Firman Mounir Yousif	F		
19	Talan Mounir Yousif	F		
20	Eilo Youkhana	M		
21	Yaqu Eilo Youkhana	M		
22	Yalda Rasho	M		
23	Basima Yalda Rasho	F		
24	Giwargis Qoryakus	M		
25	Naji Giwargis Qoryakus	F		
26	Shabo Bazna	M		
27	Shoneh Bazna	F		Wife of Shabo Bazna. Their baby girl later died in hospital
28	Samir Bazna	M		
29	Shawel Bazna	M		
30	Boutros Toma	M		
31	Yono Sliwa Toma	F		Wife of Boutros Toma
32	(child) Toma	F	5	
33	(child) Toma	M	6	
34	Alo Yousif	M		
35	Shirin Samo Yousif	F		

	Name	Sex	Age	Comments
36	Amina Alo Yousif	F	7	
37	Oraha Khamo	M		
38	Warina Oraha Khamo	F	5	
39	Rasho Warda	M		
40	Asmar Elias Warda	F		Wife of Rasho Warda
41	Rev. Ḥannā	M		Village priest
42	Guiliana Markus	M		
43	Husni	M		Driver from Zakho
44	Berro Husein	M		
45	Qamar Rasheed Husein	F		Wife of Berro Husein
46	Nadira Berro Husein	F		
47	Halima Husein	F		Mother of Berro Husein

was issued by Salam's brother 'Abd al-Rahman 'Arif, both supporters of the pan-Arabist ideology of Gamal Abdel Nasser. A rationale behind two separate amnesties was likely that the 'Abd as-Salam 'Arif regime hoped to win over the Kurds to the cause of the new government, and likewise that in the midst of the chaotic transfer of power in 1963, little information was known about opposition parties besides the more infamous and charismatic Barzani.

In reference to the physical destruction, Assyrians encountered a secondary assault due to their minority ethnic, religious and cultural status both within the government-controlled regions to some extent, and within the opposition. In a strictly demographic sense, as many of the villages abandoned by Assyrians following the 1961–3 fighting either remained empty or were resettled by Kurdish groups, (including those fighting for the government) the Assyrians were displaced once again. This situation would be furthered in the late 1970s with the creation of the collective towns, a testament to loss of homeland, creating a further dispossessed cultural entity.[69] Beyond the data, an underlying Arabisation and Ba'thification influenced large numbers of formerly independent villagers required to subsist in unfamiliar urban settings. This urban assimilation would be a side-effect of the Assyrians' attempt to survive both economically and socially, and would later help solidify their indoctrination into Arabism. In some cases of urbanisation, however, an unforeseen consequence occurred – the desire for integration became linked to high intellectual attainment and for some, the preservation and propagation of a revitalised ethno-cultural spirit.

Table 9 Assyrian village summary, 1960s

Name	Province	District	Alt. name	Schools	Religious structures	Comments
Batase	Arbil	Harīr			1	Attacked and resettled by pro-government militia
Darbandoke	Arbil	Harīr			1	Attacked and resettled by pro-government militia 1960s
Diyana	Arbil	Harīr	Diana		5	Attacked and resettled by pro-government militia
Hanare	Arbil	Harīr	Henare			Attacked and resettled by pro-government militia
Harīr	Arbil	Harīr			1	Attacked and resettled by pro-government militia
Kalate	Arbil	Harīr				Attacked and resettled by pro-government militia
Hawdian	Arbil	Rowanduz	Havdian		1	Attacked and resettled by pro-government militia
'Amēdiyāh (city)	Dohuk	'Amēdiyāh		1	2	Mass exodus
Arāden	Dohuk	'Amēdiyāh		2	4	Razed 1961
Argen	Dohuk	'Amēdiyāh	Ergin, Hargin, Argin		4	
Ashawa	Dohuk	'Amēdiyāh			1	Attacked and resettled by pro-government militia
Badarrash	Dohuk	'Amēdiyāh	Beth Darrash, Beth Durashe		1	

Barzanke	Dohuk	'Amēdiyāh				Resettled by Kurds
Baz	Dohuk	'Amēdiyāh	Bas		2	
Bebede	Dohuk	'Amēdiyāh	Be Bede, Beth Bede		2	Razed 1961 by Zebari Kurds; resettled by same tribe
Bekozanke	Dohuk	'Amēdiyāh	Beth Kozanke			Attacked and resettled by pro-government militia
Blejanke	Dohuk	'Amēdiyāh	Blejane		1	
Dohuke	Dohuk	'Amēdiyāh	Dahoki, Dohoke		1	
Eṣṣān	Dohuk	'Amēdiyāh	Ṣiyān		2	
Havintka	Dohuk	'Amēdiyāh	Hawintka			Resettled by Zebari Kurds
Hayyis	Dohuk	'Amēdiyāh	Hayis		2	Site of napalm attack, 1968
Komāne	Dohuk	'Amēdiyāh	Kowane	1	5	
Lish	Dohuk	'Amēdiyāh	Lich			
Meze	Dohuk	'Amēdiyāh			2	
Rekan	Dohuk	'Amēdiyāh				
Sarsang (city)	Dohuk	'Amēdiyāh			2	
Ṣawura	Dohuk	'Amēdiyāh	Ṣawra			
Tazhikka	Dohuk	'Amēdiyāh				
Tirwanish	Dohuk	'Amēdiyāh	Der Wanis		1	
Ṭlanīthā	Dohuk	'Amēdiyāh	Talaneetha, Dewike		2	
'Aqra (city)	Dohuk	'Aqra	'Aqra		2	Mass exodus of Assyrians beginning in 1961

Table 9 (continued)

Name	Province	District	Alt. name	Schools	Religious structures	Comments
Ba-Mishmish	Dohuk	'Aqra	Beth Shimsha		2	Attacked and resettled by pro-government militia
Barak	Dohuk	'Aqra	Barrake		1	Attacked and resettled by pro-government militia
Belembase	Dohuk	'Aqra				
Birmawa	Dohuk	'Aqra	Birmava			Attacked and resettled by pro-government militia
Cham Chali	Dohuk	'Aqra				
Dinārta	Dohuk	'Aqra	Dinārta d'Nahla			Attacked and resettled by pro-government militia
Dodi Masih	Dohuk	'Aqra	Beth Nura, Beth Nuhra		1	Attacked and resettled by pro-government militia
Garbesh	Dohuk	'Aqra	Girbish, Upper & Lower		1	Attacked and resettled by pro-government militia
Gera Sor	Dohuk	'Aqra	Sifra			
Hasaniye	Dohuk	'Aqra				
Hazarjot	Dohuk	'Aqra			1	
Kashkawa	Dohuk	'Aqra			1	100 families displaced
Khalilani	Dohuk	'Aqra	Kalilane			
Khardis	Dohuk	'Aqra	Khardes, Khardez		2	Attacked and resettled by pro-government militia
Kharjawa	Dohuk	'Aqra	Ḥarǧāwa			Attacked and resettled by pro-government militia

Khelafta	Dohuk	'Aqra	Khaleptha, Beth Hlāpe	1	
Kherpa	Dohuk	'Aqra	Ḥerpā, Kherpa d'Malka	2	Attacked and resettled by pro-government militia
Nahawa	Dohuk	'Aqra	Nūhāwā, Nūwābā	2	Attacked and resettled by pro-government militia
Nerem dRaʾawatha	Dohuk	'Aqra	Gundik, Gündük	2	Attacked and resettled by pro-government militia
Nergezwe	Dohuk	'Aqra			Attacked and resettled by pro-government militia
Ras al-'Ain	Dohuk	'Aqra	Resh 'Aina, Resha	1	
Safra Zor	Dohuk	'Aqra			
Sedar	Dohuk	'Aqra			
Sharmin	Dohuk	'Aqra	Shalmath	3	
Shush	Dohuk	'Aqra	Shush, Shushan, Bā Šōš	1	
Sian	Dohuk	'Aqra	Sanāyā, Sanāyā d'Nahlā	2	Attacked and resettled by pro-government militia
Dawrīye	Dohuk	'Aqra	Dūre, Deviry	1	Besieged 3 months, 35 (families) survived
Cham Kare	Dohuk	Dohuk			
Kora-Dere	Dohuk	Dohuk			
Malta	Dohuk	Dohuk	Maʾalthaye, Maltai	2	

Table 9 (continued)

Name	Province	District	Alt. name	Schools	Religious structures	Comments
Mangesh (town)	Dohuk	Dohuk			2	
Masike	Dohuk	Dohuk				
Bāsifre	Dohuk	Sheikhan	Be Sāpre, Beth Sāpre			
Bedul	Dohuk	Sheikhan	Be Dole		1	Attacked and resettled by pro-government militia
Betnare	Dohuk	Sheikhan	Benarink, Be Naring			Attacked and resettled by pro-government militia
Billa	Dohuk	Sheikhan	Billān, Bellan		3	Attacked and resettled by pro-government militia
Birta	Dohuk	Sheikhan	Birta, Bire		1	Attacked and resettled by pro-government militia
Kanifalla	Dohuk	Sheikhan	Kani Fala		1	
Malla-Birwan	Dohuk	Sheikhan			1	
Ishkavdal	Dohuk	Simele	Shkafdal	1		20 families displaced
Kharab-Kulk	Dohuk	Simele	Ḥarbai (?)		1	
Șoriya	Dohuk	Simele		1	1	40 families before 1969 massacre
Bahmona	Dohuk	Zakho				30 families displaced
Dar Hozan	Dohuk	Zakho				
Marzi-Khabur	Dohuk	Zakho				
Prakh	Dohuk	Zakho				
Alqosh	Ninawa	Telkeif			numerous	Attacked numerous times

Notes

1. 'History', Assyrian Levies RAF website, http://assyrianlevies.info/history.html (accessed 14 July 2014). It is possible though largely speculative that a major reason for the withdrawal of the levies was to assuage any fears Turkey or Iraq may have had concerning still-armed Assyrians within their borders.
2. Isaac Isaac, *Riyāḍīyah fī bilād mā bayn al-nahrayn* ['Sports in the Land of Mesopotamia'] (Chicago: Alpha Graphic, 2000), 364–90.
3. 'Three Lions: The Birth of Asood Al-Rafidain', http://iraqsport.wordpress.com/2013/03/09/three-lions-the-birth-of-asood-al-rafidain (accessed 14 July 2014).
4. Isaac, *Riyāḍīyah fī bilād mā bayn al-nahrayn*, 519–23.
5. Peter Sluglett and Marion Farouk-Sluglett, *Iraq since 1958: From Revolution to Dictatorship* (London: I. B. Tauris, 2001), 45.
6. Ibid., 80.
7. 'The Emblem of the Iraqi Republic', Law No. 57 of 1959, *Weekly Gazette of the Republic of Iraq*, 18 November 1959, 900.
8. Sluglett and Farouk-Sluglett, *Iraq since 1958*, 80.
9. Ismail al-Arif, *Iraq Reborn: A Firsthand Account of the July 1958 Revolution and After* (New York: Vantage Press, 1982), 86.
10. Also spelled as Baradost and Biradost.
11. Human Rights Watch, *Iraq's Crime of Genocide: The Anfal Campaign against the Kurds* (New Haven, CT: Yale University Press, 1995), 28. For a good discussion on pro-government Kurdish forces, see David McDowall, *A Modern History of the Kurds*, 3rd ed. (London: I. B. Tauris, 2004), 354–6.
12. See list and photographs in Na'aman Maher al-Kan'ani, *Ḍoh 'alla Shimāl al-'Irāq* ['A Light in Northern Iraq'] (Baghdad, 1965), 26–110.
13. Human Rights Watch, *Iraq's Crime of Genocide*, 29.
14. Edgar O'Ballance, *The Kurdish Revolt 1961–1970* (Hamden, CT: Archon, 1973).
15. This large-scale change in demography continued to effect regional policy and become specifically apparent during the creation of the Iraqi Kurdistan region following the establishment of the no-fly zone in 1991 and in Iraqi internal politics after the US invasion of 2003.
16. O'Ballance, *The Kurdish Revolt*, 81.
17. Uriel Dann, *Iraq under Qassem: A Political History 1958–1963* (New York: Praeger, 1969), 335. The Assyrian villages that were resettled by Zebari Kurds after 1961 are discussed in further detail in the following pages.

18. Mordechai Nisan, *Minorities in the Middle East*, 2nd ed. (Jefferson, NC: McFarland, 2002), 42.

19. Dann, *Iraq under Qassem*, 334–5.

20. Embassy Baghdad to Secretary of State, no subject, 16 November 1961, NA/RG59/787.00/11-199.

21. Hirmis Aboona (Alqosh), interview with author, October 2007, Mississauga, Ontario. The tradition that keeping a weapon as a means of defence of one's family is a matter of personal honour. Relinquishing that weapon was tantamount to helplessness in the minds of the mountaineer Assyrians and also their Kurdish neighbours.

22. Embassy Baghdad to Secretary of State, no subject, 16 November 1961, NA/RG59/787.00/11-199.

23. Y.C. (Darbandoke-Baghdad), interview with author, 1 September 2006, Chicago. The initial Kheit Kheit Allap was started in Habbaniyya by Ousta Mushe Khoshaba in the 1940s.

24. Sargon Yousip Potros, 'The Assyrian Rafidain Club in Basra City, Iraq', *Nineveh* 22.3 (1999), 15–17; 'Law No. 1 of 1960 for the Societies', *Weekly Gazette of the Republic of Iraq*, 23 August 1961, 665.

25. K.S. (Dūre), interview with author, 24 February 2008, Toronto.

26. O'Ballance, *The Kurdish Revolt*, 74–5.

27. Avshalom H. Rubin, 'Abd al-Karim Qasim and the Kurds of Iraq: Centralization, Resistance and Revolt 1958–63', *Middle Eastern Studies* 43.3 (2007), 369.

28. O'Ballance, *The Kurdish Revolt*, 81.

29. Baghdad to State, 'Kurdish Revolt – Continued', 22 January 1962, NA/RG59/787.00/1-2262.

30. Baghdad to State, 'Kurdish Rebel Activity in Dohuk Area', 28 December 1961, NA/RG59/787.00/12-2861.

31. Baghdad to State, 'Kurdish Revolt – Continued; Government Pretends Kurds Crushed; Reports Massacres in Christian Villages', 10 January 1962, NA/RG59/787.00/1-1062.

32. Baghdad to Foreign Office, 17 January 1962, BNA/FO/371/164231. See also Rubin, 'Abd al-Karim Qasim and the Kurds of Iraq', 369–70.

33. An associated tribal system that solidified relations between tribes in times of war in the Hakkâri region.

34. Baghdad to State, 'Kurdish Revolt – Continued; Government Pretends Kurds Crushed; Reports Massacres in Christian Villages', 10 January 1962, NA/RG59/787.00/1-1062.

35. D.T. (Blejanke) and K.S. (Dūre), interviews with author, 24 February 2008, Toronto. See also Baghdad to State, 'Kurdish Rebel Activity in Dohuk Area', 28 December 1961, NA/RG59/787.00/12-2861. According to the report, the '"Kurdish mercenaries" employed by the government have deserted and joined with the rebels'.

36. Frederick A. Aprim, *Assyrians: From Bedr Khan to Saddam Hussein – Driving into Extinction the Last Aramaic Speakers* (F. A. Aprim, 2006), 210.

37. In 1946 when Qadi Muhammad proclaimed an autonomous Kurdish region, the Mahabad Republic in Iran, he was supported by Soviet troops in Azerbaijan. The USSR did not begin to officially support the Kurds and Barzani in Iraq until June 1963. Whether such Soviet support of the Kurds (through the ICP) extended to Iraq in the 1960s is uncertain. See Sluglett and Farouk-Sluglett, *Iraq since 1958*, 29.

38. Nisan, *Minorities in the Middle East*, 43.

39. Jean-Pierre Valognes, *Vie et mort des chrétiens d'Orient: des origines à nos jours* (Paris: Fayard, 1994), 763; Dann, *Iraq under Qassem*, 335.

40. Hirmis Aboona (Alqosh), interview with author, 11 October 2007, Mississauga, Ontario. Tomas, a native of Alqosh, was born in 1924, was enlisted in the Iraq Levies as a young teenager, and became a major figure in the ICP in the 1960s. His memoirs recall his pride in his family's role in protecting refugees from the Simele massacres in 1933. For more information see Alda Benjamen, 'Negotiating Assyrians in the Modern History of Iraq' (PhD thesis, University of Maryland, forthcoming).

41. Ibid.

42. Y.C. (Darbandoke-Baghdad), interview with author, 1 September 2006, Chicago.

43. Ibid.

44. D.T. (Blejanke), interview with author, 24 February 2008, Toronto.

45. Y.D. (Annūnē) and K.S. (Dūre), interviews with author, 24 February 2008, Toronto. Like many Yezidis and Christian Assyrians, Chikko fought against an oppressive regime during the armed autonomist movement. His body was taken and buried in the Yezidi village of Sharia, where a monument was erected in his honour.

46. Y.C. (Darbandoke-Baghdad), interview with author, 1 September 2006, Chicago.

47. Ibid.

48. Ibid.

49. Robert Brenton Betts, *Christians in the Arab East: A Political Study* (Athens: Lycabettus Press, 1975), 179. This is also based on an oral tradition of some

Assyrians. Most Assyrians who converted to Islam adopted the culture/ethnicity of the most numerous Muslim group in their region, whether Turkish, Kurdish, Persian or Arab. Thus, the discussion of Assyrian Muslims is usually a moot point, since converts to Islam (as many early Assyrian converts to Christianity but in a more complete manner) lost a sense of their ancestral identity. One exception is that of the Mḥalmōyē (Maḥallmiyīn) community living in southeast Turkey in the Turabdin region and in Mardin, some of who advocate an Assyrian heritage.

50. Hirmis Aboona (Alqosh), interview with author, 11 October 2007, Mississauga, Ontario.
51. See UN Economic and Social Council report, A/5429 36th session, 11 July 1963, 109; Edmund Ghareeb, *The Kurdish Question in Iraq* (New York: Syracuse University Press, 1981), 68. Ghareeb does not mention the issue of genocide.
52. UN Economic and Social Council report, A/5429 36th session, 11 July 1963, 109.
53. Dana Adams Schmidt, 'Kurds in Iraq set up "regime" after failing to sway Baghdad', *New York Times*, 12 November 1964, 4.
54. Ian Black and Benny Morris, *Israel's Secret Wars: the Untold History of Israeli Intelligence* (London: Hamish Hamilton, 1991), 184.
55. McDowall, *A Modern History of the Kurds*, 310. George was later suspiciously killed in her sleep in 1966 (see ibid., 381), though some reference her being killed in 1969.
56. Hariri was assassinated in 2001 by Kurdish members of Ansar al-Islam. See pictures of Hariri and Barzani at kurdistan-photolibrary.org.
57. Burchard Brentjes, *The Armenians, Assyrians and Kurds: Three Nations, One Fate?* (Campbell, CA: Rishi, 1997), 65–6.
58. 'Assyria', Unrepresented Nations and Peoples Organization website, http://www.unpo.org/members/7859 (accessed 15 July 2014).
59. Aprim, *Assyrians*, 215.
60. 'Kurdish Threat against Kirkuk Oil Installations; Iranian and Israeli Support for Assyrians', Memorandum of Conversation, Foreign Relations, 1969–1976, Volume E-4, Documents on Iran and Iraq, 1969–1972, 29 May 1969. See also 'Kurdish/Assyrian Appeal for U.S. Assistance', Memorandum of Conversation, Foreign Relations, 1969–1976, Volume E-4, Documents on Iran and Iraq, 1969–1972, 13 June 1969.
61. 'Kurdish Threat against Kirkuk Oil Installations; Iranian and Israeli Support for Assyrians'.

62. Majed Eshoo, 'The Fate of Assyrian Villages Annexed to Today's Dohuk Governorate in Iraq and the Conditions in These Villages Following the Establishment of the Iraqi State in 1921', tr. Mary Challita (2004), Assyrian General Conference website, http://www.assyriangc.com/magazine/eng1.pdf (accessed 9 July 2014), 19.

63. Much of what is known about the Ṣoriya massacre is nebulous at best. Accounts by human rights NGOs that reference it are vague, with no real original source material (oral accounts) used. Fortunately, Michael Tucker presents some groundwork in his interview with massacre survivors Adam and Noah Yonan. See Michael Tucker, *Hell Is Over: Voices of the Kurds after Saddam* (Guilford, CT: Lyons Press, 2004). The accuracy of the language used by Tucker is problematic and reflects modern KDP and KRG Kurdification processes, whereby referring to these people as Kurdish Chaldean Catholics is similar to the previous trend of Arabisation. Also as a further note, the Yonan family originally hails from Harbol, an Assyrian village in the Bohtan region of Turkey. Harbol almost entirely consists of members of the Chaldean religious community who are referred to and refer to themselves in French (most living in diaspora in France) as Assyro-Chaldean.

64. Tucker, *Hell Is Over*, 104. 'Avzarook' probably refers to Avzerok (Avzarook, Avzarog) Shanno to the north, passing Baghluje (Bakhlogia), rather than Avzerok Khamo, which lies twice the distance to the south of Ṣoriya. Avzerok Shanno was later destroyed in 1975.

65. Though Table 8 is mostly based on Eshoo, 'The Fate of Assyrian Villages Annexed to Today's Dohuk Governorate in Iraq and the Conditions in These Villages Following the Establishment of the Iraqi State in 1921', the original work states only thirty-eight victims.

66. Tucker, *Hell Is Over*, 106.

67. Since the fall of the Neo-Assyrian Empire in the seventh century BC, many villages and cities in northern Mesopotamia and their names continue to reflect an Assyrian character. Many cities in Iraq today retain some form of their ancient name: Arbil (though Hawler in Kurdish) is Syriac Arbela and Akkadian Arbailu, a centre for the worship of the goddess Ishtar and later a diocese of the Church of the East in the second century AD; Kirkuk, ancient Arrapḫa and classical Syriac Karkā d-Beth Slōkh, was the metropolitan see of the Church of the East from the fifth to the fourteenth centuries, the centre of the ecclesiastical region of Beth Garmai. See Simo Parpola and Michael Porter, *The Helsinki Atlas of the Near East in the Neo-Assyrian Period* (Helsinki: Neo-Assyrian Corpus Text Project, 2001), 20, 26. See also *The Chronicle of Arbela*, written by the sixth-century

writer Mshikha-zkha, and available in an English translation at http://www. sasanika.org/wp-content/uploads/ChronicleofArbela.pdf (accessed 15 July 2014); Rubens Duval, *Īšoyahb Patriarchae III: Liber Epistularum* (Leuven: CSCO, 1962), 102, 106, J.-M. Fiey, 'Pour un Oriens Christianus Novus; répertoire des diocèses syriaques orientaux et occidentaux', *Beiruter Texte und Studien* 49 (1993), 63.

68. 'General Amnesty for Those Taking Part in the Kurdish Military Uprising', Law No. 9 of 1963, *Weekly Gazette of the Republic of Iraq* (24 July 1963), 703; and 'General Amnesty for Those Who Participated in the Events in the North', Law No. 65 of 1966, *Weekly Gazette of the Republic of Iraq* (21 December 1966), 18.

69. B.B. (Harīr), C.C. (Darbandoke), I.Y. (Diyana), P.W. (Diyana) and Elias Haroon Bazi (Hejerke-Simele), interviews with author, 17 February 2008, Toronto; D.T. (Blejanke), K.S. (Dūre), T.S. (Dūre), Y.D. (Annūnē), Y.G. (Bebede) and Z.Y. (Annūnē), interviews with author, 24 February 2008, Toronto; B.A. (Komāne), interview with author, 26 July 2008, Toronto.

5

Enduring Discord: Political Machinations and Border Clearings

Perhaps the most significant moral characteristic of a nation is its hypocrisy.

Reinhold Niebuhr

In March 1970, the Iraqi government and Kurdish parties agreed on a peace accord that would grant the Kurds some semblance of autonomy and end the ongoing armed autonomist movement. The 11 March manifesto recognised Kurdish as an official language and amended the constitution to state: 'The Iraqi people are made up of two nationalities, the Arab nationality and the Kurdish nationality.' The Assyrians had been left out of the political meetings, as the events of 1961–3 had decimated their northern villages. Despite this detail, the Iraqi government was still wary of Assyrian–Kurdish relations – so much so, that on 24 April 1970, Mar Eshai Shimun, exiled Patriarch of the Church of the East, was personally invited to meet the Iraqi President in Baghdad in a bid by the government to reconcile old differences.

The government restored his citizenship as he was greeted by thousands of Iraqi Assyrians upon arrival. The patriarch lauded president al-Bakr and gave a positive interview of that historic meeting to the *Baghdad Observer* on 30 April 1970. Iraqi officials began to play both sides against the middle. The government used this invitation to garner ecclesiastic support and to attempt to exert control over a portion of the Assyrian population by playing to its religious leaders. The regime's proposal was to fashion an Assyrian police force (reminiscent of the levies) in order to buffer foreign advances. Indeed the patriarch commented on the progressive steps of the Ba'th government under al-Bakr to grant the Kurds yet further concessions as evident in the official 11 March 1970 manifesto. It appeared as though there would be large-scale reconciliation.

Such attempts continued for a year while relations between the Kurds and the Iraqi government deteriorated. In 1971, Mustafa Barzani began appealing in earnest to the United States for aid. Because of these events, the Assyrians saw an opportunity to emerge: when Baghdad granted the Kurds the option of autonomy in Arbil and Sulaymaniyah, the Assyrians petitioned for an autonomous region in Dohuk province. The so-called Assyrian Committee (made up of Assyrians from various church denominations) began petitioning the Iraqi government through Malik Yaqo d'Malik Ismael.[2] Further as yet another step toward progress, on 16 April 1972 Baghdad offered 'Syriac-speaking nationals' limited cultural rights through decree 251, as follows:

(a) The Syriac language shall be the teaching language in all primary schools whose majority of pupils are from speakers in such language, and teaching of Arabic language shall be compulsory in such schools.

(b) Syriac language shall be taught in intermediate and secondary schools whose majority of pupils are from speakers in such language, and Arabic language shall be the teaching language in such schools.

(c) Syriac language shall be taught in the College of Arts at the University of Baghdad as one of the old languages.

(d) Special programmes in Syriac language shall be set up at the Broadcasting Service of the Republic of Iraq and at Kirkuk and Nineveh TV stations.

(e) To issue a Syriac-language monthly magazine by the Ministry of Information.

(f) To establish a society for Syriac speaking writers, and ensure their representation in literary and cultural societies and the country.

(g) To help Syriac-speaking writers and translators morally and materially by printing and publishing their cultural and literary works.

(h) To enable Syriac-speaking nationals to open cultural and artistic clubs and formulate artistic and theatrical groups for reviving and evolving their legacy and popular arts.

–Ahmed Hassan al-Bakr
Chairman of the Revolutionary Command Council[3]

Despite this decree, the regime had ulterior plans. Immediately following a surge in Assyrian cultural activities, the Ba'thist regime once again began a policy of suppression.[4] Though the 1972 decree gave Assyrians a one-hour radio broadcast in their native language, the programme was quickly usurped by Ba'thists and used for pro-party propaganda, and Assyrians deemed non-compliant or in opposition to the party's ideological views were promptly removed.[5] A cultural-linguistic association, the Syriac Academy, was created and with it the publication of a literary and poetry journal entitled *Qala Suryaya*. However, Ba'thist supporters eventually infiltrated the association and politicised the group's academic and cultural activities. The decree applied to all the private or parochial schools, including the al-Taqaddum (Qasha Khando) School, quashing the Assyrians' numerous efforts at promoting their cultural legacy, something many also did through the avenue of religious institutions.[6]

Other Assyrian communities retained a semblance of independence, especially those in remote mountain villages. As head of the Assyrian Committee, Yaqo Ismael (son of Malik Ismael), a respected former levy commander and head of the Tiyari tribe, delivered the Assyrian National Petition (arguments discussing the creation of an autonomous region for Assyrians) to the Iraqi government in 1973.[7] Meanwhile, the Kurdistan Democratic Party (KDP) garnered international monetary support. Such aid from foreign allies to the Kurds made many of the already frustrated and tribally oriented Assyrians more likely to form a closer relationship with Mustafa Barzani and his troops. This was seen unmistakably during the summer of 1972, when both Iran and Israel intensified economic support to Kurds in Iraq. Furthermore, the United States, under the instructions of President Richard Nixon and Secretary of State Henry Kissinger, funnelled more than $16 million in CIA funds to the Kurds from 1972 to 1975.[8] Much of this increase in aid followed the Iraqi–Soviet friendship treaty, signed in April 1972, which also saw the Iraqi government's slight change in policy regarding their view on a previously treasonous ICP. The United States regularly supported parties in opposition to Soviet control, and vice versa. Thus, the age-old struggle of foreign colonial powers over the Middle East would continue, but the previous positions of the French and British had now been supplanted by the Soviet Union and the United States using pawns to contend for control and authority over Iraq.

As a deterrent to potential Assyrian involvement in a rebellion, the Ba'th regime took various measures to ensure their neutrality as well as to pacify a growing anti-government sentiment among Shiites in the south that remained their immediate focus. The regime feared a fight on two fronts and concocted a plan permitting them to control the centres of religious/cultural education. They achieved this by nationalising all schools in Iraq, from predominantly Shia establishments in the south to Christian parochial schools in large urban areas and throughout the north.[9] Most foreigners were deported, and priests and nuns were forced to swear an oath of allegiance to the Ba'th regime. The nationalisation programme also succeeded in tempering the government-feared increase of growing Assyrian intellectualism and nationalism in urban areas (a counterbalance to the loss of land, language and culture during the urbanisation process – and an unforeseen circumstance) by effectively eliminating many religiously based Assyrian schools that had offered language, history and cultural classes – notwithstanding sections (a) and (b) of decree 251, as shown above. Once all the schools were deemed public, Assyrians no longer comprised a majority in their own parochial schools, effectively negating any benefit they might have drawn from those sections of the decree. In addition, many years of urbanisation and compulsory Arabic, coupled with socio-economic difficulties and institutionalised prejudice, led others to adopt an assimilatory attitude.[10]

The 1970s witnessed the targeting of specific individuals for their political leanings and influencial politics. Bishop Mar Youalah of Dūre, Barwar, was poisoned in 1972, as was Archbishop Quryaqos Mushe of 'Amēdīyāh not long after.[11] Elsewhere artists such as the Assyrian composer and singer Shlimon Bet-Shmuel were imprisoned and beaten. Born on 24 April 1950, Bet-Shmuel, a member of Nādi al-Thaqāfi al-Āthūrī (Assyrian Cultural Club), had a deep passion for music expression. On 2 August 1973, during a celebratory gathering for the third anniversary of the club, Bet-Shmuel performed the ballad 'Simele', a commemoration of the 1933 massacres. Due to increased government harassment and threat in response to promoting what was deemed Assyrian nationalist sentiment, Bet-Shmuel soon fled to Iran and eventually the United States.

As with Bet-Shmuel and others Ba'thification practice analogously besieged organisations. In 1974 the Baghdad athletic club Nādi al-Riyadhi al-Āthūrī (Assyrian Sports Club), founded in 1955 and home of national soccer hero Ammo Baba, had its name compulsorily altered to Nādi al-Tamouz (July Club) in honour of the 1968 July revolution that saw the rise to power of the Ba'th Party.[12] In true totalitarian fashion, the nationalisation process penetrated all aspects of life. Concurrently, due to decree 251 of 1972, the Assyrians were given the ability to publish and distribute a variety of magazines within government-sponsored institutions like the Syriac Academy and its journal along with the radio programme mentioned above, which received strong support and won over many Christians even those not self-identifying as Assyrian. While assimilated urbanites and some proponents of Assyrianism took the programme at face value, others were not long deceived. Writers continued their cultural promotions through the magazine *Mordinna Atouraya*, an organ of Nādi al-Thaqāfi al-Āthūrī, in 1974. The magazine became the intellectual nucleus of Assyrian thought in the 1970s and was published in both Arabic and Assyrian. *Mordinna Atouraya*, vastly more so than the Syriac Academy, fostered culture beyond intellectualism for its own sake. Articles on language and social activities provided the predominant content and engaged the living community. Artists and writers such as Akhtiyar Benyamin Mushe (born in Mosul in 1940) wrote on the value of language for identity, Mushe remarking that it was through the medium of language that people are known.[13] Few political matters were discussed in the magazine as it was monitored and printed by the Ministry of Education. Some writers frequently utilised poetic metaphor to express social or political angst, yet others were unabashedly fearless in their longings.[14] Furthermore, the Assyrian narratives were protected and disseminated. Authors like Yousip Nimrud Canon told stories of the community that painted a positive and progressive past rather than one of failed strategies and promises. As early as 1928 drama groups and writers in Baghdad flourished in a community classified as 'a foreign and unassimilable people' even amid problems of resettlement.[15] The reminder ignited feelings of pride as well as astounding possibility.

As time progressed, privileges were reduced and funding curtailed, and in some cases, organisations impaired by the influence of government supporters embedded in the strata of the association.[16] Notwithstanding this, the powerful imagery influenced a younger generation to view prospects and potential through the successes of the past, thus creating hope despite an uncertain future.

Figure 16   A cover of *Mordinna Atouraya* from 1973

A Resumption of Violence

Regional players also asserted significant influence over Iraq. This was unmistakable following the Algiers Agreement, an accord between Iraq and Iran in 1975 engendered in order to settle border disputes, when Iran's support for the Kurds had begun to diminish, at least on the surface – the involvement of Iran's secret service, SAVAK, on the other hand, continued. In addition, Israel persuaded Mustafa Barzani to begin a new offensive against the Iraqi army in 1973 – some sources believe, to keep the Kurds occupied and unable to support the Syrian army on the Golan front.[17] Violence was renewed in earnest from Kirkuk to Sinjar. At Khanaqin on 18 August, two Iraqi militarymen and ten paramilitory Kurds were killed in skirmishes along the Iranian border.[18] According to a telegram from US intelligence, an intercepted telegram from the KDP politburo to the Revolutionary Command Council (the ultimate decision-making body in Iraq) reported that the fighting in Sinjar had worsened. The KDP promised repercussions should attacks continue.[19] The situation saw greater deterioration as the months wore on with little hope of reconciliation and no end in sight. Indeed further infighting occurred. On 11 November, using a *pêşmerge* force 2,000 strong, the KDP reportedly launched attacks against communist villages in Sulaymaniyah. The KDP in turn accused the communists of receiving arms and ammunitions from the Iraqi government and attacking the KDP headquarters at Darbandikhan.[20]

In March 1974 the Iraqi government completed a draft autonomy agreement and allotted two weeks for a KDP response. The organisation rejected the agreement, which would have left the oilfields of Kirkuk under Iraqi government control. Some experts have speculated that a solution to the Kurdish question in Iraq was greatly imperilled by 'the increased Iranian–U.S.–Israeli support for Barzani'.[21] Israel's Mossad continued close relations and collaborated further on issues concerning Iraqi Kurds through the mid-1970s, at which time fighting resumed between the Barzani Kurds and the Iraqi government, causing internal fighting and forced demographic displacement, especially in the Zakho region.

In 1974, the Kurdish paramilitary movement was renewed. A new committee was created known as the High Committee of Christian Affairs, headed by Gewargis Chikko, brother of the late Hurmiz Malik Chikko. Gewargis Chikko worked in concert with Barzani and the rest of the opposition movement, attempting to provide consistent aid to non-combatants in the struggle as well as general aid for needy Assyrians. But for all his efforts, the United States made it clear that as policy they would not intervene in the internal issues of another country.[22]

Barzani, having at different times secured Israeli, US and Iranian backing, made a play for greater power in the early 1970s.[23] This backing, probably due to Barzani's anti-communist tendencies at that particular moment and the Ba'th regime's kinder treatment of the Communist Party in Iraq at the time, allowed those Kurds involved in the struggle to once again take up arms against the government. This support, most specifically from Iran, ceased in 1975 immediately following the signing of the Algiers Agreement, with the settling of border disputes and the beginning of what became known in Iraq as the border clearings.

During this time of uncertainty and questioning of Barzani's leadership of the KDP, in June 1975 a former leading member of the KDP politburo, Jalal Talabani, along with some Marxist and socialist-leaning members, formed the Patriotic Union of Kurdistan (PUK) while in Damascus.[24] The succeeding years would witness great friction between the newly formed progressive PUK and the predominantly tribal Barzani-led KDP. As a consequence, serious fighting erupted between KDP and PUK militia, which affected Kurds and also those Assyrians caught in the crossfire.

To add to the rising frictions, atleast on the Assyrian front, Dawood Malik Ismael assassinated Mar Eshai Shimun, patriarch of the Assyrian Church of the East, in San Jose, California, on 6 November 1975.[25] This blow to the Church of the East, already in exile, left a deep impression on the community that also coincided with a resumption of fighting and forced displacement in Iraq, further cleansing Assyrians from their ancestral homeland. This continued demographic shifting produced two significant by-products. Firstly, their initial relocation to Arab-dominated cities in southern Iraq severed the 'natural tie between the people and their land'.[26] Secondly, in many cases Assyrians were removed alongside Kurds and forced into collective towns where they once again became a minority to the more numerous Kurds. And further, the so-called legal confiscation of their land indicated that any future settlement could just as simply be repossessed by government officials.

Elsewhere in urban regions, pressures experienced by less compliant members of the Assyrian community continued into the latter part of the decade. The following account will serve as a case in point of the suffering visited upon Assyrian individuals by the Iraqi government. In many cases, the reason for their detention ranged from refusal to join the ruling Ba'th Party to performing Assyrian patriotic songs and poetry:

It was Wednesday, January 5, 1977, in the evening. As always (almost every day), I left home on my way to the Assyrian Cultural Club. I got to the main street and stood on the sidewalk. The next day I woke up in the trauma hospital with my brother and a friend by my side. I asked where I was and they told me that a pick-up truck hit me and I was in the hospital. Because I was sedated I went back to sleep. Because I didn't remember anything about the accident, I thought it was really a normal car accident.

My brother told me that the truck knocked me into a steel electric pole and the lights went off. He went out to see what happened and he saw me and the driver. He caught the driver until the police came and took him. A couple days later, an old man and an officer, in air force uniform, came to visit me. The old man was in tears. He said that he was the father of the driver who hit me. He asked me to drop the charges against him in order to be released from jail. I said, 'Not so fast.' The officer said that he was the brother of the boy. Three days later the officer came alone and said, 'Do you remember me? I'm the cousin of the driver. I came to ask you what is your decision regarding the charges against my cousin.' Although I was in bad shape and in pain, I remembered that he previously said that he was the driver's brother. So I felt something fishy in this case. I told him, 'I haven't made a decision yet.'

A couple days after that, the officer came to me again and said, 'Listen, Y., I am a friend of the family and if you want to get out of this hospital, you better sign these papers to drop the charges.' I immediately said, 'Give me the pen,' and I signed the papers. There was a small biscuit factory next to our house and on the main street. A while after the accident, the officer said to my father, 'I will tell you something, but you have to swear on the Bible and on the lives of your children that you not tell a soul, including Y.' My father swore. The man said that the factory was closed but he was in it, and he saw the pick-up truck idling on the side street. 'As soon as he saw Y. the truck moved and hit your son.' My father never talked about that, but he decided to leave Iraq like many others were doing. I didn't understand because he was always against leaving Iraq. After I left Iraq, my father told the story to my nephew on the day he was leaving Iraq. At that time, the Ba'th Party was ruling, but the President was Ahmed Hassan al-Bakr and Saddam Hussein was the Vice President. It was known by Iraqis that opponents were killed in accidents or would disappear mysteriously, including the son of President al-Bakr, who was a candidate to replace him.[27]

As pressure mounted, spreading rapidly through the urban populace, especially among the elite, most metropolitan Christians diffidently accepted the 'Arab' appellation for various reasons involving socio-economic and political survival. Yet not all conformed. 'Abd Salam and Abu Sargon [of the Syrian Catholic community] were arrested and tortured for identifying themselves as "Assyrian" [Ashūri] in the 1977 Iraqi census.'[28] On 19 October 1978, the Iraqi government ordered the imprisonment of five Assyrian singers, songwriters and artists, including David Esha, Sami Yako and Albert Oscar Baba.[29] To illustrate one example, Yako's imprisonment and subsequent torture came from his singing of an Assyrian song. Yako, a playwright and actor, was held between 1 and 23 November 1978, in solitary confinement, in a cell measuring approximately one by two metres. Until the time of his release, he was subject to mental and physical torment, including regular beatings with various instruments, electric shocks and mental abuse. Fleeing to Kuwait after his release, Yako left for England, where he was admitted as a political refugee:

> I didn't leave Iraq because I wanted to. We left because I was put in prison and badly tortured for a month for singing an Assyrian nationalistic song at a party. Just before I was released, one of the Ba'th officers in charge told me that he would be expecting weekly communication from me detailing the nationalistic activities of our community – in particular those who were meeting in the Assyrian Culture Club (Nadi Al Thaqafi).[30]

Out of necessity and fear, as illustrated by the government reaction above, acquiescence brought socio-economic benefit to some, being further swept along within the rising tide of Iraqi-Arab nationalism, fostered initially by the education system and print media, and later audio-visual media, controlled by the Ba'th Party.[31] Such cultural repression became prominent in cities; in other urban centres both men and women thrived. While these are individual cases and should not be assumed to be monolithic rubrics for the Assyrian experience, the policies of otherisation reverberated on a greater scale as towns and villages were destroyed, ways of life altered, further contributing to marginalisation within the Iraqi polity and indeed creating the same within the Assyrian community itself.

The Border Clearings of 1977–8

The Barwari Bala region of northern Iraq contained around eighty villages. Of these, thirty-five are entirely inhabited by Assyrians were during the 1970s. The region is principally mountainous, and many villages remained inaccessible by most motorised vehicles at the time. The region is bordered by Turkey to the north and the Sapna valley to the south, and rests between the Greater Zab to the west and the river Khabur to the east.[32] This remoteness allowed the retention of a unique identity and lifestyle distinct from families in urban center. Furthermore, the Barwar region was an ancient Church of the East enclave, and its continuous habitation and familial relations with Assyrian villages in modern Turkey speaks to both the historic continuum and the artificiality of the modern border.

The border clearings would devastate almost every village in the region, along with the symbols of their cultural heritage. As reported by Human Rights Watch (HRW), under the terms of the 1975 Algiers Agreement, Iraq began to clear a *cordon sanitaire* along its northern borders, in particular with Iran. HRW further reported, based on correspondence, that initially a 5-kilometre-wide corridor was created, later expanded to 10, then 15 and eventually 30 kilometres.[33] Families were told they were to be removed from the region to be settled with few belongings in collective towns farther south while their villages and churches were dynamited and bulldozed.[34] According to the Ba'th's own sources, some 28,000 families were removed from their villages in two months in 1978.[35] Initially, this *cordon sanitaire* was fashioned under the pretext of preventing further Iranian support to the Kurdish movement in Iraq.

Following the large-scale upheavals at the end of 1978, the demographics of the country were drastically altered once again as the culmination of the continuous displacement and eradication of ancestral villages and rural communities by government decree, followed by the creation of processing facilities, which became known as *mujamma'āt*, or collective towns, fostered the disappearance of the last vestiges of rural Assyrian life and culture (see Table 10).[36] This second wave originated in a far more ideologically Arab Iraq, which had developed through a close connection with and in tutorship from the great powers of the United States and the Soviet Union. They waged a war of influence over Iraq, and each country's funding depended on which Iraqi faction could best stem the tide of influence from the other.

Table 10 Assyrian village summary, 1970s

Name	Province	District	Alt. name	Schools	Religious structures	Year(s)	Comments
Alih	Dohuk	'Amēdīyāh				1978	Border clearings
Balūkā	Dohuk	'Amēdīyāh	Bebālūk, Beth Bālūk		1	1978, 1988	15 families displaced, site of chemical attack
Bāsh	Dohuk	'Amēdīyāh		1	2	1977–8, 1988	Border clearings, 50 families displaced
Bazif	Dohuk	'Amēdīyāh	Ba Zibe, Ba Zive, Ba Dibbe			1942, 1976	
Bequlke	Dohuk	'Amēdīyāh	Beth Qulke	1	1	1978	Border clearings, 8 families displaced
Beshmīyaye	Dohuk	'Amēdīyāh	Bishmiaye, Beth Shmayaye		2	1978	Border clearings, 50 families displaced
Betannūrē	Dohuk	'Amēdīyāh	Beth Tannūrē		1	1978	Border clearings, 24 families displaced
Birka	Dohuk	'Amēdīyāh				1977	Border clearings, 35 families displaced
Butara	Dohuk	'Amēdīyāh	Botara		1	1978	Border clearings, 8 families displaced
Challik	Dohuk	'Amēdīyāh	Challik Nasara		2	1933, 1978	Border clearings, 100 families displaced in 1978
Cham Dostina	Dohuk	'Amēdīyāh			1	1978	Border clearings, 5 families displaced
Chaqala (lower)	Dohuk	'Amēdīyāh	Chaqala Khtetha	1		1978	Border clearings, 20 families displaced
Chaqala (upper)	Dohuk	'Amēdīyāh	Chaqala Letha			1978	Border clearings, 35 families displaced

Deralok	Dohuk	'Amēdiyāh	Deira d'Luqa		4	1933, 1978, 1987–8	1978 and Anfal, used as collective town
Derke	Dohuk	'Amēdiyāh	Derka			1976	
Dohuke	Dohuk	'Amēdiyāh	Dahoki, Dohoke		1	1933, 1962, 1977, 1988	60 families displaced 1988
Dūre	Dohuk	'Amēdiyāh			4	1978	Border clearings, 100 families displaced
Hawsarek	Dohuk	'Amēdiyāh	Avsarke			1977–8	Border clearings
Helwā	Dohuk	'Amēdiyāh	Halwā, Helwā Nasara		1	1978	Border clearings, 60 families displaced
Hish	Dohuk	'Amēdiyāh	Hiche, Heesh	1	1	1978	Border clearings, 100 families displaced
Iqri	Dohuk	'Amēdiyāh	Aqri, Aqra, Keri		2	1978	Border clearings, 35 families displaced
Istip	Dohuk	'Amēdiyāh	Histip		1	1978	Border clearings, 35 families displaced
Iyyat	Dohuk	'Amēdiyāh	Yate, Iyat		2	1978	Border clearings, 40 families displaced
Kaftumardina	Dohuk	'Amēdiyāh				1976	
Khwara	Dohuk	'Amēdiyāh			1	1978	Border clearings, 16 families displaced
Komāne	Dohuk	'Amēdiyāh	Kowane	1	5	1961, 1965, 1977, 1987–8	Became collective town in 1977

Table 10 (continued)

Name	Province	District	Alt. name	Schools	Religious structures	Year(s)	Comments
Lish	Dohuk	'Amēdiyāh	Lich			1963, 1978	Affected by civil war and border clearings
Maghribiya	Dohuk	'Amēdiyāh			1	1978	Border clearings, 8 families displaced
Malakhta	Dohuk	'Amēdiyāh			1	1978	Border clearings, 15 families displaced
Māyē	Dohuk	'Amēdiyāh	Māyē Nasara		2	1978	Border clearings, 35 families displaced
Meydan	Dohuk	'Amēdiyāh	Maydan		1	1978	25 families displaced
Nerwa (lower)	Dohuk	'Amēdiyāh	Nerwa Khtetha, Lower Nerwa		1	1976, 1988	60 families displaced, 1988
Qārō	Dohuk	'Amēdiyāh	Qarou, Karou		2	1977–8, 1988	Border clearings; Anfal, 50 families displaced
Rekan	Dohuk	'Amēdiyāh				1963, 1978	Civil war, border clearings
Sardāshte	Dohuk	'Amēdiyāh			1	1978	Border clearings, 90 families displaced
Sarsang (city)	Dohuk	'Amēdiyāh			2	1961, 1972–3	1972–3, Barzani and government confiscated land
Spe	Dohuk	'Amēdiyāh				1978	Border clearings
Tashish	Dohuk	'Amēdiyāh			2	1978, 1988	Destroyed during Anfal
Tirwanish	Dohuk	'Amēdiyāh	Der Wanis		1	1961, 1977–8	Mostly Kurdish by 1960s; border clearings
Wela	Dohuk	'Amēdiyāh	Welah		2	1977, 1988	Border clearings; Anfal, 20 families displaced

Village	Governorate	District	Alternative name		Years	Notes
Zuinke	Dohuk	'Amêdiyâh			1976	
Hazarjot	Dohuk	'Aqra		1	1961, 1972, 1988	Destroyed during Simele massacre; later Arabised by regime
Badariyah	Dohuk	Sheikhan	Badliyah		1933, 1976	
Bebôze	Dohuk	Sheikhan	Beth Bôzi		1976, 1987	30 families displaced
Shkaft-Mara	Dohuk	Sheikhan	Sharkaf, Sarkafe		1975	
Avzerok Khammo	Dohuk	Simele	Lower Avzerog	1	1975	50 families
Avzerok Shanno	Dohuk	Simele	Upper Avzerog	2	1975	60 families displaced
Bajidda-Barave	Dohuk	Simele			1975, 1976	30 families displaced in 1975; Arabised 1976
Bajidda-Kandal	Dohuk	Simele			1975	
Bakhluja	Dohuk	Simele	Bachloudja		1975	8 families displaced
Dosteka	Dohuk	Simele			1933, 1976	Pillaged and destroyed in 1933 during Simele massacre
Gerqawa	Dohuk	Simele			1976	
Hawresk	Dohuk	Simele			1975	10 families displaced
Ishkavdal	Dohuk	Simele		1	1961, 1975	20 families displaced
Karrana	Dohuk	Simele			1933, 1976	Many fled to Syria in 1933 during Simele massacre

Table 10 (continued)

Name	Province	District	Alt. name	Schools	Religious structures	Year(s)	Comments
Mar Yaqob	Dohuk	Simele	Mar Yaco, Mar Ya'aqub, Qashafir	1	2	1976, 1988	Destroyed ancient monastery of the same name destroyed; 20 families displaced
Mavan	Dohuk	Simele	Mawana			1933, 1975	10 families displaced, removed for government poultry project
Muqble	Dohuk	Simele	Moqoble			1933, 1976	Mostly Yezidi by 1976
Reqawa	Dohuk	Simele	Rekawa			1933, 1974–6	
Salahiya	Dohuk	Simele				1933, 1976	Pillaged and destroyed in 1933 during Simele massacre
Slevani	Dohuk	Simele	Slewani			1976	
Şoriya	Dohuk	Simele		1	1	1969, 1975–6	40 families before 1969 massacre
Alanish	Dohuk	Zakho	Alanash		1	1975	40 families displaced
Avkani	Dohuk	Zakho	Avgni, Avgani			1976 or 1978	
Bahnona	Dohuk	Zakho				1961, 1975	30 families displaced
Bajuwa	Dohuk	Zakho				1976	5 families displaced
Bedār	Dohuk	Zakho	Beth Dara		1	1975	130 families displaced
Behere	Dohuk	Zakho				1975	

Table 10 (continued)

Name	Province	District	Alt. name	Schools	Religious structures	Year(s)	Comments
Mahate	Ninawa	'Ain Sifni				1976	Predominantly Yezidi families
Mahmouda	Ninawa	'Ain Sifni				1976	Predominantly Yezidi families
Mam Rachan	Ninawa	'Ain Sifni				1976	Predominantly Yezidi families
Baqasri	Ninawa	Sheikhan				1976	50 families displaced
Beristeke	Ninawa	Sheikhan	Beristek			1976	
'Ain Helwa	Ninawa	Telkeif				1933, 1976	Assyrian Bohtan tribes
Bendawaye	Ninawa	Telkeif	Beth Handawaya			1976	Arabised by regime
Jamboor	Ninawa	Telkeif	Janbur			1976	
Khercheniya	Ninawa	Telkeif	Khershinya			1976	
Khoshaba	Ninawa	Telkeif	Khochaba			1976	Arabised by regime
Nāṣeriyā	Ninawa	Telkeif				1976	
Qasrune	Ninawa	Telkeif				1976	
Ummairi	Ninawa	Telkeif				1976	

Village	Governorate	District	Alternative names		Year	Notes
Benakhre	Dohuk	Zakho			1975	10 families displaced
Bersive	Dohuk	Zakho	Beth Nakhre	2	1976, 1988	Transformed into a military camp and collective town
Dashtnakh	Dohuk	Zakho	Birsivi, Beth Sawe Dashta d'Nakh, Dashtatakh		1975	15 families displaced
Dehere	Dohuk	Zakho	Behere		1975	15 families displaced
Deirabūn	Dohuk	Zakho	Deir Abuna	1	1976	Destroyed; resettled by Mosul Arabs and Yezidis by government order
Derashīsh	Dohuk	Zakho	'Umra, Ūmra Shghisha		1975–6	50 families; resettled by Kurds
Feshkhābur	Dohuk	Zakho	Pešabūr, Pesh Khabur	2	1976	Destroyed; resettled by Mosul Arabs and Yezidis by government order
Istablan	Dohuk	Zakho	Stablan	1	1975	20 families displaced
Pireka	Dohuk	Zakho			1978, 1984	90 families displaced in 1978
Qarawilla	Dohuk	Zakho	Qarawola	1	1975–6	100 families, 70 homes before being destroyed
Sanaat	Dohuk	Zakho	Esnakh	2	1975	120 families displaced
Shuwadin	Dohuk	Zakho	Shudin		1975	35 families displaced
Yarda	Dohuk	Zakho		2	1975	60 families displaced
Greapan	Ninawa		Girēpān		1976	
Kandale	Ninawa	'Ain Sifni			1976	Predominantly Yezidi families
Mahara	Ninawa	'Ain Sifni			1976	

Many Assyrian and Kurdish families, including those who had deserted the army rather than take part in the wholesale destruction, became refugees in Turkey. The Ba'th regime under Ahmed Hassan al-Bakr enacted an amnesty law that would allow for the return of refugees and those referred to deserters. Under Article 1 of Law 108 of 1979, General Amnesty for Military and Civil Kurds:

> Iraqi Kurds who are related to the army, interior security forces and civil deserters outside the country shall be exempted from all offences they have committed because of Northern events and from all the substantive and subsidiary penalties issued against them because of these events. Also they shall be exempted from all the penalties provided for in the military Laws consequent to their absence, desertion, default, and violation.[37]

The amnesty, according to the government, facilitated the return and integration of Kurds who had left their posts and abandoned their battalions into their previous position with no harm and no change in salary or benefits.[38] Subsequently, Law 109 was created to extend the amnesty to all military and civilian deserters residing outside Iraq.[39] Furthermore, the promulgation of Law 187 of 1978, First Amendment to the Law of Kurdish Culture and Publication House No 29 of 1976, signified a crucial attempt by Ba'th under al-Bakr to pacify armed Kurds in the north who had begun obtaining foreign aid.[40]

Whereas concessions were made, at least in principle, to integrate and negotiate the status and position of Iraqi Kurds during various periods of Iraq's political history, the same cannot be said of the Assyrian experience during the same time periods. Contrarily, whereas the Kurds were granted legal, political and cultural concessions, the Assyrians were recognised by the regime as Syriac-speaking Arab Christians, 'Arab-Messiḥiyīn. Moreover, referring to oneself as Ashūri was a penal offence carrying with it time in prison.[41] Moreover, arrests of individuals accused of treason for practising cultural traditions such as performing folkloric and cultural songs further contributed to a sense of disparity. Constant intimidation and imprisonment became obstacles for any cultural advancement. The subsequent destruction of over ninety-five villages, sixty religious structures and schools and over 1200 families displaced including the annihilation of their economic sustainability through the destruction of their modes and ways of life from apple orchards to agricultural fields from Barwar to Zakho foreshadowed the end of any hope for pluralism in Iraq. The litmus test a failure.

Notes

1. Ashor Giwargis, 'Until when? The Assyrian ethnicity persecuted and marginalized in its own homeland', tr. Mary C., *Zinda Magazine*, 30 September 2002.
2. Vahram Petrosian, 'Assyrians in Iraq', *Iran and the Caucasus* 10.1 (2006), 134.
3. Iraq Ministry of Information, 'Granting the Cultural Rights to the Turkman and Syriac-speaking Nationals', Information Series 58 (Baghdad: Al-Hurriya, 1974), 11–12. The formation of the Syriac Academy is dealt with on pages 21–30.
4. *Iraq: Continuous and Silent Ethnic Cleansing – Displaced Persons in Iraqi Kurdistan and Iraqi Refugees in Iran* (Paris: FIDH/International Alliance for Justice, 2003), 17.
5. Y.C. (Darbandoke-Baghdad), interview with author, 1 September 2006, Chicago.
6. Ibid.
7. Petrosian, 'Assyrians in Iraq', 134; see Annexes for US government document attestations.
8. Ian Black and Benny Morris, *Israel's Secret Wars: the Untold History of Israeli Intelligence* (London: Hamish Hamilton, 1991), 328.
9. Ray Mouawad, 'Syria and Iraq: Repression – Disappearing Christians of the Middle East', *Middle East Quarterly*, Winter 2001.
10. The so-called Arab Christians of Mosul are a prime example of this assimilation practice. In the case of many of these Christians, their socio-economic situation was well above that of Muslims in the region, showing a discrepancy in the solely anti-Christian argument for the conditions faced by the Assyrians in Iraq. However, those Christians who identified as Ashūri ('Assyrian') were ridiculed and ostracised by the Arabised Christian community, itself effectively accomplishing government policy.
11. *Iraq: Continuous and Silent Ethnic Cleansing*, 58. Any indication of who murdered the bishops is still speculative. Most theories support Iraqi government responsibility for the poisoning, due to the two bishops' Assyrian-nationalist stance. This was mentioned numerous times within the oral histories recorded. This idea is coupled with or sometimes in opposition to speculation of possible Kurdish KDP involvement to distance Assyrians from the government which had began to grant concessions and possibly arms to buffer Kurdish advances.
12. It was changed back in 1987 due to continued protests from supporters and fans.

13. Akhtiyar Benyamin Mushe, 'Leshanā d-Yimmā', *Mordinna Atouraya* 3.11 (1977), 41–3. Mushe was a prolific writer, also translating works such as *The Merchant of Venice* into Assyrian.

14. This is beyond the scope of this work, but deserves attention since it illustrates the paradox of 'cultural rights' as offered by the Ba'th. See Khaziqaya Israel, 'Freedom', *Mordinna Atouraya* 1.3–4 (1974), 12–13.

15. Hanna Batatu, *The Old Social Classes and the Revolutionary Movements in Iraq* (London: Saqi, [1978] 2004), 869; Yousip Nimrud Canon, 'Tash'ītā', *Mordinna Atouraya* 1.1 (1973), 11–14.

16. Y.C. (Darbandoke-Baghdad), interview with author, 1 September 2006, Chicago.

17. Black and Morris, *Israel's Secret Wars*, 329.

18. US Intelligence Baghdad, Iraq to Secretary of State, Washington, DC, 'Deterioration of Government of Iraq–Kurdish Relations', 26 August 1973, WikiLeaks.

19. US Intelligence Baghdad, Iraq to Secretary of State, Washington, DC, 'Kurdish Conflict', 28 August 1973, WikiLeaks.

20. US Intelligence Baghdad, Iraq to Secretary of State, Washington, DC, 'Kurdish–Communist Clashes', 18 November 1973, WikiLeaks.

21. Black and Morris, *Israel's Secret Wars*, 330.

22. Department of State to Iran Tehran, Lebanon Beirut, 'Request for Aid to Assyrians', 9 May 1974, WikiLeaks.

23. George Black, *Genocide in Iraq: The Anfal Campaign against the Kurds* (New York: Human Rights Watch, 1993), 6.

24. Gareth R. V. Stansfield, *Iraqi Kurdistan: Political Development and Emergent Democracy* (London: RoutledgeCurzon, 2003), 80.

25. See 'Public Records of the Trial Proceedings of the Assassination of His Holiness Mar Eshai Shimun XXIII', Superior Court of the State of California (1975).

26. Nisan, *Minorities in the Middle East*, 190.

27. Y.C. (Darbandoke-Baghdad), interview with author, 1 September 2006, Chicago (includes follow-up email correspondence). See also Frederick A. Aprim, *Assyrians: From Bedr Khan to Saddam Hussein – Driving into Extinction the Last Aramaic Speakers* (F. A. Aprim, 2006), 233, for similar situations which occurred during the 1980s.

28. 'Northern Iraq Human Rights Field Mission', Iraq Sustainable Democracy Project, 2006, www.iraqdemocracyproject.org/pdf/Northern%20Iraq%20Human%20Rights%20Field%20Mission.pdf (accessed 16 July 2014).

29. *Amnesty International Report 1979* (London: Amnesty International, 1979), 158; Aprim, *Assyrians*, 232. See also 'World Ignores Plight of Assyrians', *Assyrian Sentinel*, April 1979.

30. Tony Kasim, 'An Interview with Sami Yako', *Nineveh* 30.1–2 (2007), 23.

31. See Batatu, *The Old Social Classes and the Revolutionary Movements In Iraq*, 40, 700, Tables A-27–A-29 (references to 'Arabised Assyrians' and 'Arabised Chaldeans').

32. S.A. (Dūre), interview with author, 2 July 2007, Toronto.

33. Black, *Genocide in Iraq*, 37. Footnote 29 mentions the work of Dr Shorsh Haji Resool (see Chapter 1, 'Key Sources'). It is evident that HRW is dependent on Resool's work for most of its information concerning the Anfal campaign and the 1978 border clearings.

34. S.A. (Dūre), interview with author, 2 July 2007, Toronto.

35. *Al-Thawra*, 18 September 1978.

36. Pictures of the displacement of people and bulldozing of the villages are available at http://www.barwar.net and more specifically http://www.barwar.net/view-article-117.html (accessed 16 July 2014).

37. 'General Amnesty for Military and Civil Kurds', Law No. 108 of 1979, *Alwaqai Aliraqiya: The Official Gazette of the Republic of Iraq*, 19 December 1979, p. 7.

38. Ibid.

39. 'General Amnesty for Militarymen and Civilian Deserters outside Iraq', Law No. 109 of 1979, *Alwaqai Aliraqiya: The Official Gazette of the Republic of Iraq*, 1 September 1980, p. 2.

40. *Alwaqai Aliraqiya: The Official Gazette of the Republic of Iraq*, 1 March 1979, p. 10.

41. As exemplified by the experience of Abu Ishtar, an urban-dwelling Syrian Catholic by ecclesiastical background. See 'Northern Iraq Human Rights Field Mission'.

6

New Movements and War
on the Horizon

It is the constant fault and inseparable quality of ambition that it never
looks behind it.

Seneca

The Iran–Iraq War

With the accomplishments and setbacks of the late 1970s in hindsight, the turn of the decade signalled yet another difficult situation for Iraq and her Assyrian inhabitants.[1] Following the Islamic revolution in Iran in 1979 and further instability in the northern region, the Kurdistan Democratic Party (KDP) revived its alliance with Tehran. On 22 September 1980, Iraq, under a fearful and power-motivated Saddam Hussein, went to war with Iran. In an attempt to eliminate future threats and possible rebel elements, the military drafted many Assyrian men and deployed them to the front lines. Many disappeared or were killed. Most of the combatants had little desire to fight in a war for an oppressive regime, yet the war effort 'involved the conscription of large numbers of Assyrian soldiers, as some forty thousand of these unwilling recruits were killed, wounded, imprisoned in Iran, or missing in action'.[2] At least 266 Assyrians were held as prisoners of war in Iran, some for more than twenty years.[3] Overall, 200,000–300,000 people, predominantly Shia Arabs from the southern regions of Iraq, were deported to Iran in 1980.[4]

It is not inconceivable that the positioning of Christians on the front lines and in difficult military situations during the Iran–Iraq War was done with malevolent purpose by the regime. Most Assyrians who survived spoke of threats against their person from their fellow Muslim combatants. In essence, it would not do for a Christian to kill a Muslim – an enemy Iranian or otherwise. As Christians, Assyrians feared a religiously motivated backlash from

Iraqi soldiers for killing fellow Muslims.[5] The Assyrians of Iranian origin in Iraq included refugees from Urmia during the Baqubah refugee camp crisis (see Chapter 2) who had lived in Iraq since the end of the First World War, as well as those recent refugees following the 1978–9 Islamic revolution in Iran and ousting of Muhammad Reza Shah Pahlavi.[6] In the latter case, most families were visited briefly by an army officer, told to retain only the clothes on their person, packed into buses, and then driven to the border of Iran and forced into exile in a inhospitable region.[7] Thus, in most cases, the deportees lost all of their material possessions, including homes and land. The demography of Iraq in relation to the Assyrians was, thus, again altered during the early 1980s.

The Calm before the Storm

The destruction wrought by the war spanned various regions and ethnic and religious groups, and affected the entirety of Iraq simultaneously. In its midst and immediate aftermath the government made a conscious decision to increase economic prosperity at the expense of cultural plurality. As such during the early 1980s, Assyrians became an easy target for Ba'thist scrutiny. Targeted as individuals and as groups, they were increasingly frustrated with such government policies. Their frustration garnered a strong nationalist reaction from kin living both in and outside Iraq, especially those involved in political and cultural activities.[8] It was here at the turn of the decade that a grassroots opposition movement began. Among the Assyrian political and cultural groups that most strongly supported the development of the Assyrian Democratic Movement (ADM) was the predominantly diaspora-based (with some Iranian-Assyrian links) Assyrian Universal Alliance (AUA). Due to the assumed link between the ADM and the AUA, many Assyrians in Iraq came under suspicion of working with foreign powers. Furthermore, the Iraqi government now employed a new level of espionage to record Assyrian activities in the United States, Europe and elsewhere. The government regularly infiltrated Assyrian cultural centres and churches and influenced members towards pro-Ba'th sentiments, furthering discord, especially in regard to influencing church officials:

> Influence the clergy in the Assyrian community and use them in a manner
> to cause damage to the activities of the group. Hire some clergy to infiltrate

and have access to their precincts in order to gain information from the families of those who have fled [deserters].[9]

Such influence would sow discord and fear within the ranks of those working in political and cultural circles and as said fear escalated, many marginalised fled Iraq willingly during this persecution, and in many cases, escaped to Iran. For predominantly political reasons, an estimated 330 Assyrians fled to Iran in 1984 alone, in an attempt to escape oppression.

Assyrians amid the opposition

Throughout the 1980s, many Christians who identified as Assyrians continued to face political, ethnic and socio-economic oppression. The decades of government policies of acculturation and inculcation, which instilled fear and desperation in the Assyrians through urbanisation (effectively Arabising them), had an unforeseen consequence: an increase in the number of Assyrian young men and women in higher education. This allowed for an intellectual movement, despite the government's attempts to eliminate possible dissident ideas fostered by an isolated tribal system still prevalent in rural areas of Iraq, especially in the northern and southern extremes. A few of these intellectual movements gained ground, allowing for an armed resistance movement during the 1960s alongside the Kurds, and the later establishment of the ADM in 1979.

The Assyrian Democratic Movement, or Zowaʻa Demoqratāyā Athorāyā (ADM/Zowaa), was established on 12 April 1979 from among various smaller cultural-political and student groups, including Akhunwāthē Athorāyē (Assyrian Brothers in 1969). Among these cultural groups, and even among church and religious groups, especially in the Mosul region, a national awakening was ignited.[10] Interestingly, the ideology of the ADM was heavily synthesised from an Assyrian cultural awareness that had developed much earlier in Urmia, Iran, and in Harput, Turkey, independently. By this period in the development of Assyrian nationalist thought, both the AUA, which existed mostly in diaspora with some members in Iran – and by extension the Assyrian Democratic Organization (ADO) with strongholds in Turkey, Syria and Europe – and the ADM resolutely supported an Iraq-based Assyrian political movement. The general hope of all parties was reflected in their defence of Assyrian ethnic, political and cultural rights within a country known for its continued violations thereof.

It is most commonly believed that the ADM launched its opposition in 1982, sending supporters to northern Iraq during the Iran–Iraq War. As their supporters and numbers were not vast, and with the 1978 destruction of 'Amēdīyāh still fresh in their minds, the ADM 'militiamen' were used defensively, predominantly to protect villages in light of the consistent targeting of their kin, rather than in any offensive manner (see Figures 17 and 18). During that first year, the ADM launched its first official periodical, *Bahra*. The ADM began its true push into the opposition and gained the support of many Assyrians as well as the respect of the Kurdish and Communist parties, from whom they had adapted their structural basis while in exile in the northern mountains. Much of this growth led to the regime's keen interest in any mention of Assyrian cultural and political groups, the ADM in particular. The Ba'th's physical retribution was silent and swift and focused on villages and cultural edifices.[11] On 14 July 1984, the Saddam regime attacked ADM locations in Baghdad, arresting more than 150 members of the movement. Of those arrested, twenty-two were sentenced to life imprisonment, and four were sentenced to death.[12] Not long after, the regime also attacked the villages of Hejerke and Pireka, where militiamen died attempting to safeguard residents. Other members of the opposition suffered analogously, and their families marked by the regime. In some cases relatives of known or presumed dissidents were imprisoned in Abu Ghraib, including elderly men and women, while entire families were exiled to the Iran–Iraq border and stripped of citizenship.[13]

In the months following the Ba'th devised an abiding plan to control the ADM and other Assyrian parties believed to have questionable loyalties. 'The security agencies are charged to squash any organisation within the ranks of the Assyrians and keep them from progressing, especially inside the cities.'[14] Infiltrators were tasked to

> prepare a list of all influential individuals within the ranks of Assyrians in the church and among the general community. The list should be updated on regular basis. The prominent individuals among them in the community will be provided personal and financial help etc. [to become Ba'th informants].[15]

Figure 17   Assyrian Democratic Movement militia near Mar Mattai in 1987
(Courtesy of Hormuz Bobo and Nineveh Center for Research and Development,
Qaraqosh, Iraq)

To further their control Ba'th was assiduous in its courting of individuals within religious organisations and would spend a good portion of its
resources on bribery. Further, it sought not only to penetrate but to initi-
ate inter- as well as intra-community conflict. The security services were
charged to 'increase the personal conflict between the mentioned group and
the disloyal Kurdish Democratic Party. Seek all ways to create disunity and
disagreement among sides of the enemy.'[16] That included infiltrating and
marking printing and distribution facilities: 'Locate the printing facilities
of this Assyrian group, since their publishing style resembles the newspaper
published by the disloyal Communist Party.'[17]

The Assyrians made inroads with other opposition groups, but even
there they remained relegated to the margins. In the case of attempts by
Assyrian political parties to work towards a united front alongside the
Kurds in the 1980s, the failure of Assyrian nationalism in Iraq to minimise or amalgamate tribal and religious components allowed the Kurds to

Figure 18   ADM militia in the ruins of an Assyrian village in Barwar during the 1980s (Courtesy of Hormuz Bobo)

dismiss their former allies or, from the perspective of Kurdish leader Idris Barzani concerning Assyrian–Kurdish collaboration, to effectively subsume them as part of the Kurdish forces in 1984. According to Iraqi government correspondence:

> The Beth Nahrain party agreed to take responsibilities of military functions and mediate between the Assyrian National Front and the Democratic Front. They also opened negotiations with the Kurdish Democratic Party in order to work with each other, even though the AUA has previously requested from the traitor Idris al-Barzani to fight under the Assyrian name. Idris replied that if they wanted they could fight, but under the condition that they fight under the Kurdish name and not under [an] Assyrian or any other front.[18]

This lack of political authority guaranteed the Assyrians a continued minor role in any opposition movement in the years that followed. Moreover, the socio-economic, geographic and ethnic distinctions the Iraqi regime placed on both Assyrians and Kurds – which, for the Assyrians, included religious affiliation – gave the regime further excuse to ignore their basic human rights in the midst of a project in state homogenisation. Since the Assyrians were not acknowledged as a separate ethnic group, those in the northern region were further disregarded as part of a troublesome Kurdish element by a government wishing to create public animosity towards what they perceived as a foreign element in an otherwise homogenous Iraq. One of the many pitfalls of progress is the institutionalising of agency of minority communities, where in effect one becomes the hegemonic power (i.e. the Kurdistan Regional Government (KRG) in post-1991 Iraq) they aided to counter.[19] Furthermore, many Assyrians, like Kurds, maintained tribal and feudal relations despite integration into a larger nation-like structure. Yet unlike Kurds, the geopolitical situation assured them a relatively negligible role in the opposition movement, especially on the international stage.[20]

To return to the opposition parties, while the Assyrians' travails were generally ignored by larger media outlets, they were recalled within their own community. Some of those individual stories are recounted here; the first among them concerns Jamil Matti, an ADM member, born in Baghdad in 1953. Matti began political work in 1976 by working in an underground Assyrian organisation in Baghdad. In 1982, he joined the ADM and became active in its labours towards the recognition of Assyrian ethnic and cultural rights in Iraq. Matti played an active role in both the political and military affairs of the ADM, including various humanitarian aid missions to regions under scrutiny by the Ba'th regime. Along with Sheeba Hami, who was born in 1956 in the village of Babilu, Dohuk province, and joined the ADM in 1983, Matti led an operation to defend the populace of Hejerke village in Simele against the Iraqi army in 1984. During the operation in Hejerke, Matti was killed and Hami was severely wounded, later dying on 4 December 1984. Their operation reportedly saved the lives of twenty-six Assyrian civilians.[21]

The conditions faced by those captured and accused of 'traitorous acts' are best illustrated by the arrest and torture of eighteen members of the ADM (mostly from Baghdad and Kirkuk) during that same year. For the first seven days, the individuals were placed in tiny cells of dimensions less than $4 \times 4 \times 4$ feet. While food was offered twice daily, the detainees suffered beatings with wooden rods, having the arms tied at the wrists behind their backs with a rope from which they were also suspended while beatings occurred, and electric shocks to the genitals and other areas. Following the initial seven-day period, the detainees were placed together in Baghdad for six months in a cell that only allowed space for nine to sleep at a time.[22]

Of the traumas suffered by ADM members at the hands of the Ba'th regime, perhaps the most prominent and public was the February 1985 execution of: Yousef Toma Zibari, Youkhana Esho Shlimon and Youbert Benyamin. The government itself confirmed these executions and accused the three of 'having committed the crime of creating a hostile and separatist movement aimed at threatening the independence and unity of Iraq . . . They transported weapons and carried out acts of sabotage.'[23] Many of those original eighteen not executed remained in detainment for the following ten to fifteen years.

Few survived to tell the tale of their capture and imprisonment. One survivor, born in September 1951 in Kirkuk, was among the eighteen individuals captured and imprisoned in 1984. After spending two years in Abu Ghraib prison, where he was subjected to regular questioning and physical and mental torture, the young man was released and eventually fled Iraq on 9 August 1991.[24]

The anecdotes mentioned above serve as an example of how Assyrian political and cultural movements were viewed during the 1980s. This was evident in previous decades, with attempts at infiltration and coercion in both Kheit Kheit Allap I and II and Nādi al-Thaqāfi al-Āthūrī (Assyrian Cultural Club). The case of the ADM illustrates the ongoing policies and patterns of violence and marginalisation that the Assyrians faced in the 1980s.[25] Even individuals considered apolitical, were targeted during this period. In many cases the ruling regime found any Assyrian cultural activity suspect and exploited the fear of a growing opposition as a pretext to arrest persons judged a possible threat. As expected, targeting extended to intimidation and harassment of family members of suspected individuals. An Amnesty International (AI) report mentions the case of the brothers Mirza and Mardan Rasho, who were arrested in al-Sheikhan district in July 1985 aged six and thirteen, respectively. The motive for arrest was the accusation that the two boys' father was a member of the *pêşmerge*.[26]

Christian clergy members who remained outside Ba'thist influence, especially those with opposition propensities, were targeted for their feared charisma or political views. In 1985, Younan Kena, a priest in the Church of the East, was murdered by poisoned coffee in Kirkuk. Not long after, Father Youḥanna Abdulahad Sher was assassinated in front of a church in the town of Shaqlawa on Good Friday, 28 March 1986. Fellow cleric Archbishop Stephanos Kacho of Zakho was pursued by a military vehicle and killed in 1986, again in peculiar circumstances. These attacks led to widespread fear among Iraq's Christian communities.[27]

Renewed International Interest in Iraq: the Anfal Campaign

Since 1963, consecutive Iraqi regimes, whose authoritarian and in some cases totalitarian stance left little room for a pluralist state, targeted non-Arab citizens and at times non-compliant Arabs such as Shiites and those with communist leanings. The politically Ba'th-dominated governments utilised a policy of acculturation through physical destruction (in the case of villages and cultural sites) and socio-economic threat as well as compulsory urbanisation and over time inculcation through educational and media-based propaganda. In more recent memory, the invasion of Kuwait in August 1990 by the Iraqi army and the American counterattack some six months later marked a new page in the history of Iraq and the Middle East. During the 1980s, despite regular pleading from Iraqis and some international NGOs concerning widespread fear and crimes against humanity in Iraq, the United States government was hesitant to act against a country it was supplying with arms during its war with Iran from 1980 to 1988. Immediately following the US-led attack on Iraqi forces in Kuwait in 1991, news emerged and circulated evidence gross human rights violations committed, especially against Iraq's Kurdish and Shiite populations, throughout the previous decade. Statistics on the gassing and bulldozing of villages hit political and academic circles, and the general public was given a glimpse of images from the gassing of a town, Halabja, near the Iranian border, on 16 March 1988, which claimed over 3,200 lives.[28]

The Halabja gassing was part of the Anfal campaign, which took place from 23 February 23 to 6 September 1988 and has been defined as 'a campaign by Saddam Hussein's regime to eliminate the Kurds as a threat to the government once and for all'.[29] The reasons given for why this campaign was carried out vary, though most suggest that in view of the collection of material that supports Kurdish cooperation with Iran during the Iran–Iraq War, it can be attributed to retribution for the Kurds' rebellion against the Iraqi state. The campaign was characterised by various atrocities and human rights violations, including: mass executions and disappearances; chemical weapons attacks on civilian populations; bulldozing villages; salting the earth; razing crops; destroying cultural property, including dynamiting schools, churches, monasteries and mosques; looting and land appropriation; forcibly displacing hundreds of thousands of persons, including urbanising large populations of rural dwellers; arbitrarily jailing suspect persons; and establishing 'collective towns' and 'prohibited zones'.[30]

It is well accepted that the term *anfal*, meaning 'spoils', is taken from the eighth sura of the Koran, which discusses spoils of war in the conflict of the believer versus the 'unbeliever'.[31] This sura promises that Allah will 'cast terror into the hearts of those who disbelieve. Therefore strike off their heads and strike off every fingertip of them' and it was evident modern political dissidents equally fitted into the regime's scheme for 'military chastisement'.[32] For most historians, Anfal is divided into eight major campaigns. The official military operations are categorised as follows:

> First Anfal: 23 February–19 March 1988 (Halabja attacked
>   16 March 1988)
> Second Anfal: 22 March–1 April 1988 (Qara Dagh)
> Third Anfal: 7–20 April 1988 (Germian village, Qader Karam)
> Fourth Anfal: 3–8 May 1988 (Lesser Zab region)
> Fifth, Sixth and Seventh Anfals: 15 May–26 August 1988 (Shaqlawa
>   and Rawanduz)
> Final Anfal: 25 August–6 September 1988 (Bahdinan)[33]

Ali Hassan al-majid, secretary-general of the Ba'th party's northern region beginning in March 1987, executed and enforced a military terror campaign against its own citizens.

There were a reported 150 Assyrian Christian and Yezidi disappearances in seven villages during the Final Anfal, which included the regions of Sarsang, Doski, Barwar, Deralok and Nerwa/Rekan, alongside 632

Kurdish disappearances in thirty-six villages.[34] In a January 2003 report, the International Federation for Human Rights (FIDH) and the International Alliance for Justice (AIJ) included in their statistics a record of 115 Assyrians who disappeared in August 1988, and 141 Muslims whose fate could not be determined. Another list compiled by FIDH and the AIJ mentions thirty-five villages destroyed in the Garmian region during the Anfal campaign.[35] Most Kurdish organisations and research cite the destruction of more than 4,000 villages and 182,000 victims.[36]

Dr Shorsh Haji Resool, a Kurdish researcher for Human Rights Watch (HRW) who also served as a *pêşmerge* soldier, tallied 3,739 Kurdish villages ('any group of houses in a particular location . . . that had a name and was known to local people as a village') destroyed from 1963 to 1988, excluding some villages in the Mosul and Dohuk regions, and 70,000 to 100,000 victims.[37] Though Resool built on Iraqi documents and hundreds of interviews he conducted, it is evident that all subsequent estimates of Kurdish village destruction, including those done by human rights groups, are based on these PUK statistics.[38] Similarly, the documents concerning Assyrians have mostly been compiled by the ADM but never studied or analysed. Despite their attempts to remain apolitical, it is evident that in most cases, these very political (nationalist) institutions have assembled the basic research on the Anfal. This is reflected in the compilation of material in the FIDH and AIJ report, *Iraq: Continuous and Silent Ethnic Cleansing – Displaced Persons in Iraqi Kurdistan and Iraqi Refugees in Iran*' as well as most of the work conducted by HRW.

While the demographic and cultural blow of the terror and devestation wrought by the campaign itself was staggering, the terminologies utilised by the regime and indeed collection of the data was and still is largely suspect. The created timeline of Anfal events, for instance, neglects earlier programmes from 1987 as well as those following in 1989. Another dilemma research faced the extent of the destruction of the Anfal campaign – owing mostly to appellative problems. In the Arab-controlled regions and up as far as Arbil province, Assyrians were generally referred to as 'Christian Arabs', which may explain the general lack of material specifically mentioning the term *Assyrians*. Such a lack of distinction would allow the Ba'th Party to exploit the weakness of this minority. Similarly, Assyrians living in the northern regions, in Iraqi Kurdistan and elsewhere, were generally termed 'Christian

Kurds' by both the Iraqi regime and the Kurdish authorities, which furthered this problem.[39] Kurds and Assyrians were certainly not the only victims of the campaign. Many leftist Arab Iraqis, ICP members, and Ba'th members who detested the governmental initiatives and rule of the Saddam Hussein regime were targeted for their alleged conspiracy and treason. It slowly became discernible that the major motive behind the campaign was to stifle any dissident movement in Iraq. The northern region, still home to Kurds and Assyrians, was the chief target, being the primary area to which various Iraqi government dissidents fled in the years leading up to the Anfal operations. In the case of the Kurds, collaboration with the Iranian government during the Iran–Iraq War was tantamount to treason, as defined by most governments. Consequently, the brunt of the Saddam-led Ba'thist anger was directed towards the Kurdish movement, which was supported both militarily and financially by foreign powers.

Many Assyrian and Kurdish villages were destroyed beginning in 1987, using various tactics including air raids and napalm attacks, and even more met with forced evacuation during the period. The Ba'th schema of the Anfal operations destroyed more than eighty Assyrian villages during this period and displaced thousands of families from their ancestral lands. The elimination of Syriac liturgical and cultural material also increased during this period, and its extent remains largely unknown. Furthermore, since a large percentage of the villages targeted during the 1980s had also targeted been in the 1960s and 1970s (some since 1933), this leaves little doubt that a continuous campaign of both physical and cultural (spiritual) devastation. Whether the ruin was consciously or subconsciously constructed, the effects on the Assyrians remain (see Table 11).[40]

At the same time to the south, Shia Arabs suffered tremendously under the Ba'th regime and were also dramatically displaced in the 1980s. For the Assyrians, despite the violence wreaked against thousands of civilians and the destruction of various villages and between forty and fifity cultural and historical sites, including ancient churches and monasteries, as well as some 2,000 reported deaths in the 1987–8 gas campaigns, few reports surfaced in the mainstream media or in NGO publications.[41] On 19 June 1992, a priest of the Assyrian Church of the East from Dohuk spoke with HRW in an interview about the April 1987 annihilation of Bakhitme:[42]

Table 11 Assyrian village summary, 1980s

Name	Province	District	Alt. name	Schools	Religious structures	Year(s)	Comments
Armota	Arbil		Armota, Armūṭā, Harmota	1	1	1988	Dynamited and bulldozed during Anfal; 50 families displaced
Alolen	Dohuk	ʿAmēdīyāh				1987	
Annūnē	Dohuk	ʿAmēdīyāh	ʿAin Nūnē, Kani Masi	1	2	1988	140 families displaced
Arāden	Dohuk	ʿAmēdīyāh		2	4	1961, 1987–8	Razed 1961, 1987–8; 220 families displaced
Argen	Dohuk	ʿAmēdīyāh	Ergin, Hargin, Argin		4	1961, 1988	Destroyed during Anfal
Atrush	Dohuk	ʿAmēdīyāh	Atrosh		4	1933, 1988	25 families displaced
Badarrash	Dohuk	ʿAmēdīyāh	Beth Darrash, Beth Durashe		1	1961, 1987	
Balūkā	Dohuk	ʿAmēdīyāh	Bebālūk, Beth Bālūk		1	1978, 1988	15 families displaced, site of chemical attack
Banasora	Dohuk	ʿAmēdīyāh				1987	
Bāsh	Dohuk	ʿAmēdīyāh		1	2	1977–8, 1988	Border clearings; 50 families displaced
Baz	Dohuk	ʿAmēdīyāh	Bas		2	1961, 1988	20 families displaced, 1988
Bebede	Dohuk	ʿAmēdīyāh	Be Bede, Beth Bede		2	1961, 1987–8	Razed and resettled in 1961 by Zebari tribes; 75 families displaced, 1987–8

Table 11 (continued)

Name	Province	District	Alt. name	Schools	Religious structures	Year(s)	Comments
Benāta	Dohuk	'Amēdiyāh	Benātha, Beth 'Ainātha			1987	
Blejanke	Dohuk	'Amēdiyāh	Blejane		1	1961, 1987	28 families displaced, 1987
Bubawa	Dohuk	'Amēdiyāh	Bibava			1987	32 families displaced
Chammike	Dohuk	'Amēdiyāh				1988	4 families displaced
Dawodiya	Dohuk	'Amēdiyāh	Daudiya		2	1988	Anfal, 82 families displaced
Dehe	Dohuk	'Amēdiyāh			3	1988	Anfal, 50 families displaced
Deralok	Dohuk	'Amēdiyāh	Deira d'Luqa		4	1933, 1978, 1987–8	Used as collective town, 1978 and Anfal
Dere	Dohuk	'Amēdiyāh		1	2	1987	70 families displaced
Derigni	Dohuk	'Amēdiyāh	Derigne, Dirgin	1	1	1988	40 families displaced
Derishke	Dohuk	'Amēdiyāh	Derishk	1	2	1988	Destroyed during Anfal; 50 families displaced
Dohuke	Dohuk	'Amēdiyāh	Dahoki, Dohoke		1	1933, 1962, 1977, 1988	60 families displaced, 1988
Eşsān	Dohuk	'Amēdiyāh	Şiyān		2	1961, 1987–8	
Hamziya	Dohuk	'Amēdiyāh			2	1987	32 families displaced
Hayyis	Dohuk	'Amēdiyāh	Hayis		2	1968, 1988	Site of napalm attack, 1968; 50 families displaced, Anfal
Inishke	Dohuk	'Amēdiyāh	Inishk, Enishke			1986	Lands confiscated by government, 1980s

Village	Governorate	District	Alternative name			Dates	Notes
Jadide	Dohuk	'Amēdīyāh			1	1988	13 families displaced during Anfal
Kani Balav	Dohuk	'Amēdīyāh	Kani Balaf		2	1988	70 families displaced
Komāne	Dohuk	'Amēdīyāh	Kowane	1	5	1961, 1965, 1977, 1987–8	Became a collective town, 1977
Madude	Dohuk	'Amēdīyāh	Mahude			1988	8 families displaced
Meristak	Dohuk	'Amēdīyāh	Meristeg			1987	5 families displaced
Merkajiya	Dohuk	'Amēdīyāh				1988	1970, village headman assassinated
Meze	Dohuk	'Amēdīyāh	Mosaka		2	1961, 1988	35 families displaced
Musaka	Dohuk	'Amēdīyāh			1	1988	60 families displaced, 1988
Nerwa (lower)	Dohuk	'Amēdīyāh	Nerwa Khtetha, Lower Nerwa		1	1976, 1988	Border clearings, Anfal; 50 families displaced
Qārō	Dohuk	'Amēdīyāh	Qarou, Karou		2	1977–8, 1988	30 families displaced
Sardarawa	Dohuk	'Amēdīyāh			1	1987	37 families displaced
Sikrīne	Dohuk	'Amēdīyāh				1987	
Tajika	Dohuk	'Amēdīyāh				1987	Destroyed during Anfal
Tashish	Dohuk	'Amēdīyāh			2	1988	45 families displaced
Ten	Dohuk	'Amēdīyāh	Tin		1	1987	10 families displaced
Tuthe-Shemaya	Dohuk	'Amēdīyāh	Tishambik		1	1988	Border clearings, Anfal; 20 families displaced
Wela	Dohuk	'Amēdīyāh	Welah		2	1977, 1988	

Table 11 (continued)

Name	Province	District	Alt. name	Schools	Religious structures	Year(s)	Comments
'Aqra (city)	Dohuk	'Aqra			2	1961, 1988	Mass exodus of Assyrians beginning in 1961
Bilmand	Dohuk	'Aqra	Bilmandi			1987–8	
Cham 'Ashrat	Dohuk	'Aqra	Cham Shirte		1	1933, 1988	
Cham Chali	Dohuk	'Aqra				1961, 1988	
Cham Rabatke	Dohuk	'Aqra				1987	45 families displaced
Guhana	Dohuk	'Aqra				1986	45 families displaced
Hazarjot	Dohuk	'Aqra			1	1961, 1972, 1988	
Hizane (lower)	Dohuk	'Aqra	Hizane (Khretha), Hizanke	1	1	1987–8	110 families displaced in total (upper, lower)
Hizane (upper)	Dohuk	'Aqra	Hizane (Eletha), Hizanke			1987–8	110 families displaced in total (upper, lower)
Kalilane	Dohuk	'Aqra	Khalilan, Khalilani			1961, 1987	
Kashkawa	Dohuk	'Aqra			1	1961, 1987	100 families displaced
Meroke	Dohuk	'Aqra	Maroke, Marogue, Mar Ogin			1987	35 families displaced

Suse	Dohuk	'Aqra	Barraka d'Qaddisha		1	1988	
Turkaye	Dohuk	'Aqra	Takhed Turkaye			1987–8	
Zouli	Dohuk	'Aqra	Zuli			1987	34 families displaced
Gund Kosa	Dohuk	Dohuk			1	1933, 1988	
Malta	Dohuk	Dohuk	Ma'althaye, Maltai		2	1961, 1987–8	Turned into a collective town
Peda	Dohuk	Dohuk				1987	
Armashe	Dohuk	Sheikhan	Armash, Harmache		2	1987	55 families displaced
Azakh	Dohuk	Sheikhan	Adhekh		2	1987	50 families displaced
Bebōze	Dohuk	Sheikhan	Beth Bōzi			1976, 1987	
Deze	Dohuk	Sheikhan	Dizze		1	1933, 1987	90 families displaced
Tilla	Dohuk	Sheikhan	Tella, Tillan	1	3	1987	
Badaliya	Dohuk	Simele			1	1983, 1987	60 families displaced
Bakhitme	Dohuk	Simele	Beth Khatme, Bekhitme		3	1987	140 families displaced
Hejerke	Dohuk	Simele	Hizeerke		1	1933, 1984, 1987	
Kharab-Kulk	Dohuk	Simele	Ḥarbai(?)		1	1933, 1961, 1987	
Kherbasla	Dohuk	Simele				1987	

Table 11 (continued)

Name	Province	District	Alt. name	Schools	Religious structures	Year(s)	Comments
Mar Yaqob	Dohuk	Simele	Mar Yaco, Mar Ya'aqub, Qashafir	1	2	1976, 1988	Destroyed Ancient monastery of the same name destroyed, 20 families displaced
Sheze	Dohuk	Simele	Shiyoz	1	2	1987	80 families displaced
Surka	Dohuk	Simele	Sorka	1		1987	Christians and Yezidis, 30 families displaced
Bersive	Dohuk	Zakho	Birsivi, Beth Sawe		2	1976, 1988	Transformed into a military camp and collective town
Levo	Dohuk	Zakho			2	1988	140 families displaced
Mala 'Arab	Dohuk	Zakho			1	1988	60 families displaced
Mergasūr	Dohuk	Zakho	Margasūr			1988	60 families displaced
Nav-Kandal	Dohuk	Zakho	Naf-Kandal		1	1988	110 families displaced
Pireka	Dohuk	Zakho				1978, 1984	90 families displaced, 1978
Sharanish	Dohuk	Zakho	Sharanish Nasara		2	1987	80 families displaced
Taftiya(n)	Ninawa	Sheikhan	Totiyan			1988	5 families displaced

I was told that they would destroy Bakhtoma [*sic*] because they had already destroyed most of the surrounding villages. It was around noon when I went to the church of St George to remove the furniture, but the Iraqi army tanks and bulldozers were already beginning to roll into the village. I was the last one to pray in the church. After finishing my prayers, I removed the furniture to take it with me to Dohuk. It was a very sad day. The Iraqi soldiers and army engineers put the equivalent of one kilo of TNT at each corner of the church. After five minutes, they blew up the building and then went on to demolish every house in the village. Later they paid me compensation of 3,000 dinars. I went to the head of the Ba'th Party in Dohuk to ask why they were destroying our villages. He replied, 'You are Arabs, and we decide what you should do. That is all there is to it.' I left his office then. What could I say?[43]

As Assyrians were seen as Arabs or Kurds, the dearth of information concerning them is evident. There are other conceivable reasons for the neglect of Assyrians – their geopolitical insignificance, their ecclesiastical divisiveness, general apathy within their community, or lack of information about them – that could be used to justify their exclusion from human rights and academic literature. Yet the question must be posed that if there is both physical and oral evidence available, why have both scholarship and international NGO work neglected these atrocities and the people who were subjected to them, especially when AI itself has criticised the lack of attention concerning the half-million Kurds and Assyrians who were forcibly relocated by the Iraqi government?[44] HRW's criticism of the United States government's failure to act on certain issues that befell Iraq in the late 1980s (especially Halabja) illustrates the plight of Iraqi minorities. However, it is remarkable that while HRW points to the US government's failure to acknowledge the atrocities of the Anfal, the organisation refers to the September 1988 targeting of Christians and Yezidis following an amnesty decree as a 'brutal sideshow . . . to the Kurdish genocide'.[45] The term 'sideshow' insinuates others targeted by the Ba'th were somehow secondary, and by extension, so too was their suffering.[46]

Some Assyrian-populated areas were targeted by the Ba'th regime due to their proximity to what were deemed Kurdish insurgent areas. Yet the targeting of specific Assyrian community leaders speaks to a goal of eliminating explicitly ethno-cultural influence. Overall, more than a thousand Assyrians were either abducted or disappeared under sometimes mysterious circumstances during the Anfal period.[47] One individual example, Raphael Nano (Esho), born in 1946 in the village of Blejanke in the province of Dohuk, was a leading member of the ADM. One of the group's top liaisons, Nano found his house surrounded by military personnel and was subsequently arrested in 1987, at the beginning of the Anfal campaign. He spent one year in various prisons and was hanged on 7 January 1988 in Abu Ghraib prison in Baghdad. His entire village was destroyed as a consequence of his reportedly anti-government activities.[48] As with Nano, 'Abd al-Massiḥ Y.' was marked for elimination by the regime for reportedly working with opposition parties and was specifically accused of being 'agents of Iran', for which he was executed on 14 August 1988 in Arbil province. A secret police document requesting the arrest of his nine family members was circulated among government officials. In gaining information about his familial relations, the officials were told to 'take action and do what is necessary' to ascertain their whereabouts and arrest them.[49] Members of the clergy were not immune to malicious attacks during this period, as illustrated by the murders of Younan Kena, Youḥanna Abdulahad Sher and Stephanos Kacho earlier in the decade. During the Anfal campaign Curate Zaya Bobo Dobato fled to Iran after numerous foiled attempts on his life, including the final incident involving a car chase by military officials in the Mosul region. Dobato died in exile in the Urmia region in 1989.

While some individuals and families made the trek to Iran, others crossed the northern border. On 6 September 1988, the Iraqi government made a call for a general amnesty to all refugees who had fled to Turkey during the Anfal operations. Despite the seemingly positive nature of this government action, Assyrians who returned along with Kurds were captured and later disappeared while government forces coerced others into collective towns. The Ba'th government used the amnesty to deprive the returnees of their civil and social rights within the system.[50] The reason for the arrest of the Assyrians was based on the amnesty itself, which was addressed solely to Kurds and did not extend to other ethnic groups. The story of 'Isho', the father of four brothers from the Sarsang region, was recorded by HRW in Arbil in July 1992. Isho's family had fled their village just prior to the Anfal operations, and three of his four sons had defected from military duty. All four brothers surrendered during the grace period following the amnesty announcement and were taken to Fort Nizarkeh in Dohuk. As with most Christians and Yezidis, the four detainees disappeared during this period of amnesty. The story was more recently corroborated by a string of letters from the sister-in-law of the brothers, who were still missing after surrendering themselves in Dohuk on 10 September 1988. 'The information provided by the central security committee stated that the above mentioned people and the prisoners with them were transferred via military vehicles and gathered to the fort of Dohuk-Mosul. They were relocated to Darman fort on the path to Kirkuk and then to Topzawa fort.'[51] Later a response from the security forces stated that there was no record of these individuals. It became evident some of the actions taken during the amnesty were not reported to the headquarters in Baghdad. Nevertheless, the whereabouts of the four men, like hundreds of others, remains unknown.

Another example of the amnesty-spawned misfortune is reflected in the story of a potter from the village of Komāne. Following their return from Turkey in the wake of the general amnesty, the local potter's son, daughter-in-law and six grandchildren disappeared after they had surrendered themselves into the hands of the Iraqi authorities. The psychological and emotional pain induced the man to become mute.[52] There were a reported thirty-three Assyrians who mysteriously disappeared during the official amnesties after returning from refugee camps in Turkey and Iran in 1988 and 1989 and numerous other reputed but never recorded.[53] In addition, Vicar Shimon Shlemon Zaya of Bersive was hanged in 1989 after returning from a refugee camp in Diyarbekir during the general amnesty. In March 1990, another general amnesty was declared for Kurds living abroad. In response to the call, in April and June of that year, some 2,900 Iraqi Kurds, Assyrians and Turkomans reportedly returned from Turkey to Iraq. Many were arrested and later disappeared.[54] Yet if the Assyrians were no threat, why then the need for removal and extermination?

One plausible explanation is this: these obstinate minorities had refused to be part of the national ranks, as defined by the Iraqi authorities. To aggravate their crime, they also refused to accept the regime's designation of their ethnicity. Not only did they want to be treated as Kurds, they acted as bad Arabs. Accordingly, they were considered traitors on two counts and punished accordingly.[55]

The above statement, though conceivably a rational behind the governmental policy as to the treatment of Assyrians in general, does not answer the question of what happened to the hundreds of families, including women and men, children and elders, who vanished, despite intense searches conducted by their kith and kin. Furthermore, if they had been treated as Kurds as stipulated by the amnesty then they (theoretically) would have been able to return as Kurds, and not told, 'You are Arabs and we decide what you should do.'[56] Simply understood, the Ba'th regime used the opportunity to further cleanse the region of one possibly irritating component. It is perhaps interesting to note that from an Assyrian perspective, Joseph Stalin's 1945 amnesty in the USSR, which released thousands of gulag prisoners, may have appeared more honourable than the amnesty issued by the Ba'th regime.[57]

Post-Anfal repercussions: end of a trend?

Ambitions for power and the violent policies driving them did not cease following the Anfal campaign – neither in the areas under Kurdish control above the 36th parallel nor in those under the central regime in post-1991 Iraq. As with the Iran–Iraq War, the Saddam Hussein-driven Iraq regime continued a policy of conscripting Assyrians and other dissidents, who were then forcibly stationed on the front lines of the invasion of Kuwait.[58] Such activities marked a continued trend of discrimination and of neglect for the lives of those who served as fodder for a dispassionate Iraqi regime.

The year 1991 marked the division of the country into three sections, following the implementation of the United Nations no-fly zones.[59] Though the details are beyond the scope of this research, it is of intrinsic importance to illustrate the clear historical continuity of repression following the Anfal campaign. That year saw the brutal deaths of more than 200,000 Shia Arabs in the south. The marsh peoples specifically were also devastated and lost perhaps 100,000 to direct action and more as a result of government policy, not to mention the attempted destruction of the marshes themselves, one of the most diverse ecosystems on the planet.[60] As a result of the outbreak of the Iraq-Kuwait War and the following Gulf War, an estimated 100,000

Assyrians fled to neighbouring countries during 1990 and 1991.[61] This meant not only persistent demographic shifting but also possible disappearances and deaths during the exodus.[62]

Various non-governmental and US government agencies reported on the Assyrians in the formative years after the first Gulf War:

> In 1994, the Special Rapporteur stated that in late 1993 the Iraq regime dismissed or expelled hundreds of Assyrian teachers and students from universities and public positions . . . Assyrians are an ethnic group as well as a Christian Community and [have] a distinct language (Syriac). Public instruction in Syriac, which was to have been allowed under a 1972 decree, has never been implemented. The Special Rapporteur reported continued discrimination against Assyrians throughout 1995. According to opposition reports, many Assyrian families were forced to leave Baghdad after they had fled to that city for safety following the regime's suppression of the northern uprising in 1991.[63]

Concurrently, during 1992 and 1993, all Assyrian teachers and professors whose families originated from modern Turkey (i.e. those whose families originated in Hakkâri) were forced to retire, and some families faced deportation to Istanbul.[64] Such discrimination strongly echoed the situation those Iranian-born, as mentioned earlier.

Such conditions also persisted in the north, in Iraqi Kurdistan where in some repects the KRG simply supplanted the Ba'th party. Kurds from Meristak and nearby villages confiscated land in the town of Dere after the Assyrians fled, following the Anfal operations.[65] In 1993, the KDP leadership reportedly allowed the illegal building of 500 houses on the agricultural lands east of Sarsang for Kurds from the Assyrian village of Chiya in the Arbil province.[66] In the following years, the continued displacement by the newly formed Kurdish regime became reminiscent of the Iraqi regime of previous years, from suborning local clergy to imposing discriminatory socioeconomic conditions. This is exemplified in the experience of an Assyrian man, Abu Ishtar, who was hospitalised after being beaten for opposing the KDP move to absorb the Nineveh Plain region of Mosul. 'The Ba'th, in a program of cultural genocide, made it illegal to be an Assyrian. As the recent beating and hospitalization of Abu Ishtar shows, very little has changed for these people from 1977 to 2006.'[67]

The continuing cultural destruction and demographic upheaval following the Anfal campaign is evident as well. It is estimated that the number of Assyrians dwindled from over one million to 300,000–400,000 between 1961 and 1991.[68] The 1991 Gulf War saw a dramatic increase in refugees and asylum seekers in neighbouring countries. Furthermore, the new state-building process in Iraqi Kurdistan created its share of enduring cultural complications such as land expropriation, especially in relation to villages forcibly abandoned in the previous three decades.

> There are outstanding issues of Assyrian villages and lands, which were vacated under Baghdad's forced repatriations during the 1970s and '80s . . . Those issues had not been resolved when the Kurdish authorities took over and they are a bone of contention between the two groups.[69]

Thus, reflective of the political climate in Iraqi Kurdistan, a new state- and nation-building experiment had commenced. In recent years Assyrians living in the larger cities of southern Iraq have been forced back to their former territories in the northern region under both the central government and the KRG, due to ethnic and more predominantly religious persecution. Thus, a reverse demographic shifting took place following 2003, a situation and topic in need of further study.

Notes

1. By distant extension another reminder of the callousness with which the regime dealt with dissidents became frighteningly apparent in November 1978 at the convening Eleventh World Congress of the Assyrian Universal Alliance (AUA) in Sydney. The five-member delegation attending from Iraq offered Iraqi sweets to the other delegates, nine of whom suffered adverse physical symptoms due to what Australian health officials later determined was poison. See 'City man is located after candy warning', *Assyrian Sentinel*, December 1978.

2. Mordechai Nisan, *Minorities in the Middle East*, 2nd ed. (Jefferson, NC: McFarland, 2002), 191.

3. For a partial list of 266 names see 'Iraqi-Assyrian POW's in Iran,' *Assyrian*

Sentinel, April 1983. Much of the research data and hundreds of photographs were collected from a mission to Iran by AUA representatives Atour Golani and Afram Rayis.

4. *Iraq: Continuous and Silent Ethnic Cleansing – Displaced Persons in Iraqi Kurdistan and Iraqi Refugees in Iran* (Paris: FIDH/International Alliance for Justice, 2003), 7.

5. Y.C. (Darbandoke-Baghdad), interview with author, 1 September 2006, Chicago. It has been suggested that the Assyrians accepted military positions with personal zeal since they wished to display their 'fighting prowess' for their country. This assumption was not corroborated by any of this study's interviews with members of the Assyrian community, but it is possible that it may have been true among a few individuals attempting to procure favour from the regime. See Anthony O'Mahony, 'The Chaldean Catholic Church: The Politics of Church–State Relations in Modern Iraq', *Heythrop Journal* 45.4 (2004), 443.

6. 'Iranian-Assyrians banished from Iraq', *Assyrian Sentinel*, June 1980.

7. More than 5,000 cases of such treatment had been reported: see *Assyrian Sentinel*, June 1980. Similar treatment was meted out to many Shiite families in Iraq as well.

8. Assyrians who had lost siblings during the war were especially disgusted with the regime and led them further into the opposition movement. See (Figure 40) concerning the ill treatment of an individual Assyrian which received attention at the international level, 'Dear Lawyer Helina', UNHCR file no. 3284 (Afram Rayis private archive).

9. See Security Major, Sulaymaniyah District Security Manager to all Administrative Departments, 'Assyrian National Front', September 1984, ADM Archives, Ba'th Secret Files and Correspondence, Iraq.

10. R.B. (Kirkuk), interview with author, 16 January 2008, Toronto.

11. 'Reign of terror sweeps Iraq's Christian churches', *Assyrian Sentinel*, February 1982.

12. Meghan Clyne, 'Kana's Iraq', National Review Online, 19 May 2004, http://www.nationalreview.com/articles/210717/kanas-iraq/meghan-clyne (accessed 16 July 2014).

13. P.D. (Dūre, Hayyis), interview with author, 26 July 2008, Toronto.

14. Security Major, Sulaymaniyah Security Directorate to all Security Divisions, 'Assyrian Democratic Movement', 14 October 1984, ADM Archives, Ba'th Secret Files and Correspondence, Iraq.

15. Ibid.

16. Security Major, Sulaymaniyah District Security Manager to all Administrative Departments, 'Assyrian National Front', September 1984, ADM Archives, Ba'th Secret Files and Correspondence, Iraq.

17. Ibid.

18. Security Major, Sulaymaniya District Security Manager to all Administrative Departments, 'Assyrian National Front', September 1984, ADM Archives, Ba'th Secret Files and Correspondence, Iraq.

19. The continuity of this thread, especially in a more basic bureaucratic fashion, became more widely available post-2010. See Michael Rubin, 'Kurdish officials need a code of conduct', Kurdistan Tribune, 28 December 2013, http://kurdistantribune.com/2013/kurdish-officials-need-code-of-conduct (accessed 16 July 2014).

20. Scholars have recently spoken of parallels between Kurdish disregard towards Assyrian travails, at least politically, and Armenian inattention to Greeks and Assyrians in reference to the devastation of the First World War. See 'Affirmation of the United States Record on the Armenian Genocide Resolution', House Resolution 252, 17 March 2009, http://www.gpo.gov/fdsys/pkg/BILLS-111hres252ih/pdf/BILLS-111hres252ih.pdf (accessed 16 July 2014). Armenian scholars and laity have often promoted parallels with the Holocaust, while omitting shared suffering during the First World War. See ibid., Findings, section 2(15). Into the more recent decades, the Assyrians of Turkey remain unrecognised as a minority and are sometimes referred to as 'Semitic Turks'. See Mehlika Aktok Kaşgarlı, *Mardin ve yöresi halkından Turko-Semitler* (Kayseri: Erciyes Üniversitesi, 1991), 7–9.

21. Personal notes and records of Afram Rayis and the AUA. Eshoo, 'The Fate of Assyrian Villages', 24 has a variant date and marks the death of Hami in 1983.

22. R.B. (Kirkuk), interview with author, 16 January 2008, Toronto.

23. David Korn, *Human Rights in Iraq* (New Haven, CT: Yale University Press, 1990), 58.

24. R.B. (Kirkuk), interview with author, 16 January 2008, Toronto. The ADM also found itself at odds with the KDP following the establishment of the no-fly zone in 1991. *Iraq: Human Rights Abuses in Iraqi Kurdistan since 1991*, Amnesty International, February 1995, 90–6, for the story of ADM member Francis Shabo, who was assassinated in May 1993 in Dohuk, according to AI most probably by KDP First Liq assassins, for his labour on the issue of Assyrian villages in the Bahdinan region.

25. The treatment of ADM members in Iraq mirrors that of the Syrian government's handling of members of the ADO from 1960 to 1990.

26. *Amnesty International Report 1989* (London: Amnesty International, 1989), 259.

27. *Iraq: Continuous and Silent Ethnic Cleansing*, 58.

28. Human Rights Watch, *Iraq's Crime of Genocide* (New Haven, CT: Yale University Press, 1995), 72, 327 n35. This is based on the research of Kurdish researcher Shorsh Resool.

29. Edmund A. Ghareeb, *Historical Dictionary of Iraq* (Lanham, MD: Scarecrow Press, 2004), 13.

30. Adapted from Human Rights Watch, *Iraq's Crime of Genocide*, 1–2.

31. Ibid., 1.

32. Qur'an 8:12, Electronic Text Center, University of Virginia Library, http://etext.virginia.edu/toc/modeng/public/HolKora.html (accessed 17 July 2014).

33. Human Rights Watch, *Iraq's Crime of Genocide*, 262–4.

34. Ibid., 267–8.

35. *Iraq: Continuous and Silent Ethnic Cleansing*, 47–57.

36. Kerim Yildiz, *The Kurds in Iraq: Past, Present and Future*, rev. ed. (London: Pluto Press, 2007), 65–6; Human Rights Watch, *Iraq's Crime of Genocide*, xv.

37. Personal correspondence, 3 July 2008. Most of the research by Resool was published in a study entitled *The Destruction of a Nation*, released by the PUK in 1990. See Joost Hiltermann, 'Case Study: The 1988 Anfal Campaign in Iraqi Kurdistan', Online Encyclopedia of Mass Violence, 3 February 2008, http://www.massviolence.org/Article?id_article=98&artpage=10 (accessed 17 July 2014). Resool had worked in the media relations department of the PUK in northern Iraq in the late 1980s, joining Human Rights Watch analysts who examined the Iraqi state documents in the early 1990s. Resool most recently served as chairman of the Goran Party in the Iraqi parliament.

38. General numbers given by human rights groups and scholarship concerning Kurds speak of more than 4,000 villages destroyed from 1963 until the Anfal, with more than 2,000 destroyed specifically in the 1980s. See Yildiz, *The Kurds in Iraq*, 65–6; Human Rights Watch, *Iraq's Crime of Genocide*, xv. Whether or not these estimates include Assyrian villages remains unclear.

39. This may be the reason for the lack of material on the Assyrians during the Anfal, as the majority of reports lump them among Kurdish statistics.

40. The villages are those reported by Assyrians as eliminated due to their historical and cultural significance. According to official Ba'th Party documents, between

25 April and 15 July 1987, Ali Hasan al-Majid reported the destruction of 1,441 prohibited villages and the forced expulsion of 26,399 families. While there is no reference pertaining to the ethnic makeup of these villages, these reports alongside Assyrian and Kurdish ones illustrate quite staggering devastation.

41. 'The Chaldoassyrian Community in Today's Iraq: Opportunities and Challenges', Human Rights Without Frontiers Mission Report, November 2003, http://www.aina.org/reports/hrwf.htm (accessed 17 July 2014), 4. In AI's annual reports from the 1980s, Assyrians are referred to briefly in the 1985 report, and glossed in the 1986 one, which briefly discusses opposition parties, but nowhere else.

42. Assyrian towns/villages referred to by outside sources are frequently incorrectly written, and some even inaccurately located. In this instance, Bakhitme is incorrectly referred to as 'Bakhtoma.'

43. Human Rights Watch, *Iraq's Crime of Genocide*, 211.

44. The US State Department made it clear that the US ambassador to Baghdad discussed such issues with Iraqi officials in 1988 and 1989. See Korn, *Human Rights in Iraq*, 107.

45. Human Rights Watch, *Iraq's Crime of Genocide*, 236.

46. A conference entitled 'The Genocide on Kurds in 1988' was held on Thursday 2 April 2009 in the European Parliament. The event was organised by Olle Schmidt, an MEP from the Alliance of Liberals and Democrats in Europe, and the Kurdish Gulan association from Sweden. The aim of the conference was to raise awareness about the Anfal. According to complaints raised at the meeting, when the Assyria Council of Europe, also in attendance, spoke up that they, too, were targeted and suffered during the Anfal, they were immediately verbally assailed and their comments curtailed. Email correspondence with Assyria Council of Europe, 3 April 2009.

47. For a preliminary list of 115 recorded Assyrians who were abducted or disappeared during the Anfal operations see *Iraq: Continuous and Silent Ethnic Cleansing*, 56–7.

48. Frederick A. Aprim, *Assyrians: From Bedr Khan to Saddam Hussein – Driving into Extinction the Last Aramaic Speakers* (F. A. Aprim, 2006), 235.

49. Confidential Telegram to all Security Units of the Region, No. 4618, Concerning the Whereabouts of Family Members of Executed Individual, 1 September 1988, ADM Archives, Secret Files and Correspondence, Iraq, also found in the North Iraq Data Set of the Iraq Memorial Foundation collection at the Hoover Institute.

50. Dina Rizk Khoury, *Iraq in Wartime: Soldiering, Martyrdom, and Remembrance* (New York: Cambridge University Press, 2013), 120.

51. M.T., Baghdad to President Saddam Hussein, Concerning Relatives Missing Following Returning under the Amnesty Decree, 16 February 1989, ADM Archives, Ba'th Secret Files and Correspondence; General, Presidential Palace Security, Baghdad to General Intelligence Army Service, Northern Region Intelligence Service, Concerning Relatives Missing Following Returning under the Amnesty Decree, 16 February 1989, ADM Archives, Ba'th Secret Files and Correspondence; Captain, Northern Region Intelligence Service to General, Presidential Palace Security, Baghdad, A Citizen's Request, undated (between 8 and 12 March 1989), ADM Archives, Ba'th Secret Files and Correspondence.

52. Conversation with Professor Amir Harrak, 10 February 2008.

53. *Amnesty International Report 1991* (London: Amnesty International, 1991), 123.

54. Ibid.

55. Human Rights Watch, *Iraq's Crime of Genocide*, 213.

56. Ibid., 211.

57. According to the sentiments of several interviewees.

58. Stephen Zunes, 'The US Obsession with Iraq and the Triumph of Militarism', in Tareq Y. Ismael and William W. Haddad (eds), *Iraq: The Human Cost of History* (London: Pluto Press, 2004), 192.

59. Recall the similar division of the region into three provinces under the Ottomans: Mosul, Baghdad and Basra.

60. *Iraq: Continuous and Silent Ethnic Cleansing*, 8.

61. Nisan, *Minorities in the Middle East*, 191.

62. *Iraq: Continuous and Silent Ethnic Cleansing*, 58.

63. Anthony H. Cordesman and Ahmed S. Hashim, *Iraq: Sanctions and Beyond* (Boulder, CO: Westview Press, 1997), 122, 118.

64. 'Assyrian Human Rights Report', Assyrian International News Agency, 1997, http://www.aina.org/reports/ahrr.htm (accessed 17 July 2014).

65. Assyrian Academic Society, 'Field Mission Iraq 2004'.

66. Ibid.

67. 'Northern Iraq Human Rights Field Mission', Iraq Sustainable Democracy Project, 2006, www.iraqdemocracyproject.org/pdf/Northern%20Iraq%20Human%20Rights%20Field%20Mission.pdf (accessed 16 July 2014)

68. Anthony O'Mahony cites a fall from one million to 150,000 between 1961 and 1995 (O'Mahony, 'The Chaldean Catholic Church', 438).

69. Hania Mufti of Human Rights Watch, quoted in Glen Chancy, 'Christians for Saddam?', Orthodoxy Today, 2003, http:// www.orthodoxytoday.org/ articles/ChancyIraq.php (accessed 17 July 2014). See also Fred Aprim, 'Kurdish official denies Assyrian, Turkomen land claims', Assyrian International News Agency, 3 November 2007, http://www.aina.org/guesteds/20071103124836. pdf (accessed 17 July 2014), for the more recent land issues.

7

State Formation, State-building and Contentious Pluralism

It may be that when we no longer know which way to go that we have come to our real journey. The mind that is not baffled is not employed. The impeded stream is the one that sings.

Wendell Berry

Evil does not arrive from outside of our civilization, from a separate realm we are tempted to call 'primitive'. Evil is generated by civilization itself.

Michael Mann

How and why violence is done is a critical question in the case of this research and while violence can have multiple meanings, it is the idea of injustice, or an unjust exercise of power, and how it may be remedied or at least guarded against that defines the *so what?* of this book. Violence varies in its forms both structurally and individually – physical, cultural, political, academic, spiritual etc. – and includes less-considered emphases such as harm to meaning, content or intent. Yet in every case it is initially a sense of adverse otherisation and secondly a value assessment which leads to violence in thought, word and deed. And while physical harm may be more discernible, injury to meaning harms the spirit or nature of things and occasionally holds a more sinister quality.

There are various determinants for why states and nations (whether ethnic or civic) engage in violent and non-violent homogenisation during the nation- and state-building process. Michael Mann cites nine motives used by perpetrators of violent crimes (including states), most of which can be extended to perpetrators of non-violent crimes: ideology, bigotry, violence for its own sake, fear, careerism, materialism, discipline, comradeship and bureaucracy.[1] Since people are the true power behind the state, individual and professional reasons for homogenisation often overlap through social influence, creating perpetrator campaigns of both violent and non-violent justification often spearheaded by nationalist elites. In many cases, when the victim becomes involved in the nationalist thrust for recognition, they apply similar motives for denying other victims, thus continuing the hierarchy of marginalisation and suffering.

Such homogenisation is also a result of the age of democracy since the notion of rule by the majority began to entwine the *demos*, 'all the ordinary people', with the dominant *ethnos* or ethnic group.[2] As Iraq became Arab (as it arguably had been since the foundation of the Iraqi state) the Assyrian ethnos could not compete with the dominant ethnos turned demos. On the other hand, the Kurds were able to contend against this trend simply by virtue of their numerical strength or critical mass.

Iraq was formed in a crucible of competing colonial powers and rising ethno-nationalist sentiments. In the absence of an accurate account (which in reality does not exist), 'the fragments imagine the nation', as Sami Zubaida put it. In this case, however, the nation of Iraq, and studies concerning it, unimagined one of its fragments – the Assyrians. It has been argued that they have remained absent within academic and political literature due in large part to internal matters, further contributing to subjugation, in some cases self-subjugation. Yet, with the substantiation presented in this study, the lacuna of critical attention towards this group can be explained by a three-part structure. The first element is the traditional hostility created by ultra-nationalism in the state- and nation-building process: 'The necessity of using force in the establishment of unity in a national community, and the inevitable selfish exploitation of the instruments of coercion by the groups who wield them, adds to the selfishness of nations.'[3] The second element is the mendacity of the perpetrators and benefactors of the events that caused the ethno-cultural, social and political ruination of this people. This deception is exhibited by attempts to minimise the importance of the events by adjusting the details with denialist political argot in order to protect interests in the region. The final element is the silence surrounding or neglect of events in which the Assyrians played a major role, such as the 1961 armed autonomist

Table 12 Instances of internal violence against Iraqis by state, political party or military, 1933–91[4]

Event	Target	Year
Simele massacres	Assyrians	1933
Farhud	Jews	1941
Executions	Communists	1949, 1959, 1963, 1966, 1978
Armed autonomist movement	Kurds, Assyrians, Communists	1961–3
Mass expulsion	Shiite Arabs	1969–71
Armed autonomist movement (cont.)	Kurds, Assyrians	1974–5
Border clearings	Assyrians, Kurds	1977–8
Anfal prelude	Assyrians, Kurds, Yezidis	1987
Anfal	Assyrians, Kurds, Yezidis	1988
Gassing of Halabja	Kurds	1988
Massacre following intifada	Shiite Arabs	1991

movement, the border clearings of the 1970s, and the Anfal period of the late 1980s (See Table 12). This stems from the acceptance or apathy towards the mendacity as espoused by past literature (both academic and political)[5] and by more recent works.

Situating the Assyrian Experience

When understood, the Assyrian case in Iraq can also be employed to comprehend the similar struggles of the Iraqi Kurds (prior to 1991), Jews (prior to 1948), Shiites (prior to 2003), Turkomans, Mandeans, Yezidis and others. The dismissal or neglect of events in Kurdish history and the dismissal by the international community of the Soviet–Mongolian accusation of genocide by the Iraqis against the Kurds plays a similar role to the neglect of Simele with one major exception – today the Anfal is generally treated as a Kurdish genocide where Simele is, at best, infrequently memorialised, and in reality, by no one other than the Assyrians themselves.[6] Furthermore, had it not been in the best geopolitical interests of Western powers to demonise Iraq in 1991, Halabja too would barely be a footnote in history.[7]

Considering the roles performed by the Assyrians since the start of the twentieth century, the question remains: why have they been relatively neglected by most studies concerning these transformative periods of Iraq's history? Additionally, what role does acquiescence play? There are several hypotheses for this silence, including one which purports that the oversight of the Assyrian case is tied to British imperial guilt following Britain's negligence in ensuring minority protection provisions after its withdrawal from Iraq. The source of this British guilt would be the inaction concerning violence at Simele in particular, barely two decades after the onslaught against Christians in eastern Anatolia.[8] Was the Assyrian tragedy simply the outcome of circumstance? Had the Assyrians become collateral damage in the programme of a pro-British, independent Iraq whose unified national makeup had to necessarily absorb, deny, eliminate or unimagine this relatively small minority in order to allow the larger ethnic and religious groups to construct a functioning and formidable nation-state?[9]

The disintegration and loss of the spirit of the Assyrian people has complemented the scarcity of information concerning their trials within Iraq. This process, beginning with the First World War, has subdued the Assyrians and ensured their relative absence in documenting the destruction of their people and culture, especially evident in Western scholarship.[10] This trend, whether malevolent or innocent, ensured that future generations would find it difficult to substantiate their experiences and those transmitted by their elders. Thus, denial would have a traumatic effect on the Assyrian psyche.

This continues to affect them, since as a numerical and political minority they lack the power to impel scholars to document their trials. In instances where Assyrians themselves have documented atrocities, they are usually disregarded (for example, Yusuf Malek's *The British Betrayal of the Assyrians*), proving their undervalued position in scholarship. Furthermore, there is also the tendency of using one's own sufferings as justification for reciprocity.[11] While this trend has become more apparent in recent decades, the unfortunate side-effect to such crimes against humanity (perhaps 'crimes against life' would be better here) as a component in nation- and state-building is the justification inevitability. This again stems from the basis of 'might makes right' inherent in the commodification and commoditisation of peoples.

Agency, Failed Strategies and Transdenominationalism

There are numerous reasons for the Assyrians' failure to elicit a positive political response for their demands at Versailles in 1919 (where arguably, they had the greatest chance for success), as well as in subsequent treaties and conferences. They were plagued by internal disputes as much as by simple dismissal by larger authorities, as religious and tribal adherence would add to distrust and outright enmity. The Chaldean Assyrians, such as General Petros Elia and Malik Kambar Warda of Jilu, were linked to France and Rome; the Nestorian Assyrians, led by Patriarch Mar Eshai Shimun, his aunt Surma and tribal chiefs, among them Malik Ismael of Upper Tiyari, were linked closely to the British Crown, the Archbishop of Canterbury, and the Church of England; the Jacobite Assyrians, from Abraham K. Yoosuf to Archbishop Barsoum, occupied a more nebulous position; and the Protestants, from Joel Werda to Malik Khoshaba of Lower Tiyari, were linked to the American missions.[12] While some of the delegations' claims and desires seemed far-fetched and 'totally out of touch with the true state of affairs', the element of inclusivity with seemingly strong historical and geographical veracity may be argued as progressive.[13] For instance the inclusion of Islamised Assyrians and the entreaty for territory that was shared by said groups was arguably not only inter- or trans-ecclesiastical, which the delegates themselves were, but inter- or trans-denominational in the sense of inter or trans-religious as well.[14] Additionally, and very much to the contrary of the conflicts mentioned above, General Petros Elia (Catholic) and General David Shimun (Nestorian/Church of the East), brother of Patriarch Benyamin, led the two flanks of the Assyrian Volunteers in the First World War; Elia and Malik Khoshaba (Protestant) came to the aid of the besieged Urmia plainsmen in February 1918; Kambar Warda (Catholic) was part of the Patriarchal faction that supported Mar Eshai Shimun (Nestorian/Church of the East) in 1933, despite his earlier apprehension concerning Surma in 1919 when Eshai had just become Patriarch;[15] and finally Archbishop Barsoum (Jacobite) spoke for and proposed an Assyrian homeland in 1920, adding his support to that of almost the entire Harput diaspora community of Massachusetts (Jacobites) for Mar Eshai Shimun raising funds, to be sent to the 'patriotic leader for a new Assyria' despite the terror that gripped the

Assyrian communities following the Simele massacres in 1933. These are all evidence of and testament to the importance of situationalism in the complex and indeed perplexing decades from the advent of the First World War through the 1930s.[16]

Yet the Assyrian quandary was not without its external advocates. Raphael Lemkin's usage of the terms 'crimes of barbarity' and 'crimes of vandalism' as put forth in 1933 following the Simele massacres (and influenced by the devastation during the First World War) inspired widespread work within the international arena. For Lemkin such violence denoted a calculated effort, involving

> different actions aiming at the destruction of essential foundations of the life of national groups, with the aim of annihilating the groups themselves. The objectives of such a plan would be disintegration of the political and social institutions, of culture, language, national feelings, religion, and the economic existence of such groups, and the destruction of the personal security, liberty, health, dignity, and even the lives of the individuals belonging to such groups. Genocide is directed against the national group as an entity, and the actions involved are directed against individuals, not in their individual capacity, but as members of the national group.[17]

This definition would come to be used in its international form in the Convention on the Prevention and Punishment of the Crime of Genocide (1948). Article 2 of the convention defines genocide as

> any of the following acts committed with intent to destroy, in whole or in part, a national, ethnical, racial or religious group:
>
> (a) Killing members of the group;
> (b) Causing serious bodily or mental harm to members of the group;
> (c) Deliberately inflicting on the group conditions of life calculated to bring about its physical destruction in whole or in part;
> (d) Imposing measures intended to prevent births within the group;
> (e) Forcibly transferring children of the group to another group.[18]

Though there is a lack of consensus surrounding the convention's definition, particularly regarding its scope, it has been supplemented by various international mechanisms in the form of international treaty and customary law, which will be referred to in the following passages.

Since its early introduction by Lemkin, the definition and scope of genocide has been deeply rooted within the confines of the state as the key actor and facilitator of genocidal campaigns and other related crimes against humanity. This is evidenced by the emphasis placed on the state as the primary agent in the varying definitions found in major works on the subject, namely those of Helen Fein, Donald Horowitz, Vahakn Dadrian and Jack Porter.[19] A focus on the nation-building processes employed during the emergence of newly formed states has been a prevalent theme within existing discourse, as the state has been the focal point of analysis. For Eric Weitz, the state is at the core of such violent marginalisation, and further its distinguishing element becomes the pervasiveness of calculated, state-induced policies perpetuated by nationalist elites, as seen during the waning of the Ottoman Empire and the emergence of the Young Turks, Nazi Germany, the Khmer Rouge in Cambodia and the former Yugoslavia, and the current Israeli treatment of Palestinians. A point of differentiation from previous pogroms and massacres that characterises Weitz's theory in the twentieth century has been the ability and capacity of the state to systematically devise and execute policies on an unprecedented scale, to 'mobilize and unleash their bureaucrats, armies, and loyal citizenry to carry out extreme acts of violence, which may appear random at the moment they occur'.[20] Thus, the state, with its capacity to mobilise and utilise state resources, becomes the central actor and agency that propagates and implements genocide within its structures and institutions, often mobilising civilians and labelling perceived targets and threats. Such an atmosphere sets the stage whereby the state, operating as the ultimate sovereign, categorises perceived undesirables along social and racial lines, resulting in the elimination of state laws protecting the weak in the name of progress and evolution.[21]

Similarly, Arjun Appadurai claims that 'the idea of a "national ethnos"' is one of the most dangerous notions of, and indeed an innate element in, the ideology of the modern nation-state. A 'national ethnos' feeds the notion that the sovereignty of the state is built upon some form of ethnic genius.[22] The undesirable and the weak can be quickly incorporated into the vernacular of justification and legitimisation of absolutist state polices that advocate purging and eliminating groups perceived as enemies during the nation-building process, or at times of upheaval in already established states. The events of the various violent campaigns in Iraq are a product of both the state-building process and the development of a national ethnos.

Simele Revisited

> They are to the majority of 'Iraqis an alien race with an alien religion, bound to 'Iraq by no strong ties of patriotism or loyalty and having originally no claim to the special consideration of the 'Iraqi Government.[23]
>
> George Antonius

The termination of the British mandate in Iraq in 1932 and the creation of Iraq as a sovereign territory required the newly formed government to legitimise its claim by asserting its sovereignty. Simele, thus, came to symbolise the tenacious power and valour of the young Iraqi military to eliminate what they perceived to be the last vestiges of European power.[24] Indeed it epitomised the requisite for social discipline steeped in an Arab nationalism generated by Sāṭiʿ al-Ḥuṣrī, who held 'that general military service is one of the most important means of teaching social education and increasing a spirit of unity and discipline in the individuals of the nation'.[25] The country had perceived a foreign martial threat in the Assyrians and this military action against them stirred a largely incoherent and fragmented Iraqi populace behind an instrument of homogeneity and authority. Al-Ḥuṣrī's yearning was realised: the military had done a service by massacring the Assyrians, and their rise to supremacy as a tool for political control was recognised for future coups, as is patently obvious in Iraq's history.

Rebellions by the Kurds in the north from 1930 to 1932 and the Shia majority in the south in 1920 and again in 1935 created an unstable political environment, thus minimising the sphere of tolerance for dissidents and minorities. For Michael Mann, such an environment provides the justification for the state, as a factionalised, radicalised and unstable geopolitical entity, to perpetuate 'murderous cleansing . . . calling for tougher treatment of perceived ethnic enemies'.[26] The unbridled targeting of Assyrians in 1933 framed a clear linear development that would affect other minorities in the newly created state. The overlooking of exterminatory military and governmental tactics again created a rift in the understanding of the armed autonomist movement, border clearings and Anfal campaign in the decades that followed. The use of the Iraqi military in the operations of the 1960s and 1970s has been dismissed by some scholars, who argue that the true destruction was the fault of the targeted, rather than shifting the focus and the blame to the main culprit, the Iraqi state/military and its propaganda apparatus.[27] This dismissal of the state's violent actions towards its citizens as perceived enemies of the state is a common justification for perpetrators and deniers of mass violence.[28]

The systematic massacre of the male population of Simele village on 11 August 1933 ensured the silence of this already distraught native community.[29] The Assyrians and in fact the very idea of *Assyrian* was portrayed as the equivalent of British marionettes with teeth; tools which could be used to destroy the new and independent Iraqi state which the British had time and again opposed. Other Iraqis were incited by a large propaganda campaign, which circulated reports that armed Assyrians returning from Syria had mutilated the bodies of Iraqi soldiers, despite contrary reports that the French had disarmed the Assyrians. The accusations of them mutilating bodies of fallen soldiers and the call by the Ikha al-Watani (National Brotherhood) party in Mosul to eliminate all foreign elements are part and parcel of the government's marketing and its policies of violent authoritarianism and totalitarianism.

The initial destruction and the killing of more than 300 unarmed individuals, the looting and razing of more than 100 villages and the eventual death toll of up to 6,000 was one of the two sets of events within the lifetime of a young Raphael Lemkin to influence his presentation to the League of Nations in 1933 in Madrid, arguing that such events be considered a crime according to international law.[30] Due to the volatile nature of his argument (at least relating to possible repercussions levelled at more powerful nations), Lemkin was forced by the Polish Foreign Minister to resign from his post as public prosecutor of the district court of Warsaw not long after, in 1934. Thus, it is unambiguous that the international community was still unable or unwilling to inquire into such acts of malice, though these acts would become the foundation for the Genocide Convention, which was later adopted by the newly established United Nations in 1948.

> Even in the highest circles there was talk of the 'rid me of this turbulent priest' order. 'Let all the Assyrian men be killed,' they cried, 'but spare the women and children as the eyes of the world are on us. Let the Arabs and Kurds be raised against the Assyrians. Let trouble be stirred up in Syria against the treacherous French.'[31]

Regardless of whether or not the highest circles issued a final decree in such bold words (most bodies committing exterminatory acts rarely leave a concrete paper trail), the actions taken by the Iraqi army and the experience of Assyrian civilians amount to the same. The data suggests these were not simply words, but a premeditated plan created by the government and army against Assyrians of the region. Whether the government feared the highly trained and armed levies as a political threat, the data indicates certain elements of their identity were ameliorated during the period. The Assyrians were targeted – otherised as both a Christian religious minority (with ties to Western Christianity) and for being ethnic Assyrians. Elias Haroon Bazi's eyewitness observation, 'either become Muslim or we will kill you', is a vivid reminder of the anti-Christian religious persecution, reverberating with an ethnic anti-Assyrian sentiment, where 'it was enough for them to be Assyrians to be shot' and 'it was evident by now that the Army Command was quite certain in its own mind [of] its decision to wipe out the Assyrians'.[32] In fact it was this anti-Assyrian sentiment that caused the various ecclesiastical Christian sects to begin (forcibly and of their own volition) to detach themselves from their ethnic identity (since they were also in the process of being persecuted for their religious beliefs) and as an alternative, to identify solely with their religious denominations to avoid retribution.[33]

The effect of the Simele massacre and subsequent community fragmentation[34]

If, as a British diplomat, Gerald de Gaury stated that 'it was enough for them to be Assyrians to be shot', what chance of survival did the community have at its disposal?[35] Such a statement by de Gaury, a major champion of the Arabs and friend to the Saud family, carries a great deal of weight as he was not lightly dismissing the maltreatment of the Assyrians. Yet it elucidates the problem: Assyrians were being slain simply for being Assyrian. The answer became palpably uncomplicated: stop being Assyrian – which is precisely what many did. This identity denial was made more pronounced by intra-religious enmity, which had been fostered by a longstanding Catholic hostility towards the Church of the East for its 'Nestorian heresy', one of the many undying and ancient Christian enmities, and vice versa.[36]

Following the initial massacre, and perhaps under pressure from the Iraqi regime, two Chaldean clerics (Mar Yousef VI Emmanuel II Thomas of the Chaldean Church and Priest Wadisho of Alqosh) and one Syrian Orthodox cleric (Athanasius Thoma Kassir, Bishop of Mosul) sent letters of support to the Iraqi regime, as reported by *al-Ikha al-Watani* in Baghdad on 20 August 1933. The American resident minister, Paul Knabenshue, related to the US Secretary of State that 'the exaction of false testimonials from the various Christian dignitaries, virtually at the point of the pistol, is a sad testimonial to the integrity of the Iraq government'.[37] Whether or not this duress was genuine, the end result was as authoritative as it was flagrant. 'Assyrian' as an identity and culture became increasingly identified with the Nestorians alone (mostly due to the political involvement of Mar Eshai Shimun) and more so as 'those Nestorian foreigners' brought into Iraq by the British rather than the descendants of the ancient Assyrians whose history successive regimes in Iraq (and Syria as well) would appropriate as part of a larger but vague Arab *ummah* (nation) or *sha'b* (people).

The Chaldean Church had been part of the Nestorian Church, or Church of the East, until 1552/3. Most of its adherents in Iraq were descended from people who had been converted in the 1800s by Dominicans. Now it began in earnest to distance itself from the Nestorians, who were now seen as the 'uncouth Assyrians' as British parlance had sometimes referred to the tribal society of the Hakkâri mountaineers. During this period, many members of the Chaldean Church began to be identified and to identify themselves solely by their religious community, and later as Iraqis, Iraqi Christians, or Arab Christians, rather than part of a larger Assyrian community. This is also true of the Syrian Orthodox Church, which, prior to the events, considered itself part and parcel of a transnational and trans-ecclesiastical Assyrian heritage.[38] The Chaldean Church has generally had continuous positive relations with successive governments of Iraq, in part because its members were predominantly found in relative proximity to large, Arab-dominated cities. Migration from rural northern villages to large cities in the central and southern regions was part of an attempt by the Assyrians 'to demonstrate their desire of integration into the country and to adopt its agenda'.[39] Such intentions (whether sincere or otherwise) aided the Chaldean Church community to survive and at times prosper, economically, socially and politically, within greater Iraqi Arab society, with former vice president Tareq 'Aziz as a example.

Furthermore, following the transfer of the patriarchal see of the Syrian Orthodox Church to Homs, Syria, the Jacobite clergy also became influenced by a rising tide of Syrian nationalism and Arabisation.[40] The events at Simele had repercussions for Syria, since some 1,350 armed Assyrians had crossed the border and settled in the Khabur basin. Thus, the desire to seem distinct from its militant brethren was an additional reason for the Syrian Orthodox Church to further distance itself from its former identification as Assyrian. In fact it was the former Bishop Severius who initiated the change in identity. He became Patriarch Ignatius Afram Barsoum of the Jacobites in 1932, the year the patriarchal residence was moved to Syria from Deir Za'afaran in Mardin, Turkey. Beginning first in 1933, following the tragedy of Simele, Barsoum and the church adopted an increasingly anti-Assyrian stance as they distanced themselves from anything Assyrian-related. By the early 1960s, all the Jacobite churches in the United States, previously bearing the official name 'Assyrian Apostolic Church of Antioch', had changed their names to 'Syrian Orthodox Church of Antioch', with the exception of Paramus, New Jersey and Worcester, Massachusetts.[41] The fallout was immense and included excommunications such as that of Farid Elias Nuzha, born in Hamah, Syria in 1895. Nuzha, then living in Buenos Aires, was the head of Centro Afremico Asirio and the publisher of *al-al-Jam'iah as-Siryaniyah* (*Asociación Asiria*). He demonstrated his disgust in an answer to a letter from a Jacobite living in Iraq which asked him to modify or erase the Spanish name of the magazine (*Asiria*) as it was reflective of a different people (i.e. the Assyrians of Hakkâri) and further as it did not please the government of Iraq. Nuzha responded by highlighting the problem in equating the Assyrian identity solely with Nestorians rather than more properly to Jacobites and Chaldeans as well.[42] This concern or adaptation is not evident prior to 1933, illustrating the blatant sectarianisation of the Assyrians, particularly in post-Simele Iraq.

On a broader scale, the official Iraqi yearbook of 1936 mentioned four ethnic groups in Iraq: Arabs, Kurds, Turkomans and Persians, reflecting (1) the tendencies of states to centralise and view exclusively numerically and/or politically significant constituencies, and (2) a methodical political indifference – a form of subtle assimilation, exacerbated by (3) actions on the part of the churches, perhaps initially a method of self-preservation, that marked the beginning of an unforeseen loss or unimagining of Assyrian identity.[43] Thus the Assyrians played an active role in the slow degradation of their own culture, becoming in some cases their own worst enemy. Additionally, the political environment coupled with a general fear of the Iraqi government exacerbated the ecclesiastical animosities. The propensity for such tensions between the various churches speaks to a strong tie between ecclesiastic organisations and larger cultural ones, especially in the Middle Eastern/Islamic world context. State and non-state actors, including individual Assyrians vying for power or indoctrinated by an appealing ideology, exploited this tension to the detriment of the development of an integrated and recognised Assyrian identity. While I concur that there are various layers to identity, or to use the trendy term hybridised identities, there are objective elements which create the subjective identity and those objective elements are in many cases imposed by subjective notions of reality and so forth. The problem of assigning culpability is one of the adage of contradiction: both choice (subjective) and design (objective) exist simultaneously.[44]

As discussed above in great detail, 1933 was a watershed for the contemporary sectarianisation of the Assyrians by ecclesiastical adherence. Yet the Assyrian ethno-cultural identity has retained a trans-ecclesiastical or trans-denominational nature; many individuals and organisations from among the non-Nestorian/Church of the East (and, more to the point, the non-Mar Shimun-related) denominations continued to provide succour for their kin and remember the attacks on their community while the official hierarchies of the Chaldean and Jacobite churches began the process of slow disassociation. Immediately following the tragedy, Simele was remembered and recounted by Assyrians around the world. Why is apparent, but how and by whom less so.

Despite the growing anti-Assyrianism of the Chaldean and Jacobite churches and their clergy, also strongly linked with growing Arab nationalism as well as country-specific nationalisms through the years, some lay and clergy individuals in those churches retained ethno-cultural solidarity with their brethren.[45] The composer Gabriel Asaad (1907–97), born in Qamishli, Syria, composed the song 'Sohdē d-Oṯur' ('Martyrs of Assyria') in 1933 about the victims of Simele after hearing the news while he was in Tabariya, Palestine. Further confirmation of this is offered through the poetry of Paulos Bedari, a Chaldean priest living in north Iraq who did not share the sentiments of his hierarchy. Bedari wrote a poem titled *Ūlītā l-gunkhā d-Simelē* ('Lamentation on the Simele Massacre') not long after the event had occurred. The first section illustrates matters of fraternity and identity:[46]

Bkhī ya gani b-khasha w-dim'é twira:	Weep, o my soul, in sorrow and tears and in shattered heart,
'al parpasta d-umtan khqirta mart iqara.	About the splintering of our noble nation so honourable.
	The heavens and earth weep about a most bitter massacre:
Shmaya w-ar'a bkho 'al gunkhā chim marīra:	Assyria, mother of lions and all the mighty, has fallen.
Npīlah Ātur yimma d-aryé w-d-kul gabbara.	

Bedari's usage of 'Assyria' and reference to community or nation possessively alludes to two axioms: that there continued to be individuals within the church structure who did not adhere to a growing self-segregation from the Assyrian identity, at least early on; and possibly that the public comments made by Chaldean and Jacobite church leaders early in this chapter may have reflected a mask of seeming; not being. Yet the consequences reaped for such an action would shake the foundation of the Assyrian community and the narratives generated around it would create a newly illusory record.

Though the religious and ethnic basis for external targeting is strongly apparent, it was fear and the desire for self-preservation in a hostile environment, alongside more selfish aspirations, that motivated internal divisions:

> You have seen what happened to the Assyrians just as soon as they ceased to be of use to the British. You read how the English ministers stood up in their Mejliss at Westminster and disowned any claims made by their fellow Christians, pleading for their wives and children to be safe from rape and slaughter.[47]

Years later, with fear remaining a motivating factor, many Assyrians became embedded in the Arab mainstream (Kurdish, Persian and Turkish, as well), and being Assyrian became as foreign to them as being Arab had been to their parents and grandparents. This became a reality for a variety of reasons and can be illuminated by another look at the terms *emic* (a native designation) and *etic* (non-native designation) in identity formation and propagation. Despite the simplified definition above, one must consider the fact that what academics including historians and anthropologists view as *emic* terms today are in fact created by *etic* power structures and later adopted by the community (making vigilance against anachronism a must). This issue is related to the understanding expressed by political scientist Alexander Wendt that identity is defined by both the self and the other and is in fact propagated or sustained within community structures, the most powerful of those structures being the state.[48] Thus once the Assyrian community had become truly sectarianised within the infrastructure and under the influence of the Iraqi state apparatus, new counter-Assyrian identities would form and be transmitted to secondary and tertiary generations. The mask would become the face of a new identity:

> There's a fundamental connection between *seeming* and *being* ... We understand how dangerous a mask can be. We all become what we pretend to be ... The truth is deeper than that. It's like everyone tells a story about themselves inside their head. Always. All the time. That story makes you what you are. We build ourselves out of that story.[49]

Part of the Assyrian experience in Iraq is an intertwining of distinct campaigns aimed at accomplishing a similar goal: the assimilation by acculturation and indoctrination or the destruction of a distinct community, a benefit to the indivisibility of the state. The state is portrayed as the totality and the Assyrians as other: trespassers and aggressors.

As for the physical massacres, Iraqi governmental denial and redistribution of the blame on the Assyrians is of note.[50] The argument of wartime chaos could feasibly make finding a true motivation tricky. Yet according to international law, communities are also protected from such situations: 'Individual or mass forcible transfers, as well as deportations of protected persons from occupied territory to the territory of the Occupying Power or to that of any other country, occupied or not, are prohibited, regardless of their motive.'[51] Deportation during armed conflict is classified as a crime against humanity in light of the ethnic cleansing campaigns implemented in former Yugoslavia.[52]

In Drazen Petrovic's study on the methodology concerning ethnic cleansing, he defines the act simply as policies and practices aimed at achieving security through displacement of an ethnic group from a particular territory which may or may not include violence.[53] Additionally, Ilan Pappé provides a pertinent paradigm of ethnic cleansing when analysing the impact of Zionism on the resettlement of Palestine by Jewish settlers. For Pappé, the ethnic cleansing of Palestine was not a cause and effect of war, but rather a fundamental element of Jewish resettlement – which was ingrained in the origins of Zionism as the ideological cause for the ethnic cleansing that took place prior to the creation of the state of Israel in 1948.[54]

The atrocities of Simele certainly were not enacted under a war paradigm, as 'there was no war in sight in 1933 when the Assyrians were being martyred because Britain feared for her oil in Mosul'.[55] The data here would support Pappé's paradigm of ethnic cleansing, since in 1933 there was no justification of wartime acts, no threat to the Iraqi state. To speak more of issues concerning intentionality we return to the question of the regime's blueprint both pre- and post-massacre:

> Here and there in the mountains they came up with fugitive Assyrians. And every Assyrian they caught they shot out of hand. Clearly by now the Army had decided that the Assyrians, as far as possible, were to be exterminated. No pretence was made that these operations had any purely military objective, for the Army Intelligence officers did not even take the trouble to cross-question the captured Assyrians, who were simply shot as they were rounded up . . . it was evident by now that the Army Command was quite certain in its own mind that, in its decision to wipe out the Assyrians, it would . . . be backed not only by Arab public opinion, but by the Baghdad Government.[56]

Colonel Stafford's narrative of events reveals that on 9 August, the Iraqi Air Force bombed the Kurdish village of Ziwa, killing a woman under the false pretence that Assyrians had attacked the village. After further investigation, the Kurds stated that they had never seen an Assyrian in the village. Evidently the possibility of eliminating Assyrians wherever they might be stirred the

Iraqi military into a lethal frenzy, as they never substantiated the reports prior to attacking the village. Also, as the army had planned to continue the massacres with Alqosh and other non-Nestorian villages (as many in the region of Alqosh were predominantly Chaldean), the entire event clearly spoke of a frenzy of pan-Assyrian paranoia and desired state-sponsored destruction of the entire community, of which, despite attempts at dissection, the Chaldeans, or at the very least Alqosh, were a part.[57]

An American missionary in Dohuk, Roger Cumberland, in a letter to Paul Knabenshue, stated that Simele ushered in a variety of consequences:

> One is that the reputation of the Assyrian warrior has vanished. Second, the tribes have seen with their own eyes that the British armed forces, whether land or air, took no part in the recent operations. Third, old animosities between Muslims and Christians have been aroused and new ones created in recent months. Fourth (of local significance in the Dohuk district only, unless it should spread), two of the Kurdish tribes have quarrelled over spoil, and it would take only a small incident to set them upon each other. Fifth (a seemingly absurd thing, but nevertheless significant), there is a shortage of eligible Kurdish girls at present; a good bride costs about 300 dollars; and whether the young Kurds would consciously start out to get brides by conquest or not, the situation does make them restless. Sixth, the Semeil massacre and similar events have gone far to destroy the confidence of the Assyrians and other minority groups, especially Christians, in the good faith of the Government. Seventh, there seems not to be the personal integrity in the government services to form a stable administration. To be sure, we as Americans are not in a position to throw stones; but the objective fact remains that corruption is the rule rather than the exception in this country, and that it is not condemned by any body of public opinion that is strong enough to check it.[58]

Cumberland's first four points speak of what could be termed a gendercidal campaign as Assyrian men of fighting age, the focus of the army, were simply eliminated wherever they were found.[59]

> The soldiers then remained in the village, remaining about to find any male person and shoot him down. About evening they entered the places (i.e.,

the fort and other houses where the women and children had gathered together). Among the women and children there were nearly about hundred men and grown-up boys, who, being without arms to save themselves, had put on women's clothes. They were all discovered by the soldiers and police (as every woman and other person in female dress was examined by the soldiers and the police) and they were all killed. I saw the police-sergeant also dashing the priest's two children of 4 and 6 years of age against the wall because they were clinging to their father and screaming after him as he was being taken away. Qasha Ishmail was taken outside, where he joined another priest, Qasha Irsanis [Arsanis], whom the police had found in another house. They were both murdered just below the fort in front of a house known as of Khishaba [Khoshaba]. Their beards were cut off and their hair was dashed in their mouths.[60]

Regarding Cumberland's fifth point, 'whether the young Kurds would consciously start out to get brides by conquest or not, the situation does make them restless': if all the men in the Simele region were eliminated and, further, if the women and children that remained feared for their safety without the men, then they would be forced either to marry Kurds (effectively making them Kurds themselves) especially amid a shortage of Kurdish girls of marriageable age, or to leave the country since, as expressed in Cumberland's points six and seven, the 'events have gone far to destroy the confidence of the Assyrians and other minority groups, especially Christians, in the good faith of the Government . . . there seems not to be the personal integrity in the government services to form a stable administration'. The Assyrians had no faith left in the British and far less in the Iraqi government.[61]

Analogous international cases recognised

The internationally unrecognised massacres of Simele echo the internationally recognised killing, during the Bosnian War, of more than 8,000 Bosnian Muslims, mainly men and boys, in and around the town of Srebrenica in Bosnia and Herzegovina, by units of the Army of Republika Srpska under the command of General Ratko Mladić. The event became known as the Srebrenica genocide in July 1995. The massacre was described by the secretary general of the United Nations as the worst crime on European soil since the Second World War. An excerpt from the 2004 trial reads as follows:

> I consider that the alleged requirement for proof of intent to destroy the group physically or biologically was met by the disastrous consequences for the family structures on which the Srebrenica part of the Bosnian Muslim group was based. The Trial Chamber was correct in finding that the Bosnian Serb forces knew that their activities 'would inevitably result in the *physical disappearance* of the Bosnian Muslim population at Srebrenica'.[62]

As for the Assyrians, the official notes of Raphael Lemkin spoke of the atrocities in detail, laying blame on the Iraq army for having carried out genocidal acts. Further, the premeditated nature of the event was illustrated by the fact that ten Arab families, living alongside the 100 Assyrians in Simele, were told to leave prior to the massacre. In addition, the Assyrians were disarmed and surrounding Kurdish tribesmen were given more than a thousand rifles by the army to instil fear in those wishing to flee, effectively keeping them in the village, increasing the terror factor and guaranteeing a high death toll.[63]

Through corroborating sources, the data validates Iraq attempted to solidify its homogeneity as a nation through the purging of those Assyrians at Simele and the surrounding districts, epitomising the complexity of a situation in which the envisaged state-building could only progress via 'nation-destroying' of the Assyrians.[64] Once the last vestiges of their physical power in the form of the levies was stemmed, more subtle forms of homogenisation, such as acculturation and assimilation, could be used in place of physical obliteration: a proverbial 'survival of the fittest' paradigm as enacted by state policies where the marginal group must be either eliminated or absorbed by the dominant group for the sake of progress. Forced homogeneity in state- and nation-building would continue with the subsequent maltreatment of minorities (in a variety of manifestations) throughout Iraq's tumultuous history.[65]

Development and Consequences of Urbanisation and Arabisation

> Nebuchadnezzar stirs in me everything relating to pre-Islamic ancient history. And what is most important to me about Nebuchadnezzar is the link between the Arabs' abilities and the liberation of Palestine. Nebuchadnezzar

was, after all, an Arab from Iraq, albeit ancient Iraq.[66]

Saddam Hussein (1979)

The development and propagation of Iraqi nationalism (as a segment of Arab nationalism) and Pan-Arabism had a lasting impact on the non-Arab minorities in Iraq.[67] Though Arab nationalism was intrinsically embedded within Iraqi nationalism, the two did differ in some respects, especially in reference to the reigning power. Whereas Qasim's regime used ancient Mesopotamian iconography, the Ba'th Party furthered this process by combining it with Arab symbolism, making the two virtually inseparable.[68] Arguably even Qasim Arabised Mesopotamian standards, evident in the usage of the 'Arabic' sun as 'the emblem of Justice ancient Iraqis adopted before Christ'.[69] This ideology, though not problematic in and of itself, when imbedded into Iraqi educational patterns became indoctrination. This combination overwhelmed Assyrian cultural history, which became frailer with each new governmental policy directed towards education and social status, and with each demographic shift, starting with the disparity left following the Simele massacres.

The concepts of an alien race or alien religion and of savages, in accordance with the Arab nationalist sentiment of George Antonius, also dominate missionary reports, as seen earlier, and colonial British commentaries concerning the Assyrians formerly of the Hakkâri region living in Iraq following the First World War.[70] The arbitrary borders created by Western powers furthered this alienness, despite thousands of years of Assyrian culture and religion in the newly created Iraq – a Christianity built by the same ethnic Assyrians who happened to fall 'south of the border', driving a wedge between the two Assyrian factions. The promotion and propagation of such negative or biased material concerning the Assyrians can be credited to Western- and Arab-controlled media outlets, which normalised intra-ethnic and intra-religious enmity. These normalised hatreds influenced socio-economic standing and developed into an everyday deprecating vernacular, in which the Assyrians were referred to as *fellehi* (Arabic 'farmer' or 'peasant'), a term applied to them by their urbanised brethren.[71]

To say the ideologies of Arab nationalism and Pan-Arabism in Iraq were standard shows but a fraction of the picture. Early on, some radical writers demanded identification of pre-Arab, pre-Islamic civilisations with Iraq and as part of its Arab heritage. Others, such as 'Abd al-Raḥman al-Bazzaz, President and Prime Minister of Iraq in the mid-1960s for a brief period and a prolific writer, saw such early civilisations as part of the history and land of Iraq, but certainly not part of the modern Iraqi Arab identity. The greatest attempt to identify the pre-Islamic Mesopotamian cultures with modern Iraqi Arab identity was done mostly by the regime itself, and more extensively during the Iran–Iraq War, most likely to garner greater solidarity.[72] Arab nationalism and Arabisation used subtle ideas inserted in the educational system to influence a populace that was both ethnically and culturally diverse. Slogans of the Ba'th Party became part and parcel of the system and the forced indivisibility of Iraqi identity was blatantly evident: *l'Umma 'Arabiyya Wāḥda, wḍāt Risāla Khālida* ('One Arab Nation, with an Eternal Message').[73] This occurred quite early in the formation of the Middle East:

> This was done in the 1920s by postulating Arabia as the cradle of all the Semites who had migrated over the centuries and paved the way for the latest wave of Arab immigration, or by co-opting all pre-Islamic cultures of the Near East into an evolving Arab identity.[74]

Thus, the 'Semitic' Assyrian cultural identity (including from the ancient and Syriac Christian eras) was appropriated as part of a greater Arab identity, which defined Iraqi Arab nationalism. Nationalists, like Sāṭi' al-Ḥuṣrī, Director of General Education from 1922 to 1927, believed that that Arabic language and common history had to be indoctrinated within the population and 'only by removing the child from the family and the village and subjugating him to a nationalist education and military training could his loyalty be reoriented toward the nation'.[75]

Since various Arab intellectuals spoke of conflicting views concerning this appropriation, the Arabism of the later government, an assimilatory Arabism, won out over all others despite attempts to contain it. Under Qasim, secular left-leaning Iraqi nationalism allowed for the inclusion of various cultures as Iraqi, but not as Arab. To the non-Assyrian Iraqi populace, the Assyrians were portrayed as foreign people. This ideology, taken a step further, gave the events of Simele a facade of inevitability and necessity (though Antonius himself never goes so far, and in fact condemns the violence and atrocities that occurred). Such notions are prevalent in anti-indigenous literature of colonial states. This otherisation, in essence a form of dehumanisation, is echoed in L. Frank Baum's comments concerning the Lakota in the United States in the 1890s:

> The pioneer has before declared that our safety depends upon the total extermination of the Indians. Having wronged them for centuries, we had better, in order to protect our civilization, follow it up by one more wrong and wipe these untamed and untamable creatures from the face of the earth . . . Otherwise, we may expect future years to be as full of trouble with the redskins as those have been in the past.[76]

Baum's words were received in a similar light to Antonius's statement, whether they were aptly a reflection of the author's sentiments or of the general attitude of the masses. While some may argue against the need for such parallels, it seems evident that likening Eastern (sometimes ethnic) state violence against its own local populations, including dictatorships, to that committed by Western 'civic democracies', where ethnic 'cleansing and democratisation proceeded hand in hand', is pertinent.[77]

As mentioned briefly, the Simele massacres bear an uncanny resemblance to the Battle at Wounded Knee in South Dakota in December 1890, when 500 troops of the US 7th Cavalry surrounded and massacred a band of Lakota Sioux for fear of a spiritual movement called the ghost dance. From the broken land treaty, which angered the Lakota, to their later disarmament, and finally to the initial number of casualties at around 300, the attacks at Wounded Knee and Simele are methodically similar in their intent to destroy the Sioux ghost dancers and mountaineer/warrior Assyrians respectively. Furthermore, the reactions in the aftermath of the US government and the Iraqi government are peculiarly analogous. The American cavalry troops were venerated with eighteen Congressional Medals of Honor, parallel to the parades held for the victoriously returning Iraqi troops following the murders at Simele.[78] In most cases, local Americans, already suspicious of 'savage redskins', saw the event through an ethno-religious lens – similar to the local 'Iraqi' general distrust of these alien and rural community, which was furthered by government and media propaganda. This idea of savagery and rebellion was also promoted by the Iraqi government, as attested in a US Department of State document which stated, 'Rebels mutilated dead and

wounded, burned bodies [of] officers and killed some women and children,'
an almost identical tactic to Khaldun Husry's attempt to subvert the blame
for the Assyrian massacre by creating tales of Assyrians mutilating the bodies
of Iraqi army officers.[79] Similarly, the US military attempted to blame the
Lakota for the genocidal massacre. As some historians have attempted to
blame the Assyrian victims for the Iraqi military action at Simele, citing
premeditated rebellion (Husry being the most prominent), a similar case has
occurred regarding the Lakota and Wounded Knee:

> Many historians have argued that the Sioux changed Wovoka's originally
> peaceful movement into a militant one, thus ultimately leading to the battle
> at Wounded Knee, but Ostler flatly denies this and claims that the idea
> originated in the army's attempts to justify the suppression of the Ghost
> Dance.[80]

The violence at Wounded Knee is rightfully interpreted as a colonialist action
by the government. 'It was not the Lakota Ghost dancers who were becoming
hostile or threatening to use force . . . it was the United States.'[81] One wonders
whether the fact that the Lakota and Assyrians were partially armed remains
a sufficient pretext for their near annihilation. To return to Baum, while the
intent with which he employed his remarks is highly contested,[82] Barbara
Chiarello asserts that this white Anglo-Saxon Protestant American nationalist ideology was unmistakably reflected by (and in many cases developed by)
American authorities, including President Theodore Roosevelt, who stated:

> All men of sane and wholesome thought must dismiss with impatient
> contempt the plea that these continents should be reserved for the use of
> scattered savage tribes, whose life was but a few degrees less meaningless,
> squalid, and ferocious than that of the wild beasts with whom they held
> joint ownership . . . The most ultimately righteous of all wars is a war with
> savages, though it is apt to be also the most terrible and inhuman. The rude,
> fierce settler who drives the savage from the land lays all civilized mankind
> under a debt to him. American and Indian, Boer and Zulu . . . in each case
> the victor . . . has laid deep the foundations for the future greatness of a
> mighty people.[83]

Roughly speaking, Iraq in the 1960s–1980s was in a similar position to the United States in the 1890s. While the state had been formed, it had not been totally consolidated. In order to become so, it began changing people's ways of life physically, whether through urbanisation or literally changing the topography. As rural modes of living were eradicated, people were forced into urban centres that would by default carry a stronger element of Arabisation.

State-sponsored Acculturation

The experience of the Iraqi Assyrians vis-à-vis state-solidifying in Iraq is best conceptualised within the framework of state-sponsored acculturation. When they had dissolved into general obscurity, with neither numerical nor political strength, they became targeted by the Iraqi regime, as with other factional groups, through a more subtle elimination of their distinct ethno-cultural identity.

> Genocide has two phases: one, destruction of the national pattern of the oppressed group; the other, imposition of the national pattern of the oppressor. This imposition, in turn, may be made upon the oppressed population which is allowed to remain, or upon the territory alone, after removal of the population and the colonization of the area by the oppressor's own nationals.[84]

The propagation of Arabisation and Ba'thification, which subsumed the Assyrians as well as other communal groups into a monolithic identity, resulted in the elimination of any modes of identification of these groups outside the acceptable norms of Ba'thism and Arabism. For the Iraqi Assyrians, this meant the state ceased to officially recognise them as an ethnic minority, thereby eliminating them as a separate group. This is analogous to the assimilatory policies, with intent to purge, of various nations (both ethnic and civic) against indigenous populations in settler states. Eliminating millennia-old churches and monasteries, statues, inscriptions and books; burning apple, walnut and almond orchards; and salting the earth were deliberate attempts to destroy this people's sustainability and way of life.

Therefore extermination, in its cultural shape, speaks to a social death, when 'one group begins to feel that the very existence of the other group is a danger to its own survival'.[85] Thus, logically extending the argument, one may claim that the Iraqi government feared the Assyrian minority. The question remains as to why. A likely answer reflects on the idea that 'ethnocide and ethnic cleansing are among the most significant markers or sources of indigenous identity'.[86] It is therefore probable that the Iraqi government's attempt to absorb the Assyrians into Iraqi Arab society, see them as outcasts and label them as Kurds, or eliminate their ancestral ties to the land through such policies of acculturation, solidified a policy of stabilising an insecure national identity in order to consolidate and justify political, military and economic control of the country. This includes the appellative issue of referring to them as *Āthūri* rather than *Ashūri* to sustain a distinction between the alien 'Nestorians' and the ancient Assyrians, progenitors of an Iraq that had begun to appropriate its historic navel. Being an ancient Assyrian (or descendant thereof) granted almost nominal indigeneity to a troublesome people, something the Iraqi government could not allow.

Since Iraqi Arab nationalism saw the Arabs as the inheritors of ancient Mesopotamian civilisation (dogma most Iraqi nationalists also adhered to), then Assyrians could not be an entity separate from the Arab identity, a situation which left them simply as Christians. The type of Christian was determined by their loyalty to Iraq and their geographic distribution: the urban Arab Christian element in areas of 'Arab' Iraq on the one hand, and those who were lumped geographically with the rural and 'rebellious' Kurds and considered traitors to the regime. The hardening of Arabisation following the Ba'thist rise to power ensured that acculturation, both violent and subtle, became part and parcel of successive government policies as tools and mechanisms by which the government could suppress, assimilate and silence its population without purging them physically, as they had done in 1933. This building of a coerced collective 'Iraqi' identity, with all of its sub-texts, would demonstrate the solidification of systematic and subsequent policies of assimilation and homogenisation in an otherwise pluralistic society. This attempt at ethno-cultural homogenisation '*constituted* the states system, for it has been constructed in large measure on the exclusionary categories of insider and outsider'.[87]

Thus, the usual rhetoric of the Assyrians as being 'some forty thousand persons who were brought to Iraq from Turkey' has led to the view of this people as 'outsiders' or non-Iraqis, which would contribute to the

justification of their massacre in 1933. The incessant labelling of these mountaineer Nestorians as 'Assyrians' (and as outsiders) furthered the rift between
Assyrians of various ecclesiastic sects, as many reinvented themselves as Iraqis
and as insiders rather than Assyrians, equivalent to foreigners. Cultural genocide or ethnocide is an apt term for the continued denial of their existence
in Iraq as a distinct entity, sometimes furthered by modern scholarship in
questioning their distinctive culture, particularly when self-identification as
Assyrian (*Ashūri* or *Āthūri* in Arabic, in relation to descent from ancient
Assyria) results in imprisonment and torture. Through ideas of development
and progress according to its national and socialist principles, members of the
Ba'th Party desired a public reinforcement of belief in God and knowledge
of Arabic and Islamic culture.[88] In reality, this aided the ethnos/demos mud-
dling and indeed confused it even further.

A telltale result of the cultural-genocidal campaign within Iraq was evident in the fracture within the Assyrian community, with some showing
partiality toward the more Arabised segments of the populace and, in fact,
ridiculing the Assyrian identity as peasant oriented and abased. Thus, the
cultural chasm widened, and vocabulary such as *fellehi* in Christian Arabic
became commonplace to refer to those who spoke some ancient language,
dressed strangely and retained notions of a distinct ethnic and cultural identity. At first in the period of 1920–50, especially in the wake of the atrocities
at Simele, those persons of Assyrian heritage who had no direct connection
to the Assyrians involved completely cut any possible ties, both publicly and
privately. They wore a mask of Arabism. They *seemed* as Iraqi and, by extension, as Arab as possible. 'We understand how dangerous a mask can be. We
all become what we pretend to be.'[89]

The specific treatment of Assyrian asylum seekers returning from Turkey
to Iraq under amnesty decree no. 736 of 8 September 1988, illustrates the
original Clause 3 of the Genocide Convention as proposed by Lebanon,
which stated that 'subjecting members of a group to such conditions as would
cause them to renounce their language, religion, or culture' should be considered genocidal in scope.[90] Though the total number of persons who went
missing during the aforementioned time period is unclear, from government
documents and oral estimates it can be surmised that thousands of Assyrians
disappeared following the Anfal campaign and that many more were forcibly

assimilated. Furthermore, it is probable that on being told that only Kurds were subject to the amnesty, for survival purposes many Assyrians living in Iraqi Kurdistan were forced to adopt a cover of a Kurdish identity. Thus, the identity conundrum came full circle. Arab identification became commensurate with strong socio-economic stature, forcibly attracting many Assyrians and Kurds alike. Yet the drawback for Assyrians was twofold, because at specific times and in particular locales, identifying as a Kurd guaranteed even greater socio-economic prowess (in Iraqi Kurdistan) and was seemingly (according to the government census) safer than being a non-Kurd. Also, the unchecked and unreported Arabisation tactics faced by the Assyrians became a precursor to some Kurdification processes under the Kurdistan Regional Government, just as the relative silence surrounding Simele allowed the Iraqi government to continue its suppression of other minorities, including the Kurds.[91]

In addition to cultural destruction, it is beyond contestation that thousands of Assyrians lost their lives during the period 1961–91, either physically or spiritually or mentally (through forced assimilation), and that thousands more were ethnically cleansed from their ancestral lands. Any assertion and/or proliferation of Assyrian culture and identity, denied through policies, census accounts and so forth, was punishable by imprisonment and torture. There can be few cases of mental harm greater than the denial of one's existence.

This process of ethnic cleansing, under a guise of integration, was first used by the British on the highland Assyrians of Hakkâri, who had established a cohesive settlement in the region of Diyana, then still under British dominion. These Assyrians were 'given orders to move from Di[y]ana' and 'moved to the lowlands well south of the Zab' before the end of the mandate.[92] Malik Ismael, the tribal leader of Upper Tiyari, in his response to the news of the termination of the British mandate and Hakkâri Assyrians' removal yet again out of their cohesive settlement in the highlands stated, 'Now we have to meet death at long last,' a reference to a social or identity death – a death of being Assyrian. Such demographic shifting to unknown regions, alongside the deliberate infliction of conditions of cultural degradation such as the elimination of villages, churches, livestock and orchards, provided a dramatic illustration of British policies.[93] Such alterations would eventually cause many cultural or lifestyle elements of this people, much dependent on their geography and local environment, to wane. Of course, this was done only in part, as not all Assyrians were physically eliminated by such policies – with the exception of Simele, which, according to the data collected, was an attempt to physically eliminate a portion of Assyrians from Iraq.

Such geopolitical plots assured the appropriation and redefinition of a nascent Assyrian identity in Iraq by the state (and later internalised), owing in part to the strength of Arab and Kurdish nationalisms and the relative weakness of Assyrian nationalism. Their weaker political power was/is due not necessarily to the Assyrian people's unwillingness to absorb ethnic nationalism, but rather to governmental policies, and the lack of external aid, as discussed in the preceding chapters. Yet prior to the rise of modern Middle Eastern nation-states, the Assyrians in diaspora, and even in the remoter regions of the Ottoman Empire, were able to see and further develop a transnational and transreligious/ecclesiastical Assyrian identity.[94] In that sense, Joseph Yacoub's description of the Assyrian predicament as a *dynamisme démographique* is an apt designation as it speaks to constant migration which in reality lead to continuous fluctuation in identity.[95]

While at first glance they may seem out of place, some of the most meaningful interpretations of ideas concerning sanctity of place come from Patrick Curry, a scholar of ecological philosophy. In his conclusion to a book on Middle-Earth and ecology entitled 'Hope without Guarantees', Curry reminds the reader about the core connection of people to place and its integral sanctity by alluding to the physical destruction in the wake of the Bosnian war. He refers to the Old Bridge in Mostar, built in 1566, which collapsed due to repeated shelling in 1993. Quoting Slavenka Drakulić, he states, 'The bridge is us.'[96] By extension, such places need not be man made, but even natural: forests, springs, rivers, mountain ranges etc., and those non-human animals which dwell there are equally part of the sacredness of place, which is undeniably linked to the community, 'its modes of life and [the] thought of a people who are different from those who carry out this destructive enterprise'. Such destruction aimed at those elements of life interconnected to the human often 'kills their spirit'.[97]

Likewise, the initial meeting of Assyrians with 'the white man' was with those Western missionaries who desired to develop a simple language and culture for the Assyrians in order to facilitate a speedy evangelisation process. Furthermore, the benefits of what was too lightly termed integration were vastly overshadowed by the imminent assimilation of a political/social/economic and numerical minority, which Malik Ismael could see after a close look at his brethren who had lived for hundreds of years in metropolitan centres and lost their cultural Assyrianness. Like all 'progress', it had proved a double-edged sword. Demographic shifting and, thus, urbanisation produced the state and non-state actors' desired effect on the Assyrians. As a direct result of urbanisation, attributed to ethnic cleansing campaigns, Assyrians were indoctrinated into the language, traditions, clothing, lifestyle and names of Arab Iraq (and in some cases, Kurdish Iraq). The desired result was accomplished through both direct and indirect Arabisation. It is of note that more than one million Assyrians resided in northern Iraq prior to the demographic shifting following 1961, a number that had declined to fewer than 200,000 by the mid-1990s.[98]

The Iraqi state and its policies in the twentieth century can be explained by closely examining the Assyrian minority. The policies directed against the Assyrians are a microcosm of the larger situation, which affected various political, cultural, ethnic, linguistic and religious minorities. The treatment of the Assyrians initially by the British colonial government and then by the new Iraqi government was the litmus test for nation- and state-building and the international response thereto. The cost of the establishment of Iraq and the attendant subordination of minorities to a Sunni Arab elite by the British for strategic purposes guaranteed that the 'identity chosen for Iraq was unrepresentative and exclusionary'.[99]

Cultural genocide/ethnocide, introduced by Lemkin as an act of vandalism, is essential in examining the consequences of the Arabisation policies on the Assyrian community in Iraq following the Ba'th's rise to power in the 1970s. According to UNESCO's Declaration of San José, 'Ethnocide means that an ethnic group is denied the right to enjoy, develop, and transmit its own culture and its own language, whether collectively or individually.'[100] The declaration further stated, 'Ethnocide, that is cultural genocide, is a violation of international law equivalent to genocide.'[101] Ethnocide is created in a crucible of yearning for hegemonic control first evident in a state's push to secure a national identity; this yearning is evidenced by various policies of assimilation (as opposed to integration) designed to eradicate major cultural distinctions such as language, dress, folklore, art and music, and by 'rival claims to sovereignty that arise from first occupation of a territory. Its goal is the elimination of knowledge of, and attachments to, distinct and incontinent ways of life.'[102] According to Human Rights Watch, the stress of simply being Assyrian in Iraq forced large numbers of people to effectively stop or deny being Assyrian for fear of physical or socio-economic retribution or reprisal:

> The teaching of the Assyrian language, even in churches, is forbidden, and Assyrian Christians who identify themselves as such suffer official discrimination. However, other Christians and those Assyrians who identify themselves as 'Arab' seem to face no particular discrimination. In fact, many Muslim Iraqis consider Christians to be a favored minority under the Ba'th regime.[103]

Such acts are imbedded in deeply rooted predilections that contain an inherent link to each other. Lawrence Davidson lists them as:

Natural localism: People tend to classify or identify themselves in geographical terms – by their everyday surroundings, and therefore everyday activities in such a state are natural or normal. (Not inherently problematic.)

Closed information environments: Because of such identification, information that locals or inhabitants tap into (apparently even in the internet age) usually comes from within that same defined region and is cast and stereotyped based on it.

Thought collectives: And since the information which is filtered into a specific population is generally closed off from 'other' knowledge or experience networks then particular ways of thinking about oneself and everyone and everything else becomes a product of an incomplete and coloured lens.

A *natural localism* left to its own ignorance in fear or arrogance creates *closed information environments* and leads to a restricted body of knowledge referred to as *thought collectives*. In this work, one can think of a general clash between competing localisms that 'breed cultural paradigms'.[104] The powerful localism of the aggressive (or the predatory identity as argued by Arjun Appaduri) versus the non-aggressive can be viewed in this work in many ways including Arab/Assyrian, Kurdish/Assyrian, Iraqi/Assyrian, Ba'th/Assyrian among other relationships.[105] Thus, this synthetic Iraqi identity as fostered and disseminated by the state through *natural localisms* and enforced upon a multicultural, multi-ethnic, and multi-religious region through *closed information environments* assured the violent nature of its state formation as a likely consequence of authoritarian, and further, totalitarian and rigid *thought collectives*. It was 'an imagined political community, and imagined as both inherently limited and sovereign'.[106] In actuality, this imagined community also gave hope to non-Muslim religious communities to become part of a larger secular community that would not discriminate on the basis of religious adherence. To urban Christians who in many cases had but their Christianity as a matter of distinctiveness, it permitted a semblance of equality with their Muslim neighbours in a land they had inhabited for millennia.

In terms of framing the patterns of destruction, the villages discussed throughout this study have been those with known historical and cultural significance.[107] Almost 200 Assyrian cultural sites – including ancient churches and monasteries, schools, shrines and reliefs – were destroyed between 1960 and 1980 as a result of political manoeuvring by majority groups, including both state and non-state actors. As with the relatedness of Simele and Wounded Knee, the scheme of the *mujamma'āt*, the collective towns and processing centres during the Iraqi government's continuous campaigns in the north, was not dissimilar ideologically to those created by the German army (perhaps the first modern idea of a *konzentrationslager*, or 'concentration camp') when dealing with the Herero people in Namibia at the beginning of the twentieth century.[108] The *mujamma'āt*, however, were probably more in line (treatment-wise) with the internment camps, also known as 'war relocation camps' and 'assembly centres', that the United States and Canadian governments used to detain citizens of Japanese descent during the Second World War.[109] In the cases of both East and West, thanks to the ideology promoted by the 'collective camps,' the negative stigma and socio-economic ramifications attached to being Kurdish or Assyrian in Iraq, or Italian, German or Japanese in the United States and Canada, became a social and economic deterrent that compelled many people among these ethnic groups to distance themselves from their ethno-cultural identity.

The specific trend of forced demographic shifting by both state and non-state actors follows similar trends observed during the Second World War in the United States. The Iraqi use of wartime powers, which created collective towns and destroyed entire regions of Assyrian villages, have many well-documented parallel situations in the United States, which are illustrated by Executive Order 9066, signed by President Franklin D. Roosevelt on 19 February 1942, permitting authorised military commanders to designate military areas within the United States at their discretion, 'from which any or all persons may be excluded'.[110] Under this order, many US citizens of German and Italian ancestry were targeted by the military for detainment. This corresponds directly to the border clearings in Iraq during the 1970s. Regions in which Assyrian villages predominated were dynamited and bull-dozed as part of 'security measures' to protect the territorial integrity of Iraq as the United States did with the military zones, again on the coast or border regions. In the case of the Assyrians, most of the population was removed and in most instances offered no compensation.

The effort in the United States and Canada was directed toward an ethnic group within the country perceived as a possible threat by many political leaders, in all likelihood to disguise a programme of ethnic cleans-ing. The case of the Assyrians in Iraq followed this pattern as well, and did further damage by identifying the Assyrians as Kurds (who were seen as separatists) and rebellious Arabs. Thus, not only were they processed in such camps, they were denied even their self-identification, something akin to the experience of First Nations peoples in the United States and Canada. The Assyrians experienced a social death under the guise of socio-economic empowerment and integration similar to that of many First Nations peoples in Canada, through residential schools only recently terminated in 1996.[111] Decree 251 of 1972 under Ahmed Hassan al-Bakr depicted a cohesive image of the country amid growing concerns illustrating the contrary. In actual-ity, the decree eliminated all private Assyrian schools (including classes in culture and history) and instruction in Aramaic or Syriac. Such assimilatory practices disguised as progressive measures share their misfortune with the treatment of other indigenous communities, such as those of Brazil, where the 'Service for the Protection of Indians was actually found to be destroying them'.[112]

Ulterior motives, dwelling behind the facade of a cultural decree, are quite common. The Iraqi regime, like a multitude of others, sometimes circumvented scrutiny following physical destruction or the targeting of individuals (after its military actions early on in and around Simele) by enacting policies of acculturation intended to affect the social or spiritual life (identity) of a community considered troublesome. The Iraqi government's engagement in village clearings, including destroying churches, monasteries, schools and agricultural fields, and seizing livestock – attacking all means of a stable livelihood – and expelling and resettling Assyrians into urban areas ensured the forfeiture of the Assyrian way of life.[113]

Notes

1. Michael Mann, *The Dark Side of Democracy: Explaining Ethnic Cleansing* (Cambridge: Cambridge University Press, 2005), 27–9.
2. Ibid., 3.
3. Rienhold Niebuhr, *Moral Man and Immoral Society: A Study in Ethics and Politics* (New York: Charles Scribner's Sons, 1960), 89.
4. It should be noted that while Sunni Arabs are not specifically mentioned during these periods, they were targeted as part of the Communist Party.
5. In many cases there is little separation between the two.
6. Most Assyrians designate 7 August as a day of commemoration for the fallen.
7. More recent Kurdish political prowess (perhaps based largely on an economic boom as well as the cultural and political development made possible by their geopolitical significance) has remedied much of such past academic negligence.
8. Elie Kedourie, *The Chatham House Version, and Other Middle East Studies* (New York: Praeger, 1970), 3–4, 27–8.
9. The terms 'imagined' or 'unimagined' are based on Benedict Anderson's concept of nations/communities/identities being constructed and deconstructed. In itself the term is not a value judgement. I use the term 'unimagining' in reference to the Assyrians more in the secondary sense of the political attempt to at first eliminate, then suppress and artificialise, and finally recreate their identity through forced assimilation policies.

10. This, coupled with the erasure of the accounts of the Assyrian massacres from the French translation of the 'Blue Book' presented to the Paris Peace Conference, further distorted the historical record (Hannibal Travis, '"Native Christians Massacred": The Ottoman Genocide of the Assyrians during World War I', *Genocide Studies and Prevention* 1.3 (2006), 331). Furthermore, the original title of the Blue Book (*Papers and Documents on the Treatment of Armenians and Assyrian Christians by the Turks, 1915–1916, in the Ottoman Empire and North-West Persia*), a 'compilation of American and European eyewitness testimony and documentation of the Armenian and Assyrian genocides', was amended to *The Treatment of the Armenians in the Ottoman Empire 1915–1916*. The record was only set straight when the 2005 edition edited by Ara Sarafian, which includes the information on the Assyrians, was republished under the altered name *The Treatment of Armenians in the Ottoman Empire, 1915–16: Documents Presented to Viscount Grey of Fallodon by Viscount Bryce (Uncensored Edition)* (London: Gomidas Institute, 2005). This tension has reverberated in the literature surrounding the events in Iraq during the decades that followed. For an excellent basic discussion on the overshadowing of the Assyrians in the First World War see Samuel Totten and Paul R. Bartrop, *A Dictionary of Genocide, vol. I: A–L* (Westport, CT: Greenwood Press, 2008), 25–26.

11. For a description of this trend see Idith Zertal, *Israel's Holocaust and the Politics of Nationhood*, tr. Chaya Galai (Cambridge: Cambridge University Press, [2002] 2005).

12. See Aryo Makko, 'The Historical Roots of Contemporary Controversies: National Revival and the Assyrian "Concept of Unity"', *Journal of Assyrian Academic Studies* 24.1 (2010), 1–29 for a more focused discussion of the internal issues.

13. See John Joseph, *The Modern Assyrians of the Middle East: Encounters with Western Christian Missions, Archaeologists, and Colonial Powers* (Leiden: Brill, 2000), 157. Joseph, a student of Philip Hitti, was highly influenced by the American Presbyterian schools as well as the American University of Beirut, a bastion of Arab nationalism: see Betty S. Anderson, *The American University of Beirut: Arab Nationalism and Liberal Education* (Austin: University of Texas Press, 2011), 1–3.

14. Joel E. Werda, *The Flickering Light of Asia or The Assyrian Nation and Church* (Joel E. Werda, 1924), 199–202, 205.

15. Malik Yaqo d'Malik Ismael, *Aturayé w-tre plashe tibilayé* ['Assyrians and the Two World Wars'] (Tehran: Assyrian Writers Board, 1964), 223.

16. See Sargon Donabed, 'Neither Syriac-speaking nor Syrian Orthodox Christians: (K)Harputli Assyrians in the United States as a Model for Ethnic Self-Categorization and Expression', in H. G. B. Teule, E. Keser-Kayaalp, K. Akalin, N. Doru, N. and M. S. Toprak (eds), *Syriac in its Multi-cultural Context* (Leuven: Peeters, forthcoming).

17. Raphael Lemkin, *Axis Rule in Occupied Europe: Laws of Occupation, Analysis of Government, Proposals for Redress* (Washington, DC: Carnegie Endowment for International Peace, 1944), 79.

18. Convention on the Prevention and Punishment of Genocide, http://www.hrweb.org/legal/genocide.html (accessed 21 July 2014).

19. Adam Jones, *Genocide: A Comprehensive Introduction* (London: Routledge, 2006), 19.

20. Eric Weitz, *A Century of Genocide: Utopias of Race and Nation* (Princeton, NJ: Princeton University Press. 2003), 7.

21. Ibid., 37.

22. Arjun Appadurai, *Fear of Small Numbers: An Essay on the Geography of Anger* (Durham, NC: Duke University Press, 2006), 3.

23. George Antonius, *The Arab Awakening: The Story of the Arab National Movement* (Philadelphia: J. B. Lippincott, 1939), 365. Despite this comment, Antonius did condemn the actual violence. See also *Special Report by His Majesty's Government in the United Kingdom of Great Britain and Northern Ireland to the Council of the League of Nations on the Progress of Iraq During the Period 1920–1931*, CO 58 (London, 1931), 266.

24. This is fascinating for a variety of reasons including that the Iraqi state and elements of it such as the royal family and the military were in and of themselves 'vestiges of European power'. Similarly the evidence corroborates the assertion that the Assyrians were neither a physical nor existential threat to Iraq with one feasible exception: their existence as Assyrians on ancestral lands and possible future claims.

25. Sāṭi' al-Ḥuṣrī, "Al-Khidma al-'Askariyya w-'l-Tarbiya al-'Amma', speech delivered in Baghdad in 1934, in *Mudhakkirātī fi al-Iraq* (Beirut: Dar al-Taliah, 1967–8), vol. 2, 312–13, quoted in Phebe Marr, 'The Development of a Nationalist Ideology in Iraq 1920–1941', *Muslim World* 75.2 (1985), 91.

26. Mann, *The Dark Side of Democracy*, 7.

27. See Sami Zubaida, 'Contested Nations: Iraq and the Assyrians', *Nations and Nationalism* 6.3 (2000), 370. Though some local Arabs and Kurds continued looting villages and killing Assyrians in the region, to assume that this was not

at the urging or in the least, under the watchful eye of the army and the government would be insincere.

28. Jones, *Genocide*, 352.

29. Recall here Elias Haroon Bazi's observation that young Assyrian men were dressed and presented as young women to protect them from the campaign.

30. Richard Kleiner, 'Lemkin's 35-year crusade against genocide reaches successful end', *La Crosse Tribune*, La Crosse, WI, 22 September 1949.

31. R. S. Stafford, *The Tragedy of the Assyrians* (London: George Allen & Unwin, 1935), 162.

32. Ibid., 154.

33. Mark K. Tomass, 'Religious Identity, Informal Institutions, and the Nation-states of the Near East', *Journal of Economic Issues* 46.3 (2012), 719. Tomass provides the most intricate discussion of identity-sharing and resource-sharing groups. See also Sargon George Donabed and Shamiran Mako, 'Ethno-cultural and Religious Identity of Syrian Orthodox Christians', *Chronos* 19 (2009).

34. A portion of this section was originally presented in Sargon George Donabed, 'Rethinking Nationalism and an Appellative Conundrum: Historiography and Politics in Iraq', *National Identities* 14.4 (2012), 407–31.

35. Gerald de Gaury, *Three Kings in Baghdad: The Tragedy of Iraq's Monarchy* (London: I. B. Tauris, [1961] 2008), 89.

36. Hirmis Aboona, *Assyrians, Kurds, and Ottomans: Intercommunal Relations on the Periphery of the Ottoman Empire* (Amherst, NY: Cambria Press, 2008), 279.

37. Paul Knabenshue, US ambassador to Iraq, to Secretary of State, 'Christian Religious Heads and Assyrian Massacres' (no. 167), 23 August 1933, 890g.4016 Assyrians/84

38. Donabed and Mako, 'Ethno-Cultural and Religious Identity of Syrian Orthodox Christians', 108.

39. Vahram Petrosian, 'Assyrians in Iraq', *Iran and the Caucasus* 10.1 (2006), 125.

40. Tomass, 'Religious Identity, Informal Institutions, and the Nation-states of the Near East', 718.

41. Donabed and Mako, 'Ethno-cultural and Religious Identity of Syrian Orthodox Christians', 78, 106–7.

42. See ibid., 78–9; Aprim Shapera, 'A great message from a great Assyrian man', Zinda, 12 August 2002, http://www.zindamagazine.com/html/archives/2002/8.12.02/index.php (accessed 21 July 2014).

43. *Al-Dalīl al-ʿIrāqī* ['The Official Directory of Iraq'] (Baghdad, 1936).

44. I am reminded of the explanation of all the events that had befallen Tanis Half-Elven and his companions given by the god/wizard Paladine/Fizban: 'I set the stage, lad. I didn't give you a script. The dialogue has been all yours.' See Margaret Weis and Tracy Hickman, *Dragonlance Chronicles, vol. 3: Dragons of Spring Dawning* (Lake Geneva, WI: TSR, [1985] 1994), 372.

45. This is seen most clearly outside the Middle East or at the very least outside the capitals and centres of conflicting nationalisms.

46. Paulos Bedari, 'Lamentation on the Simele Massacre', *Nineveh* 36.3–4 (2012). In the 1960s Bedari was an advocate for the anti-government leanings of Assyrian, Communist and Kurdish groups in the north of Iraq. See Gabriele Yonan, *Assyrer heute* (Hamburg: Gesellschaft für Bedrohte Völker, 1978), 99. Interestingly, he was one of two Chaldean priests, along with Father Akhikar, who were known to be pro-Mar Shimun before the events of Simele and considered to be undesirable Assyrians (secret memorandum, serial no. 125 from Special Service Officer, Mosul, to Air Staff (Intelligence), Air Headquarters, 5 August 1933, AIR 23/655).

47. Douglas V. Duff, Poor Knight's Saddle (London: Herbert Jenkins, 1938), 150.

48. Alexander Wendt, *Social Theory of International Politics* (Cambridge, Cambridge University Press, 1999), 225–35.

49. Patrick Rothfuss, *The Name of the Wind* (New York: DAW, 2007), 716.

50. See *Iraq Times*, 29 August 1933. Khaldun Husry remarks that the Assyrians mutilated the bodies of Iraqi soldiers in Deirabun. In the following sentence he contradicts this statement with a quote from R. S. Stafford, who admitted freely that such accusations 'may or may not have been true' (Khaldun S. Husry, 'The Assyrian Affair of 1933 (I)', *International Journal of Middle East Studies* 5.2 (1974), 176).

51. Article 49, Geneva Convention Relative to the Protection of Civilian Persons in Time of War of 12 August 1949, http://www.icrc.org/eng/assets/files/publications/icrc-002-0173.pdf (accessed 22 July 2014).

52. Updated Statute of the International Criminal Tribunal for the Former Yugoslavia, September 2009, http://www.icty.org/x/file/Legal%20Library/Statute/statute_sept09_en.pdf (accessed 22 July 2014); Rome Statute of the International Criminal Court, July 1998, http://www.icc-cpi.int/NR/rdonlyres/ADD16852-AEE9-4757-ABE7-9CDC7CF02886/283503/RomeStatutEng1.pdf (accessed 22 July 2014).

53. Drazen Petrovic, 'Ethnic Cleansing: An Attempt at Methodology', *European Journal of International Law* 5.4 (1998), 2–3.

54. Ilan Pappé, *The Ethnic Cleansing of Palestine* (Oxford: Oneworld, 2007), 7.

55. Ibid., 151.

56. Stafford, *The Tragedy of the Assyrians*, 154.

57. Ibid., 155. See also secret report by Major C. J. Edmonds, Ministry of the Interior, Baghdad to Mr G. A. D. Ogilvie-Forbes, British embassy, Baghdad, 24 August 1933, AIR 23/656.

58. Paul Knabenshue, US ambassador to Iraq, to Wallace Murray, containing letter from Mr Cumberland to Secretary of State, 13 September 1933, 890g.4016 Assyrians/110.

59. Daniel Silverfarb, *Britain's Informal Empire in the Middle East: A Case Study of Iraq 1929–1941* (New York: Oxford University Press, 1986), 42.

60. 'Statement Made by Miryam, Wife of David Jindo, a Corporal in the Iraq Levies, Exhibit D to Supplementary Petition, Dated September 24 1933, from the Mar Shimun, "Catholicos" Patriarch of the Assyrians to the League of Nations', *League of Nations Official Journal* 14 (1933), 1826.

61. Ibid. The evidence for this is abundant. See Carol Prunhuber, *The Passion and Death of Rahman the Kurd: Dreaming Kurdistan* (Bloomington, IN: iUniverse, 2009), 141, 143, 146. The focus of the work is Abdul Rahman Ghassemlou, a Kurdish nationalist with an Assyrian mother who was forcibly converted to Islam (see pages 136 and 141), and took on a new name. Ghassemlou is a prime example of what happens to succeeding generations in most intermarriages between Muslim Kurds and Christian Assyrians.

62. Prosecutor vs Krstić, ICTY Appeals Chamber Judgment, case no. IT-98-33, 19 April 2004, para. 33, http://www.icty.org/x/cases/krstic/acjug/en/krs-aj040419e.pdf (accessed 22 July 2014).

63. Raphael Lemkin Collection, box 9, folder 2, Armenians and Assyrians, undated, The Assyrian Case, notecards 40, 44, 45.

64. Zoë Preston, *The Crystallization of the Iraqi State: Geopolitical Function and Form* (Bern: Peter Lang, 2003), 251.

65. The Simele massacres bear an uncanny resemblance to the massacre at Wounded Knee Creek, South Dakota, in December 1890, when more than 300 Lakota men, women and children were killed by the United States 7th Cavalry in the midst of the 'taming of the West', yet another act of homogenisation and consolidation.

66. Fu'ād Maṭar, *Saddam Hussein: A Biographical and Ideological Account of His Leadership Style and Crisis Management* (London: Highlight, 1990), 235.

67. The trend of Arabisation is perhaps succinctly illuminated by the Middle Eastern historian Hanna Batatu in his descriptions of nationality ('nation'), based on the various data tables throughout his exhaustive study on Iraq. The case of Iraqi Jews is difficult as the community outside northern Iraq was predominantly Arabised. See Hanna Batatu, *The Old Social Classes and the Revolutionary Movements in Iraq* (London: Saqi, [1978] 2004), 258. Batatu refers to the Jews in the entirety of Iraq. Most Aramaic-speaking members of the Jewish religious community living in the northern regions intermarried regularly with Christians and had mostly identical language, customs and traditions to those other Assyrians of the region.

68. Reeva Spector Simon, *Iraq between the Two World Wars: The Militarist Origins of Tyranny* (New York: Columbia University Press, 2004), 160.

69. Law no. 57 of 1959, *Weekly Gazette of the Republic of Iraq* (November 1959), 900. Fascinatingly the reference to 'before Christ' leads one to assume there would be a reference to Iraqi Christians and their link to ancient Mesopotamia but there is not.

70. Antonius, *The Arab Awakening*, 365; Matthew Frye Jacobson, *Whiteness of a Different Color: European Immigrants and the Alchemy of Race* (Cambridge, MA: Harvard University Press, 1998), 267. This is also true of Winston Churchill's conception of the Kurds when he stated in 1919, 'I am strongly in favour of using poisoned gas against uncivilised tribes,' something he desired to do once again against the Germans in 1944.

71. For earlier occurrences of this see Dina Rizk Khoury, *State and Provincial Society in the Ottoman Empire: Mosul 1540–1834* (Cambridge: Cambridge University Press, 1997), 190.

72. Amatzia Baram, *Culture, History, and Ideology in the Formation of Ba'thist Iraq 1968–89* (Basingstoke: Macmillan, 1991), 28.

73. Joseph Sassoon, *Saddam Hussein's Ba'th Party: Inside an Authoritarian Regime* (Cambridge: Cambridge University Press, 2012), 9.

74. Youssef M. Choueiri, *Arab Nationalism: A History – Nation and State in the Arab World* (Oxford: Blackwell, 2000), 25.

75. Phebe Marr, 'The Development of a Nationalist Ideology in Iraq', 90–1.

76. Barbara Chiarello, 'Deflected Missives: Zitkala-Ša's Resistance and Its (Un) Containment', *Studies in American Indian Literatures* 17.3 (2005), 9, based on *Aberdeen Saturday Pioneer*, 3 January 1891. See also Reneau H. Reneau, *Misanthropology: A Florilegium of Bahumbuggery* (Inglewood, CA: Donlázaro Translations, 2003), 161.

77. Michael Mann, *The Dark Side of Democracy*, 4.

78. This is the most medals ever awarded in a single US military action. See Scott L. Pratt, 'Wounded Knee and the Prospect of Pluralism', *Journal of Speculative Philosophy* 19.2 (2005), 153.

79. See Husry, 'The Assyrian Affair of 1933 (I),' 168.

80. Francis Paul Prucha, 'Wounded Knee through the Lens of Colonialism', *Diplomatic History* 29.4 (2005), 727. This article is a review of Jeffrey Ostler's *The Plains Sioux and US Colonialism from Lewis and Clark to Wounded Knee* (Cambridge: Cambridge University Press, 2004). The ghost dance was a spiritual belief based on the prophetic vision of a Paiute elder Wovoka, which contested that the white man would soon be removed from the land and it would be given back to the native peoples. The idea gained strong backing among the Lakota in the late 1800s. For more information see Pratt, 'Wounded Knee and the Prospect of Pluralism', 151.

81. Jeffrey Ostler, *The Plains Sioux and US Colonialism from Lewis and Clark to Wounded Knee* (Cambridge: Cambridge University Press, 2004), 287–8.

82. Some scholars have pointed out to critics of Baum that they should remember the intrinsic sarcasm and mockery in much of his writing.

83. Jacobson, *Whiteness of a Different Color*, 218. Also quoted in Chiarello, 'Deflected Missives', 10.

84. Lemkin, *Axis Rule in Occupied Europe*, 79.

85. Appadurai, *Fear of Small Numbers*, 88–9.

86. Ibid., 56.

87. Heather Rae, *State Identities and the Homogenisation of Peoples* (Cambridge: Cambridge University Press, 2002), 14 (original emphasis).

88. 'Regulation No. 30 for the Year 1978 Primary Schools', *Alwaqai Aliraqiya: The Official Gazette of the Republic of Iraq*, 1 September 1980, p. 4.

89. Rothfuss, *The Name of the Wind*, 716.

90. *Summary Record of the Fourteenth Meeting of the Ad Hoc Committee on Genocide*, UN ESCOR, Doc. E/AC.25/SR.14 (1948), 13.

91. See 'Northern Iraq Human Rights Field Mission', Iraq Sustainable Democracy Project, 2006, www.iraqdemocracyproject.org/pdf/Northern%20 Iraq%20Human%20Rights%20Field%20Mission.pdf (accessed 16 July 2014)

92. A. M. Hamilton, *Road through Kurdistan: The Narrative of an Engineer in Iraq*, new ed. (London: Faber & Faber, 1958), 217.

93. Article 2(c), Convention on the Prevention and Punishment of Genocide.

94. This refers back to the late 1800s in places of relative freedom, from Harput, Urmia and Tbilisi to the United States.

95. Joseph Yacoub, *Les Minorités dans le monde: faits et analyses* (Paris: Desclée de Brouwer, 1998), 691.

96. Patrick Curry, *Defending Middle-Earth: Tolkien, Myth and Modernity* (Boston: Houghton Mifflin, 2004), 144.

97. Mario Sáenz, *The Identity of Liberation in Latin American Thought: Latin American Historicism and the Phenomenology of Leopoldo Zea* (Lanham, MD: Lexington, 1999), 18. See also Pierre Clastres, *Society against the State: Essays in Political Anthropology*, tr. Robert Hurley (New York: Zone, 1988), 52.

98. Joseph Yacoub, *Les Minorités: quelle protection?* (Paris: Desclée de Brouwer, 1995), 241.

99. Preston, *The Crystallization of the Iraqi State*, 252.

100. 'Unesco and the Struggle against Ethnocide', Declaration of San José, December 1981, http://unesdoc.unesco.org/images/0004/000499/049951eo. pdf (accessed 22 July 2014). It was first codified in Article 7 of the United Nations High Commissioner for Human Rights Draft Declaration on Rights of Indigenous Peoples (1994). Following the adoption of the declaration in 2006, the act was reworded to indirectly characterise it as part and parcel of genocide.

101. 'Unesco and the Struggle against Ethnocide'.

102. Ronald Niezen, *The Origins of Indigenism: Human Rights and the Politics of Identity* (Berkeley: University of California Press, 2003), 5, 55.

103. Middle East Watch, *Human Rights in Iraq* (New Haven, CT: Yale University Press, 1990), 35.

104. Lawrence Davidson, *Cultural Genocide* (New Brunswick, NJ: Rutgers University Press, 2012), 112.

105. This can also be seen within the Assyrian peoples and could be structured in terms of ecclesiastical or sectarian partitions.

106. Benedict Anderson, *Imagined Communities: Reflections on the Origin and Spread of Nationalism*, 2nd ed. (London: Verso, 1991), 6.

107. The coverage in this study is by no means exhaustive and future work must be undertaken in Iraq including forensic research and a proper oral history of the Assyrians.

108. Jones, *Genocide*, 81.

109. For the case of Canada see Franca Iacovetta, Roberto Perin and Angelo Principe (eds), *Enemies Within: Italian and Other Internees in Canada and Abroad* (Toronto: University of Toronto Press, 2000), 11.

110. 'Brief Overview of the World War II Enemy Alien Control Program', National Archives website (USA), http://www.archives.gov/research/immigration/enemy-aliens-overview.html (accessed 22 July 2014)

111. 'Residential schools apology too late, say survivors', CBC Online, 11 June 2008, http://www.cbc.ca/news/canada/prince-edward-island/residential-schools-apology-too-late-say-survivors-1.719268 (accessed 22 July 2014).

112. Vernon Van Dyke, *Human Rights, Ethnicity, and Discrimination* (Westport, CT: Greenwood Press, 1985), 81.

113. One way to counteract the inattention to the Assyrians in the vacuum created by the political focus on the modern nation-state is to characterise and group them as a transnational indigenous people. See Timo Koivurova, 'Can Saami Transnational Indigenous Peoples Exercise Their Self-determination in a World of Sovereign States?', in Nigel Bankes and Timo Koivurova (eds), *The Proposed Nordic Saami Convention: National and International Dimensions of Indigenous Property Rights* (Oxford: Hart, 2013).

8

Conclusion

As long as there are slaughterhouses, there will be battlefields.

Leo Tolstoy

We recall our terrible past so that we can deal with it, to forgive where forgiveness is necessary, without forgetting; to ensure that never again will such inhumanity tear us apart.

Nelson Mandela

No one is born hating another person because of the colour of his skin or his background or his religion. People must learn to hate, and if they can learn to hate, they can be taught to love, for love comes more naturally to the human heart than its opposite.

Nelson Mandela

Ultimately, by highlighting the history of the Assyrians in twentieth-century Iraq, this work hopes to create a model that can be used for analyses of minorities across the region, where violence to marginalised communities is aleviated by their inclusion in mainstream history. This creation, if successful, was accomplished by demonstrating the importance of minorities to generally accepted 'major' events, which in turn was achieved through the application of (and in turn substantiated by) an inclusive paradigm where all experiences are vital to and exist in symbiosis with all others in order to illuminate a reality (or past) which is both holistic and intrinsically boundless and unknowable in its entirety (*panenhistoricism*). This essential interdependence thereby safeguards those experiences on the margins (i.e. the Assyrians and others) against subsumption (*subordinating narrativisation*) by the mainstream ('Iraqi history') through policies of acculturation tied to the destruction of place and ways of life, the building blocks of identity and community.

This work simultaneously serves as an alternative narrative about Iraq in the twentieth century as well as an Assyrian history of the region. It has looked outside the prism of the state and attempted to use the Assyrian situation to present another view of the historical events – a retelling of how and why they occurred, and why such issues, from a minority perspective, are essential to a panenhistorical reality or paradigm. It is a duty of scholarship to examine the story left untold. Unfortunately many still appear to adhere to the sometimes-subconscious view that 'at best, history is a story of power, a history of those who won'.[1] There is the need for a shift in how we view reality and meaning that would allow history to be seen as an ever-expanding puzzle with each piece or narrative a distinct manifestation of historical truth vital to its totality. Otherwise, the quandary of the inadequate material or lacunae concerning the Assyrians in academia is simply dismissed as a scarcity of scholarly interest or feigned ambivalence, likely manipulated by the political ambitions for authority and supremacy in the modern nation-state, both Eastern and Western. This includes the fears of powerful Western states to tackle the problem of crimes against humanity (and perhaps broaden it to crimes against life) and the violations of minorities and indigenous peoples' rights, which would in turn force them to face their own gross human rights violations against minorities and indigenous populations. I refer here to 1988, and the nearly forty years that it took the United States to ratify the Genocide Convention bill.[2] And still the majority continues to steamroll the opposition in the name of progress.

More broadly this further reflects the reluctance of Western states to confront how authoritarian and totalitarian states in the Middle East treated their own citizens in exchange for maintaining geostrategic interests in the region, from the Anglo-Iraqi Agreement for oil through the neglect of and possible British military succour in the massacre at Simele in 1933 to the blatant disregard of the Shia uprisings in 1991. This setback has further contributed to the lack of scholarly and political influence held by the Assyrians, which is a matter embedded in a process of marginalisation beginning with both Eastern and Western scholarship and political powers at the start of the 1900s. In most cases, scholarship was (and is) embedded in the political ambitions and processes of states. The same can be said for the Assyrian predicament in Iraq in the twentieth century – a long tale that requires greater examination from various perspectives.

Moreover, the onus placed on marginalised groups in the Middle East to research and write their own history in order to be heard is a scapegoat for poor inquiry, abject neglect or both. It is a case of laying the burden for animals sent to slaughter at their own feet – by virtue of their agreeable taste they are regrettably doomed to become a meal for the higher species.[3] It becomes a detached commodification and commoditisation of life. In choosing and attributing value based on larger groups' assessment of the worth of those considered lesser – be they plant, animal, human, land, water, air, metal – all things become relegated to mere 'resources.' It is intriguing that such unvoiced ideology is as rampant in the constructivist approach as in the objectivist/positivist one. At core both have a normative claim that inevitably sidelines select communities or individuals. What is more perplexing is the fact that the way to circumvent the issue for the post-modernist scholar and their paradigms is sometimes more damaging as in order to refrain from nullifying their ontological worldview, they deconstruct minority communities and unauthenticate them as such, providing themselves an escape clause from their ethical responsibility to the truth of existence and substantiation of meaning.

Since pursuit of the academy was and still is to a large extent an elitist endeavour embedded in the politics of nation-states, indigenous peoples and minorities have traditionally lacked the means by which to approach the echelons of academic authority. The entire system remains a hegemonic institutional framework, is far from apolitical, and gives priority to certain dominant methods. Thus, people's histories and self-histories unquestionably must occur in greater magnitude as these numerically and politically marginal groups will always bear the brunt of the burden and responsibility for improving their present predicament. Over time, the powerful grow more authoritative and those others less so. Others become a roadblock to 'progress', a speed bump on the path to 'development' and greater dominance. Desire for power and the illusion of control and indeed arrogance of more significance, rooted in a learned idea or behaviour, are the culprits of this global pandemic of violence against communities, places and the land itself. Furthermore, rationalising criminal or malevolent acts does not somehow make them virtuous and employing an extenuous vocabulary does not make one objective. Neither does hiding behind perceived neutral terms like 'archives' and 'institutions', which are essentially state apparatus for telling its own version of history, and what it views as culture.

This is also a reflection on the interconnectivity of people and place. Demographic displacement and dispossession are precursors to disconnection and hopelessness, which in turn distance people, in this case Assyrians, from writing their own history, their own struggles. In the absence of political, economic or social influence minorities and indigenous cultures rely on various means of cultural resistance. Yet, without constant vigilance and compassion outside commodities and resources, it may be, as the Lakota ghost dancers came to comprehend, that 'in the end, songs and dancers were no match for dollars and guns'.[4] Accordingly it should be the enduring role of the academy to engage in unknown/marginal histories while realising that those who take such steps may expose themselves to contempt and short careers. In the words of Edward Said:

> This role has an edge to it, and cannot be played without a sense of being someone whose place it is publicly to raise embarrassing questions, to confront orthodoxy and dogma (rather than produce them), to be someone who cannot easily be co-opted by governments or corporations, and whose raison d'être is to represent all those people and issues that are routinely forgotten or swept under the rug.[5]

Any event or act or thought can be justified – heinous and delightful are often a matter of perspective – and feigning or assuming to be above perspective is in and of itself grounded in perspective. Research on recent Iraqi state formation is incomplete without a close examination of the significance of the Assyrian case as both equal to and a catalyst for continued treatment of those communities on the margins of history. To weave a historical narrative devoid of an authentic appreciation for place is inadequate. Time and place are inextricably interconnected: Assyrian villages and homes in Iraq as much as the place of Assyrians in modern discourse on Iraq and the Middle East. Furthermore, homogenisation, both overt and subtle, whether by nationalist ideology or uncritically accepted American exceptionalism etc. codified in museums and education systems and reinforced by mass media, or by academic studies which intentionally or unintentionally unimagine or marginalise what are deemed societies and individuals of lesser significance, rob us of visible and invisible things which have meaning to us, they devalue our longitudinal wisdom and erase the fragments from which to piece together the stories of nature and history through which our humanity is fed. They stunt our sensibilities and starve our imagination.[6]

In summation, demonising peoples, cultures etc. is not the refrain of this work. Rather reforging or reshaping history is. Furthermore, policies of marginalisation, both violent and (seemingly) non-violent, are embedded in a more basic unethical ambition for power, while the attainment of that absolute control creates the paranoid fear of losing it to others, especially those considered of lesser significance to the matter, be it trivial or ultimate. As Patrick Curry notes:

> The precise nature of that power – whether primarily economic, religious, political, or whatever mixture of these – is entirely secondary to its intended monism, universalism and homogeneity. The effects of such an enterprise, regardless of the intentions of those who carry it out, are necessarily evil.[7]

A return to Tolstoy's remark above reminds us that it is only after a further look at this learned desire for control, based in fear, arrogance and lack of reverence, that humanity may glimpse one of its fundamental flaws and remedy it. While it may be an unpopular position in society, it must be pursued. There is the need for a shift in how humans view reality, truth and meaning. For if such adverse thoughts or behaviours, learned or instinctual, whether by states or individuals, are inherent to knowledge lacking wisdom, power lacking mercy and humility, then there is a solution: they can be unlearned by people reimagining or reforging the fragments of knowledge into wisdom. As Nelson Mandela movingly intoned, people 'can be taught love, for love comes more naturally to the human heart'. Insight is born of accepting an ever-growing and changing portrait of reality, inclusive and interdependent, with each and every hue and thread (and story and experience) essential to the grand tapestry. And wisdom appears when finally it is acknowledged that this tapestry (or as much of it as can be seen and experienced) is constrained only by the fact that it is a shadow, a lesser reflection of that entity which it has aimed to capture – and yet the reflection, the shadow, the individual stories have meaning in and of themselves as they have the power to remind us of the unfathomable whole which they represent. One might ask, 'But where can one find them?'

> You find them where I found them, and they will be there forever, the race of man, the part of man, of Assyria as much as of England, that cannot be destroyed, the part that massacre does not destroy, the part that earthquake and war and famine and madness and everything else cannot destroy.
>
> This work is in tribute . . . to the race of man everywhere, to the dignity of that race, the brotherhood of things alive . . . I am thinking of seventy thousand Assyrians, one at a time, alive, a great race. I am thinking of Theodore Badal, himself seventy thousand Assyrians and seventy million Assyrians, himself Assyria, and man, standing in a barber shop, in San Francisco, in 1933, and being, still, himself, the whole race.[8]

Notes

1. Michel-Rolph Trouillot, *Silencing the Past: Power and the Production of History* (Boston: Beacon Press, 1997), 5.
2. See 'Convention on the Prevention and Punishment of the Crime of Genocide: Declarations and Reservations', United Nations Treaty Collection, website, https://treaties.un.org/Pages/ViewDetails.aspx?mtdsg_no=IV-1&chapter=4&lang=en#EndDec (accessed 23 July 2014). The signing came with conditions. Reservation one essentially stipulates that no party can bring charges against the United States in an international court without its agreement.
3. In this case, the superior human community, culture or people.
4. Elaine Eastman, 'The Ghost Dance War', in Stephen Duncombe (ed.), *Cultural Resistance: A Reader* (London: Verso, 2002), 194.
5. Edward Said, *Representations of the Intellectual: The 1993 Reith Lectures* (London: Vintage, 1994), 9, as quoted in Giles Mohan and Gordon Wilson, 'The Antagonistic Relevance of Development Studies', *Progress in Development Studies* 5.4 (2005), 264. Mohan and Wilson translate as 'Said urges intellectuals to retain their amateur status. That is, to maintain a critical distance from the largely statist agendas of the research funders.'
6. Sue Clifford and Angela King, 'Losing Your Place', in *Local Distinctiveness: Place, Particularity and Identity*, quoted in Patrick Curry, *Defending Middle-Earth: Tolkien, Myth and Modernity* (Boston: Houghton Mifflin, 2004), 145.
7. Curry, *Defending Middle-Earth*, 146.
8. William Saroyan, 'Seventy Thousand Assyrians' (1934).

Glossary

Chaldeans – An ecclesiastical sect of the Assyrian people. Former Nestorians (or members of the Church of the East) who first began converting to Catholicism in 1553. 'Chaldean' was synonymous with 'Catholic'

Chatta (Turkish 'militia', also 'robber' or 'thief') – Term used by Kurds and Assyrians living in northern Iraq to refer to the pro-government Kurdish irregulars

Fursan (Arabic mounted 'knights') – Term used by the regime to refer to the *chatta* (see above), dubbing them *fursan Salahadin*, or the 'knights of Saladin'

Gippa (Assyrian) – Cave, grotto

Jacobites – An ecclesiastical sect of the Assyrian people. Also known as members of the Syrian/Syriac Orthodox Church Orthodox Church and its offshoot, the Syrian/Syriac Catholic Church

Jaḥsh (Arabic 'foal/young donkey') = *chatta*

Mar (Assyrian) – Saint (m)

Mart (Assyrian) – Saint (f)

Naṣara (Arabic) – Literally 'Nazarene' or more simply 'Christian'. Many villages in northern Iraq are in fact split between Assyrian and Kurdish inhabitants. They are sometimes designated as *naṣara* (Christian Assyrian) and *islami* (Muslim Kurdish). The term gained notoriety in the summer of 2014 as the Arabic letter N was spray-painted by the Islamic State on the houses of Christians in Mosul

Nestorians – An ecclesiastical sect of the Assyrian people. Also known as members of the Church of the East/East Syrian Church/Assyrian Church of the East and the Ancient Church of the East

Pêşmerge (Kurdish) – 'Those who face death'. A term for the fighters in resistance against the Iraqi regime

Qasha (Assyrian) – Priest

Shamasha (Assyrian) – Deacon

Sūrayt/Sūreth – Assyrian-Aramaic; the language spoken by the Assyrians today. Sometimes called Modern Assyrian Neo-Aramaic, Neo-Syriac, Modern Aramaic

Yezidis – A distinct ethno-religious community native to Jebel Sinjar in northern Iraq and extending into southeastern Turkey with ties to Assyro-Mesopotamian heritage through their religious beliefs, which include the seven greater angels who were placed in charge of the earth by a divine being. The greatest of this order of angels is known as Tawuse Melek and referred to in English frequently as the Peacock Angel

Names

Adde – Thaddeus

Aprim – Ephraim

Gewargis – George

Luqa – Luke

Mari – Bartholomew

Maryam – Mary

Mattai – Matthew

Oraha (*Auraha, Awraha*) – Abraham

Quryaqos – Cyriacus

Yawsep – Joseph

Yonan – Jonah

Youḥannan/Youkhanna – John

Appendix A: Village Data[1]

Description of Villages Affected in the 1960s by Region

The following data illustrates the Assyrian villages affected by the autonomist uprising of 1961–3, including notes on material and cultural significance, and population statistics where known and applicable. Numbers of families or persons reflect the native numbers in all cases (unless otherwise noted), sometimes distinguishing between Nestorian/Assyrian Church of the East and Chaldean/Catholic when known. The villages and towns affected are listed below by province and district.[2]

Arbil Province[3]

Harīr District

Batase

The sister village of Harīr, Batase (sometimes Batas), located in the district of the same name, was home to followers of Mar Shimun, mostly from the Nochiya region, who fled there following the First World War. In 1938, there were fifty-three families (303 persons), along with a variety of livestock and agricultural equipment: 172 goats, 147 sheep, 85 oxen, 33 donkeys, 9 mules, 8 buffalo and 16 ploughs.[4] Prior to its destruction, there were thirty Assyrian households in Batase, with the ancient church of Mar Stephanos as their religious centre. Though not built by its then resident Assyrians, the old Church of the East edifice is testament to previous Assyrian presence in the region. The villagers were attacked and forced out in 1963 by pro-government Kurdish forces, who then resettled the area.[5] Many fled to the major cities or Iran during this time, but none returned.

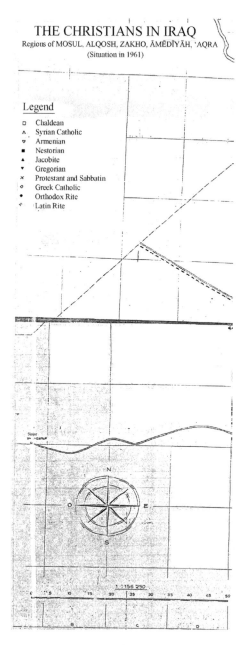

THE CHRISTIANS IN IRAQ
Regions of MOSUL, ALQOSH, ZAKHO, ĀMĒDĪYĀH, ʿAQRA
(Situation in 1961)

Legend

▫	Chaldean
ʌ	Syrian Catholic
▽	Armenian
▪	Nestorian
▲	Jacobite
▼	Gregorian
×	Protestant and Sabbatin
◦	Greek Catholic
•	Orthodox Rite
✦	Latin Rite

Figure 19   Key to the Dominican map of Father Josephe Omez translated into English. The legend displays Christian ecclesiastical communities in north Iraq. Omez's work recorded predominantly Chaldean and Nestorian villages, which are the primary focus of this study. While not based on population, it is unclear why he chose the order of ecclesiastical designations in the key

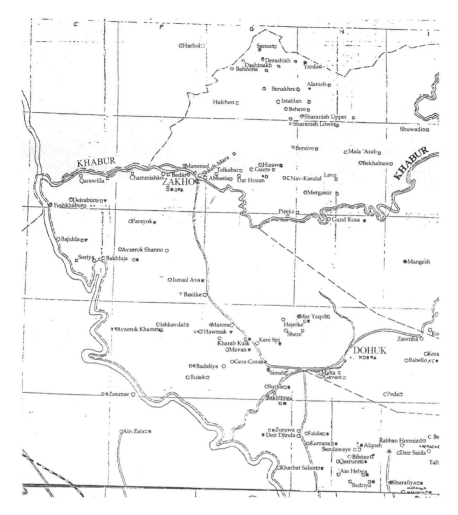

Figure 20   Omez's map showing northwestern Iraq – Dohuk, Simele and Zakho

Darbandoke

Most of the Christian inhabitants of Darbandoke or Derbandok ('enclosed place' in Kurdish) are of the Nochiya tribe, though Assyrians of other regions dwelled there as well, alongside a Kurdish population. The village is the birth-place of the Patriarch of the Assyrian Church of the East, Mar Dinkha IV, born in September 1935. It is also the birthplace of Emanuel Kamber PhD, physicist and former secretary general of the Assyrian Universal Alliance (AUA). In 1938, fifteen families totalling 108 people lived in the village,

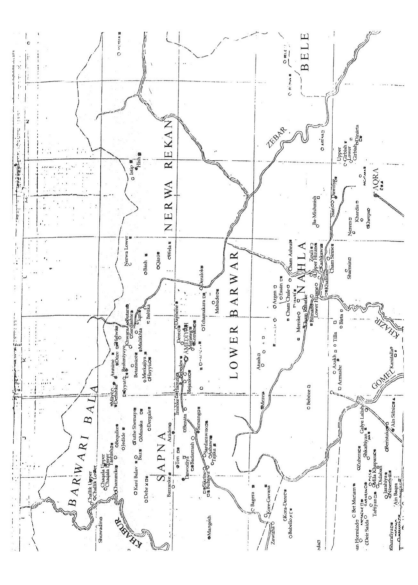

Figure 21   Omez's map showing the Barwari Bala, Sapna/Sarsang, Nerwa/Rekan and 'Aqra/Nahla subdistricts

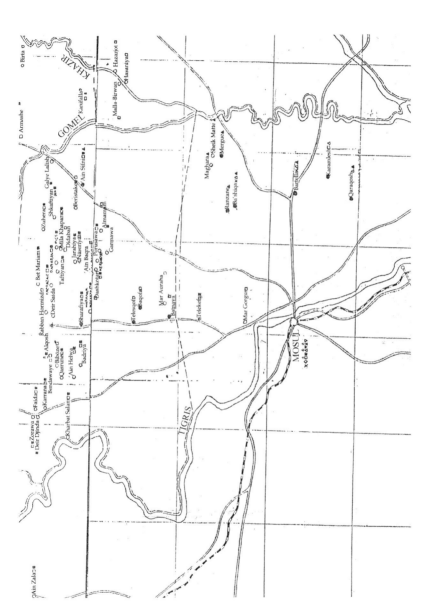

Figure 22   Omez's map showing the Mosul region

along with a variety of livestock (and other animals) and agricultural tools, including 100 sheep, 60 goats, 10 oxen, 5 horses and 5 ploughs.[6] According to most interviewees, the majority of Assyrians lived in relative peace in the region prior to the uprising in the early 1960s. In 1963, the entire village's population, approximately fifteen households, either fled, never to return, or was killed. Of those killed, five names are known: Shamoun, Hajji, Qusha, Yoab and Iktu, who was killed in a government air raid.[7] The church of Mar Quryaqos was annihilated at the same time. The Assyrian quarter of the village was resettled by pro-government Kurds.[8]

Diyana

Diyana (or Diana) was built by levy officers and their families under the British administration. According to League of Nations statistics, the village held 126 families (totalling 569 persons), along with 298 goats, 59 sheep and 20 ploughs.[9] Prior to its destruction in 1963, Diyana contained more than 125 Assyrian households and the following churches: Mar Quryaqos, two churches sacred to Mar Gewargis, and two older churches, Mart Maryam and Mar Stephanos.[10] Its population fled in 1963 while air and ground forces attacked the region. Though some natives returned, their homecoming was short lived, as the village was attacked again in 1974, whereupon its remaining Assyrians inhabitants fled a second time.[11]

Hanare

Hanare (also Henare, Hanara) was home to twenty-two families (136 persons) in 1938, along with a significant amount of livestock.[12] It contained twelve households prior to its destruction in 1963. The village and its inhabitants encountered the same fate as those of Batase, Darbandoke, Diyana, Harīr and Kalate.[13]

Harīr

Harīr village was rebuilt by Nestorian-rite from Hakkâri following the First World War. Included in the building process was the church of Mar Yohanna. In 1938, Harīr had seventy-eight families (485 persons), twenty manual ploughs and a large amount of livestock, including 672 goats, 374 sheep, 80 oxen, 12 horses, 6 buffalo, 6 mules and 2 donkeys.[14] Prior to its destruction in 1963, the total number of Assyrian households numbered above ninety.[15] Little else is known of the village, although according to a report from the Kurdish Center for Human Rights, on 18 February 2006 the Kurdistan Regional Government's Minister of Human Rights discussed the uncovering of a mass grave in which some thirty-seven bodies were identified as Assyrians originally from Harīr.[16]

Kalate

The village of Kalate (sometimes Qalana Soran in League of Nations reports) was reported to have been home to ten Assyrian families (eighty-four persons), along with 200 sheep, 106 goats, 10 oxen and 2 mules in 1938.[17] The village was attacked in 1963 by pro-government Kurdish forces and its Assyrian inhabitants were forced to flee during the infighting. None returned, and their homes were confiscated and resettled by pro-government militia.[18] No major cultural or religious structures are mentioned with respect to Kalate.

Rowanduz District

Hawdian

Hawdian (also Howdian, Havdian) is famous for its immediate proximity to≈the Shanidar Cave in northeastern Iraq. In 1938, twelve Assyrian families (ninety persons) resided in the village, along with 105 goats and 25 head of cattle.[19] Between 1957 and 1961, Ralph Solecki and a team from Columbia University excavated the site, unearthing the first adult Neanderthal skeletons in Iraq; the remains were dated to between 80,000 and 60,000 years BP. Also referred to as Zawi Chemi Shanidar, or to Assyrians as Gippa d'Hawdian (the Cave of Hawdian), the cave was mentioned extensively by the British road engineer A. M. Hamilton in the early 1930s. Hamilton questioned, Yaqo Ismael, about what he knew of the cave's history:

> You have heard little of what is said to be in the Baradost cave, sir, but
> evidently you have not heard of the mill that grinds flour for ever and
> never stops, yet with no man or woman to feed it; you have not heard of
> the fire that burns eternally, nor of the secret vault that holds the treasure
> of the ancient kings of Assyria, looted from enemies when ours was the

mightiest nation on earth, thousands of years ago, when men in Europe and in England were mere savages in the forests. I am a descendant of those ancient kings! The remnant of our nation that survived the war is now wandering homeless in Iraq. Some of us serve you as British soldiers. Yet once all these lands were ours, as the carvings at Batas, at Amadiyah and Nineveh must prove to you.[20]

Of the findings from the excavations, the various 'Christian ware' ceramics, along with a metal medallion from Constantinople dated AD 500 and a shallow stone-cut pool carved (most probably) by monks, speak to the history of a continuous Christian settlement. The name Shanidar may partially reflect the Assyrian-Aramaic term *deyra* ('monastery'), which would lend further evidence to the site as an Assyrian Christian settlement.[21] The church of Mar Oraha (Abraham) of the Church of the East was destroyed in 1963, along with the rest of the village and its twenty households, by pro-government militia.[22]

Dohuk Province

'Amēdīyāh District
'Amēdīyāh

The town, now city, of 'Amēdīyāh is located east of the Barwari mountain range, roughly 50 miles north of Mosul. The *Encyclopedia Judaica* reports approximately 1,800 Jewish inhabitants as late as the 1930s.[23] In 1835–6, Syriac sources tell the tale of the besieging of 'Amēdīyāh for seven years by a Kurdish chief, Mira Kora.[24] There were three Catholic families reported in 1850.[25] There once existed an old church dedicated to Mar Yozadek, an Assyrian Christian saint, though until recently it remained in ruins.[26] The city's Dominican convent was destroyed and rebuilt more than once.[27] 'Amēdīyāh is generally referred to as the site of the beginning of the Kurdish autonomist struggle. Here, the Barzanis fought the Iraqi army, supported by the Zebari, Surchi, Bradost and Herki Kurdish tribes.[28] Though some Assyrians fought alongside Kurdish guerrillas in Barwar – including the first casualty in the struggle, Ethniel Shleimon of Dūre village – many remained neutral. Following consistent fighting between the Barzani autonomists and the pro-government forces from October through the winter of 1961, many of those neutral Assyrians began to flee. By January of 1962, 4,500 Assyrians had been forced to flee to other parts of Iraq.[29]

Ashawa

Ashawa, located in the Sarsang sub-district, was settled most recently by refugees from Hakkâri in the 1920s.[30] According to the 1957 census, its Assyrian population stood at 619. Though taken and resettled by pro-government Kurdish irregulars during the uprising in 1961, Ashawa was later bulldozed by the Ba'th regime, and a presidential palace was erected on its lands.[31]

Badarrash

Badarrash (also Badrashk), located about one mile north of Sarsang, was settled by Nestorian and Chaldean refugees of the Baz tribe in the 1920s. In 1938, the village was home to twenty-seven families (eighty men and seventy-two women), along with livestock: 100 goats and 50 sheep.[32] Mar Gewargis Chaldean Church, built in 1925, suffered ruination during the village raiding in 1961, which also destroyed all the farms and apple orchards. Adherents of both the Church of the East (Nestorian Church) and the Chaldean Church occupied the village until many fled under threat during the civil war. Badarrash was home to thirty households in 1961.[33]

Havintka

There are few references to Havintka (also spelled Hawintka) before the settlement of refugees of the Lower Tiyari tribe in 1920. In 1957, there were approximately sixty people in the village. Havintka was abandoned in 1961.[34]

Sarsang (city)

The city of Sarsang (also spelled Sarseng and Sarsank) was most recently settled by 100 families (40 households) of refugees from the Tiyari tribe, adherents of the Church of the East, in 1922.[35] In 1933, the population shrank to about 150. By 1938, fifty-five families (166 men and 135 women) resided in the city, along with livestock: forty goats and twenty sheep.[36] A church dedicated to Mar Mattai was built in 1955 for the Assyrians in Sarsang. It is also a popular tourist destination for people from throughout Iraq. In 1961, the town numbered 150 families (80 households), totalling 700 people.[37] Most of the Assyrian lands began to be confiscated in 1972 and 1973 by pro-Barzani Kurdish villagers from Upper Arāden and Kani-Chinarke.[38] Many Assyrians fled following threats and attacks during that period.

Ṣawura
Ṣawura (sometimes spelled Ṣawra) was divided into upper and lower districts. It is the well-known site of the school of Babai the Great, a Christian religious figure, which served both the region and Eastern Christianity generally for many years, producing scholars in theology and philosophy.[39] It was settled by Nestorians of Upper Tiyari from the village of Rumtha in the 1920s. The then *mukhtar* (mayor) of the village was Mame Beth Semano.[40] Following the massacre at Simele in 1933, many villagers fled or were robbed and killed.[41] In one particular case more than twenty Assyrians were killed.[42] Ṣawura's population was forced out in 1961 and fled the region.[43]

Tazhikka
Tazhikka was resettled by refugees from Hakkâri in the 1920s. Its population numbered 123 in 1957 and its villagers abandoned it under threat in 1961.[44]

Ṭlanīthā
The name Ṭlanīthā may be based on the Assyrian-Aramaic word for 'shadow' or 'shade', though the village is sometimes known as Dewike. In 1850 Badger wrote the settlement name as Ṭalneetha; at the time it was home to between six and twelve families, a priest and a church. Ṭlanitha was within the Church of the East diocese of Mar Abraham of Gündük (Nerem), in the mountains south of Jebel Gara.[45] The village, along with the churches of Mart Shmuni and Mar Quryaqos, was left in ruins after the rebellion of 1961 when Zebari tribesmen ransacked it.[46]

'Aqra District
'Aqra
'Aqra's etymology may trace to an Assyrian-Aramaic word meaning 'root', perhaps, in the case of the city, as the root or foot of the mountain. The

city is mentioned in Neo-Assyrian sources as Kurbail.[47] Many of its original inhabitants were religiously Christians and Jews. Its people were known as artisans – weavers and jewellers. Prior to the fourteenth century, the region was part of the diocese of Margā and under the jurisdiction of the Church of the East's metropolitan see of Adiabene.[48] Most villages in and around 'Aqra were Nestorian until the beginning of the nineteenth century. Dominican proselytising during the mid-1800s caused a drastic decline in the Nestorian community and a surge in Catholic converts. By 1913, the Chaldean Church in the 'Aqra district consisted of nineteen villages, ten churches, sixteen priests, and approximately 2,400 people.[49] The town itself contained at least 250 Chaldean-rite families, with two priests, a church and a school. The churches of Mart Maryam and Mar Gewargis illustrated the combined Chaldean/Jacobite/Nestorian character of the region. Persons of Jewish faith left Iraq between 1948 and 1949, whereas the Christians began their exodus after 1961, as a result of the pressure against them by the Iraqi authorities and irregular Kurdish forces. 'Aqra's diocese closed after its population had left the town. Nearby are the remnants of the Mar Quryaqos Monastery, overlooking the Assyrian village of Birta, which is located 20 kilometres from 'Aqra. In the period of the timeline covered by this research, most of the families of 'Aqra became internally or externally displaced.

Ba-Mishmish

Also known as Beth Shimsha or 'House of the Sun', this village is located in the Nahla region northwest of Dawrīye. It is known from a book of hymns and benedictions copied there by a priest named Bahrīn in or around 1741.[50] In 1850, it was home to between fifteen and twenty-two families and one active church.[51] Following the increase in Catholic missions in the region, in 1913 there were 150 converts to Catholicism (Chaldeans) with a church and chapel.[52] By 1918, there were forty-nine Assyrians (twelve households) left in total, with a Kurdish majority. The last Assyrians left the village in 1961 during Kurdish and Iraqi government fighting, and at that time, the church of Mart Maryam and the chapel to Mar Youḥannan were left in a state of ruin. The village was also home to a shrine to Mar Yawsep.

Barāk

Barāk, also spelled Barrāke, located southwest of Kharjawa and known for its tobacco, was once settled by Assyrians. Following attacks on the village in 1961, which saw the destruction of the church of Mart Maryam, its inhabitants fled, and Kurds subsequently resettled it.[53]

Dawrīye

Dawrīye, also referred to as Dūre (not to be confused with the Barwari Bala region of the same name), has long been an Assyrian settlement in the Nahla or Nahla d'Malka region of 'Aqra. Early on, Thomas of Margā mentions it in his section concerning Youḥannan of Dēlūm,[54] who worked as keeper of a monastery situated in the village.[55] In 1913, it was home to fifty Chaldeans, with a priest serving one church.[56] By 1918, there were only two families (eleven people) left in the village. In 1922, refugees from Lower Tiyari resettled Dawrīye, and by 1957, the village population totalled 134. Zebari Kurdish irregulars employed by the government surrounded the village in 1961 and besieged it for three months. Four villagers were killed, including Yacoub and Ishaq Yalda, and Khoshaba Kako, as well as a fourteen-year-old girl. Thirty-five families survived, fleeing to Mosul and 'Aqra following the siege.[57] The church of Mart Shmuni, in the centre of the upper part of the old village, was damaged.[58].

Dinārta

According to a League of Nations report, in 1933 Dinārta, or Dinārta d'Nahla, was home to 113 people.[59] The village was mixed Assyrian and Kurdish before its Assyrian inhabitants abandoned it. In 1961 the remaining Assyrians fled following attacks from both pro-government militia and neighbouring tribes.[60]

Dodi Masih

It is also referred to as Upper Dodi or by its ancient name, Beth Nura. In 1913, there were eighty people in the village, but by 1918 their number had decreased to only twenty-three (three families), due to conflicts with the Herki tribe of Kurdish origin.[61] In 1957, the Assyrian population numbered seventy-three. The village was forcibly abandoned in 1961, and its church, dedicated to Mar Gewargis, destroyed.[62]

Girbish

Girbish (spelled also as Garbesh and Garbish), an old settlement, was divided into upper and lower districts. Just prior to the First World War, Girbish had a mostly Catholic (Chaldean) makeup, alongside a Nestorian contingent. In 1922, the tribe of Lower Tiyari settled Girbish.[63] In early 1938, approximately thirty Assyrian families of Church of the East ecclesiastical background dwelled in the village, along with 229 sheep and 530 goats.[64] Later that same year, their number decreased to twenty-six families (121 persons), most likely due to a widespread malaria outbreak.[65] By 1957, the village population totalled 374, with 182 in Upper Girbish and 192 in Lower Girbish. In 1961, Zebari Kurdish irregulars surrounded and besieged the village for months. At this time, the 210 families were forced to flee their houses, numbering approximately seventy-five, which were in turn settled by the besieging Zebaris. The church of Mart Shmuni (rebuilt in 1949 over its older ruins) was also left in disrepair.[66]

Khardis

Khardis, or Khardas, is mentioned in a 1698 Syriac manuscript that attests to its continued settlement and importance. A copy of the *Hudra*[67] was penned in the village not long after in 1715.[68] In linear order, from the northwest to the southeast of Khinnis/Bavian, the village lies fifth, following Sharmin, Shush, Nerem and Sheikhi, and is followed by Resha and, finally, Kherpa.[69] In 1913, it was home to 120 Catholics, served by a priest and a single chapel.[70] By 1918, the population of Khardis had decreased to fifty-six (ten families). Khardis suffered damage, as did the local churches, dedicated to Mart Maryam and Mart Shmuni. Its population fled when Kurdish forces attacked it in 1961.[71] Villagers have also mentioned a monastery built inside a cavern in the valley behind the village.[72]

Kharjawa

In 1918, there were thirty households (142 people) in the village of Kharjawa (Ḥarğāwa), with a mud-brick church dedicated to Mar Youḥannan (St John the Baptist). This church was rebuilt with stone in 1952. There was also a shrine to Mar Pius. Though David Wilmshurst believes the village to have had a Chaldean contingent at the end of the nineteenth century, Tfinkdji does not mention it in his 1913 study.[73] Wilmshurst does, however, mention another church, dedicated to Mar Yawsep.[74] Kharjawa's entire Assyrian population was forced to flee during the infighting in 1961. The village is missing from the 1961 Omez map.

Khelafta

Khelafta, also Khaleptha or Beth Ḥlāpe, is mentioned in Thomas of Margā's *Book of Governors* and was located in the Sapsāpā or Shapshāpā ecclesiastical district, just west of the ʿAqra region.[75] It is mentioned as being attacked by a certain ʿAmran bar-Muhammad hailing from Bebōze, who also laid waste to Birta, Shush, Kherpa and other villages in the Sapsāpā region.[76] A few miles south of Khelafta are the ruins of the ancient monastery of Rabban Bar ʿEdta. The village was destroyed in 1961 and resettled by its attackers but never by Assyrians, as it is absent from the 1961 Dominican map.[77]

Kherpa

Kherpa, also written Ḥerpā and Kharpa, was once an Assyrian settlement and has an archaeological mound referred to as *tella d'malka*, 'the King's hill'. In 1868, when Zebari Kurdish irregulars attempted to ransack the village it had four priests, testament to a large population.[78] In 1913, according to Tfinkdji, the settlement was home to 200 Assyrian Catholics, with a priest, church and school, but by 1918 its population had decreased to 114 (twenty-one families).[79] The village was abandoned in 1961 and seized by Zebari Kurd irregulars employed by the government.[80] The church of Mart Maryam (restored in 1952) was damaged as was the chapel of Mar Youḥannan, built around a cave shrine in 1918.

Nahawa

Located in the ʿAqra region and the sub-district of Girdasin, Nahawa (also Nūhāwā or Nūwābā) is an important Assyrian settlement. Wilmshurst mentions Nahawa as the location where three manuscripts were copied during the second half of the nineteenth century.[81] In 1913, Nahawa was home to 150 Chaldean-rite residents, with one priest serving one church.[82] Many had originated in the Urmia region of Iran and immigrated in the late eighteenth century. The church of Mart Maryam and a shrine to Mar Pius were severely damaged during the 1961–3 period, when the entire village population was forced into other regions of Iraq.[83]

Nerem

Nerem, or Nerem d-Ra'awatha, called Gundik or Gündük (Kurdish for 'village') by Badger, was an Assyrian village of great significance as the location of a Church of the East bishopric in the mid-nineteenth century. The then bishop, Mar Awrahem (Awraha or Auraha), had originally been of Chaldean religious affiliation, but reportedly returned to Nestorianism (Church of the East) around that time.[84] In 1850, Nerem was home to between twelve and eighteen Church of the East families, served by a priest and one church.[85] By 1913, there were more than 100 Catholic-rite families, again with a single priest and church.[86] The number who remained faithful to the Mar Shimun Patriarchal line of the Church of the East at that time remains unknown. By 1918, the Assyrian population of Nerem had decreased to sixty-six (fourteen families), who made up about half the population of the village, along with Kurds and a small number of adherents of Judaism with their own synagogue. These Jews left during the expulsions of 1949–51, and government militia forces drove the Christians out of Nerem in 1961.[87]

The ancient monastery of Mar 'Abdisho' is located less than one mile northwest of Nerem in the direction of Shush. Though the monastery's original date of construction is unknown, it is mentioned in a Syriac manuscript dating from 1610. The monastery, with grottos dedicated to Ambusk and Mar Youhannan, was partially destroyed and fell into ruin following the opposition movement and civil wars from 1961 to 1963. The grotto of Mar Youhannan is famed for possessing an ancient wall relief. As Badger recounts:

> To the left of the cave we discovered the object of our search, viz a rock tablet bearing on its surface the representation of a man in the act of spearing a wild sheep or ibex, and beneath this a procession of six figures standing in various attitudes. The style is not unlike that of the sculptures dug up at Nimrood, but the costume is different, and may be found to belong to a distinct age and people.[88]

According to villagers, the early monastery of Mar Quprios is also located in the vicinity, which is likely the case, since a monk by the name of Cyprian, a disciple of Narsai, is extensively mentioned by Thomas of Margā as living in the region and performing various deeds of note.[89]

Ras al-ʿAin

Ras al-ʿAin was known as Rēš-ēni during the Neo-Assyrian period and as Resh ʿAina or Resha in Syriac sources.[90] The village, situated close to Khelafta, is mentioned in Thomas of Margā's *Book of Governors*. In 1865, there were four households in the village, which had been converted to Catholicism through Dominican persuasion. In 1918, it was home to twenty-three Assyrians (five families). Though Fiey mentions the lack of a Christian population from 1945 to 1955, some families resided in the area and regularly attempted to rebuild their property until 1961, when those inhabitants were forcibly expelled, most likely by pro-government militia, and the village not resettled, as it is absent from the Dominican map of 1961.

Safra Zor

Safra Zor, or Sifra, was home to thirty-five people in 1933.[91] In 1938, its population numbered forty-seven, along with three sheep and thirty-eight goats.[92] Its residents were forced to flee in 1961 during the civil war.[93]

Sharmin

Sharmin, or Shalmath, is mentioned extensively by Thomas of Margā. It dates back to the eighth century, and once housed a thirteenth-century manuscript at one of its three churches.[94] At one time, it was home to nearly 1,000 Assyrians. In 1850 there were between thirteen and twenty-one families, Church of the East adherents, served by two priests, and in 1913 there were 250 villagers, with a priest and a school.[95] It is unknown how many of Sharmin's inhabitants remained faithful to the Church of the East (Nestorian) at that time. By 1918, only sixteen Assyrian families (sixty-two people) were left in Sharmin, but their numbers were replenished by refugees from Lower Tiyari in the 1920s. In 1961 (probably just prior to the armed resistance), Fiey mentions ninety-six Assyrians (Chaldean-rite) and a few Kurdish families, with an Assyrian village chief. The last Assyrians were

forced out of Sharmin in the following year by Zebari Kurds, who resettled the village. The church of Mar Aḥḥa survived for at least a few years,
as Fiey describes it as relatively intact.[96] Fiey briefly mentions two 'other'
churches, suggesting that the ruins of one were visible during his research and
that the second became the village mosque following the events of 1961.[97]
These churches, the first dedicated to Mar Sawa (previously unnamed) and
the second previously unknown, were no longer visible at the turn of the
millennium.[98]

Shush

Shush, also known as Shushan and Bā Šōš, is mentioned extensively by
Fiey in *Assyrie chrétienne*, though curiously it is left out of the Dominican
map of 1961, meaning it most likely was never resettled. Believed to have
been continuously inhabited from at least 720 onward, Shush was the site
of a school built by Rabban Babai.[99] In 1850, it was home to between three
and five Christian families and more than 200 Aramaic-speaking Jewish
families, early Assyrian converts to Judaism.[100] Fiey also mentions that, circa
1861, the then owners of much of the valley were the family of Aḥmed
Mšīḥāyā or Aḥmed the Christian, an indication of the possible forced conversion of many Shush Christians to Islam.[101] The Assyrian population,
however, did increase over the decades. The fortified castle of Shush was
used as a protective fortress in 1914 during the period of massacres against
Assyrians, Greeks and others in the fading Ottoman Empire. The Jews of
the settlement fled between 1949 and 1951 during their exodus from Iraq,
and its Assyrian inhabitants abandoned it in 1961 when attacked by pro-
government militia.[102]

Sian

Sian is also known as Sanāyā or Sanāyā d'Nahlā. In 1913, Lower Sian consisted of approximately 100 Chaldean-rite Assyrians, with one church served
by a priest.[103] By 1918, there were only thirty-nine people (four households)
left in Lower Sian. Both Upper and Lower Sian were originally inhabited
by Assyrians, but it is unclear when they fled Upper Sian. The churches of
Mar Gewargis and Mar Zaya (fifth century) were left in ruins when the last
Assyrians were forced out in 1961.[104]

Dohuk District

Cham Kare

Little is known of Cham Kare's early history other than the 1922 settlement of Nestorian-rite Assyrians from Lower Tiyari. In 1933, the villagers moved to another nearby village, Gund Kosa, where they repelled various attacks by Baqr Sidqi and the Iraqi army. Most of the remaining villagers fled or were killed around 1961.[105]

Kora-Dere

Though the village was destroyed in 1961, the etymology of the name Kora-Dere, which contains the Assyrian-Aramaic term *deyra,* suggests it to be the location of a monastery complex.[106]

Mangesh (town)

Mangesh has been the home of notable figures since the 1950s, such as Francis Yousif Shabo (of the Assyrian Democratic Movement (ADM)) and Lazar Mikhael (of the Iraqi Communist Party), who were both assassinated in 1993. In 1850, there were 150 families, served by three priests. In 1913, there were 1,100 Chaldean-rite Assyrian, with four priests serving one church and a school.[107] By 1920, the number of households had risen to 230, and in 1947, the population numbered 1,195. In 1961, there were 600 families in Mangesh, but many left due to the attacks on the village by both Barzani-led pêşmerge and Iraqi government infighting, so that by 1965 the population had shrunk to 959 people. In 1970, there were 1,390 people in Mangesh.[108] The town's religious structures include a church dedicated to Mar Gewargis, which includes a manuscript library, and a shrine to Mart Shmuni. It is worth noting that from 1950 to 1997 (when six men were killed), more than forty individuals from Mangesh were assassinated, including mayor Rayis Hanna in the late 1950s.

Masike

Masike was settled in 1920 by refugees from Baz in the Hakkâri Mountains. In 1957, its population totalled 105, but it was abandoned in 1961 when its inhabitants faced an onslaught from government forces.[109]

Sheikhan District

Bāsifre

Bāsifre, also written Beth Sāpre, possibly meaning 'place of books or scribes', is located east of Mosul, just southeast of Birta at the foot of mountainous country once reportedly resplendent with gardens and vineyards.[110] It is mentioned in Syriac manuscripts in 1685 as having a sizeable community and three priests. According to Fiey, the inhabitants have found traces of a large castle situated just in front of the church of Mar Youḥannan, which suffered during the battles of 1961.[111] Fiey also records that just north of Bāsifre lies a village named Kalwaka, which may contain the ruins of a church dedicated to Mar Abdisho'.[112] In 1913 there were thirty individuals in the village.[113] Little is known about the Assyrians of the village following the armed autonomist movement of 1961–3.

Bedul

Bedul, or Be-Dole, may derive from the Assyrian-Aramaic meaning 'place of buckets'. Mentioned by Badger, Bedul is located in the Mezuriyeh district close to Meze and Deze, behind the Yezidi religious centre of Sheikh 'Adi. In 1850, it was home to between twenty and thirty Chaldean-rite families, with a church.[114] The last Assyrians were forced to flee the village during the attacks of 1961–3.[115]

Billān

Billān, also known as Billa, is mentioned in Syriac manuscripts as early as the ninth century and again in 1656.[116] In 1913, Tfinkdji tallied 300 Chaldean (Catholic) converts, one priest serving the village church, and a school.[117] The last Assyrians were forced to abandon the village in 1963.[118] The church of Mar Sawa was destroyed, along with the shrine of Mart Shmuni. There was also an ancient monastery dedicated to Mar Gregorious in a valley north of the village, which retains the place name Gali Dera, 'the valley of the monastery'. E. A. Wallis Budge mentions a shared connection with the village of Tilla. Though it is tempting to assume an association between Billa and Bar Bellī, mentioned by Wilmshurst, this is probably not the case.[119]

Kanifalla

Kanifalla is mentioned as the home of Syriac manuscripts copied in 1713 and 1723. The village name finds its etymology in Kurdish as *kani* 'spring' or 'source' and *fallah* 'Christian(s)'.[120] The famous copyist and writer David d'Barzane mentioned the hardships endured by his family and other villagers during the period just prior to 1854, which he attributed to the injustices of the Zebari tribesmen.[121] In 1913, there were 120 inhabitants in the village, with a priest.[122] They were later joined by refugees from Lower Tiyari. Kanifalla's Assyrian residents were forced to flee the pro-government retribution, which became most evident after 1961. The old church of Mar Akha, which was utilised by both Nestorian and Chaldean-rite villagers, was almost completely destroyed; the village was resettled by Iraqi government militia (*fursan*).[123]

Malla-Birwan

Prior to the First World War, Malla-Birwan was served by a single priest, with a school, and was inhabited by 120 families.[124] At that time, there were also four Muslim and five Jewish households. Between 1920 and 1933, thirty-five individuals from Jilu in Hakkâri were settled in Malla-Birwan.[125] The old village church, dedicated to Mar Sawa, was destroyed in 1963, and most of the population forced to flee as it was resettled by pro-government militia.[126]

Zakho District

Dar Hozan

Though the 1957 census numbered Dar Hozan's Assyrian population at 244, the majority fled in 1961.[127]

Marzi-Khabur

Marzi-Khabur is located in the sub-district of Rizgari. Little is known about the village, except that its Assyrian villagers fled under duress from 1961 to 1963.[128]

Prakh

According to the 1957 census, Prakh's population totalled 139, but its Assyrian inhabitants were forced out in 1961.[129]

Ninawa Province

Telkeif District
Alqosh

The town of Alqosh is an ancient settlement located 30 to 40 kilometres north of Mosul, in the Qardu mountain range. The etymology of Alqosh is largely contested. Theories include tracings to the Turkish *al* 'scarlet' and *kuş* 'bird' and to the Akkadian *elu* 'god' and *qushtu* 'bow'. The great monastery of Rabban Hormizd was founded here in the sixth or seventh century and became the patriarchal see for the Church of the East (Nestorians). It, as a Christian hub, witnessed recurrent maltreatment over the centuries. In 1743, it was pillaged by the Persian armies of Nādr Shāh.[130] It suffered numerous attacks during the nineteenth century, including in 1828 and 1832 by Mira Kora, who, according to a Syriac colophon, 'killed 172 local men, not counting women, children and foreigners, and pillaged it'.[131] The town was attacked again in 1840 and 1842 by Isma'il Pasha, who also assaulted the Rabban Hormizd monastery.[132] Following the massacres of Bedr Khan Beg between 1843 and 1846, many Nestorians took refuge in Alqosh, still the see of one of the patriarchal lines of the Church of the East. It was at this time that many were coerced into becoming Chaldeans (Catholic) by the Dominicans, who aided only those willing to accept the supremacy of the Pope.[133] According to Tfinkdji, approximately 7,000 Chaldean-rite Assyrians lived in Alqosh, with six priests, three churches and two schools in 1913.[134] In 1937, Father Estefan Kaččo (later bishop) conducted a census of the town and recorded the population at 8,475. In 1950, Father Raphael Bidawid (later Patriarch) conducted another census, at the request of Bishop Estefan Kaččo, and reported the population at 9,500. In 1961, Giwargis 'Awwad put the population at 7,000. Due to its pro-communist sympathies, It was attacked by pro-government Kurdish *fursan* in 1961. Alqosh suffered attacks again in 1969.[135]

Description of Villages Affected in the 1970s by Region

The 1977–8 Campaign

As reported by Human Rights Watch (HRW), under the terms of the 1975 Algiers Agreement, Iraq began to clear a *cordon sanitaire* along its northern borders, in particular with Iran. Initially a 5-kilometre corridor was created, later expanded to 10, then 15, and eventually 30 kilometres.[136] Families were told they were to be removed from the region. As they left with whatever they could carry for collective towns farther south, their villages and churches were dynamited and bulldozed.[137] According to the Ba'th's own sources, some 28,000 families were removed from their villages in two months.[138] Initially, this 'corridor' was fashioned in the hopes of preventing further Iranian support to the Kurdish movement in Iraq. The question is why regions such as Barwar, along the Turkish border and heavily Assyrian, were targeted.

Dohuk Province

'Amēdiyāh District
Bazif

Bazif (also spelled Ba Zive, Ba Zibbe and Ba Dibbe) may derive from the Assyrian-Aramaic 'place of bears', Bears are a common predator of the Barwari livestock, which in Bazif in 1938 numbered 131 sheep and 42 goats.[139] The village was first abandoned in 1942 due to pressure from other local populations. This period saw the murder of four villagers during attacks on the village.[140] Bazif was then destroyed and confiscated in 1976 by pro-government forces, who resettled the region.[141] The village is absent from the 1961 Dominican map.

Bequlke

In 1850, Bequlke was home to five Assyrian families, adherents of the Church of the East.[142] By 1938, four families dwelled in the village with their livestock: forty-three goats and six sheep.[143] In 1957, its residents numbered seventy-four, including a few Kurdish families. The village was almost emptied of its inhabitants during the 1960s uprising, but a few residents remained. In 1978, the village was home to eight families, who were forcibly deported by the government as it was marked for demolition. Bequlke's school and the church of Mar Abraham were both destroyed during the process.[144]

Beshmīyaye

In 1850, Beshmīyaye (Beth Shmīyaye) was home to six families adherents of the Church of the East, served by a priest, with one functioning church and a shrine dedicated to Mar Ephrem d-Aqrwé (St Ephraim of the Scorpions).[145] During the First World War, Beshmīyaye suffered significantly, with half its population killed as a result of the fighting and massacres.[146] In 1938, it is mentioned in the League of Nations documents as Shamayila, having twenty-five Hakkâri Assyrians (among others), along with considerable livestock.[147] In 1957, the village population had reached 163. In 1961, there were sixty families in approximately thirty houses in the village. By 1978, fifty families dwelled in Beshmīyaye, before they were forcibly expelled during the border-clearing urbanisation policy of the Ba'th regime.[148]

Betannūrē

Betannūrē (also spelled Be-Tannūrē and Beth Tannūrē), meaning 'place of stone ovens', is an ancient Assyrian stronghold containing the ruins of an old fortress.[149] Mentioned as a religiously Jewish village by Badger during his travels in the mid-nineteenth century, Betannūrē is located east of Hayis on the Bedu rivulet.[150] In 1938, there were four Nestorian-rite families of the Tiyari tribe (plus seventy-five goats and sixty-four sheep) in the village, along with a number of Jewish inhabitants.[151] Prior to 1949, when the Jews were forced out of the country, it was home to fifteen Jewish families. The village contained the remains of an ancient fort and a tenth-century synagogue.[152] Many adherents of the Church of the East had lived alongside their Jewish counterparts, and remained after 1949. In 1957, its population totalled twenty-nine, and in 1961 there were fifteen families (five households) in the village. Prior to being destroyed in 1978 by pro-government militia, it was home to twenty-four families.[153]

Butara

Butara, or Botara, has long been an inhabited village in the Barwari region. In 1938, one family resided in the village, along with twenty-five goats.[154] In 1957, its population totalled forty-three, and in 1961, there were twelve Assyrian families (six households) in the village, as well as a small number of Kurds. Prior to being destroyed along with the church of Mar Gewargis in 1978 by the Ba'th regime, it was home to eight Assyrian families.[155]

Challik

Challik (also Tchallek, or Tcalluk, as referred to by Badger) is divided into upper and lower districts and is located near Tashish in the western part of the Barwar region. In 1850, it was home to between forty and sixty families, with the church of Mar Mushe, served by a priest.[156] Most of Challik's residents fled to Urmia for safety during 1915 and 1916, though half of its population perished due to wounds and exposure.[157] By 1933, there were approximately 200 inhabitants living in the village. By 1938, fifty-five families dwelled in the village, along with their livestock: 564 goats and 290 sheep.[158] In 1957, its population totalled 519. In 1961, there were 400 families (200 households) in the village, and prior to its destruction in 1978, around 100 families still dwelled in the village, which had a school.[159] The church of Mar Mushe (first built in 1100 and restored in 1860) suffered heavy damage during the campaigns and was mostly destroyed.

Cham Dostina

In 1961, there were three families dwelling in Cham Dostina at the onset of the civil war. Though the village was affected during this period, little detailed information remains. Just prior to its destruction in 1978 by the border clearings, it was home to five families.[160] The village is not mentioned on the 1961 Omez map.

Chaqala, Lower and Upper

Located east of Tashish, Chaqala (or Jaqala) is divided into an upper and lower district. In 1938, fifteen families lived in the village, along with their 125 goats and 58 sheep.[161] In 1957, the combined population of Upper and Lower Chaqala totalled 103 individuals, and prior to its destruction in 1978 during the border clearings, Upper Chaqala was home to thirty-five Church of the East-rite families and Lower Chaqala to twenty.[162] Following the village's destruction, most of its inhabitants fled the region to Turkey, Iran and other regions of Iraq.

Dūre

The village of Dūre lies along the border of Iraq and Turkey, not far from the Lower Tiyari villages of Līzān and Zerni, with which it shares many ancestral ties. The region has many ancient sites, including the remains of a fortress on the western mountain said to date from an earlier period, which gives some insight into the probable etymology of the village name: it may be Akkadian *dūrum* 'fortress'. As early as Badger's mid-nineteenth-century trips to the region, there had been longstanding animosity between the Assyrians and Kurds, which was voiced by the Barwar region's then bishop, Yeshu'yab. The region had already been emptied of half its Nestorian population in the 1850s.[163] It was quite apparent that the Dominican missions had caused a negative situation, even in these remote regions, as Bishop Yeshu'yab mentioned to an English missionary, Rev. F. N. Heazell. Thus, this period saw a host of new religious problems brought in by the French-led Catholic Church missions on the one hand, and the English-led Protestant missions on the other. The internal divisions that these interventions fostered would become unfavourable for the Assyrians internally, and create external conflicts with Kurds and others.[164] The Church of the East bishop Mar Youalah (Yab-Alaha) occupied his episcopal see in Dūre until the 1970s; the last bishop to carry the name *Youalah* was poisoned in 1972.

In 1850, Dūre was home to between twenty and forty families with four priests serving two ancient churches.[165] Thirteen bishops sat on the episcopal see of Dūre in recent history, making the village a significant religious centre of Eastern Christianity. During the First World War, Dūre was home to about 200 inhabitants. During the war, thirty of its residents were either killed or carried off (specifically women and children), and ninety died in the vicinity of Urmia.[166] By 1957, the village population totalled 296. Dūre has long been important as both a religious and a secular location for Assyrians. In 1938, thirty-five families, along with 348 goats and 195 sheep, dwelled in the village.[167] Due to its strategic importance, the village took the brunt of a napalm attack in 1968, along with other Assyrian villages of the Barwar region. Prior to its demolition on 8 August 1978, 100 families (seventy-five households) dwelled in Dūre.[168] The village also had a school and its two churches: Mar Gewargis (first built in 909) and the fourth-century monastery of Mar Qayyoma, known also as the burial place of nine bishops of the Church of the East. Some of the manuscripts of the church have been preserved, including 'The Usefulness of Aristotle's Writings', dated to 1224, which speaks to the long cultural and intellectual history of the region.[169] Two shrines, to Mart Maryam and Mar Pius, and four cemeteries were situated within the village. The churches, along with all the houses, were first dynamited and then bulldozed by the Iraq regime during the border clearings of the late 1970s. Simultaneously, the entirety of the village's farms and apple orchards were burned.[170] This same fate was faced by all the Assyrian villages of the Barwari Bala district between 1960 and the Anfal campaign. In some cases, villages faced destruction numerous times during that thirty-year span.

Dūre is also home to the *gippa d-miyya*, 'cave of water', which is said to contain ancient wall paintings, and the *gippa d-dermana*, 'cave of medicinal compounds', named for its concentration of potassium nitrate and what is probably sulphur, both key components in the production of gunpowder.[171] Though some villagers were offered recompense for their homes after their removal from the region, it was a paltry sum in comparison with the destruction. Many of the families were sent to the collective town (*mujamma*) or resettlement camp of Baṭufa, further evidence of the ethnic cleansing

Figure 23   Ruins of Mar Qayyoma, Dūre (Courtesy of Yourem Mako)

Figure 24   Mar Gewargis, Dūre, prior to destruction on 8 August 1978 (Courtesy of Yourem Mako)

Figure 25   The last vesitges of Mar Gewargis following the border clearings of 1978 (Courtesy of the late Yacoub Khoshaba)

Figure 26   Ruins of houses in Dūre, 1978 (Courtesy of the late Yacoub Khoshaba)

campaign.[172] The village was also the birthplace of the first personage to be killed during the 1961 armed resistance movement, Ethniel Shleimon.

Hawsarek

Hawsarek, or Avsarke, in the vicinity of Annūnē (Kani Masi), was destroyed by the Ba'th government during the 1977–8 border clearings. The village is absent from the 1961 Dominican map.

Helwā

In 1850, Helwā (also Halwā or Helwā Naṣara) was home to between seven and eleven families, with a church served by a priest of the Church of the East.[173] In 1938, twenty-five families lived in the village with their livestock: 348 goats and 305 sheep.[174] By the census of 1957, its population numbered 194. At the time of the armed autonomist movement of 1961–3, researcher Majed Eshoo reported forty families in the village.[175] These residents suffered tremendously, causing some to flee the region. Before its elimination by the Ba'th regime in 1978, Helwā was home to the old church of Mar Yonan (razed by the authorities), and its sixty families were forcibly relocated to urban areas during the government's ethnic cleansing campaign.[176]

Hīsh

Hīsh, or Heesh, is located on the border with Turkey. In 1850, between ten and fifteen families, served by a priest, lived there. By 1876 one priest served fifteen families in one church.[177] In 1938, sixteen families dwelled in the village with their livestock: 526 sheep, 244 goats, 15 oxen, 7 mules and 2 donkeys.[178] By 1957, the population numbered 286 individuals.[179] By 1961, there were eighty families (twenty-two households), and prior to the final evacuation of the village by the Ba'th regime in 1978, there were 100 families and a school.[180] The churches of Mar Bacchus, Mar Abraham and Mar Khnana of the Church of the East still lie in ruins.

Iqri

Iqri (sometimes Kiri) has been an important village for many years, and was the seat of Bishop Mar Yonan of Barwar (1820–1906) of the Church of the East. Some of the village's residents assert that their families originated in the Arbil region but fled during a wave of persecution in the twelfth or thirteenth century. Local legend traces the etymology of the name to a modern Assyrian word for 'turtle', a creature found in abundance in the river Zab. A second etymology sees the village name derived from the Assyrian-Aramaic word *qaretha* or *qarra* 'gourd', as the village was shaped like one. In 1850, Iqri was home to between twenty and thirty families, served by a priest, with one functioning church, according to Badger.[181] Iqri suffered considerably during the First World War, in 1915 and 1916. During that period, most of its inhabitants were massacred or carried off by marauders.[182] In 1938, twelve families resided in the village with their livestock: 117 goats and 29 sheep.[183] In 1961, the village was home to forty families (twenty-five households). Preceding its demolition in 1978, thirty-five Assyrian families still called Iqri home.[184] The ancient churches of Mart Maryam and Mar Yonan were both bulldozed during the government attempts to ethnically cleanse this rural district of its Assyrians.

Istip

Istip, or Histip, is located on the border with Turkey. In 1850, between twenty-five and thirty-eight families, with a priest, lived there. By 1876 Edward Cutts reported one priest serving eighteen families in one church.[185] In 1961, there were forty-seven families (twenty-four households). Prior to the final evacuation of the village in 1978, there were thirty-five families, with a Church of the East church dedicated to Mart Shmuni.[186]

Iyyat

In 1850, Iyyat, or Yate, was home to between five and eight families, served by a priest and a church.[187] Half of Iyyat's population was murdered during 1915 and 1916, amid the skirmishes of the First World War.[188] In 1938, twenty-five families resided in the village alongside their 136 goats and 77 sheep.[189] By 1957, its population numbered 169. In 1961, there were thirty-five families (twenty households) in Iyyat.[190] During the border clearings in 1978, approximately forty families were residing in Iyyat at the time of its destruction.[191] Its entire population was forcibly uprooted and resettled in urban centres.[192] The church of Mar Gewargis, built in 920, was destroyed, along with all the village's dwellings.[193]

Khwara

In 1938, the League of Nations report cites fifteen families, along with fifty-three goats and twenty-three sheep.[194] According to the 1957 census, Khwara's population totalled ninety-two, and in 1961, the village had ten households.[195] Prior to being destroyed in 1978, it was home to sixteen families of the Assyrian Church of the East religious community.[196]

Maghribiya

In 1957, Maghribiya's population numbered approximately twenty Church of the East-rite families. According to Majed Eshoo's research, in 1961 only five families dwelled there. The village suffered during the internal fighting from 1961 to 1963, but some Assyrian villagers managed to remain. About eight families resided in the village when it was finally eliminated by the government border-clearing campaign in 1978.[197] The village is absent from the 1961 Dominican map.

Malākhta

Malākhta is an old Assyrian settlement, famous for its numerous salt deposits, which provide the etymology of the village name, 'the salty one'. In 1850, it was home to between five and eight families.[198] Like Iqri, Malākhta suffered damage during the First World War, seeing most of its inhabitants massacred or taken by Kurdish tribes during the fighting.[199] By 1938 eight families dwelled in the village with their livestock: forty-eight goats and twenty-two sheep.[200] In 1957, its population totalled twenty-eight. In 1961, there were five households in the village, and prior to being destroyed in 1978, it was home to fifteen families, ecclesiastically belonging to the Church of the East.[201] The village was bulldozed and its ancient church of Mar Khananiya was dynamited in 1978.

Māyē

In 1850, Māyē, or Māyē Naṣara, probably Assyrian-Aramaic for 'the waters', contained between fifteen and twenty-two families.[202] By 1915, in the midst of the First World War, eyewitness Rev. Shlemon reported that of Māyē's 140 residents, 90 had been killed, with 50 managing to flee toward the Assyrian region of Urmia in Iran.[203] In 1938, fifteen families resided in the village alongside 184 goats and 110 sheep.[204] By the census count of 1957, the village population was slowly recovering from its losses, and tallied eighty residents, an indication of its inhabitants' continued persecution. By 1961, there were thirty families (fifteen households) in Māyē. The churches of Mar Quryaqos and Mart Maryam of Church of the East jurisdiction were destroyed in 1978, and Māyē's thirty-five remaining families forcibly moved to urban centres.[205]

Meydan

Meydan (or Maydan or Maldani, as it is referred to in League of Nations documents) like Hīsh and Istip, it is located on the border with Turkey, and is seven hours' walk from the nearest road.[206] In 1938, three families dwelled in the village, along with their livestock: ninety-two goats, forty-one sheep, nine oxen and seven mules.[207] In 1957, according to the government census, thirty-one individuals lived in the village. By 1961, there were nine families (four households).[208] During the border clearings of 1978, which affected the entire Assyrian-populated regions of Nerwa and Rekan, there were twenty-five families living in Maydan.[209] The church of Mar Gewargis of Church of the East distinction was destroyed along with the village in the same year.[210]

Sardāshte

Sardāshte accepted an influx of refugees from Lower Tiyari following the First World War. The birthplace of bounty hunter Gewargis N'Belatha Benasimo, the village is also home to the old church of Mar Youḥannan. According to the 1957 census report, 250 individuals lived in Sardāshte. Approximately forty families resided in the village prior to the resistance movement. In 1961, Abdul-Wahid Hajji Malo, a tribal leader loyal to Mustafa Barzani, massacred thirty-two of the village's men, including the priest, during the Kurdish armed autonomist movement.[211] Its ninety families were displaced following the border clearings and ethnic cleansing of the region.[212]

Tirwanish

Tirwanish, or Der Wanis, is named after a monastery dedicated to Mar Iwanius. It also hosted six other monasteries or churches.[213] Its land title belongs to Malik Khoshaba Yosip of Lower Tiyari and to the brothers Khammo and Sliwo Be-Zizo.[214] Since the displacement of the late 1970s, its Assyrian population has been discouraged from returning. The village is absent from the Omez map of 1961.

Simele District

Avzerok Khammo

Avzerok (Avzerog) Khammo, also known as Lower Avzerok, was largely Armenian. The village's name is etymologically Kurdish, meaning 'yellow water'. According to the 1957 census, it had 176 inhabitants. Many of these Armenians arrived as refugees from Turkey during the First World War. The village was destroyed in 1975 along with its sister village, Upper Avzerok (Avzerok Shano), and its fifty families were displaced.[215] The government allotted the village lands to Arab tribes during the Arabisation period of the 1970s. The village originally contained one church, dedicated to St Vartan, and one school.

Avzerok Shano
Avzerok (Avzerog) Shano, also known as Upper Avzerok, was entirely inhabited by Assyrian in the period of this work. Before the government-sponsored destruction of many villages in 1975, its population comprised sixty families.[216] The old church of Mar Gewargis, also known as Mar Mansour, was targeted during the military operations. The government resettled the village with an entirely Arab population.

Bajidda-Barave
Bajidda-Barave is located in the Slevani sub-district of Simele. The village had both an Assyrian and a Kurdish population and a school within village grounds. According to the census, its Assyrian inhabitants numbered 199 in 1957. In 1975, the village was attacked, and many houses were destroyed. Some of its thirty remaining Assyrian families were forced to flee.[217] In 1976, the demography changed as the regime settled several Arab families in the village.[218]

Bajidda-Kandal
In 1957, the Bajidda-Kandal Assyrian population numbered 127 persons. The village was destroyed in 1975 along with its sister village, Bajidda-Barave.

Bakhluja
The village of Bakhluja (or Bachloudja, according to the 1961 Dominican map) is located east of Ṣoriya and southwest of Zakho, bypassing Avzerok Shanno. In 1957, its population numbered 209 inhabitants, and in 1975, it was home to eight families.[219] In 1976 Arabs were settled in the village as part of the government's ethnic cleansing campaign of northern Iraq.

Hawresk
Hawresk contained an Assyrian population with a tiny Armenian segment for many years during the twentieth century. By 1957, its population included 238 Assyrians. Prior to its destruction in 1975, Hawresk was home to ten families.[220] It was known as the village of Leon Pasha al Armani, who had

accompanied the Assyrian leader (Agha) Petros Eliya in his battles with Turkish forces during the First World War.[221]

Ishkavdal

Ishkavdal (mentioned in *Assyrie chrétienne* as Škafdalé) faced destruction on numerous occasions, notably in 1961 and again in 1975, when the village's twenty remaining families were displaced.[222] J. M. Fiey mentions the hamlet briefly as seeing the return of some Assyrian families, most likely following a ceasefire.[223] Prior to its annihilation in 1975, the village was also the site of a local school.[224]

Karrana

Karrana was settled by refugees of the Hakkâri Baz tribe in 1920. It was first razed during the Simele genocide in 1933. Later, 110 people returned to rebuild the village.[225] Karrana was destroyed again in 1976, and its population displaced.

Mavan

In recent history, Mavan (or Mawana) was settled by Nestorian-rite Assyrian from the Tkhuma region and Rumta in Upper Tiyari, in 1920.[226] Its inhabitants fled to Syria after the 1933 massacres, but the village was later settled by other Assyrian families. In 1957, its population totalled sixty-one. By 1975, the remaining ten families who had managed to survive the various conflicts in the region were forced to flee their village. Some returned following the government-sponsored destruction, only to be forcibly removed again in 1984.[227]

Reqawa

Reqawa, or Rekawa, was most recently settled in 1920 by refugees, predominantly adherents of the Church of the East, from Baz, Nochiya and Mar Bishu in Hakkâri. Most of these settlers fled again to the Khabur basin in Syria after the 1933 massacres. Those who remained were finally forced out from 1974 to 1976 during an increase in government military activity and external threats. The village was immediately resettled by Kurdish militia and their families.[228]

Zakho District
Alanish
Alanish, sometimes Alanash, is located in the sub-district of Sindi. In 1913, it was home to seventy Catholics, with a priest, a church and a small chapel.[229] By 1957, the population had risen to 264 inhabitants. In 1975, government forces targeted the village during the infighting between forces loyal to Mustafa Barzani and those loyal to the government of Iraq. Alanish's ancient church, Mar Adde, and school were destroyed at this time. Its forty families who escaped were never able to return.[230]

Avkani
Avkani's name (also spelled Avgni and Avgani) is Kurdish, meaning 'spring water'. The village was destroyed in 1976 during the border clearings, and its Assyrian inhabitants displaced. It is not mentioned on the 1961 Dominican map.

Bahnona
Bahnona is located close to Alanish in the Sindi sub-district of Zakho. Both Jews and Christians lived in the village until the expulsion of Jews from Iraq in 1948. It was home to 111 inhabitants at the time of the 1957 census. In 1975, the village was destroyed, and its thirty families displaced.[231]

Bajuwa
Bajuwa was mostly settled by Assyrians from the village of Yarda in the Zakho region.[232] In 1957, its population numbered seventy-nine, and in 1976, when the village was finally sacked, it was home to five families.

Bedār
The village of Bedār, possibly Assyrian-Aramaic for 'place of battle' or 'place of the sheepfold', is well known for being the birthplace of the Syriac scholar Father Paulos Bedari.[233] The village is located approximately 60 miles north of Mosul within the Catholic diocese of Jezirah. In 1850, between fourteen and twenty-one families dwelled in the territory, with one church.[234] In 1913, its inhabitants numbered 400 Chaldean-rite villagers, with a

priest, church and school.[235] By 1957, the population of Bedār had grown to 508, and in 1961 it reached 868 (ninety-five families). Just before its demolition in 1975 by the Iraqi regime, there were 130 Assyrian families in Bedār.[236] The old church of the Virgin Mary also suffered ruin during this period.

Benakhre

Approximately ten families dwelled in the village of Benakhre prior to its destruction in 1975, during the government-sponsored military offensives in the region.[237]

Dashtnakh

The meaning of Dashtnakh (also spelled Dasht-Nakh and Dashtatakh) stems from *dashta d'Nakh*, or the 'field of Noah', following the story that pieces of a ship were found in the region that were later connected to the biblical flood narrative. Such naming of villages is prevalent not only in Iraq, but also in Turkey in the Jebel Cudi mountain range. Dashtnakh was settled by Assyrians from nearby Esnakh (Sanaat), three miles to the east, and was destroyed during the border clearings in 1975. Prior to that, it was home to fifteen families.[238]

Deirabūn

Deirabūn, meaning 'monastery of our Father', is situated close to Feshkhābur on the Iraqi border with Syria. The village became infamous during the ethnic cleansing of the Assyrians in 1933. According to the 1957 census, it had a population of 657 inhabitants. In 1976, Arabs forcibly resettled Deirabūn, along Feshkhābur, three miles to the west. Though the village was predominantly Christian Assyrian, the Arabisation tactics of the regime transferred some Arabised Yezidi families into the region during that same year.[239]

Derashīsh

Derashīsh, also known as ʿUmra and ʿUmra Shghisha, originally a Church of the East enclave, is mentioned by Tfinkdji in 1913 as home to 200 Chaldean converts, with a single church.[240] By 1957, the population had increased to 361 but then decreased drastically in the years of the armed autonomist movement from 1961 to 1963. By 1975, at the time of its destruction, the village was home to fifty families, with a school and the ancient church of Mar Ephrem.[241]

Feshkhābur

In the valley west of Zakho, Feshkhābur (also spelled Pešabūr) is located on the river Tigris on the Iraqi border with Syria and Turkey, approximately 30 miles south of Jezirah. The village's name may derive from the Kurdish meaning 'against the river Khabur'. During his journey to the region, Badger mentions the village as part of the Jezirah diocese of the Chaldean Church. At that time (1850), between sixty and ninety families lived in the village, served by two priests and one active church.[242] By 1913, Tfinkdji reported 1,300 Catholic families in the town, with two priests serving one church and a school.[243] During the First World War, Feshkhābur was attacked on 11 July 1915 by the sons of Muhammad Agha Atroshi.[244] Four days later, according to French Dominican missionary Father Jacques Rhétoré, 900 people were killed when the Miran tribe sacked the town.[245] Feshkhābur witnessed the passage of Malik Yako Ismael and his group from the Tigris to Syria during the 1933 uprising. According to the 1957 census, Feshkhābur had a population of 899 residents. It contained 175 homes, and 150 families were still living in the village after the remainder had fled in the aftermath of the 1961 uprising. In 1963, the Syrian army entered the village and Kurdish mercenaries, *fursan*, burned it down. In 1974, as a result of the renewed tensions, its inhabitants fled to Syria, crossing the Tigris, and remained there for six months. They returned to rebuild the village a year later. However, in 1976 the village was evacuated and its inhabitants forced to leave, due to its highly important military location near the Turkey–Syria border. Immediately following this incident, Arab families from Mosul were resettled in the region by the Iraqi regime. The village's cultural and religious structures suffered during the civil war and during the relocation and destruction, including the fourteenth-century church of Mart Maryam. A church dedicated to Mar Gewargis was built in 1964 after the civil war.

Istablan

Istablan, or Stablan had a population of five Assyrian families in 1961, which increased to twenty families by 1975.[246] Following the destruction of numerous border villages in the Zakho region in 1974–5, the village was destroyed, and its church of Mar Addai was left severely damaged.

Qarawilla

Qarawilla, or Qarawola, lies on the river Khabur on the Turkish border. In 1957, 334 individuals dwelled in this village. The previous regime destroyed it in 1975 and displaced its 100 families, destroying their seventy homes and the church of Mart Maryam. The village was resettled by Yezidis, who were displaced the to area by the Iraqi regime.

Sanaat

Esnakh, as Sanaat is referred to in the native Assyrian-Aramaic of the region, probably finds its meaning in the phrase 'wall of Noah' (as it sits on the mountainside), in reference to the biblical legends of Noah's Ark found throughout the region (compare the derivation of Dashtnakh above). In 1913, it was home to 600 Chaldean-rite (150 families), with a priest, church and school.[247] In 1957, the population totalled 585, and prior to its destruction in 1975 by the Ba'th regime, it was home to 120 families, with a school.[248] The ancient churches of Mart Maryam and Mar Sahdona were also destroyed. Due to its proximity to the border with Turkey, inhabitants of Sanaat would regularly visit villages in the Bohtan region and would traditionally marry people from the village of Harbol. This borderless image of the region was commonplace to Assyrians before the Western colonial division of the modern Middle East, showing that current borders are not reflective of the continuous Assyrian settlements of northern Mesopotamia and Anatolia.[249]

Shuwadin

Shuwadin, or Shudin, is located approximately 3.5 miles west of Bazif. Approximately 120 inhabitants dwelled there in 1957. During the renewed internal strife Shudin was destroyed in 1975, and thirty-five families forced to flee.[250]

Yarda

Yarda, its name Assyrian-Aramaic for 'well' or 'tank', is located in the sub-district of Sindi. In 1913, it was home to 250 converts to the Chaldean Church, with a priest and two churches.[251] In 1957, the population totalled 280, and prior to its destruction in 1975 by the Ba'th regime, it was home to sixty families with a school.[252] The ancient church of Mar Addai was destroyed along with the village.

Ninawa Province

Telkeif District

Bendawaye

Bendawaye, or Beth Handawaya, is a small village three or four miles west of Alqosh. The village is close to an Assyrian bas-relief known as Šero Malakta, which is also the site of many monastic grottos.[253] In 1913, this village contained 100 Chaldean-rite villagers, with one priest serving one chapel.[254] Though Tfinkdji seems only concerned with the Catholic population, it is clear some Nestorians dwelled in the village, as well. During the Simele genocide in 1933, 124 people dwelled in the village, in thirty-six houses.[255] By 1938, three families (numbering fifteen persons) of the Ashita clan retuned to the village, alongside the largely Yezidi population still living there.[256] The church of Mar Gewargis once contained a New Testament, written circa 1772. Arabs were resettled in the village in 1976.[257]

Nāṣerīyā

In 1938, there were two, Church of the East-rite families of the Jilu tribe (ten persons), along with some Catholics and Yezidis.[258] Fiey briefly mentions in his study that the village had three Catholic households and an ancient church dedicated to Mar 'Abdisho', most likely the same monk who had given his name to the monastery of Nerem.[259] The village was looted and destroyed during the Simele massacres, when it contained forty-one people in eighteen houses.[260] Nāṣerīyā met with a similar fate as that of its surrounding villages from 1974 to 1975.

Description of Villages Affected in the 1980s by Region

Arbil Province

Koy Sinjaq District
Armota

Armota, Armūṭā or Harmota, lies just outside Koy Sinjaq, a two-hour drive from Sulaymaniyah. The village is a remote farming settlement and part of the Chaldean diocese of Kirkuk. In 1843 there were between twenty-five and thirty-eight families, with a priest serving one church.[261] In 1913, Armota had around 100 Catholic adherents, with a priest who served the village church.[262] Yohānnan Hormizd had converted three villagers, 'Ainkāwā ('Amkābā), Armota and Shaqlāwā, to Catholicism in 1779.[263] The village's name is explained in the local Assyrian-Aramaic dialect as meaning 'land of death'. The etymology is based on a local legend of a plague that had once slain all of the villagers, or on a large battle between Christians and Muslims of the region. Another explanation may be a derivation *ara'* and *nūṭā* (with a shifting of 'n' to 'm'), meaning 'land of oil'. A fourth-century monastery, located in the mountainous region overlooking the village,[264] faced numerous ravages including dynamiting during the Anfal campaign in 1988 while the village was transformed into an army camp.[265] There was also a local school in the village. Villager Sabah Hana spent ten years in Abu Ghraib prison, and his brother was executed during this period.[266]

Dohuk Province

'Amēdīyāh District
Annūnē

Annūnē, or more specifically 'Ain Nūnē – Assyrian-Aramaic for 'source of fish', which is also reflected in its Kurdish name, Kani Masi – has been the centre of the Barwari-Bala sub-district since 1934. In 1850 between twenty and thirty families resided in the village, with one functioning church and a priest.[267] During the First World War, Annūnē had approximately 350 residents; some twenty were killed, ten women were taken, and another 120 died in the Urmia region during the winter of 1915–16.[268] Iskharia Gewargis was the town's resident *mukhtar* in 1926–7, during the building of the first school in the Dohuk region. The building began at the behest of Qasha

Oraha Shlimun in 1924 and was completed in 1928. Classes were taught in Assyrian, English and French. Since Arabic was not spoken by many Assyrians in the north of Iraq, it was only added to the curriculum at a later date when required by the Iraqi government. When that occurred schoolmaster in Annūnē brought Rabi Hanna of Tel Esqof to instruct in Arabic. By the mid-1930s, there were more than 300 students from the Barwari region and two teachers, Qasha Dawid Toma and Gewargis Bikko.[269] In 1938, seventy families dwelled in the village, along with their livestock: 743 goats and 247 sheep.[270] According to the 1957 census, the village population then stood at approximately 400 individuals. As early as 1958, there were 612 students and 12 Assyrian teachers at the school in Annūnē.[271]

In 1961, during the onset of fighting in Iraq, Mustafa Barzani and 400 of his men requested permission to traverse the village toward Zakho and Syria. The village elders allowed passage only near Hayyis, rather than directly through the major Assyrian villages.[272] Upon returning, Barzani's numbers had swollen to more than 3,000 fighters, who then attacked Annūnē and killed every male above the age of fifteen, including two priests.[273] The Assyrians of numerous Barwari villages came to the aid of the besieged Annūnē and repelled the attack from Barzani's men, while the Iraqi government officials remained safe in the village centre.[274] In 1968 Annūnē suffered napalm attacks by government forces.

Prior to its destruction by the regime on 27 February 1988, there were 180 families living in Annūnē (between 84 and 100 houses), with two schools and the two churches of Mart Shmuni and Mar Sawa.[275] Mar Sawa dates from the tenth century with a restoration period in 1742. As with the entire Barwari region of Assyrian villages, the fields were eliminated and the apple orchards, the area's greatest resource, burned indiscriminately. On one occasion, an Assyrian interviewee had been told that his house and land were to be confiscated and that he would be paid 30 dinars (approximately $90 US) for each of the 1,000-plus trees in his orchard. The man never received the payment.[276]

Arāden

Arāden has always been a culturally significant village in the Sapna region, to the south of Barwari Bala.[277] The large village is located within the 'Amēdīyāh diocese of the Chaldean church, along with the regional villages of Mangesh, Dawodiya, Ten and Inishke. Arāden is approximately 160 kilometres north of Mosul.[278] Locals believe the etymology of Arāden as being *'ar'a d-a'den*, or 'the land of Eden'. The village sits at an altitude of more than 1,100 metres above sea level.[279] In 1850, it was home to between fifty and seventy-five families, with a priest serving one church.[280] In 1913, there were approximately 650 Catholic converts, with two priests and two schools.[281] Around 1933, there were 515 Assyrians in total in Arāden.[282] The town's population in 1954 numbered 474 families, approximately 5,000 people.[283] In 1957, Arāden's population totalled 1,049, and in 1961 there were 350 families, around 3,000 inhabitants.[284]

Arāden is a pilgrimage hub for Assyrians of various denominations. There are three Chaldean churches in the village: one dedicated to the third-century saint Mart Shmuni, another to the fourth-century saint Sultan Mahdokht, and the third to Mar Awda, also from the fourth century. The church of Sultan Mahdokht is dedicated to a princess by the same name and her two brothers, who were baptised by Mar Awda but later martyred. When the churches were initially built is uncertain, but it is possible that one or all may be a millennium old. A more recent church was built and dedicated to the Sacred Heart of Jesus. Feast days in Arāden include the 15 May *shera* ('vigil') and the 12 January *dookhrana* ('remembrance') of Sultan Mahdokht. Some of Arāden's major personalities include Chaldean Bishop Francis, Chaldean Bishop Toma, Rayis Hermiz Sana and the former AUA secretary general Afram Rayis.

In the 1960s, the village was first bombed and then razed by 700 government forces; Kurdish irregulars under the leadership of Zabir Muhammad Zebari murdered at least seven villagers, including Nona Daniel.[285] Though Arāden was rebuilt over the years, continued targeting resulted in the assassination of the Shimshun Elisha in 1974, and the murders of Sami Goriel and Salem Dawood in 1975. Dinkha Eshaya, the village *mukhtar*, was later assassinated in 1981.[286] The Ba'th regime destroyed the village again in 1987, at which time it accommodated an estimated 220 families and two schools.[287]

Argen

Argen, alternately Argin or Hargin (or Ergin, as referred to by Badger), is located in the mountainous region south of Jebel Gara near Ṭlanitha,

Armashe and Meze. In 1850, between ten and fifteen families made the village their home, with one operational church.[288] By 1918, there were six families who had converted to Catholicism, numbering forty-one people, and seven families who remained faithful to the Church of the East (Nestorian). According to a League of Nations report, two families (seven men and five women) resided in the village along with their livestock: ninety-two goats and twenty-two sheep.[289] In 1957, the population of Argen totalled seventy-nine. The village suffered much damage in the early 1960s, and though many of its inhabitants fled, some remained to rebuild.[290] The village was then eliminated in 1988. Argen is of great importance as a cultural site due to its four churches: Mar Gewargis, Mart Maryam, Mar Abraham and Mar Quryaqos, which were all laid waste during the Anfal campaign.

Aṭush

Aṭush's name is said to derive from a word meaning 'spring of the mulberry trees.' As early as 1850, there were between eleven and sixteen families in the village, with two functioning churches.[291] In 1938, ten families (nine men and five women) dwelled in the village along with their livestock: eighteen goats and one sheep.[292] By 1957, it was inhabited by seventy-five individuals. Prior to its destruction in 1988, there were twenty-five families in Aṭush. The churches of Mar Gewargis, Mar Abraham, Mart Maryam, and Mart Shmuni of the Church of the East all suffered complete destruction during the Anfal campaign.

Balūkā

Balūka, also known as Bebāluk or Beth Bāluk, lies near the Turkish border and is not accessible by most vehicles. In 1850, it was home to between ten and fifteen families, served by a Nestorian priest and one functioning church.[293] Around 1915, almost the entirety of Bālūka's population was forcibly converted to Islam.[294] By 1938, fourteen families lived in the village, along with their livestock: 176 goats and 116 sheep.[295] In the years leading up to the census of 1957, some of its surviving Christian Assyrian residents returned, numbering an estimated fifty individuals. According to Majed Eshoo's research, by 1961 there were twenty-five families (ten households) in the village and during the chaos in the region its headman and some villagers were killed in an air raid by the Iraqi army. Prior to its destruction in 1976–8 during the border clearings, Bālūka was home to fifteen families, who were all forcibly removed from their homes.[296] The church of Mart Maryam was destroyed during the same period. Though the village was emptied, a few families managed to return and attempted to rebuild until the Anfal operations. The air bombings took out the Bālūka Bridge and also left any stragglers to contend with a chemical cloud. The village was then taken over by pro-government Kurdish militia.[297]

Bāsh

Bāsh is located on the Iraq–Turkey border. In 1850, there were between twelve and eighteen families with a priest of the Church of the East.[298] According to League of Nations documentation from 1938, Bāsh had ten Assyrian families of the Nestorian religious community (including approximately thirty men[299]), along with a variety of domesticated animals: 335 goats, 95 sheep, 7 oxen and 2 donkeys.[300] In 1957, there were 150 individuals living in the village. By 1961, there were sixty Assyrian families (thirty-six households).[301] Prior to the village's initial destruction by the regime in 1977–8, there were fifty families and a school. Bāsh was rebuilt in 1981 by twenty families who had returned but was destroyed again in 1988.[302] The churches of Mar Zakka (seventh century) and Mar Dawūd were destroyed, along with the rest of the village, and its inhabitants fled to Turkey. More than thirty-four villagers surrendered and attempted to return to Bāsh after the announcement of a general amnesty, but were never heard from again.[303]

Baz

Baz, or Bas, is located in the sub-district of ʿAmēdīyāh.[304] In 1938, five families called the village home, along with their 104 goats and 12 sheep.[305] In 1957, it was home to 130 individuals, and in 1961 there were forty families (twenty households) in the village. In 1961, the village suffered attacks by pro-government troops, Kurds loyal to Mustafa Barzani and the armed autonomist movement from the neighbouring village of Benaveh, which took possession of the historic church of Mar Abraham and later converted it into a mosque.[306] The church of Mar Youhanna survived in ruined condition until 1988, when the entire village, then home to twenty families, was destroyed.[307] At least five villagers from Baz were reported missing during the Anfal campaign.[308]

Bebede

Bebede, or Beth Bede, lies at the foot of the city of 'Amēdīyāh and is built close to ruins of one of the most ancient Assyrian castles in the Sapna valley. The people of Bebede, skilled in ceramics, refer to themselves as *aslaye*, or 'originators', for having lived in the village for millennia, whereas many villages in the Sapna valley had been abandoned and resettled, some on numerous occasions.[309] Badger mentions the village as having twenty families, a church and a priest, but he also says that the village was destroyed and emptied of Assyrians during his travels.[310] Whether the statistics given are pre- or post-destruction is unknown. According to a League of Nations report, in 1933 there were approximately 250 individuals living in the village.[311] In 1938, ten families (twelve men and twenty-four women), along with fifteen goats and seven sheep, resided in the village.[312] Bebede, which falls within the old Nestorian diocese of Mar Yeshuyau of Barwar,[313] also became the headquarters for Patriarch Mar Eshai Shimun following the migration from his original home in Quchanis (Hakkâri) until 1933, when he was exiled with his family to Cyprus. In 1957, the inhabitants of Bebede numbered 480, and in 1961, there were 100 families.[314] The village was razed in 1961 by mercenaries under the leadership of Muhammad Zebari.[315] Some Assyrians returned in 1963 and following years, but constant struggles with neighbouring Kurds (mostly from Arāden Islam, Upper Arāden) left little room for stability and development. In 1987, Bebede was destroyed, along with its school and the sixth-century church of Mart Shmuni, and its seventy-five families were displaced.[316]

Bebede's notable personalities include Toma Yosip Toma, chairman of the city council of 'Amēdīyāh in 1914 and during the First World War. According to Majed Eshoo, Toma was executed in Mosul by Ottoman authorities, along with his companion Petto Rayis from Arāden.[317] The village attained a reputation for its school, which was established in 1908 by the English missionary Rev. William Wigram. The school was destroyed by the Ba'th regime in 1988 and its foundation materials were appropriated for building an army barracks.[318]

Benāta

Benāta (also spelled Beth 'Ainātha), or 'place of sources', gets its Assyrian-Aramaic name from the variety of water springs in the vicinity. The *Book of Governors* describes the ninth-century village as being mentioned in a vision of Maran-'Ammeh.[319] In 1913 it was home to approximately 150 Catholic-rite Assyrians, with a priest and a chapel.[320] Prior to 1961, there were still sixty families (thirty households) in the village. Following 1988, Benāta was emptied of Assyrians.

Blejanke

Blejanke (also Blejane) is well known among Assyrians as the home of Yousif Toma Hermiz Zebari and Rafael Nanno, members of the ADM who were later killed by the Iraqi regime. In its recent history, Church of the East-rite Assyrians of the Tkhuma region in Hakkâri settled Blejanke in the nineteenth century. In 1850, it was home to between eight and twelve families, with a Church of the East dedicated to Mar Gewargis.[321] The villagers at that time came originally from Erdel (in Arbel province), which also had a Church, a priest and fourteen families.[322] Erdel was evacuated by Agha Petros Elia when he sacked the nearby Kurdish stronghold of Barzan during the First World War. By 1938, four families (eleven men and twelve women) resided in Blejanke, along with their livestock: fifty-seven sheep and thirty-nine goats.[323] In 1957, Blejanke had 238 inhabitants. When the village was attacked in 1961, there were approximately thirty houses.[324] During the initial raid on the village that year, two villagers were injured and three killed; the remaining Assyrians fled to Sarsang. During this time, the government forces also fired various rounds of ammunition at the nearby monasteries of Mar Qardagh and Mar 'Abdyeshu', causing large-scale damage.[325] Though some returned to the village, it was destroyed again in 1987 by the Ba'th regime, specifically for being the known home of several prominent nationalist leaders; its twenty-eight families were then displaced.[326]

Bubawa

In 1938 Bubawa, also spelled Bibava, was home to nine families, adherents of the Church of the East (thirty-two men and twenty-five women), along with their livestock: 213 goats and 55 sheep.[327] The village was more recently settled by the inhabitants of Daragale (located between Hayyis and Musake), who were forced to flee their village in Barwari-Bala in 1950. At the time of the 1957 census, eighty-five Assyrians resided in Bubawa. It was home to thirty-two families (twelve households) in 1987, when the Iraqi military destroyed it in order to build an artificial lake.[328]

Chammike
Chammike was resettled by displaced families from Lower Tiyari in 1920. By 1938, eight families resided in the village, along with eighty-one goats and four sheep.[329] In 1961, there were twenty families (ten households) in the village, and prior to its destruction in 1988 by the Ba'th regime, Chammike was home to four families (two households).[330] The village was abandoned due to constant pressure from neighbouring tribes.

Dawodiya
Dawodiya, or Dawudiya, lies in the far west of the Sapna valley region and is built on an archaeological mound dating to the fifth century BC. The name of the village is said to derive from a monastery dedicated to Mar Daudo, located an hour north of the present village on the Hasn Birka road.[331] In 1840, an unknown military leader built a military barracks in the town.[332] In 1850, between thirty and forty-five Chaldean-rite families called Dawodiya home.[333] By 1913, the population reached 300 people, with a school and a church served by a single priest.[334] According to a League of Nations report following the 1933 massacres, 275 Assyrians lived in the village.[335] In 1957, there were eighty households, totalling 524 people, and in 1961, there were 150 families, in 120 households.[336] The village was destroyed in 1987, at which time there were eighty-two families and a school.[337] The church of Mar Youḥannan, originally built in the seventeenth century, was destroyed in 1987. There was also a shrine dedicated to Mart Shmuni, which was damaged during the military campaign. Approximately five adults from Dawodiya disappeared during the Anfal operations from August to October 1988.[338]

Dehe
Located in the Dohuk region and sub-district of Sarsang, Dehe, though on the map of Father Josephe Omez, seems more a part of the Barwar

region and is shown as lying just southwest of Baz. As early as 1850, there were between ten and fifteen families in Dehe, served by a priest.[339] In 1920, an influx of Church of the East-rite families from the Upper Tiyari tribe settled there. At the time of the Simele massacres in 1933, there were 140 Assyrians in the village.[340] Five years later, only twenty-nine people (both indigenous and non-indigenous) remained.[341] By 1957 the population had recovered to 292 residents; and prior to the war in 1961, there were 100 families (twenty-two households), totalling approximately 600 people. The village, including its two schools, was destroyed in 1987, and the fifty remaining families were forced to flee.[342] Around the village, there are ruins of churches dedicated to various saints, some from the tenth century. The fifth-century church of Mart Shmuni also suffered ruin during the uprooting process.[343]

Deralok

Deralok, or Deira d-Luqa, 'monastery or church of St Luke', is situated on the Upper Zab River. The town's name derives from the ruins of a monastery dedicated to Mar Luqa located in the surrounding area. It was settled by Nestorians of the Baz tribe in 1920 following their expulsion from their villages in the Hakkâri region. Many fled to the Khabur basin in Syria after the massacres of 1933. Prior to that, 130 individuals resided in Deralok.[344] The regime turned Deralok into a collective town (*mujamma*) in 1978, settling there the displaced inhabitants of villages in the Nerwa and Rekan sub-districts. The people originally hailed from Qārō (thirty households), Lower Nerwa (five households) and Derigni (five households), with the rest originating from Wela.[345] Originally, forty-five houses were built for Assyrians. A church dedicated to Mar Khnana was built in 1979. During the Anfal operations, the village was once again turned into a collective town.

Dere

The village of Dere (Assyrian for 'monasteries' or, more literally, 'dwellings') lies quite close to its sister village, Komāne; they are often referred to as a pair, Dere w-Komāne. Its etymology can most likely be traced to the area's status as the site of the Mar 'Abdyešu' and Mar Qardagh monasteries. The fourth-century monastery of Mar ʻAbdyešuʻ, at one time served by forty-two monks living in the nearby caves, was reportedly partially ruined during Badger's initial visit in 1843. In 1850, however, Badger records that the villagers had restored it.[346] In 1850, Badger recorded between twelve and eighteen families residing there, with one functioning church.[347] In 1938, a League of Nations report cited forty-five autochthonous Assyrian families (425 people) living in the village (owned by them), along with livestock: 317 goats and 160 sheep.[348] By the 1957 census, the population had grown to 323 residents. In 1961, there were 100 families (60 households) there, but many left the village due to the autonomist movement.[349] Mar ʻAbdyešuʻ was also destroyed.[350] In 1987, government soldiers destroyed Dere and the Mar ʻAbdyešuʻ monastery for the second time in less than thirty years (after its restoration following the 1961 campaign), and its remaining seventy families were forced to flee yet again.[351] The majority of families who fled moved to nearby ʻAmēdīyāh, but found that also to be unsafe. After Anfal, a Dutch researcher, J. C. J. Sanders, recalls:

Figure 27   Mar ʻAbdyešuʻ monastery in Dere, 1991 (Courtesy of Hormuz Bobo)

I saw a new church with a white dome and a cross on top which had been bombed [a result of the Anfal]. The roof hung down to the ground . . . The church itself had two naves, the first sized ten by three and one-half meters, devoted to Saint Qardagh, pupil of Mar Awdisho/Odisho ['Abdyešuʻ], the one to whom the second nave, nine by four meters wide, was devoted.[352]

Sanders also mentions the possible entrance to a cave-shrine or monastery in the rock face of the mountain.

Derigni

The village of Derigni (also spelled Derigne and Dirgin) lies in the Sapna plain, three miles east of Dere. In 1850, Derigni was home to between forty and sixty Nestorian-rite families, with a single church and two priests.[353] By 1938, twenty families (sixty men and fifty-seven women) resided in the village with livestock: 288 goats and 55 sheep.[354] In 1957, the village was home to 130 Assyrians, and prior to its final destruction in 1988, there were forty families (thirty households) in the village, with a school.[355] During the Anfal campaign, the ancient church of the Virgin Mary, built in 885, sustained damage in the village destruction. At least twelve citizens from Derigni disappeared during the campaign, including a mother and her six children.[356]

Derishke

Derishke Naṣara lies just west of ʻAin-Nune, along with its Kurdish counterpart, Derishke Islam. The etymology of the village name suggests a possible monastic community in the region. This village was famous for its iron deposits, which were mined and used to forge agricultural tools and other necessary implements. In 1850, it was home to between fifteen and twenty-two families.[357] In 1915, during the massacres of the First World War, only 30 of Derishke's 130 residents survived.[358] In 1938, fifteen families, along with 158 goats and 72 sheep, called the village home.[359] By the 1957 census, the village population had again risen to 167 persons. Prior to its destruction by the Baʻth regime in 1988, there were fifty families (thirty households), with a school.[360] The churches of Mar Youhanna (built in 1810) and Mar Shukh-Alaha lie in ruins. Interestingly, although the Assyrian village of Derishke

Naṣara was destroyed by air raids in 1988, Derishke Islam, inhabited by Kurds, was left unharmed.[361]

Dohuke

Following the Simele massacres, part of Dohuke's population, of the Tkhuma tribe, fled to Syria. In 1936, thirty families inhabited Dohoke.[362] By 1938, 22 families (fifty-eight men and fifty-nine women) inhabited the village, along with their livestock: 218 goats and 185 sheep.[363] According to the 1957 census, roughly 120 people inhabited the village, and by 1961, approximately sixty families resided there.[364] The village was burned in 1962, but some of its population returned to rebuild in 1964. The villagers were forced to flee again in 1965, but returned once more following the 11 March 1970 peace agreement, which briefly pacified anti-government forces. The fighting resumed in the mid-1970s, when pro-government militia attacked and destroyed the village from 1974 to 1977 and began confiscating its lands.[365] Some villagers managed to return, but were expelled once again during the Anfal operations in 1988, which destroyed the village yet again and saw its surviving 60 families displaced.[366]

Eṣsān

Eṣsān, or Ṣiyān, is the former home of no fewer than seven metropolitans. The local church is dedicated to Mar Quryaqos. Another church, dedicated to Mar Zaddiqa, lies at the summit of the Gara Mountains at an elevation of more than 2,000 metres.[367] According to Badger, in 1850 Eṣsān had between forty and sixty families and a church served by a single priest of the Church of the East.[368] By 1918, there were twelve families, numbering ninety people, who had converted to Catholicism. In 1957, the population of Eṣsān totalled 249, and in 1961, it was destroyed for the first time.[369] The annihilation of the village in 1987 and 1988 included the destruction of its two churches and led to the displacement of its remaining population.

Hamziya

Hamziya had two churches, both dedicated to Mart Shmuni, built in the sixth century and twentieth century respectively.[370] As early as 1850, between six and nine Nestorian-rite families lived in the village,[371] and in 1913, its population stood at 200, with a priest and a school.[372] Around 1933, there were only fifty individuals in the village.[373] In 1957, the population of Hamziya was approximately a hundred. In 1987, the then population of thirty-two families fled when the village was targeted for being the known home of dissidents, among them Youkhana Esho Shimon Jajo, one of the founding members of the ADM, who was executed by the Iraqi regime in Abu Ghraib prison in 1985.[374]

Hayyis

In 1850, Hayyis was reported as having between fifteen and twenty-two Church of the East families and one church.[375] During the First World War, Hayyis fared better than many of the Barwari villages, as only one-third of its population perished.[376] In 1938, a League of Nations report mentioned thirty-five families, along with 242 goats and 104 sheep, residing in the village.[377] By the time of the Iraqi census of 1957, its population was listed at 194 individuals. In 1961, there were sixty families (thirty-five households). Hayyis was attacked in 1968, along with several other villages of the region. The destruction was quite severe, due to the amount of napalm dropped in the area. The village was not attacked in the 1977–8 border clearings, since, besides being quite remote, it remained within the region of Barwar under pro-Barzani pêşmerge control. In 1988, Hayyis, along with the Assyrian villages of Merkajiya and Musake, was the site of a chemical weapons attack. At the time of its destruction during the Anfal operations, it was home to fifty families (twelve households), with a school and the churches of Rabban Pithion and Mar Gewargis, which were levelled during the devastation.[378]

Inishke

During G. P. Badger's travels in 1850, Inishke (also Enishke) was home to between twenty and thirty families, with a priest serving one church.[379] In 1913, there were reportedly some 250 Chaldean-rite individuals, with a priest serving one active church, and a school.[380] By 1938, twenty families were residing in the village, amounting to thirty men and forty women, along with their livestock: fifty-five goats and forty sheep.[381] In 1957, Inishke's population numbered 333, according to the Iraqi census.

Figure 28   Ruins of Hayyis, Barwar, destroyed in 1988 (Courtesy of the Nineveh Center for Research and Development, Qaraqosh)

By 1961, it was home to 120 autochthonous Assyrian families (fifty households).[382] The village was not completely destroyed by the Ba'th regime, but its lands were confiscated, and a presidential palace complex was built upon them. The five churches in the village included the newer Mart Shmuni church; the old Mart Shmuni church (last restored in 1885); Mar Gewargis church (last restored in 1830); Mar Quryaqos monastery; and the tenth-century 'Red Monastery' of Mar Yosip Busnaya on a nearby hilltop all left in ruins.[383]

Jedide
In 1850, Jedide was home to between five and eight families adherent to the Church of the East.[384] In 1938, eight families resided in the village with their livestock: 101 goats and 40 sheep.[385] By 1961, there were 24 families accounting for the village's ten households, along with five Kurdish families.[386] Prior to its destruction in 1988 by the Ba'th regime, it was home to thirteen families.[387]

Kani Balav
As early as 1850, there were between twenty and thirty families in the village, with an old church dedicated to the Virgin Mary. Around 1933, the village population numbered 110 inhabitants, including a large number of newer settlers from the town of Ashitha in Turkey.[388] Twenty families resided in the

village in 1938, along with a number of livestock: 282 goats and 51 sheep.[389] Prior to 1949, there were mentions of a tiny Jewish community in the village. In 1957, there were 190 Assyrians in Kani Balav; in 1961, there were seventy families residing in thirty-five houses.[390] In 1988, the village was destroyed, along with its school and church. The villagers were then deported.[391]

Komāne

The sister village of Dere, Komāne (also Kowane) had been a large settlement. Its cultural and religious edifices included the church of Mar Ephrem (Sassanid period), an eighth-century monastery dedicated to Mar Quryaqos, and a perhaps fourth-century monastery to Mart Maryam. There is also an old cave-shrine or grotto dedicated to Mar Sawa in the Gara mountains opposite Komāne.[392] In 1850, there were between thirteen and twenty families in the village, with a priest and a church dedicated to the Virgin Mary that held allegiance to the Church of the East archdiocese of Mar Yeshu'yab of Barwar.[393] By 1913, most of the village had been converted to Catholicism, and Tfinkdji counted sixty Chaldean-rite Assyrians, with a chapel to Our Lady of Light and Life, while the number of Church of the East-rite individuals was unknown.[394] By 1938, four families (nineteen people) resided in the village with their livestock: fifty-three goats and forty-one sheep.[395] In 1957, Komāne had grown to 550 residents, and in 1961 contained about 150 families. In 1963, a primary school was built but, lamentably, the village and many of its antique buildings were looted and burned down by the pro-regime Zebari Kurds, led by Zubir Muhammad Zebari, in 1965.[396] In 1977, the Iraqi government built 100 new houses in and around Komāne, turning it into a refugee collective town for eighty Kurdish families and twenty Assyrian families who had been forced out of their villages in the Nerwa region.[397] A new church dedicated to the Virgin Mary was built in 1978 for the Church of the East of Nerwa, from the village of Wela, who also had their own priest. During the Anfal period, the village was used once again as a collective town.[398]

Mahude

Little is known about Mahude, which is located near the Assyrian village of Havintka. It was settled by displaced families of the Lower Tiyari tribe in 1920. In 1938, six families lived in the village, along with farm animals: 278

goats and 102 sheep.[399] There were around eight Assyrian families residing there, along with several Kurdish families, at the time of its destruction in 1988.[400]

Merkajiya

Merkajiya is located in the Barwari Bala sub-district of 'Amēdīyāh. In 1957, it was home to forty-nine individuals. As with all the Barwari villages, Merkajiya was not left unscathed by the events of the 1960s. It was the site of napalm attacks in 1968. In 1970, the headman, Yukhanna Odisho Zaia, was assassinated in order to intimidate the villagers into leaving. Prior to its ruination in 1988 by the Iraqi military, twenty families residing in twelve households called the village home.[401] Merkajiya was also the site of a known chemical attack during the Anfal offensive.[402]

Meze

Meze is located just south of the Gara Mountains in the old Church of the East diocese of Mar Abraham of Nerem. As early as 1850, between thirty and forty-five families (seven of them converts to Catholicism) resided in Meze ('Mezi' in Badger), served by a priest of the Church of the East.[403] By the time of Tfinkdji's arrival in 1913, the number of Chaldeans had increased to 100 individuals, including a priest.[404] In 1957, Meze was inhabited by 179 people, who fled in 1961. The Chaldean church of Mart Shmuni and Mart Maryam of the Church of the East both lay in ruins following an attack by pro-government Zebari militiamen, who later squatted on its lands.[405] The village was reportedly attacked and destroyed again in 1987.[406]

Musaka

Musaka is located in the Barwari Bala sub-district of 'Amēdīyāh. In 1938, nineteen families called the village home, alongside their 124 goats and 43 sheep.[407] In 1957, it was home to 128 villagers. Little remains of the ancient church dedicated to Mar Yosip, which was destroyed, along with the school and the remainder of the village, in 1988, displacing its thirty-five families.[408] Along with Hayyis and Merkajiya, Musaka was the site of a known chemical attack.[409]

Figure 29   ADM figures among the ruins of a village in Nerwa

Nerwa (Lower)

Lower Nerwa is a five-hour walk from the nearest road.[410] In 1938, it had seven Church of the East families (including approximately twenty-five men), along with a variety of domesticated animals: 144 goats, 73 sheep, 4 donkeys, 2 oxen and a mule.[411] According to the 1957 census, 149 Assyrians lived in Lower Nerwa, and in 1961 there were thirty-two families (approximately twenty-five households).[412] Prior to the final evacuation of the village by the Saddam regime in 1978, there were sixty families living in Lower Nerwa.[413] During the border clearings, the seventh-century church of Mar Khnana was eliminated along with the village. Many Assyrians from Lower Nerwa who survived the destruction were forcibly moved to the collective town of Deralok.

Qārō

In 1850, there were between ten and fifteen Church of the East-rite families in Qārō, with one priest.[414] In 1938, League of Nations documentation identifies nine Assyrian families of the Nestorian religious community (including approximately forty men), along with a variety of domesticated animals: 397 goats, 83 sheep, 7 oxen, 2 donkeys and a mule.[415] In 1961, there were forty-two Assyrian families (eighteen households). Prior to Qārō's first destruction by the regime in 1977–8, there were fifty families and a school.[416] In 1981, parts of the village were rebuilt by a small contingent of returnees. The entire village was once again ruined in 1988, and the remaining families were forced to flee. More than thirty-five Assyrians of the village had fled and attempted to return during the general amnesty offered by the Iraqi government, but none were seen or heard from again.[417] Qārō's three churches – Mar Gewargis, originally built in the seventh century and last restored in 1810; Mar Quryaqos; and Mar Younan – still lie in ruins.

Sardarawa

Sardarawa (sometimes spelled Sardawara or Sirdarao) was resettled by Assyrian refugees from Hakkâri after the First World War. In 1938, eight families (fifteen men and fifteen women) dwelled in the village, alongside nine goats.[418] According to the 1957 Iraqi census, its inhabitants numbered ninety-nine people. Sardarawa was destroyed by the Saddam regime in 1987, along with its church. The thirty remaining families were forced to flee to Assyrian areas elsewhere in Iraq. A presidential palace was later built on the villagers' land, further solidifying Sardarawa's total destruction.[419]

Sikrīne

In 1920, Sikrīne (also Segrin) was settled predominantly by Assyrian refugees of the Tkhuma tribe, who then fled to Syria after the 1933 massacres. In 1938, four families (ten men and seven women) resided in the village, along with their livestock: ninety-eight goats and three sheep.[420] Just prior to the exodus from the village, the population numbered approximately sixty-five. Other Assyrians later resettled Sikrīne, and in 1957, the population stood at 475. In 1987, the Ba'th regime destroyed the village, along with its school, and its thirty-seven families were displaced.[421]

Tāshish

In 1850, Tāshish, or Tārshish, was home to between twenty and thirty families, served by a Church of the East priest and one functioning church.[422] By 1938, sixty families dwelled in the village, alongside their 320 sheep and 122 goats.[423] In 1957, its population totalled 163 individuals. In 1961, there were sixty families (thirty households) in the village, and prior to being attacked by the pro-regime militia during the Anfal operations, it was home to seventy families, with a school.[424] The church of Mar Quryaqos (restored in 1850) and a shrine dedicated to Mart Shmuni were once part and parcel of the village.

Ten

Referred to as Keni on some British topographical maps, Ten, or Tin, is a fifteen-minute drive from the monastery of Abraham, which is 'now a 100 meter by 50 ruin, called "House of the Painters".'[425] Ten has long been inhabited and contains many markers of its cultural significance. In 1850, between thirty and forty-five families and a priest serving one church dwelled in the village.[426] By 1913, the population of Ten had increased to 450, served by two Chaldean-rite priests and a school.[427] Following the 1933 massacres, there were 200 Assyrians living in Ten.[428] By 1938, thirty-three people resided in the village with their livestock: ninety-three goats and forty-six sheep.[429] In 1957, the village population totalled 362, and in 1987, when the Ba'th regime destroyed it, there were forty-five families dwelling in the area.[430] The ancient church of Mart Shmuni was also eliminated at this time. An hour's drive from Ten, in Zawitha, west of the village of Bamarne, is the famous monastery of Mar Abraham ('Abraham the weeper'), dating back to at least the tenth century, whose ruins were still visible as late as 1956.[431] Two Assyrians from Ten were abducted and disappeared during the Anfal operations from August to October 1988.[432]

Tuthe Shemaye

Tuthe Shemaye's (written as 'Toshambic' in some League of Nations documents) etymology may be connected to an abundance of *elana d'tuthe*, or mulberry trees, in the region. It was part of *athran meetha*, 'our dead land', a term for the Assyrian region of Barwari Bala, which lost its tribal independence and fell under the jurisdiction of various Kurdish aghas. During G. P. Badger's wanderings in Mesopotamia in 1850, he remarked that between ten and fifteen Assyrian families lived in Tuthe Shemaye.[433] In 1938, nineteen families, thirty-three sheep and thirty-three goats resided in the village.[434] By 1957 its population totalled forty-five individuals. In 1961, there were fifteen Assyrian families (six households) living in the village, as well as three Kurdish families.[435] Prior to its destruction in 1988 by the Ba'th regime, it was home to ten Assyrian families and the old church of Mar Gewargis, which met with the same fate as the rest of the village structures.[436]

Wela

In 1850, Wela (also Welah) had between ten and fifteen families, with one priest and one church.[437] In 1938, there were seven families in Wela, consisting of twenty-six males and an unknown number of females, along with a variety of livestock including 145 goats, 87 sheep, 7 oxen, 1 donkey and 1 mule.[438] By the 1957 census, there were fifty-nine individuals in Wela. Later, in 1961, there were sixteen families (nine households), and prior to the evacuation by the Ba'th regime in 1977, twenty families resided in Wela.[439] The churches of Mart Shmuni (perhaps seventh century) and Mart Maryam were first destroyed at this time.[440] The village met with devastation yet again in 1987 and 1988 during the Anfal operations.

'Aqra District

It may be of note to mention the Nahla d'Malka or 'valley of the king' sub-district as having a longstanding and continuous Assyrian habitation. Though much of it was abandoned for years due to persecution, the resettlement of Hakkâri Assyrians was in a sense a remigration into the region.

Bilmand

The village of Bilmand was rebuilt by Assyrians from Lower Tiyari in 1920 following their exodus from Hakkâri. By 1938, ten families resided in the village, comprising forty men and thirty-six women and children, along with 354 sheep and 333 goats.[441] In 1957, the village population totalled ninety-one. One of its residents, Odisho Iyut, saw his nearby lands in Korawa village confiscated and occupied by neighbouring Kurds in 1959.[442] There were approximately 150 Assyrians living in the village in 1977.[443] At the time of its destruction in 1987, Bilmand was residence to 35–40 families, with a school.[444] The village is absent from the 1961 Dominican map.

Cham 'Ashrat

Cham (also Chamme) 'Ashrat was settled in 1922 by refugees from Upper Tiyari. Numbering around seventy people, most of these settlers fled to Syria and settled in the Khabur basin after fleeing the massacres at Simele and surrounding villages in 1933.[445] Cham 'Ashrat was later settled by tribesmen of Lower Tiyari, and by 1957, the village population totalled ninety-five, approximately twenty-five families, living in thirteen homes.[446] The village was destroyed during the Anfal period in 1988, along with its one church dedicated to Mar Ephrem, and its remaining twenty-five families were displaced.[447]

Cham Chale

Cham Chale, located in the Nahla sub-district, was settled in 1922 by tribesmen from Lower Tiyari. In 1938, it was home to thirteen families (twenty-nine men and thirty-six women), along with their livestock: 168 goats and 90 sheep.[448] According to the 1957 Iraq census, the village population numbered fifty-one inhabitants. Cham Chale was initially plundered in 1963, and its population fled following the civil war. The village was repopulated and in 1977 had sixty persons dwelling within it before it was destroyed yet again in 1988 as part of the Anfal operations.[449]

Cham Rabatke

The name of Cham Rabatke may derive from Kurdish for 'river of the monks', speaking to a historic monastic community in the region.[450] Through the centuries, people left and emigrated to and from the region. More recently it was settled by refugees from Lower Tiyari in 1920. Following the 1933 massacres, an estimated ninety Assyrians survived in the village.[451] In 1938, six families remained, with sixteen men and twenty-six women and children, along with 368 goats and 273 sheep.[452] By 1977, ninety-eight people resided in the village.[453] Before being destroyed in 1987, Cham Rabatke was home to forty-five families (thirty households).[454] The Assyrians of the former village were relocated to 'Aqra and left there by military and government forces to build dwellings from raw materials found in the area. Most villagers lived months in tents with no forthcoming government aid.[455]

Cham Sinne

In 1922, following the First World War, Assyrians from Lower Tiyari settled Cham Sinne. A report by the League of Nations mentions forty families of the Church of the East ecclesiastical background before a malaria outbreak later that year which decreased their number to twenty-five (142 persons).[456] By 1957, the village population numbered approximately 130 inhabitants. When the village and church of Mar Ephrem were destroyed by the regime in 1987, there were thirty families in Cham Sinne.[457]

Guhana

Some nine families were settled in Guhana (also Kohana) in 1938.[458] Local Assyrians purchased the land in 1955 from the Iraqi government, and by 1961 there were twenty families who called the village home.[459] In 1986 Guhana was targeted and its thirty-five families were forced to flee.[460]

Hazarjot

The village of Hazarjot (also Hazarjift), as well as all the adjacent farming land, was purchased in 1925–6 under the supervision of the Chaldean church for refugees from the village of Sat in Hakkâri. Between 1920 and 1933, Nestorian-rite families from Lower Tiyari in Hakkâri also settled in Hazarjot.[461] In 1938, Hazarjot included thirteen Assyrian families, ten Jewish families and twenty Kurdish families. The non-human animals numbered ninety goats and fifty sheep.[462] According to the 1957 census, the population stood at 178 people. There were more than twenty-five families living in the village when it was exposed to burning and plundering by Zebari irregulars from 1961 to 1963.[463] Though the majority of its population remained, that tragedy was repeated in 1972, causing more residents to flee. Much of Hazarjot's population returned in 1975 and remained. The village was destroyed again in 1988, along with the church of Mart Maryam. Prior to the destruction of the Anfal campaign, Hazarjot was home to thirty-five families, with a school.[464]

Hizane, Lower and Upper

Hizane (sometimes Hizanke), in the Nahla region, was resettled by Assyrians from Lower Tiyari in 1920. By 1938 Lower Hizane had five families comprising fifteen men and ten women and children, along with 251 sheep and 187 goats, while Upper Hizane had twenty-eight families numbering seventy-seven men and seventy-eight women and children, along with 293 sheep and 281 goats as livestock.[465] In 1957, the village's population numbered 254 inhabitants: 210 in Lower Hizane and 44 in Upper Hizane. In 1961, there were forty-two households in Hizane. The village was razed and burned in 1964 and 1969 by government irregulars.[466] By 1977, Upper Hizane numbered twenty people and Lower Hizane 145.[467] In 1987, it was home to 110 families, with a school.[468] The old church of Mar Gewargis (restored in the 1950s) was also destroyed by the Ba'th regime.[469] Some individuals of the village who were targeted include Yalda Eshoo Zadoq, Toma Enwiya Toma, Eshoo Goriel Khoshaba and Mikhael Lazar Mikhael.[470]

Kashkawa

Kashkawa was settled by families from Lower Tiyari in 1920 (along with the majority of the Nahla region). In 1933, 134 inhabitants lived in the

Figure 30   Ruins of Mar Gewargis, Hizane (Courtesy of Hormuz Bobo)

village.[471] By 1938, there were twenty families (131 persons).[472] According to the 1957 census account, approximately 180 villagers dwelled within Kashkawa. When attacked by pro-government Kurdish irregulars in 1963, its thirty households were burned and inhabitants forced to flee, since the village was known to have significant sympathisers involved in the anti-government activities of Assyrians, Kurds and others.[473] Among those men singled out for elimination were Daniel Toma, Moshe Zaia and Youkhana Shammas, who were all eventually killed. Some of its population returned following the ceasefire on 11 March 1970, but were soon to be threatened once again.[474] Before being destroyed along with its church Mart Shmuni again in 1987, Kashkawa was home to 100 families, with a school.[475]

Khalilani

Khalilani is located in the sub-district of Nahla (or Nahla d'Malka). It was settled by families from Lower Tiyari in 1920. In 1938, seven families, amounting to twenty-four men and twenty women and children,

Figure 31   Ruins of Kashkawa, 1987 (Courtesy of Hormuz Bobo)

resided in the village, alongside 144 goats and 143 sheep.[476] In 1957, the village population was twenty-eight; by 1977, it had risen to seventy-three.[477] The population increased further to twenty-five families by the time of the village's destruction in 1987 during the start of the Anfal operations.[478]

Meroke

Meroke (also Merugee and Miroki), most likely a corruption of *Mar Awgen* or 'St Eugene', was settled by Assyrians from Lower Tiyari in 1920. In 1938, eight families dwelled in the village, amounting to twenty-six men and thirty women and children, along with 219 sheep and 188 goats.[479] In 1957, the village held around seventy residents. Meroke was home to thirty-five families (fifteen households), with a school, just prior to being bulldozed by the military operations of 1987.[480]

Suse

Suse, the name probably derived from the Assyrian for 'horses', is also known as Cham Suse and Barraka d'Qaddisha. It was home to a cultural structure called *gippa d-qaddisha*, 'the saint's cave'. According to a League of Nations report concerning the settlement of the Assyrians following the 1933 massacres, 200 people inhabited the village.[481] It was destroyed during the Anfal operations.

Zouli

Zouli, or Zhouli, was settled by families from Lower Tiyari in 1920, and usually divided into upper and lower regions. In 1957 the village population totalled eighty-eight. In 1977, Upper Zouli numbered thirty inhabitants and Lower Zouli twenty-five.[482] Before being destroyed in 1987, Zouli was home to thirty-four families, who were forced to flee to Mosul and other regions populated by Assyrians.[483]

Dohuk District

Babilo

Babilo was settled by the Baz tribe in the 1920s. Around 1933, they numbered sixty-five people. In 1957, the village population stood at 111, and in

1961 there were twenty-five families (sixteen households). In 1988, Babilo was destroyed as part of the Anfal campaign and its thirty-five families were left homeless.[484] There is reportedly an old grotto church dedicated to Mar Yosip near Babilo.[485]

Chavrik

Chavrik, or Avrik, was divided into an upper and lower region, both settled by Assyrians. The village was destroyed by the Hussein regime in 1987 during the Anfal operations.

Der-Alush

Little is known of Der-Alush, though its name indicates that it may have been the site of a monastery. The village was destroyed in 1987.

Gund Kosa

Gund Kosa, its name probably partially derived from the Kurdish word for 'village', *gündük*, lies along the river Khabour in the sub-district of Doski. In recent history, Gund Kosa and three nearby villages were settled by Lower Tiyari tribesmen in 1922. After the events of 1933, only 150 Assyrians remained in the village.[486] The settlers of the four villages garnered some help from neighbouring Kurds in the village of Akmala and managed to form a small militia that repelled various attacks against the Assyrians in the region, thus saving Gund Kosa from the Doski Kurdish tribe and granting refuge to numerous families fleeing the Simele atrocities.[487] The population of the village in 1938 consisted of twenty-eight families and their livestock: 345 goats and 217 sheep.[488] The population of another village, Spindarok,[489] who survived the Simele massacres fled to and settled in Gund Kosa. More than 170 families dwelled in the village then. At the time of the 1957 Iraqi census, 136 people resided in Gund Kosa. It is the birthplace of curate Zaia Bobo Dobato of the Church of the East, who was targeted by the government, including with various assassination attempts. Dobato escaped to Urmia, and there worked to bring the Assyrian predicament to the attention of various NGOs and the international community.[490] In 1988, Gund Kosa was home to eighty families, with a school and church, when it was targeted during the Anfal operations.[491] At least thirty-three villagers disappeared during the destruction of the village.[492]

Malta

Malta, or Maʿalthaye, is located west of the Rabban Hormizd monastery of Alqosh, on the mountainous border. It is part of the Catholic diocese of ʿAmēdīyāh. Its name comes from the Assyrian-Aramaic word meaning 'gateway', as it is literally the gateway to the mountainous region north of Nineveh. Above the village are four reliefs carved into the mountain by the ancient Assyrian king Sennacherib, as well as a monastic hermitage. According to Badger's accounts, as early as 1850 there were between twenty and thirty _families in Malta, with one active church.[493] In 1957, there were thirty households (130 people) and in 1961, there were seventy families.[494] The village was destroyed again in 1986 along with the churches of Mar Zaya and Mar Awda.[495] Due to its proximity to Dohuk, Malta was used as a collective town for hundreds of Kurdish families brought from villages ruined by the Iraqi regime during the Anfal campaign.[496]

Peda

Assyrians had lived in the area of Peda for many decades. Peda was destroyed by the Baʿth regime in 1987. The population at the time of expulsion is unknown.

Sheikhan District
Armashe

Armashe, also spelled Harmash, possesses an ancient Assyrian stele carved into the rock face nearby. In 1850, there were between fifteen and twenty-two families and a church within the village, all under the Church of the East diocese of Mar Abraham of Gündük (Nerem), in the mountainous region south of Jebel Gara.[497] Many of its villagers originated from the Tkhuma region in Hakkâri. In 1913, there were 310 Chaldean converts, with a priest serving one church.[498] In 1957, the village population totalled 204 (thirteen households), and before being destroyed in 1987 by the Baʿth regime, Armashe was home to fifty-five families, with a school.[499] Assyrian villagers of both Armashe and Azakh were resettled in Atrush, which had been set up as a collective town.[500] The church of Mart Theresa suffered some damage during the Anfal period. There is also a small church to Mar Ephrem dating back to the seventh century.

Azakh

In 1850, Azakh, or Adekh, contained between fifteen and twenty-two families and a church. The village, like Armashe, Meze and Ṭlanitha, lay in the mountains south of Jebel Gara.[501] By 1913, there were 300 Chaldean-rite individuals, with a priest and a school, though the number of Church of the East adherents was unclear at that time.[502] In 1957, the village population totalled seventy-eight individuals, and before being destroyed in 1987, Azakh was home to a total of fifty families (twenty households).[503] The church of Mar Gewargis, first built in 1535, and the grotto dedicated to Mar Abraham were once part of the once-thriving town before being bulldozed during the Anfal.

Bebōze

Bebōze, or Beth Bōzi, is part of the region known as Shemkān. In 1850, there were between ten and fifteen families and one church in the predominantly Catholic village.[504] The village's existence is also attested to in Syriac manuscripts, as in 1888 a monk named Nicholas Nōfāl of Tel Keppe copied a manuscript in the village for the monastery of Rabban Hormizd.[505] By Tfinkdji's time in 1913, there were 120 Chaldean-rite villagers, with one priest.[506] Bebōze was first destroyed in 1976.[507] The village was resettled but, along with the thirteenth-century church of Mart Shmuni and the seven shrines dedicated to her children, was devastated again in 1987 by the Iraqi military.

Birta

Birta (sometimes Bire), a half-hour walk from Tilla, is located in the western part of the old Church of the East ecclesiastical region of Margā.[508] Birta's name derives from the Akkadian word *birtu* 'fortress' and the village is the location of a burial complex belonging to an Akkadian king. This village is but one of many sites referred to as Birta, due to the ruins of a fortress in close proximity. In 1913, sixty people lived in the village.[509] While under attack during the armed resistance movement in 1961, Birta's people abandoned the village, which was later settled by Iraqi government irregulars from the Zebari tribe.[510] The ancient monastery of Mar Gewargis and the fifth-century hermitages around the village had been continually damaged by military and paramilitary activity and fell into further disrepair after 1961.[511]

Deze

Deze, or Dizze, has had a longstanding Nestorian and Chaldean ecclesiastical presence. Located not far from the Yezidi shrine of Sheikh Adi, Deze lies in the same region as Bedul, Beboze, and Meze, all part of the Chaldean diocese of 'Amēdīyāh. In 1850, it was home to between twenty and thirty families.[512] By 1913, there were eighty Chaldeans in the village, but the number of Nestorian adherents was unknown.[513] The original inhabitants fled in 1933 because of the local persecution, and the ownership of the lands passed into the hands of Kurdish landowner Ibrahim Haj-Malo Mizouri.[514] In 1974, Assyrians from Shuwadin (near Zakho) settled in Deze to work its fields. Prior to its destruction by the Ba'th regime in 1987, there were ninety families (thirty households) in Deze, with a school. The ancient stone church of Mar Christopher was also destroyed.[515]

Tilla

Tilla, or Tella, walking distance from Birta, is mentioned quite early in Syriac sources as the place of origin of a copy of the *Book of Superiors*, dated to 1701, and a book of hymns dated to 1720.[516] According to Georg Hoffmann, Tilla was also referred to as 'Tellā Bīrtā', perhaps since both *Tella* and *Birta* refer to various sites with ancient lineage in the region; Tilla is one of many sites of the same name. In 1913, there were 340 Chaldean-rite villagers in Tilla, with a priest serving one church, and a school.[517] Tilla was destroyed in 1987, along with its three churches; the third-century church of Mar Isḥaq, and another dedicated to Mart Maryam, were among those eliminated. A mound dedicated to Mart Shmuni (a remnant of an older ancient religious site), from which Tilla's etymology probably derives (*tella* meaning 'mound' or 'hill'), was also despoiled during the village's destruction.

Simele District

Badaliya

Jilu tribesmen settled in Badaliya (or Badariyah or Badriyah) in 1920, but fled to Syria after the 1933 massacres, and an Arab landowner, Muhammad Beg, took ownership of the village. By 1938, fifteen families had returned to the village, totalling seventy-five persons.[518] By the 1957 census, its Assyrian population stood at 234. Before the last Assyrians were evacuated in 1987 to make way for a government-run poultry project, sixty families inhabited the village, with a school.[519]

Bakhitme

Bakhitme, or Beth-Khatme, 'the place of the seals' (probably in reference to a place where documents or deals were signed or agreed to), is famous for being the location of the martyrdom of Mar Daniel, to whom a church was later dedicated (rebuilt in 1984).[520] In its more recent history, Nochiya tribesmen settled Bakhitme in 1920, but fled to Syria after the massacres

Figure 32   Ruins of Mar Gewargis church, Bakhitme (Courtesy Father Emmanuel Youkhanna)

Figure 33   Ruins of Bakhitme (Courtesy Father Emmanuel Youkhanna)

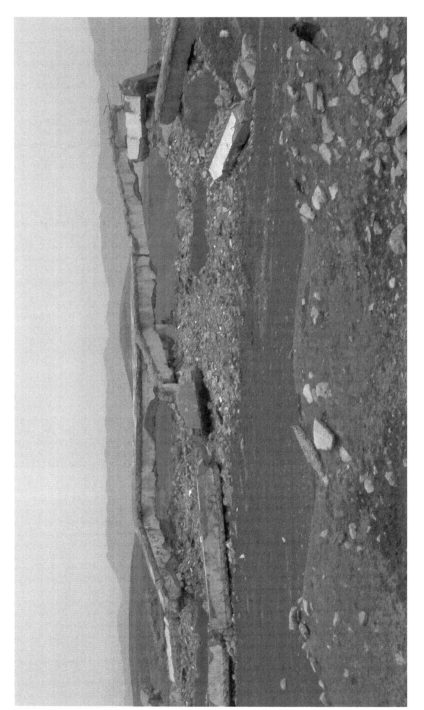

Figure 34 Ruins of Bakhitme (Courtesy Father Emmanuel Youkhanna)

of August 1933. The village was again settled by eighty Assyrian families in 1956. Bakhitme was purchased in 1957 from the Arab sheikhs who owned it, giving its approximately 230 residents hope for continued growth.[521] However, in April 1987, the village was entirely destroyed, including two schools and three churches (Mart Maryam and Mar Gewargis), and its 140 Assyrian families deported.[522]

Gera-Gora

Gera-Gora is referred to as Kera-Gora by Eshoo. Some of its more recent inhabitants hailed from Tkhuma and Rumta in Upper Tiyari and settled in the village following the First World War.[523] After the massacres of 1933, many of the villagers fled to Syria, and the village was immediately resettled by other Assyrians from the neighbouring towns. According to the census account of 1957, approximately 200 villagers dwelled in Gera-Gora. Most recently, according to information gleaned by the AAS field mission in 2004, the village was forcibly abandoned in Badaliya in 1987.[524]

Hejerke

Hejerke (also Hizeerke and Hizirki), located just northwest of Sheze, was settled by Baz tribesmen following the First World War. In 1933 there were approximately eighty-five individuals in the village, and in 1938 the League of Nations reported twenty-five families along with significant livestock: 572 goats and 180 sheep.[525] By 1957, the population had been reduced to forty-one.[526] The Iraqi regime attacked the village in 1984, and later destroyed it in 1987, when Hejerke's remaining eight families were forced to flee.

Kharab Kulk

Kharab Kulk can possibly be identified as the Ḥarbai mentioned in Syriac sources. The monastery of Mar Isaac is located nearby.[527] Kharab Kulk was settled by Nestorian-rite Assyrians from the former patriarchal see of Qochanis in Hakkâri following the massacres of Assyrians, Greeks and Armenians in Asia Minor during the First World War.[528] The village was first overrun in 1961 during the civil war, and again in 1987.

Mar Yaqob

Mar Yaqob, or Mar Yaqo, is located east of Hejerke and northwest of Sheze. According to Majed Eshoo, it sits just atop a mountain referred to by Assyrians as *Bakhira*, or *Beth Khira*, loosely translated as 'place of freedom'.[529] Mar Yaqob is known in Kurdish as Qashafir. During Badger's journeys in 1850, Mar Yaqob was home to between twenty-one and thirty-two families, with a chapel and later a school, served by a priest.[530] During Tfinkdji's travels in early 1913, he recorded 150 Chaldean-rite Assyrian villagers with a chapel and a school but no priest.[531] The Dominicans later built a large monastic academy in the 1920s. A monumental grave was built for the Dominican Father Besson, who died during an epidemic in the region.[532] Mar Yaqob was damaged first in 1976 and finally destroyed in 1988, at which time it was home to twenty Assyrian families.[533] The mausoleum of Father Besson was also destroyed.[534]

Sheze

Sheze, or Shiyoz, is located just north of the village of Simele. Like Malta and Mar Yaqob, Sheze lies along the mountain range to the west of Rabban Hormizd, within the ʿAmēdīyāh diocese. In 1850, between twenty and thirty families lived in the village, but Badger does not mention a functional church, quite peculiar for a village of approximately 150 people.[535] In 1913, there were approximately 210 villagers, with a Chaldean-rite priest serving the

Figure 35   Ruins of Sheze, circa 1987 (Courtesy the Nineveh Center for Research and Development, Qaraqosh, Iraq)

church of Mar Gewargis, along with a school.[536] In 1957, there were a total of 417 Assyrians in Sheze, but in 1987 the village was destroyed, along with its school and church. The eighty families that remained were forced to flee to friendlier territory.[537] The ruins of a monastery dedicated to Mar 'Ishoyab also lie near the village.

Surka

Surka was originally inhabited by both Christians and Yezidis. In 1957, the village's population totalled 196. In 1987, before its inhabitants were evacuated to make way for a poultry project by the Iraqi government, there were thirty families in the village, with a school.[538]

Zakho District
Bersive

The name Bersive may be rooted in the Assyrian *bera d'sawa*, or 'old man's well'. The village was settled by refugee families from what is now Turkey, descendants of Mamo, a priest in the fourteenth century.[539] In 1913, there were 400 residents in the village, served by a Chaldean-rite priest and a church.[540] In 1957, the census accounts estimated 786 inhabitants; in 1961, there were a total of 240 families (220 households).[541] Bersive was attacked numerous times in the 1960s by passing warplanes. Some of its population fled and later returned after a lessening of hostilities in the civil war. By 1976, the Iraqi regime had turned Bersive into a collective town, settling 560 Kurdish and 40 Assyrian families who had been forced out of more than twenty villages along the border region with Turkey during the first border clearings in 1974–5.[542] The Chaldean church of Mar Gewargis, dating from the twelfth century, lies in the centre of the village. The church of Mar Ephrem of the Assyrian Church of the East (Nestorian) was consecrated in 1970 and located on the village outskirts.[543] Bersive was utilised as a collective town again in 1988.[544] In 1990, on the eve of the Gulf War, there were 160 Assyrian families in Bersive.[545]

Hizawa

The village of Hizawa is located in the sub-district of Sindi. It was turned into a collective town during the Anfal period, changing its demography.[546] Little is known about its two original ancient churches.

Figure 36   Ruins of Levo following the Anfal operations, 1988 (Courtesy the Nineveh Center for Research and Development)

Levo
According to the 1957 census, Levo had a population of 616 residents (350 families, 150 homes). During the rebellion in 1961, the village was targeted by various air raid bombings. Levo continued to be targeted by raids, lootings and bombings, by both state and non-state actors for the next twenty-seven years, until 1988.[547] Most physical structures suffered major damage or were destroyed completely, including its Chaldean-rite church dedicated to Mar Abraham. Three citizens were killed during the Anfal operations at Levo: Sabriya Maroge Sliwa, Amira Odisho Khosho and Jibrael Odisho Khosho. Another Assyrian, Saber Khayri Youkhana, disappeared.[548] Levo's 140 families were displaced after the Anfal operations.

Mala 'Arab
Mala 'Arab was resettled in 1916 by refugees from Lower Tiyari, but a year later they moved to Gund Kosa. In 1922, Mala 'Arab was again settled by Assyrians from the villages of the Margā region.[549] At the time of the 1957 census, Mala 'Arab's population totalled 237 individuals, and by 1961 there were approximately 120 families (fifty households) in the village.[550] The village was burned and razed by Zebari Kurds in 1963.[551] In 1970, its population returned following the 11 March ceasefire between the government and Kurdish forces, and began rebuilding the village, including a school, until

1988 during the Anfal operations, when Mala ʿArab was once again destroyed and its sixty Assyrian households dispersed.[552]

Mergasūr

Mergasūr most likely finds its etymology in an Assyrian-Aramaic phrase meaning 'pasture of Ashur'. According to the 1957 census, it was home to 186 individuals, and by 1961, there were 170 families (eighty households) in the village.[553] Prior to its demolition by the Iraqi government in 1988, Mergasūr was the dwelling place of 60 households, with a school.[554]

Nav-Kandal

Nav Kandal (Naf Kandal) is a remote village. In 1957, it was home to 240 individuals, and in 1961, there were 150 families (approximately sixty households). The old church dedicated to Mar Yawsep served as its cultural and religious centre. Just prior to its purging in 1988, Nav Kandal was home to 110 families, with a school.[555] The church of Mar Yawsep was destroyed along with the village dwellings in the same year. There are 250 families from Nav-Kandal elsewhere in Iraq and in the diaspora.[556]

Pireka

Pireka is located in the sub-district of Guli. According to the 1957 Iraqi census, it was home to 108 individuals. The village was initially destroyed during the border clearings in 1978, and at the time, was home to ninety Chaldean-rite households (approximately thirty-five households) and a school.[557] The village was rebuilt over the next few years, but was destroyed again in 1984.

Sharanish

The birthplace of the Syriac scholar Alphonse Mingana, Sharanish (French spelling Chéranésch) is possibly named after an ancient princess known as Shiranoosh. In 1913, it was home to 600 townsfolk, with a Chaldean-rite priest serving the two churches of Mart Shmuni and Mar Quryaqos.[558] In 1957, the population reached 384, and in 1961 there were eighty households when the village was destroyed and much of its lands confiscated by Zebari Kurdish irregulars.[559] Some villagers returned over time and rebuilt, and in 1978, Sharanish was home to a total of 160 Assyrian families (2,000 people), with a school.[560] The village was targeted once again in 1987 and its remaining eighty families displaced.[561] The ancient churches of Mart Shmuni and Mar Quryaqos were both destroyed during the devastation.

Ninawa Province

Sheikhan District
Haruna
Haruna was destroyed by the Ba'th regime in 1987. It was home to a majority of Yezidis, with a small Christian population.[562]

Notes

1. Much of this data can be seen in greater detail in Nicholas al-Jeloo, 'Characteristics of Pre-19th Century Assyrian Christian Architecture East of the Tigris River: An Evaluation and Analysis Based on the Study of 114 Examples from Across the Region' (MA Thesis, Faculty of Theology, Leiden University, 2006). This appendix is indebted to his meticulous study.
2. Numbers of people, churches, animals, schools etc. are given when possible. Also for the majority of village data, the Assyrians are mentioned by their ecclesiastical and tribal affiliations when known. The Dominican map served as the initial source for geographic coordinates and aided in corroborating the ethnographic data.
3. All the Assyrian villages of this region were privately owned by Sayid Taha and the heirs of Ismail Beg, with the exception of Hawdian, which was owned by Mulla Osa Agha of the Baliki tribe. The Assyrians cultivated the land and paid tribute and had been doing so since 1921. Known crops were wheat, barley, and a variety of fruits and vegetables, as well as tobacco. Note also that the wording of the League of Nations report calls the Assyrians *fellahs* or 'cultivators'. See League of Nations, *Report on the Economic Conditions of the Assyrians in the Northern Provinces in Iraq*, 21. Similar to most Native American nations, some Assyrians did not 'own' their land in the sense of having the acquired land deeds associated with it. During the early years of the United States, the US government regularly attempted to designate 'land owners' by written deed. As this trait was not one followed by Native American/Aboriginal culture (i.e., a person owning land distinguished by a piece of parchment or paper), it is generally not recognised as a legitimate marker of indigeneity. Also note this region was not reproduced on Josephe Omez's Dominican map of 1961.

4. League of Nations, *Report on the Economic Conditions of the Assyrians in the Northern Provinces in Iraq*, 21.

5. C.C. (Darbandoke), interview with author, 17 February 2008, Toronto; *Iraq: Continuous and Silent Ethnic Cleansing – Displaced Persons in Iraqi Kurdistan and Iraqi Refugees in Iran* (Paris: FIDH/International Alliance for Justice, 2003), 42.

6. League of Nations, *Report on the Economic Conditions of the Assyrians in the Northern Provinces in Iraq*, 21.

7. B.B. (Harīr), interview with author, 17 February 2008, Toronto.

8. Ibid.

9. League of Nations, *Report on the Economic Conditions of the Assyrians in the Northern Provinces in Iraq*, 21.

10. P.W. (Diyana), interview with author, 17 February 2008, Toronto.

11. Though Diyana was destroyed again in 1974, very little information could be found concerning that period, making its inclusion in this appendix more proper.

12. League of Nations, *Report on the Economic Conditions of the Assyrians in the Northern Provinces in Iraq*, 21.

13. B.B. (Harīr), C.C. (Darbandoke), I.Y. (Diyana) and P.W. (Diyana), interviews with author, 17 February 2008, Toronto; *Iraq: Continuous and Silent Ethnic Cleansing*, 42.

14. League of Nations, *Report on the Economic Conditions of the Assyrians in the Northern Provinces in Iraq*, 21.

15. B.B. (Harīr), interview, 17 February 2008, Toronto.

16. 'Kurdish minister has no objection to Assyrian Christian administrative area', Assyrian International News Agency, 26 February 2006, http://www.aina.org/news/20060225231434.htm (accessed 23 July 2014).

17. League of Nations, *Report on the Economic Conditions of the Assyrians in the Northern Provinces in Iraq*, 21.

18. Ibid.

19. League of Nations, *Report on the Economic Conditions of the Assyrians in the Northern Provinces in Iraq*, 21.

20. A. M. Hamilton, *Road through Kurdistan: The Narrative of an Engineer in Iraq*, new ed. (London: Faber & Faber, 1958), 158–9.

21. Ralph Solecki, *Shanidar: The First Flower People* (New York: Knopf, 1971), 73–5.

22. B.B. (Harīr), C.C. (Darbandoke), I.Y. (Diyana) and P.W. (Diyana), interviews with author, 17 February 2008, Toronto.

23. ''Amēdīyāh', *Encyclopedia Judaica*, 2nd ed. (Farmington Hills, MI: Macmillan Reference USA, 2007).

24. A nickname meaning 'the blind prince'. Mira Kora, originally Muhammad Pasha, was Kurdish chief of the Rawanduz region. See Amir Harrak, 'Northern Mesopotamia in a 19th Century Syriac Annalistic Source', *Le Muséon: revue d'études orientales* 119.3–4 (2006), 298–301.

25. George Percy Badger, *The Nestorians and Their Rituals* (London: Darf, [1852] 1987), vol. 2, 174.

26. J. C. J. Sanders, *Assyrian-Chaldean Christians in Eastern Turkey and Iran: Their Last Homeland Re-charted* (Hernen, Netherlands: AA Brediusstichting, 1997), 63.

27. Ibid, 64.

28. American consulate in Tabriz to Secretary of State, 19 October 1961, NA/ RG59/787.00/10-1961; Tabriz to Secretary of State, 25 October 1961, NA/ RG59/787.00/10-2561; Tabriz to Secretary of State, 1 November 1961, NA/ RG59/787.00/10-161.

29. Avshalom H. Rubin, ''Abd al-Karim Qasim and the Kurds of Iraq: Centralization, Resistance and Revolt 1958–63' *Middle Eastern Studies* 43.3 (2007), 369–70.

30. AAS, 'Field Mission Iraq 2004'.

31. Ibid.; Eshoo, 'The Fate of Assyrian Villages', 11.

32. League of Nations, *Report on the Economic Conditions of the Assyrians in the Northern Provinces in Iraq*, 10.

33. Eshoo, 'The Fate of Assyrian Villages', 9, D.T. (Blejanke), interview with author, 24 February 2008, Toronto.

34. B.B. (Harīr), C.C. (Darbandoke) and I.Y. (Diyana), interviews with author, 17 February 2008, Toronto.

35. AAS, 'Field Mission Iraq 2004'.

36. League of Nations, *Report on the Economic Conditions of the Assyrians in the Northern Provinces in Iraq*, 10.

37. Eshoo, 'The Fate of Assyrian Villages', 8.

38. AAS, 'Field Mission Iraq 2004'.

39. Budge, *The Book of Governors*, vol. 2, 633.

40. AAS, 'Field Mission Iraq 2004'.

41. For a full account of the events which occurred at Ṣawura, see details as recounted by Shabo 'Aziz d'Baz in 'Abdyešu' Barzana, *Šinnē d-'Asqūtā: Qrābā d-Dayrabūn w-Gunḥā d-Simele* (Chicago: Assyrian Academic Society Press, 2003), 232–8.

42. R. S. Stafford, 'Iraq and the Problem of the Assyrians', *International Affairs* 13.2 (1934), 176.

43. Eshoo, 'The Fate of Assyrian Villages', 14.

44. Eshoo, 'The Fate of Assyrian Villages', 11.

45. Badger, *The Nestorians and Their Rituals*, vol. 1, 392.

46. D.T. (Blejanke), K.S. (Dūre), Y.D. (Annūnē), Y.G. (Bebede) and Z.Y. (Annūnē), interviews with author, 24 February 2008, Toronto.

47. Simo Parpola and Michael Porter, *The Helsinki Atlas of the Near East in the Neo-Assyrian Period* (Helsinki: Neo-Assyrian Corpus Text Project, 2001), 19.

48. J.-M. Fiey, *Assyrie chrétienne* (Beirut: Imprimerie Catholique, 1963), vol. 1, 225–35.

49. David Wilmshurst, *The Ecclesiastical Organization of the Church of the East* (Leuven: Peeters, 2000), 362. Wilmshurst's estimates are based on numbers extracted from Joseph Tfinkdji, 'L'Église chaldéene catholique autrefois et aujourd'hui', *Annuaire pontifical catholique 1914* (Paris: Maison de la Bonne Presse, 1913), 499, and elsewhere.

50. Fiey, *Assyrie chrétienne*, vol. 1, 305–6.

51. Badger, *The Nestorians and their Rituals*, vol. 2, 392.

52. Tfinkdji, 'L'Église chaldéene catholique autrefois et aujourd'hui', 499. Tfinkdji fails to mention the chapel in his research notes.

53. Fiey, *Assyrie chrétienne*, vol. 1, 269.

54. It is mentioned also in Georg Hoffmann, *Auszüge aus syrischen Akten persischer Märtyrer* (Nendeln, Liechtenstein: Kraus, [1880] 1966), 207.

55. E. A. Wallis Budge, *The Book of Governors: The Historia Monastica of Thomas Bishop of Marga* AD *840* (London: Kegan Paul, Trench, Trübner, 1893), vol. 2, 226.

56. Tfinkdji, 'L'Église chaldéene catholique autrefois et aujourd'hui', 499.

57. Majed Eshoo, 'The Fate of Assyrian Villages Annexed to Today's Dohuk Governorate in Iraq and the Conditions in These Villages Following the Establishment of the Iraqi State in 1921', tr. Mary Challita (2004), Assyrian General Conference website, http://www.assyriangc.com/magazine/eng1.pdf, 12 (accessed 9 July 2014).

58. Frederick A. Aprim, *Assyrians: From Bedr Khan to Saddam Hussein – Driving into Extinction the Last Aramaic Speakers* (F. A. Aprim, 2006), 211.

59. League of Nations, *Settlement of the Assyrians of Iraq*, 0.69.1934.VII, Geneva, 18 January 1934, enclosure II, 9.

60. B.B. (Harīr), C.C. (Darbandoke) and I.Y. (Diyana), interviews with author, 17 February 2008, Toronto.

61. Assyrian Academic Society (AAS), 'Field Mission Iraq 2004'.

62. B.B. (Harīr), C.C. (Darbandoke) and I.Y. (Diyana), interviews with author, 17 February 2008, Toronto.

63. Ibid.

64. League of Nations, *Report on the Economic Conditions of the Assyrians in the Northern Provinces in Iraq*, C.296.M.172.1938.VII, Geneva, 10 September 1938, 17.

65. Ibid., 18.

66. B.B. (Harīr), C.C. (Darbandoke) and I.Y. (Diyana), interviews with author, 17 February 2008, Toronto.

67. A major liturgical work used by the Church of the East.

68. Fiey, *Assyrie chrétienne*, vol. 1, 251.

69. Hoffmann, *Auszüge aus syrischen Akten persischer Märtyrer*, 223–4.

70. Tfinkdji, 'L'Église chaldéene catholique autrefois et aujourd'hui', 499.

71. B.B. (Harīr), C.C. (Darbandoke) and I.Y. (Diyana), interviews with author, 17 February 2008, Toronto; AAS, 'Field Mission Iraq 2004'.

72. AAS, 'Field Mission Iraq 2004'.

73. Wilmshurst, *The Ecclesiastical Organization of the Church of the East*, 158–61.

74. Ibid., 161.

75. Budge, *The Book of Governors*, vol. 2, 296–7.

76. Ibid., 450–2.

77. B.B. (Harīr), C.C. (Darbandoke) and I.Y. (Diyana), interviews with author, 17 February 2008, Toronto; AAS, 'Field Mission Iraq 2004'.

78. Fiey, *Assyrie chrétienne*, vol. 1, 249–50.

79. Tfinkdji, 'L'Église chaldéene catholique autrefois et aujourd'hui', 499.

80. B.B. (Harīr), C.C. (Darbandoke) and I.Y. (Diyana), interviews with author, 17 February 2008, Toronto; AAS, 'Field Mission Iraq 2004'.

81. Wilmshurst, *The Ecclesiastical Organization of the Church of the East*, 161. The manuscripts can be found in MSS 'Aqra (Voste) 17 and 'Aqra (Habbi) 53, 91.

82. Tfinkdji, 'L'Église chaldéene catholique autrefois et aujourd'hui', 499.

83. D.T. (Blejanke), K.S. (Dūre), Y.D. (Annūnē), Y.G. (Bebede) and Z.Y. (Annūnē), interviews with author, 24 February 2008, Toronto.

84. Fiey, *Assyrie chrétienne*, vol. 1, 254.

85. Badger, *The Nestorians and Their Rituals*, vol. 1, 392.

86. Tfinkdji, 'L'Église chaldéene catholique autrefois et aujourd'hui,' 499.

87. B.B. (Harīr), C.C. (Darbandoke) and I.Y. (Diyana), interviews with author, 17 February 2008, Toronto; AAS, 'Field Mission Iraq 2004'.

88. According to AAS, 'Field Mission Iraq 2004', the relief was dynamited by treasure hunters at some time in the five years preceding the report. See also Badger, *The Nestorians and their Rituals*, vol. 1, 390; Taufiq Wahby, 'The Rock Sculptures in Gunduk Cave', *Sumer* 4.2 (1948).

89. Budge, *The Book of Governors*, vol. 2, 591–622.

90. Parpola and Porter, *The Helsinki Atlas of the Near East in the Neo-Assyrian Period*, 15.

91. League of Nations, *Settlement of the Assyrians of Iraq*, enclosure II, 8.

92. League of Nations, *Report on the Economic Conditions of the Assyrians in the Northern Provinces in Iraq*, 10.

93. B.B. (Harīr), C.C. (Darbandoke) and I.Y. (Diyana), interviews with author, 17 February 2008, Toronto; AAS, 'Field Mission Iraq 2004'.

94. Wilmshurst, *The Ecclesiastical Organization of the Church of the East*, 160.

95. Tfinkdji, 'L'Église chaldéene catholique autrefois et aujourd'hui', 499; Fiey, *Assyrie chrétienne*, vol. 1, 262.

96. Fiey, *Assyrie chrétienne*, vol. 1, 262.

97. Ibid., 263.

98. AAS, 'Field Mission Iraq 2004'.

99. Budge, *The Book of Governors*, vol. 2, 296.

100. Fiey believes Badger to have exaggerated the Jewish population greatly, which is highly probable. See Fiey, *Assyrie chrétienne*, vol. 1, 259; Badger, *The Nestorians and Their Rituals*, vol. 1, 389.

101. Fiey, *Assyrie chrétienne*, vol. 1, 258.

102. AAS, 'Field Mission Iraq 2004'.

103. Tfinkdji, 'L'Église chaldéene catholique autrefois et aujourd'hui', 499.

104. D.T. (Blejanke), K.S. (Dūre), Y.D. (Annūnē), Y.G. (Bebede) and Z.Y. (Annūnē), interviews with author, 24 February 2008, Toronto.

105. Ibid.

106. AAS, 'Field Mission Iraq 2004'.

107. Tfinkdji, 'L'Église chaldéene catholique autrefois et aujourd'hui', 502.

108. Eshoo, 'The Fate of Assyrian Villages', 22.

109. Ibid., 3.

110. Fiey, *Assyrie chrétienne*, vol. 1, 291.

111. Ibid.

112. Ibid.

113. Tfinkdji, 'L'Église chaldéene catholique autrefois et aujourd'hui', 499.

114. Badger, *The Nestorians and Their Rituals*, vol. 1, 174.

115. Eshoo, 'The Fate of Assyrian Villages' mentions 1961 (p. 14), whereas *Iraq: Continuous and Silent Ethnic Cleansing* mentions 1963 (p. 42).

116. Fiey, *Assyrie chrétienne*, vol. 1, 289.

117. Tfinkdji, 'L'Église chaldéene catholique autrefois et aujourd'hui', 520.

118. *Iraq: Continuous and Silent Ethnic Cleansing*, 42.

119. Wilmshurst, *The Ecclesiastical Organization of the Church of the East*, 155.

120. *Fallah* is generally used in Kurdish to refer to Assyrian Christians, even in the Tur Abdin, which would speak to its general usage in the Kurmanji dialect. The term is most likely originally a borrowing from Arabic *fallaḥ*, denoting 'worker' or 'peasant'.

121. Fiey, *Assyrie chrétienne*, vol. 1, 293–4.

122. Tfinkdji. 'L'Église chaldéene catholique autrefois et aujourd'hui', 502.

123. K.S. (Dūre) and Y.D. (Annūnē), interviews with author, 24 February 2008, Toronto. Fursan Salahaddin or the Knights of Saladin were a Kurdish mercenary group. For further information, see Habib Ishow, *Les Structures sociales et politiques de l'Irak contemporain: pourquoi un état en crise?* (Paris: Harmattan, 2003), 89.

124. Tfinkdji, 'L'Église chaldéene catholique autrefois et aujourd'hui', 499.

125. League of Nations, *Settlement of the Assyrians of Iraq*, enclosure II, 9.

126. AAS, 'Field Mission Iraq 2004'.

127. K.S. (Dūre), interview with author, 24 February 2008, Toronto.

128. AAS, 'Field Mission Iraq 2004'.

129. Ibid.

130. Wilmshurst, *The Ecclesiastical Organization of the Church of the East*, 263.

131. Harrak, 'Northern Mesopotamia in a 19th Century Syriac Annalistic Source', 301.

132. Ibid., 302.

133. Justin Perkins, *A Residence of Eight Years in Persia among the Nestorian Christians; with Notices of the Muhammedans* (Andover, MA: Allen, Morrill & Wardwell, 1843), 22–30.

134. Tfinkdji, 'L'Église chaldéene catholique autrefois et aujourd'hui', 485.

135. Hirmis Aboona, interview with author, 11 October 2007, Mississauga, Ontario.

136. George Black, *Genocide in Iraq: The Anfal Campaign against the Kurds* (New York: Human Rights Watch, 1993), 37. Footnote 29 mentions Shorsh Haji

Resool again. It is evident that HRW is dependent on Resool's work for most of its information concerning the Anfal campaign and the 1978 border clearings.

137. S.A. (Dūre), interview with author, 2 July 2007, Toronto.

138. *Al-Thawra*, 18 September 1978.

139. League of Nations, *Report on the Economic Conditions of the Assyrians in the Northern Provinces in Iraq*, 10.

140. AAS, 'Field Mission Iraq 2004'.

141. *Iraq: Continuous and Silent Ethnic Cleansing*, 42.

142. Badger, *The Nestorians and Their Rituals*, vol. 1, 393.

143. League of Nations, *Report on the Economic Conditions of the Assyrians in the Northern Provinces in Iraq*, 10.

144. *Iraq: Continuous and Silent Ethnic Cleansing*, 40.

145. Badger, *The Nestorians and Their Rituals*, vol. 1, 393.

146. William Walker Rockwell, *The Pitiful Plight of the Assyrian Christians in Persia and Kurdistan* (New York: American Committee for Armenian and Syrian Relief, 1916), 54.

147. League of Nations, *Report on the Economic Conditions of the Assyrians in the Northern Provinces in Iraq*, 10.

148. *Iraq: Continuous and Silent Ethnic Cleansing*, 40.

149. K.S. (Dūre), interview with author, 24 February 2008, Toronto.

150. Badger, *The Nestorians and Their Rituals*, vol. 1, 380–1.

151. League of Nations, *Report on the Economic Conditions of the Assyrians in the Northern Provinces in Iraq*, 10.

152. Majed Eshoo, 'The Fate of Assyrian Villages', 4; K.S. (Dūre), interview with author, 24 February 2008, Toronto.

153. *Iraq: Continuous and Silent Ethnic Cleansing*, 40.

154. League of Nations, *Report on the Economic Conditions of the Assyrians in the Northern Provinces in Iraq*, 10.

155. *Iraq: Continuous and Silent Ethnic Cleansing*, 40.

156. Badger, *The Nestorians and their Rituals*, vol. 1, 394.

157. Rockwell, *The Pitiful Plight of the Assyrian Christians in Persia and Kurdistan*, 54.

158. League of Nations, *Report on the Economic Conditions of the Assyrians in the Northern Provinces in Iraq*, 10.

159. Eshoo, 'The Fate of Assyrian Villages', 7; *Iraq: Continuous and Silent Ethnic Cleansing*, 40.

160. *Iraq: Continuous and Silent Ethnic Cleansing*, 40.

161. League of Nations, *Report on the Economic Conditions of the Assyrians in the Northern Provinces in Iraq*, 10.
162. *Iraq: Continuous and Silent Ethnic Cleansing*, 40.
163. Badger, *The Nestorians and Their Rituals*, vol. 1, 381.
164. Rev. F. N. Heazell and Mrs Margoliouth, *Kurds and Christians* (London: Wells Gardner Darton, 1913), 151–2. Such 'Western' work was as destructive of an integrated Assyrian identity and progress as governmental policies in the later Iraqi state.
165. Badger, *The Nestorians and Their Rituals*, vol. 1, 393.
166. Rockwell, *The Pitiful Plight of the Assyrian Christians in Persia and Kurdistan*, 54.
167. League of Nations, *Report on the Economic Conditions of the Assyrians in the Northern Provinces in Iraq*, 10.
168. AAS, 'Field Mission Iraq 2004'.
169. Sanders, *Assyrian-Chaldean Christians in Eastern Turkey and Iran*, 65.
170. Amir Odisho, 'Dūrī', *al-Fikr al-Masihi*, July–September 1996, 24–5.
171. K.S. (Dūre), Interview, 24 February 2008, Toronto.
172. Ibid.
173. Badger, *The Nestorians and Their Rituals*, vol. 1, 393.
174. League of Nations, *Report on the Economic Conditions of the Assyrians in the Northern Provinces in Iraq*, 10.
175. Eshoo, 'The Fate of Assyrian Villages', 6.
176. *Iraq: Continuous and Silent Ethnic Cleansing*, 40.
177. Edward Lewes Cutts, *Christians under the Crescent in Asia* (London: Society for Promoting Christian Knowledge / New York: Pott, Young, 1877), 354.
178. League of Nations, *Report on the Economic Conditions of the Assyrians in the Northern Provinces in Iraq*, 9.
179. Badger, *The Nestorians and Their Rituals*, vol. 1, 397.
180. Eshoo, 'The Fate of Assyrian Villages', 24; and AAS, 'Field Mission Iraq 2004'.
181. Badger, *The Nestorians and Their Rituals*, vol. 1, 393.
182. Rockwell, *The Pitiful Plight of the Assyrian Christians in Persia and Kurdistan*, 54.
183. League of Nations, *Report on the Economic Conditions of the Assyrians in the Northern Provinces in Iraq*, 10.
184. *Iraq: Continuous and Silent Ethnic Cleansing*, 40.
185. Cutts, *Christians under the Crescent in Asia*, 354.
186. *Iraq: Continuous and Silent Ethnic Cleansing*, 40.

187. Badger, *The Nestorians and Their Rituals*, vol. 1, 393.
188. Rockwell, *The Pitiful Plight of the Assyrian Christians in Persia and Kurdistan*, 54.
189. League of Nations, *Report on the Economic Conditions of the Assyrians in the Northern Provinces in Iraq*, 10.
190. Eshoo, 'The Fate of Assyrian Villages', 7.
191. *Iraq: Continuous and Silent Ethnic Cleansing*, 40.
192. Eshoo, 'The Fate of Assyrian Villages', 7.
193. Aprim, *Assyrians*, 212.
194. League of Nations, *Report on the Economic Conditions of the Assyrians in the Northern Provinces in Iraq*, 10.
195. Eshoo, 'The Fate of Assyrian Villages', 5.
196. *Iraq: Continuous and Silent Ethnic Cleansing*, 40.
197. Ibid.
198. Badger, *The Nestorians and their Rituals*, vol. 1, 393.
199. Rockwell, *The Pitiful Plight of the Assyrian Christians in Persia and Kurdistan*, 54.
200. League of Nations, *Report on the Economic Conditions of the Assyrians in the Northern Provinces in Iraq*, 10.
201. *Iraq: Continuous and Silent Ethnic Cleansing*, 40.
202. Badger, *The Nestorians and their Rituals*, vol. 1, 393.
203. Rockwell, *The Pitiful Plight of the Assyrian Christians in Persia and Kurdistan*, 54.
204. League of Nations, *Report on the Economic Conditions of the Assyrians in the Northern Provinces in Iraq*, 10.
205. *Iraq: Continuous and Silent Ethnic Cleansing*, 40.
206. AAS, 'Field Mission Iraq 2004'.
207. League of Nations, *Report on the Economic Conditions of the Assyrians in the Northern Provinces in Iraq*, 9.
208. Eshoo, 'The Fate of Assyrian Villages', 25.
209. *Iraq: Continuous and Silent Ethnic Cleansing*, 40.
210. AAS, 'Field Mission Iraq 2004'.
211. Eshoo, 'The Fate of Assyrian Villages', 4; K.S. (Dūre), interview with author, 24 February 2008, Toronto.
212. *Iraq: Continuous and Silent Ethnic Cleansing*, 40.
213. AAS, 'Field Mission Iraq 2004'.
214. Eshoo, 'The Fate of Assyrian Villages', 7.

215. Ibid., 41.

216. Ibid.

217. Ibid.

218. AAS, 'Field Mission Iraq 2004'.

219. *Iraq: Continuous and Silent Ethnic Cleansing*, 41.

220. *Iraq: Continuous and Silent Ethnic Cleansing*, 41.

221. Eshoo, 'The Fate of Assyrian Villages', 21.

222. AAS, 'Field Mission Iraq 2004'; Eshoo, 'The Fate of Assyrian Villages', 21.

223. Fiey, *Assyrie chrétienne*, vol. 1, 695.

224. *Iraq: Continuous and Silent Ethnic Cleansing*, 41.

225. League of Nations, *Settlement of the Assyrians of Iraq*, enclosure IV, 11.

226. AAS, 'Field Mission Iraq 2004'.

227. *Iraq: Continuous and Silent Ethnic Cleansing*, 41.

228. AAS, 'Field Mission Iraq 2004'.

229. Tfinkdji, 'L'Église chaldéene catholique autrefois et aujourd'hui', 520.

230. *Iraq: Continuous and Silent Ethnic Cleansing*, 40.

231. Eshoo, 'The Fate of Assyrian Villages', 17.

232. AAS, 'Field Mission Iraq 2004'.

233. Father Paulos Bedari was a strong advocate of the anti-government movement of the early 1960s. See photograph in Ismet Chériff Vanly, *The Revolution of Iraki Kurdistan, Part 1: September 1961 to December 1963* (Committee for the Defense of the Kurdish People's Rights, 1965), 27.

234. Badger, *The Nestorians and their Rituals*, vol. 1, 175.

235. Tfinkdji, 'L'Église chaldéene catholique autrefois et aujourd'hui', 520.

236. *Iraq: Continuous and Silent Ethnic Cleansing*, 41.

237. Ibid., 40.

238. Ibid., 41.

239. Ibid.

240. Tfinkdji, 'L'Église chaldéene catholique autrefois et aujourd'hui', 520.

241. AAS, 'Field Mission Iraq 2004'.

242. Badger, *The Nestorians and Their Rituals*, vol. 1, 175.

243. Tfinkdji, 'L'Église chaldéene catholique autrefois et aujourd'hui', 505.

244. David Gaunt, *Massacres, Resistance, Protectors: Muslim–Christian Relations in Eastern Anatolia during World War I* (Piscataway, NJ: Gorgias Press, 2006), 244.

245. Jacques Rhétoré, *Les Chrétiens aux bêtes: souvenirs de la guerre sainte proclamée par les Turcs contre les chrétiens en 1915* (Paris: Cerf, 2005), 321.

246. *Iraq: Continuous and Silent Ethnic Cleansing*, 41.

247. Tfinkdji, 'L'Église chaldéene catholique autrefois et aujourd'hui', 520.

248. Iraq: *Continuous and Silent Ethnic Cleansing*, 40.

249. See Ephrem-Isa Yousif, *Parfums d'enfance à Sanate: un village chrétien au Kurdistan irakien* (Paris: Harmattan, 1993), for a comprehensive look at the village.

250. *Iraq: Continuous and Silent Ethnic Cleansing*, 40.

251. Tfinkdji, 'L'Église chaldéene catholique autrefois et aujourd'hui', 520.

252. *Iraq: Continuous and Silent Ethnic Cleansing*, 40.

253. Fiey, *Assyrie chrétienne*, vol. 1, 551.

254. Tfinkdji, 'L'Église chaldéene catholique autrefois et aujourd'hui', 485.

255. League of Nations, *Settlement of the Assyrians of Iraq*, enclosure IV, 11.

256. League of Nations, *Report on the Economic Conditions of the Assyrians in the Northern Provinces in Iraq*, 7.

257. *Iraq: Continuous and Silent Ethnic Cleansing*, 42.

258. League of Nations, *Report on the Economic Conditions of the Assyrians in the Northern Provinces in Iraq*, 7.

259. Fiey, *Assyrie chrétienne*, vol. 1, 550.

260. League of Nations, *Settlement of the Assyrians of Iraq*, enclosure IV, 11.

261. Badger, *The Nestorians and Their Rituals*, vol. 1, 175.

262. Tfinkdji, 'L'Église chaldéene catholique autrefois et aujourd'hui', 492.

263. Badger, *The Nestorians and Their Rituals*, vol. 1, 152; Wilmshurst, *The Ecclesiastical Organization of the Church of the East*, 168.

264. AAS, 'Field Mission Iraq, 2004'.

265. Human Rights Watch, *Iraq's Crime of Genocide*, 128.

266. Marcus Stern, 'Worlds apart on Chaldean crisis', *San Diego Union Tribune*, 12 March 2003.

267. Ibid., 393.

268. Rockwell, *The Pitiful Plight of the Assyrian Christians in Persia and Kurdistan*, 54.

269. Y.D. (Annūnē), interview with author, 24 February 2008, Toronto.

270. League of Nations, *Report on the Economic Conditions of the Assyrians in the Northern Provinces in Iraq*, 10.

271. Y.D. (Annūnē), interview with author, 24 February 2008, Toronto.

272. Ibid.

273. Baghdad to State, 'Kurdish Revolt – Continued; Government Pretends Kurds Crushed; Reports Massacres in Christian Villages', 10 January 1962, NA/RG59/787.00/1-1062.

274. Y.D. (Annūnē), interview with author, 24 February 2008, Toronto.

275. Eshoo, 'The Fate of Assyrian Villages', 3; Y.D. (Annūnē), interview with author. *Iraq: Continuous and Silent Ethnic Cleansing*, 40, mentions a slight discrepancy of 140 houses.

276. Z.Y. (Annūnē), interview with author, 24 February 2008, Toronto.

277. For a brief description of village life see Georg Krotkoff, *A Neo-Aramaic Dialect of Kurdistan: Texts, Grammar, and Vocabulary* (New Haven, CT: American Oriental Society, 1982).

278. Habib Ishow, 'Un Village irakien, «Araden» en 1961', *Cahiers de l'Orient contemporain* (1966), 6–9.

279. Michel Chevalier, *Les Montagnards chrétiens du Hakkâri et du Kurdistan septentrional* (Paris: Université de Paris-Sorbonne, 1985), 112.

280. Badger, *The Nestorians and Their Rituals*, vol. 1, 174.

281. Tfinkdji, 'L'Église chaldéene catholique autrefois et aujourd'hui', 502.

282. League of Nations, *Settlement of the Assyrians of Iraq*, enclosure II, 8.

283. Afram Rayis, 'Araden: A Living Village in Garbia', *Assyrian Star* 55.1 (2003), 32.

284. Sanders, *Assyrian-Chaldean Christians in Eastern Turkey and Iran*, 64.

285. Notes from the Rayis family personal collection. See also Ishow, 'Un Village irakien, «Araden» en 1961', 6.

286. Eshoo, 'The Fate of Assyrian Villages', 9.

287. *Iraq: Continuous and Silent Ethnic Cleansing*, 40.

288. Badger, *The Nestorians and Their Rituals*, vol. 1, 392.

289. League of Nations, *Report on the Economic Conditions of the Assyrians in the Northern Provinces in Iraq*, 10.

290. Eshoo, 'The Fate of Assyrian Villages', 14.

291. Badger, *The Nestorians and Their Rituals*, vol. 1, 174.

292. League of Nations, *Report on the Economic Conditions of the Assyrians in the Northern Provinces in Iraq*, 10.

293. Badger, *The Nestorians and Their Rituals*, vol. 1, 393.

294. Rockwell, *The Pitiful Plight of the Assyrian Christians in Persia and Kurdistan*, 54.

295. League of Nations, *Report on the Economic Conditions of the Assyrians in the Northern Provinces in Iraq*, 10.

296. Eshoo, 'The Fate of Assyrian Villages', 5.

297. Human Rights Watch, *Iraq's Crime of Genocide*, 187, 264.

298. Badger, *The Nestorians and Their Rituals*, vol. 1, 393.

299. For some reason only the number of 'males' are mentioned in the report.

300. League of Nations, *Report on the Economic Conditions of the Assyrians in the Northern Provinces in Iraq*, 9.

301. Eshoo, 'The Fate of Assyrian Villages', 24.

302. *Iraq: Continuous and Silent Ethnic Cleansing*, 40.

303. Ibid., 56–7.

304. AAS, 'Field Mission Iraq 2004'.

305. League of Nations, *Report on the Economic Conditions of the Assyrians in the Northern Provinces in Iraq*, 10.

306. Eshoo, 'The Fate of Assyrian Villages', 6–7.

307. AAS, 'Field Mission Iraq 2004'; *Iraq: Continuous and Silent Ethnic Cleansing*, 40.

308. Eshoo, 'The Fate of Assyrian Villages', 7.

309. Y.G. (Bebede), interview with author, 24 February 2008, Toronto.

310. Badger, *The Nestorians and Their Rituals*, vol. 1, 199.

311. League of Nations, *Settlement of the Assyrians of Iraq*, enclosure II, 8.

312. League of Nations, *Report on the Economic Conditions of the Assyrians in the Northern Provinces in Iraq*, 11.

313. Badger, *The Nestorians and Their Rituals*, vol. 1, 393.

314. Eshoo, 'The Fate of Assyrian Villages', 10.

315. AAS, 'Field Mission Iraq 2004'; Y.G. (Bebede), interview with author, 24 February 2008, Toronto.

316. *Iraq: Continuous and Silent Ethnic Cleansing*, 40.

317. Eshoo, 'The Fate of Assyrian Villages', 11.

318. Y.G. (Bebede), interview with author, 24 February 2008, Toronto.

319. Budge, *The Book of Governors*, vol. 2, 327.

320. Tfinkdji, 'L'Église chaldéene catholique autrefois et aujourd'hui', 502.

321. Badger, *The Nestorians and Their Rituals*, vol. 1, 393. Badger does not mention a church in Blejanke.

322. Ibid., 392.

323. League of Nations, *Report on the Economic Conditions of the Assyrians in the Northern Provinces in Iraq*, 10.

324. D.T. (Blejanke), interview with author, 24 February 2008, Toronto.

325. Ibid.

326. AAS, 'Field Mission Iraq 2004'; *Iraq: Continuous and Silent Ethnic Cleansing*, 40.

327. League of Nations, *Report on the Economic Conditions of the Assyrians in the Northern Provinces in Iraq*, 10.

328. *Iraq: Continuous and Silent Ethnic Cleansing*, 40; AAS, 'Field Mission Iraq 2004'.

329. League of Nations, *Report on the Economic Conditions of the Assyrians in the Northern Provinces in Iraq*, 10. Chammike is the only one of twenty-five Barwari villages mentioned in the League of Nations report as being owned by the government and occupied by 'non-autochthonous' (non-indigenous) Assyrians – essentially settlers from Hakkâri.

330. *Iraq: Continuous and Silent Ethnic Cleansing*, 40.

331. Sanders, *Assyrian-Chaldean Christians in Eastern Turkey and Iran*, 65.

332. Harrak, 'Northern Mesopotamia in a 19th Century Syriac Annalistic Source', 302.

333. Badger, *The Nestorians and Their Rituals*, vol. 1, 174.

334. Tfinkdji, 'L'Église chaldéene catholique autrefois et aujourd'hui', 502.

335. League of Nations, *Settlement of the Assyrians of Iraq*, enclosure II, 8.

336. Eshoo, 'The Fate of Assyrian Villages', 8.

337. *Iraq: Continuous and Silent Ethnic Cleansing*, 40.

338. Ibid., 56–7.

339. Badger, *The Nestorians and Their Rituals*, vol. 1, 393.

340. League of Nations, *Settlement of the Assyrians of Iraq*, enclosure II, 8.

341. League of Nations, *Report on the Economic Conditions of the Assyrians in the Northern Provinces in Iraq*, 10.

342. *Iraq: Continuous and Silent Ethnic Cleansing*, 40.

343. AAS, 'Field Mission Iraq 2004'.

344. League of Nations, *Settlement of the Assyrians of Iraq*, enclosure II, 8.

345. AAS, 'Field Mission Iraq 2004'.

346. Badger, *The Nestorians and Their Rituals*, vol. 1, 253.

347. Ibid., 393.

348. League of Nations, *Report on the Economic Conditions of the Assyrians in the Northern Provinces in Iraq*, 10.

349. Eshoo, 'The Fate of Assyrian Villages', 10; B.A. (Komāne) and K.D. (Komāne), interviews with author, 26 July 2008, Toronto.

350. See photograph in Barzana, *Šinnē d-ʿasqūtā*, 221.

351. Ibid.; *Iraq: Continuous and Silent Ethnic Cleansing*, 40, 55.

352. Sanders, Assyrian-Chaldean Christians in Eastern Turkey and Iran, 63.

353. Badger, *The Nestorians and Their Rituals*, vol. 1, 393.

354. League of Nations, *Report on the Economic Conditions of the Assyrians in the Northern Provinces in Iraq*, 10.

355. *Iraq: Continuous and Silent Ethnic Cleansing*, 40.

356. Ibid., 56–7.

357. Badger, *The Nestorians and Their Rituals*, vol. 1, 392.

358. Rockwell, *The Pitiful Plight of the Assyrian Christians in Persia and Kurdistan*, 54.

359. League of Nations, *Report on the Economic Conditions of the Assyrians in the Northern Provinces in Iraq*, 10.

360. *Iraq: Continuous and Silent Ethnic Cleansing*, 40.

361. Y.D. (Annūnē), interview with author, 24 February 2008, Toronto.

362. Eshoo, 'The Fate of Assyrian Villages', 10.

363. League of Nations, *Report on the Economic Conditions of the Assyrians in the Northern Provinces in Iraq*, 10.

364. AAS, 'Field Mission Iraq 2004'; Y.G. (Bebede), interview with author, 24 February 2008, Toronto.

365. Ibid.

366. *Iraq: Continuous and Silent Ethnic Cleansing*, 40.

367. AAS, 'Field Mission Iraq 2004'.

368. Badger, *The Nestorians and Their Rituals*, vol. 1, 392.

369. AAS, 'Field Mission Iraq 2004'.

370. Ibid.

371. Badger, *The Nestorians and Their Rituals*, vol. 1, 393.

372. Tfinkdji, 'L'Église chaldéene catholique autrefois et aujourd'hui', 502.

373. League of Nations, *Settlement of the Assyrians of Iraq*, enclosure II, 8.

374. *Iraq: Continuous and Silent Ethnic Cleansing*, 40.

375. Badger, *The Nestorians and Their Rituals*, vol. 1, 393.

376. Rockwell, *The Pitiful Plight of the Assyrian Christians in Persia and Kurdistan*, 54.

377. League of Nations, *Report on the Economic Conditions of the Assyrians in the Northern Provinces in Iraq*, 10.

378. *Iraq: Continuous and Silent Ethnic Cleansing*, 40.

379. Badger, *The Nestorians and Their Rituals*, vol. 1, 174.

380. Tfinkdji, 'L'Église chaldéene catholique autrefois et aujourd'hui', 502.

381. League of Nations, *Report on the Economic Conditions of the Assyrians in the Northern Provinces in Iraq*, 11.

382. Eshoo, 'The Fate of Assyrian Villages', 9.

383. D.I. (Inishke), email correspondence, 10 January 2008.

384. Badger, *The Nestorians and Their Rituals*, vol. 1, 393.

385. League of Nations, *Report on the Economic Conditions of the Assyrians in the Northern Provinces in Iraq*, 10.

386. Eshoo, 'The Fate of Assyrian Villages', 5.

387. *Iraq: Continuous and Silent Ethnic Cleansing*, 40.

388. League of Nations, *Settlement of the Assyrians of Iraq*, enclosure II, 8.

389. League of Nations, *Report on the Economic Conditions of the Assyrians in the Northern Provinces in Iraq*, 10.

390. Eshoo, 'The Fate of Assyrian Villages', 6; *Iraq: Continuous and Silent Ethnic Cleansing*, 40.

391. AAS, 'Field Mission Iraq 2004'.

392. The Gara mountain range is also identified with the region of Dasen – 'which rising near Da'udiya in the west extends along to the Upper Zab and away to the east into Gebel Pir Hasan Beg' (Budge, *The Book of Governors*, vol. 2, 67).

393. Badger, *The Nestorians and Their Rituals*, vol. 1, 393.

394. Tfinkdji, 'L'Église chaldéene catholique autrefois et aujourd'hui', 502.

395. League of Nations, *Report on the Economic Conditions of the Assyrians in the Northern Provinces in Iraq*, 10.

396. Eshoo, 'The Fate of Assyrian Villages', 10; B.A., D.Y. and K.D. (Komāne), interviews with author, 26 July 2008, Toronto.

397. B.A. and K.D. (Komāne), interviews with author, 26 July 2008, Toronto; AAS, 'Field Mission Iraq 2004'.

398. Human Rights Watch, *Iraq's Crime of Genocide*, 189.

399. League of Nations, *Report on the Economic Conditions of the Assyrians in the Northern Provinces in Iraq*, 10.

400. *Iraq: Continuous and Silent Ethnic Cleansing*, 40.

401. Ibid.

402. Y.D. (Annūnē), interview with author, 24 February 2008, Toronto.

403. Badger, *The Nestorians and Their Rituals*, vol. 1, 392.

404. Tfinkdji, 'L'Église chaldéene catholique autrefois et aujourd'hui', 502.

405. Eshoo, 'The Fate of Assyrian Villages', 14.

406. *Iraq: Continuous and Silent Ethnic Cleansing*, 41.

407. League of Nations, *Report on the Economic Conditions of the Assyrians in the Northern Provinces in Iraq*, 10.

408. AAS, 'Field Mission Iraq 2004'; *Iraq: Continuous and Silent Ethnic Cleansing*, 40.

409. Y.D. (Annūnē), interview with author, 24 February 2008, Toronto.
410. Ibid.
411. League of Nations, *Report on the Economic Conditions of the Assyrians in the Northern Provinces in Iraq*, 9.
412. Eshoo, 'The Fate of Assyrian Villages', 24.
413. *Iraq: Continuous and Silent Ethnic Cleansing*, 40.
414. Badger, *The Nestorians and Their Rituals*, vol. 1, 393.
415. League of Nations, *Report on the Economic Conditions of the Assyrians in the Northern Provinces in Iraq*, 9.
416. Eshoo, 'The Fate of Assyrian Villages', 24; *Iraq: Continuous and Silent Ethnic Cleansing*, 40.
417. *Iraq: Continuous and Silent Ethnic Cleansing*, 56–7.
418. League of Nations, *Report on the Economic Conditions of the Assyrians in the Northern Provinces in Iraq*, 11.
419. AAS, 'Field Mission Iraq 2004'; *Iraq: Continuous and Silent Ethnic Cleansing*, 40.
420. League of Nations, *Report on the Economic Conditions of the Assyrians in the Northern Provinces in Iraq*, 11.
421. *Iraq: Continuous and Silent Ethnic Cleansing*, 40.
422. Badger, *The Nestorians and Their Rituals*, vol. 1, 393.
423. League of Nations, *Report on the Economic Conditions of the Assyrians in the Northern Provinces in Iraq*, 10.
424. Aprim, *Assyrians*, 230.
425. Sanders, *Assyrian-Chaldean Christians in Eastern Turkey and Iran*, 64.
426. Badger, *The Nestorians and Their Rituals*, vol. 1, 174.
427. Tfinkdji, 'L'Église chaldéene catholique autrefois et aujourd'hui', 502.
428. League of Nations, *Settlement of the Assyrians of Iraq*, enclosure II, 8.
429. League of Nations, *Report on the Economic Conditions of the Assyrians in the Northern Provinces in Iraq*, 10.
430. *Iraq: Continuous and Silent Ethnic Cleansing*, 40.
431. Sanders, *Assyrian-Chaldean Christians in Eastern Turkey and Iran*, 64.
432. *Iraq: Continuous and Silent Ethnic Cleansing*, 56–7.
433. Badger, *The Nestorians and Their Rituals*, vol. 1, 393.
434. League of Nations, *Report on the Economic Conditions of the Assyrians in the Northern Provinces in Iraq*, 10.
435. Eshoo, 'The Fate of Assyrian Villages', 5.
436. AAS, 'Field Mission Iraq 2004'; *Iraq: Continuous and Silent Ethnic Cleansing*, 40.

437. Badger, *The Nestorians and Their Rituals*, vol. 1, 393.

438. League of Nations, *Report on the Economic Conditions of the Assyrians in the Northern Provinces in Iraq*, 9.

439. Eshoo, 'The Fate of Assyrian Villages', 24.

440. *Iraq: Continuous and Silent Ethnic Cleansing*, 55.

441. League of Nations, *Report on the Economic Conditions of the Assyrians in the Northern Provinces in Iraq*, 11.

442. Mikhael Benjamin, Nineveh Center for Research and Development (NCRD), Qaraqosh, Iraq, email correspondence, 2 February 2007.

443. Leadership of Dohuk, leadership of the branch of al-Nasir division, unit leader, to the leader of al-Nasir division, Response to Letter from Bishop concerning Nahla, 15 October 1985 (1–2), ADM Archives, Ba'th Secret Files and Correspondence, Iraq.

444. *Iraq: Continuous and Silent Ethnic Cleansing*, 41.

445. AAS, 'Field Mission Iraq 2004'.

446. Eshoo, 'The Fate of Assyrian Villages', 14.

447. *Iraq: Continuous and Silent Ethnic Cleansing*, 41.

448. League of Nations, *Report on the Economic Conditions of the Assyrians in the Northern Provinces in Iraq*, 10.

449. Leadership of Dohuk, leadership of the branch of al-Nasir division, unit leader, to leader of al-Nasir division, Response to Letter from Bishop concerning Nahla, 15 October 1985 (1–2), ADM Archives, Ba'th Secret Files and Correspondence, Iraq. However, in *Iraq: Continuous and Silent Ethnic Cleansing*, 41, Cham Chale is mentioned as having been destroyed in 1963 only.

450. AAS, 'Field Mission Iraq 2004'.

451. League of Nations, *Settlement of the Assyrians of Iraq*, enclosure II, 8.

452. League of Nations, *Report on the Economic Conditions of the Assyrians in the Northern Provinces in Iraq*, 11.

453. Leadership of Dohuk, leadership of the branch of al-Nasir division, unit leader, to leader of al-Nasir division, Response to Letter from Bishop concerning Nahla, 15 October 1985 (1–2), ADM Archives, Ba'th Secret Files and Correspondence, Iraq.

454. *Iraq: Continuous and Silent Ethnic Cleansing*, 41.

455. Eshoo, 'The Fate of Assyrian Villages', 13.

456. League of Nations, *Report on the Economic Conditions of the Assyrians in the Northern Provinces in Iraq*, 17–18.

457. *Iraq: Continuous and Silent Ethnic Cleansing*, 41.

458. League of Nations, *Report on the Economic Conditions of the Assyrians in the Northern Provinces in Iraq*, 18.

459. Eshoo, 'The Fate of Assyrian Villages', 12.

460. *Iraq: Continuous and Silent Ethnic Cleansing*, 41.

461. Ibid.

462. League of Nations, *Report on the Economic Conditions of the Assyrians in the Northern Provinces in Iraq*, 21.

463. Eshoo, 'The Fate of Assyrian Villages', 13.

464. Iraq: Continuous and Silent Ethnic Cleansing, 41.

465. League of Nations, *Report on the Economic Conditions of the Assyrians in the Northern Provinces in Iraq*, 11.

466. Eshoo, 'The Fate of Assyrian Villages', 12.

467. Leadership of Dohuk, leadership of the branch of al-Nasir division, unit leader, to leader of al-Nasir division, Response to Letter from Bishop Concerning Nahla, 15 October 1985 (1–2), ADM Archives, Ba'th Secret Files and Correspondence, Iraq.

468. *Iraq: Continuous and Silent Ethnic Cleansing*, 41.

469. *Bahra* 2 (1988).

470. Eshoo, 'The Fate of Assyrian Villages', 12.

471. League of Nations, *Settlement of the Assyrians of Iraq*, enclosure II, 8.

472. League of Nations, *Report on the Economic Conditions of the Assyrians in the Northern Provinces in Iraq*, 18.

473. Eshoo, 'The Fate of Assyrian Villages', 12.

474. Ibid.

475. *Iraq: Continuous and Silent Ethnic Cleansing*, 41.

476. League of Nations, *Report on the Economic Conditions of the Assyrians in the Northern Provinces in Iraq*, 11.

477. Leadership of Dohuk, leadership of the branch of al-Nasir division, unit leader, to leader of al-Nasir division, Response to Letter from Bishop Concerning Nahla, 15 October 1985 (1–2), ADM Archives, Ba'th Secret Files and Correspondence, Iraq.

478. *Iraq: Continuous and Silent Ethnic Cleansing*, 41.

479. League of Nations, *Report on the Economic Conditions of the Assyrians in the Northern Provinces in Iraq*, 11.

480. Y.D. (Annūnē), interview with author, 24 February 2008, Toronto; AAS, 'Field Mission Iraq, 2004'; Eshoo, 'The Fate of Assyrian Villages', 13.

481. League of Nations, *Settlement of the Assyrians of Iraq*, enclosure II, 8.

482. Leadership of Dohuk, leadership of the branch of al-Nasir division, unit leader, to leader of al-Nasir division, Response to Letter from Bishop Concerning Nahla, 15 October 1985 (1–2), ADM Archives, Ba'th Secret Files and Correspondence, Iraq.

483. *Iraq: Continuous and Silent Ethnic Cleansing*, 41.

484. *Iraq: Continuous and Silent Ethnic Cleansing*, 40.

485. AAS, 'Field Mission Iraq 2004'.

486. League of Nations, *Settlement of the Assyrians of Iraq*, enclosure II, 8.

487. Eshoo, 'The Fate of Assyrian Villages', 22.

488. League of Nations, *Report on the Economic Conditions of the Assyrians in the Northern Provinces in Iraq*, 14.

489. The Assyrian villages destroyed during the Simele incident were mostly resettled by neighbouring Kurds, as was the case in Spindarok. The village was also the site of a chemical attack during the Anfal operations.

490. Eshoo, 'The Fate of Assyrian Villages', 23.

491. *Iraq: Continuous and Silent Ethnic Cleansing*, 41.

492. Ibid., 56.

493. Badger, *The Nestorians and Their Rituals*, vol. 1, 174.

494. Eshoo, 'The Fate of Assyrian Villages', 2.

495. *Iraq: Continuous and Silent Ethnic Cleansing*, 41.

496. Ibid.

497. Badger, *The Nestorians and Their Rituals*, vol. 1, 392.

498. Tfinkdji, 'L'Église chaldéene catholique autrefois et aujourd'hui', 502.

499. *Iraq: Continuous and Silent Ethnic Cleansing*, 41.

500. Eshoo, 'The Fate of Assyrian Villages', 13.

501. Badger, *The Nestorians and Their Rituals*, vol. 1, 392.

502. Tfinkdji, 'L'Église chaldéene catholique autrefois et aujourd'hui', 502.

503. *Iraq: Continuous and Silent Ethnic Cleansing*, 41.

504. Badger, *The Nestorians and Their Rituals*, vol. 1, 174.

505. Wilmshurst, *The Ecclesiastical Organization of the Church of the East*, 145.

506. Tfinkdji, 'L'Église chaldéene catholique autrefois et aujourd'hui', 502.

507. *Iraq: Continuous and Silent Ethnic Cleansing*, 42.

508. The bastion of Assyrian (specifically Church of the East) Christianity from the seventh to the ninth century, including much of northern Iraq from Zakho to Nerem.

509. Tfinkdji, 'L'Église chaldéene catholique autrefois et aujourd'hui', 502.

510. Eshoo, 'The Fate of Assyrian Villages', 14.

511. AAS, 'Field Mission Iraq 2004'.

512. Badger, *The Nestorians and Their Rituals*, vol. 1, 174.

513. Tfinkdji, 'L'Église chaldéene catholique autrefois et aujourd'hui', 502.

514. Eshoo, 'The Fate of Assyrian Villages', 13.

515. Aprim, *Assyrians*, 212.

516. Fiey, *Assyrie Chrétienne*, vol. 1, 287.

517. Tfinkdji, 'L'Église chaldéene catholique autrefois et aujourd'hui', 502.

518. League of Nations, *Report on the Economic Conditions of the Assyrians in the Northern Provinces in Iraq*, 7.

519. Eshoo, 'The Fate of Assyrian Villages', 21.

520. Mikhael Benjamin, NCRD, email correspondence, 2 February 2007.

521. Eshoo, 'The Fate of Assyrian Villages', 20; Mikhael Benjamin, email correspondence, 2 February 2007.

522. Mikhael Benjamin, email correspondence, 2 February 2007; *Iraq: Continuous and Silent Ethnic Cleansing*, 41.

523. AAS, 'Field Mission Iraq 2004'.

524. Ibid.

525. League of Nations, *Report on the Economic Conditions of the Assyrians in the Northern Provinces in Iraq*, 14.

526. Eshoo, 'The Fate of Assyrian Villages', 21.

527. Wilmshurst, *The Ecclesiastical Organization of the Church of the East*, 155.

528. Royal Government of Iraq, *Correspondence Relating to Assyrian Settlement from 13th July, 1932, to 5th August, 1933* (Baghdad, Government Press, 1933), 48.

529. Eshoo, 'The Fate of Assyrian Villages', 21–2.

530. Badger, *The Nestorians and Their Rituals*, vol. 1, 174.

531. Tfinkdji, 'L'Église chaldéene catholique autrefois et aujourd'hui', 520.

532. Professor Amir Harrak, conversation with author, 10 February 2008.

533. AAS, 'Field Mission Iraq 2004'; Eshoo, 'The Fate of Assyrian Villages', 22.

534. Professor Amir Harrak, conversation with author, 10 February 2008.

535. Badger, *The Nestorians and Their Rituals*, vol. 1, 174.

536. Tfinkdji, 'L'Église chaldéene catholique autrefois et aujourd'hui', 520.

537. *Iraq: Continuous and Silent Ethnic Cleansing*, 41.

538. Ibid.; AAS, 'Field Mission Iraq 2004'.

539. Eshoo, 'The Fate of Assyrian Villages',' 16.

540. Tfinkdji, 'L'Église chaldéene catholique autrefois et aujourd'hui', 520.

541. Eshoo, 'The Fate of Assyrian Villages', 16.

542. Ibid.

543. AAS, 'Field Mission Iraq 2004'.

544. Human Rights Watch, *Iraq's Crime of Genocide*, 190.

545. AAS, 'Field Mission Iraq 2004'.

546. Human Rights Watch, *Iraq's Crime of Genocide*, 190.

547. Eshoo, 'The Fate of Assyrian Villages', 17.

548. Ibid.

549. AAS, 'Field Mission Iraq 2004'.

550. Ibid.

551. Eshoo, 'The Fate of Assyrian Villages', 17.

552. *Iraq: Continuous and Silent Ethnic Cleansing*, 41.

553. Eshoo, 'The Fate of Assyrian Villages', 18.

554. *Iraq: Continuous and Silent Ethnic Cleansing*, 41.

555. Ibid.

556. AAS, 'Field Mission Iraq 2004'.

557. Eshoo, 'The Fate of Assyrian Villages', 17.

558. Tfinkdji, 'L'Église chaldéene catholique autrefois et aujourd'hui', 520.

559. Eshoo, 'The Fate of Assyrian Villages', 16.

560. Ibid.

561. *Iraq: Continuous and Silent Ethnic Cleansing*, 41.

562. AAS, 'Field Mission Iraq 2004'.

Appendix B: Documents Concerning Cultural and Political Organisations

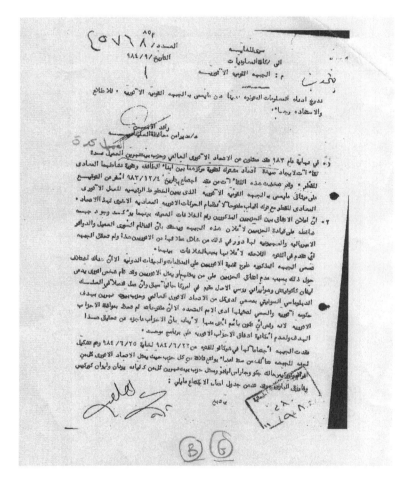

Figure 37 Security major, Sulaymaniyah district security manager to all administrative departments, 'Assyrian National Front', September 1984. ADM Archives, Baʿth Secret Files and Correspondence, p. 1

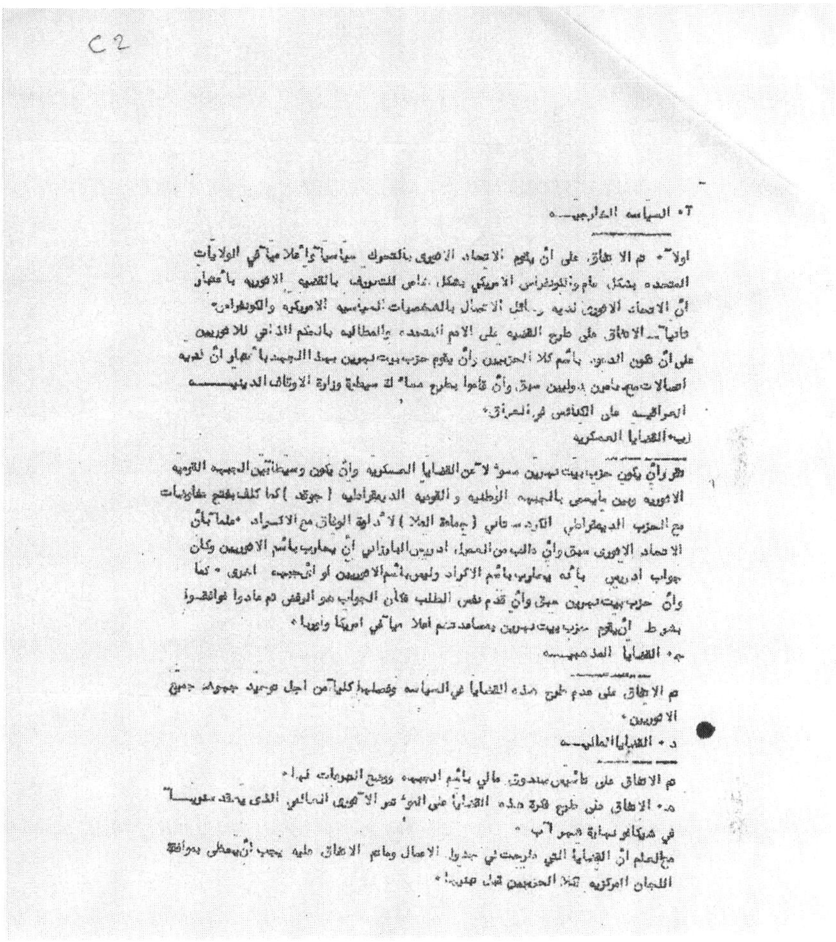

C2

٣ ٠ السياسة الخارجيه

اولاً ـ تم الاتفاق على ان يقوم الاتحاد الاشوري بالتحرك سياسياً اعلامياً في الولايات المتحدة بشكل عام ولكردستان الامريكي بشكل خاص للتعريف بالقضيه باعتبار ان الاعضاء الاشوريين لديهم رصيد الاعمال بالشخصيات لدى السياسه الامريكيه والكونغراس

ثانياً ـ تم الاتفاق على طرح القضيه على الامم المتحده والمطالبه بالدعم الذي تحظى به على ان يكون الدعم بأسم كلا الحزبين وان يقوم حزب بيت نهرين بمد الجهد بما تمار ان لديه اتصالات مهمه بامم دوليين سوف وان يقدموا يطرح بما لك سيطرة وزارة الاوقاف الدينيه والمراقبه على الكنائس في العراق ٠

ب ـ القضايا العسكريه

نظر وان يكون حزب بيت نهرين مسؤولاً عن القضايا العسكريه وان يكون وسيط بين الجبهه التربيه الاشوريه وبين مايسمى بالجبهه الوطنيه والقوميه الديمقراطيه (جوده) كما كلف بفتح مفاوضات مع الحزب الديمقراطي الكردستاني (جماعة العلا) لا دراجه الاتفاق مع الاكراد ٠ علماً بأن الاتحاد الاشوري سبق وان طرح على دالب من المعلم ادريس البارزاني ان يحارب بأسم الاشوريين وكان جواب ادريس بأنه يحاربون بأسم الاكراد وليس بأسم الاشوريين او اي جبهه اخرى ٠ كما وان حزب بيت نهرين سبق وان قدم نفس الطلب فكان الجواب هو الرفض ثم عادوا ووافقوا بشرط اشباع مزيد بيت نهرين ومساعدتهم اعلاً بما في امريكا واينها ٠

ج ٠ القضايا المذهبيه

تم الاتفاق على عدم طرح هذه القضايا في السياسه وفصلها كلياً من اجل توحيد جهود جميع الاشوريين ٠

د ٠ القضايا المالية

تم الاتفاق على تأسيس صندوق مالي باسم الجبهه ودفع التبرعات فيه ٠ هـ ٠ الاتفاق على طرح فكرة هذه القضايا على الملأ عبر الاشورى النائمي الذي يعقد سنوياً في شيكاغو بداية شهر آب ٠ مع العلم ان القضايا التي تم ادراجها في جدول الاعمال وتم الاتفاق عليه يجب ان يعطى بموافقة اللجان المركزيه لكلا الحزبين قبل طرحها ٠

Figure 38 Security major, Sulaymaniyah district security manager to all administrative departments, 'Assyrian National Front', September 1984. ADM Archives, Ba'th Secret Files and Correspondence, p. 2

Number: 45768
Date: 9/1984

Highly Confidential
To: All Administrative Departments
Subject: Assyrian National Front

We have the following information regarding what they call the Assyrian National Front. Please review and provide us with useful information.

Security Major
Sulaymaniyah District Security Manager,

First, at the end of 1983 the traitorous Assyrian Universal Alliance and Beth Nahrain Party had many meetings to find a way to unite and strengthen their position among their people and strengthen opposition activity against the country [Iraq]. As a result of those meetings both sides signed a treaty agreement called the Assyrian National Front. This treaty shows the highlights of how the Assyrians will oppose the country [Iraq], by leaving the door open to other opposing Assyrian organisation to join this alliance.

Second, even thought both parties have conflicts between them they declared their agreement. This proves that there is pressure on both leaders of the two parties to declare their front. It is assumed that the disloyal Syrian regime and the Zionist [Israel] and Imperialist [United States] agencies play a role in this through the Assyrians, since this front did not make any advancement until recent times due to conflicts between them.

This front seeks to put forward the Assyrian cause before international organisations but there is a disagreement in regards to who will represent the Assyrians. An Assyrian man by the name of Ivan Kakovich of Iranian Russian origins residing currently in the USA was previously a diplomat in the Soviet Government. He attempted to form an Assyrian government with both parties to be represented before the United Nations, but his proposal did not receive an approval from any Assyrian party since he refused to represent the name of any of the parties, he did not believe that any of the Assyrian political parties could fulfill this goal because the Assyrian political parties can not agree on a united political agenda.

The Assyrian front hosted a meeting in Chicago between 22/6/1984 until 21/6/1984 and a formation of a committee of six people was formed, three people from each party. The Assyrian United Alliance was presented by Afram, Gewargis Malik Chikko and Geras Awador. The Beth Nahrain party was represented by Giliana Younan, Ewan Gewargis and Faroq Al-Bazi. The meeting contained the following:

a) Foreign Affairs:
First: an agreement that the AUA acts politically to create awareness regarding the Assyrian cause by doing general advertisements as well as

within Congress. The Assyrian Alliance has associations with political figures in the United States and Congress.

Second: an agreement to propose the cause before the United Nations and plea for an administrative region for the Assyrians. This plea will be proposed under the name of both parties. The Beth Nahrain party is well connected with international lawyers that have opposed the control of the Iraqi Ministry of Religion over Iraqi churches.

b) Military Affairs:
The Beth Nahrain party agreed to take responsibility of military functions and mediate between the Assyrian National Front and the Democratic Front. They also opened negotiations with the Kurdish Democratic Party in order to work with each other even though the AUA has previously requested from the traitor Idris al-Barzani to fight under the Assyrian name. Idris replied that if they [Assyrians] wanted they could fight but under the condition that they fight under the Kurdish name and not under Assyrian or any other front.

The Beth Nahrian party had previously requested the same thing, but they [Kurds] rejected at first, and then they agreed under the condition that the Beth Nahrain party would promote them [Kurdish Democratic Party] in America and Europe.

c) Religious Affairs:
They agreed to not discuss it [religious denominations] in politics and separated it completely for the sake of uniting all Assyrians.

d) Financial Affairs:
They agreed to form a financial account in the name of the Front, receive donations for it and agreed to propose these issues at the annual Assyrian Convention meeting in Chicago that takes place during the end of August.

The case proposed in the agenda of the meetings should be granted by an agreement of the caucus of both parties before approving them.

Figure 39   Translation of 'Assyrian National Front'

Figure 40   Security major, Sulaymaniyah Security Directorate to all security divisions, 'Assyrian Democratic Movement', 14 October 1984. ADM Archives, Ba'th Secret Files and Correspondence

In the name of God the merciful and compassionate
Suleimaniyeh Security Directorate
Number: 54648
Date: 1984/10/14

Top Secret and personal and to be opened by the addressee
To: all Security Divisions

Subject: Assyrian Democratic Movement

The autonomy security directorate, through its letter, number 26846, dated
1984/10/06, has informed us that the following was ordered:

1. The security agencies are charged to squash any organisation within the
ranks of the Assyrians and keep them from progressing, especially inside cities.

2. Prepare a list of all influential individuals within the ranks of Assyrians in
the church and among the general community. The list should be updated on
regular basis. The prominent individuals among them in the community will
be provided personal and financial help etc. [To become Ba'th informants]

3. Identify the individuals who are not likely to reform. [Those who resisted
in becoming loyal Ba'th party supporters]. Provide us with their names and
information about them and what is recommended in each individual case.
Give this subject the utmost attention and keep us informed.

[Signature]
Major, Security
For/ Security Directorate/Suleimaniyeh Governorate

Figure 41   Translation of 'Assyrian Democratic Movement'

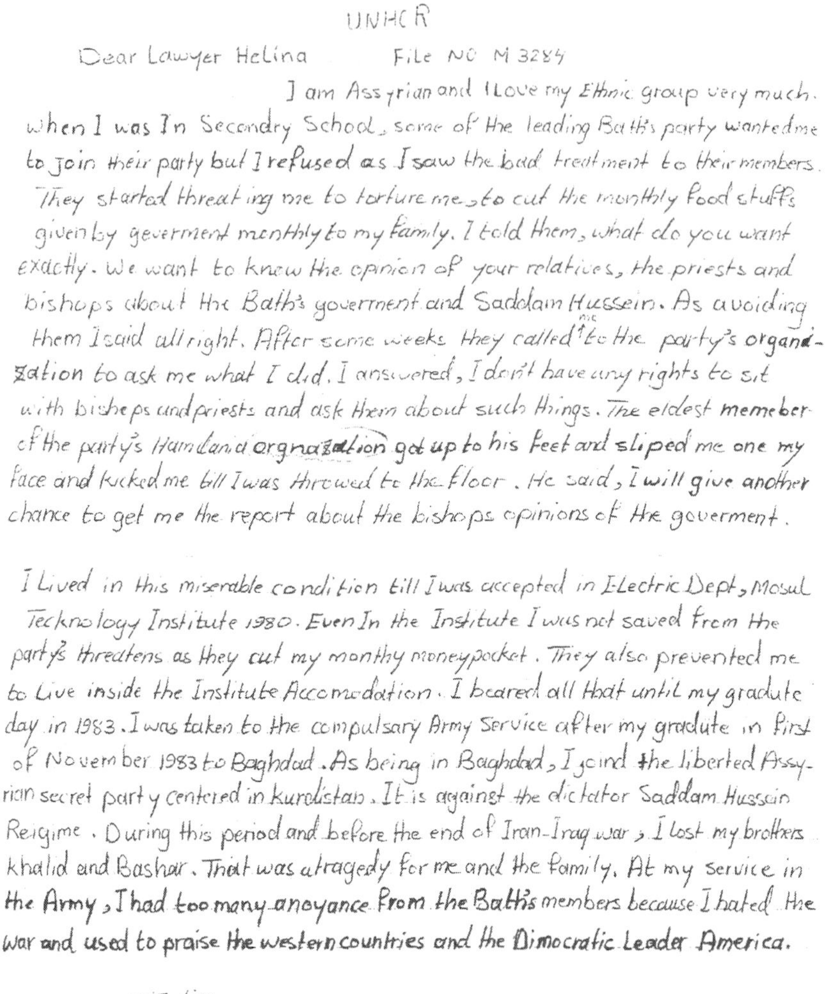

UNHCR

Dear Lawyer Helina   File NO M 3284

      I am Assyrian and I Love my Ethnic group very much.
when I was In Secondry School, some of the leading Baths party wanted me
to join their party but I refused as I saw the bad treatment to their members.
They started threating me to torture me, to cut the monthly food stuffs
given by geverment monthly to my family. I told them, what do you want
exactly. We want to know the opinion of your relatives, the priests and
bishops about the Baths government and Saddam Hussein. As avoiding
them I said allright. After some weeks they called¹ to the party's organ¹-
zation to ask me what I did. I answered, I don't have any rights to sit
with bishops and priests and ask them about such things. The eldest memeber-
of the party's Hamdan organazation got up to his feet and sliped me one my
face and kicked me till I was throwed to the floor. He said, I will give another
chance to get me the report about the bishops opinions of the goverment.

I Lived in this miserable condition till I was accepted in ILectric Dept, Mosul
Tecknology Institute 1980. Even In the Institute I was not saved from the
party's threatens as they cut my monthly moneypocket. They also prevented me
to Live inside the Institute Accomodation. I beared all that until my graduate
day in 1983. I was taken to the compulsary Army Service after my graduate in first
of November 1983 to Baghdad. As being in Baghdad, I joind the liberted Assyrian secret party centered in kurdistan. It is against the dictator Saddam Hussein
Reigime. During this period and before the end of Iran-Iraq war, I lost my brothers
khalid and Bashar. That was a tragedy for me and the family. At my service in
the Army, I had too many anoyance from the Baths members because I hated the
war and used to praise the western countries and the Dimocratic Leader America.

¹ organization

Figure 42 Document concerning the ill treatment of an individual Assyrian which
received attention at the international level. UNHCR file no. 3284 (Afram Rayis
private archive)

Bibliography

Archive Collections and Reports

1. Public Record Office, London

Air Ministry
AIR 2 Air Ministry and Ministry of Defence registered files
AIR 23 Air Ministry and Ministry of Defence: Royal Air Force overseas commands, reports and correspondence 1922–32
Military Report on Iraq (Area 9) Central Kurdistan, 1929

Cabinet Office
CAB 24 First World War memoranda; interwar memoranda

Colonial Office
CO 58 *Special Report by His Majesty's Government in the United Kingdom of Great Britain and Northern Ireland to the Council of the League of Nations on the Progress of 'Iraq During the Period 1920–1931*, 1931
CO 59-65 *Special Report by His Majesty's Government in the United Kingdom of Great Britain and Northern Ireland to the Council of the League of Nations on the Progress of 'Iraq for the Period January to October, 1932*, 1933
CO 537 Colonies, general 1921–2
CO 730 Iraq, correspondence

Foreign Office
FO 371 General correspondence 1906–66; correspondence between London and Baghdad; interdepartmental correspondence on Iraq
FO 608 Records of conferences, committees and councils 1918–20; Peace Conference: British delegation, correspondence and papers

FO 839 Records of conferences, committees and councils 1922–3: Lausanne
The Weekly Gazette of the Republic of Iraq

2. League of Nations Archive, Geneva

League of Nations Official Journal 14 (1933), 1823–8
League of Nations Secretariat, *League of Nations Questions*, 1935.
Report by the UK to the League of Nations on the Administration of 'Iraq for the Year 1930, Colonial No. 62, London: 1931
'Report of Mar Shimun, Catholicos Patriarch of the Assyrians, Oct 8, 1933', in *Protection of Minorities in Iraq*, 31 October 1933
Report of the Committee of the Council on the Settlement of the Assyrians of Iraq in the Region of the Ghab (French Mandated Territories of the Levant), League of Nations Publications, Series I: Political, vol. 1935.VII.12.3.
Report on the Economic Conditions of the Assyrians in the Northern Provinces in Iraq, C.296.M.172.1938.VII, 10 September 1938, 1–31
Settlement of the Assyrians of Iraq, 0.69.1934.VII, 18 January 1934
Textes des pétitions et observations y relatives des puissances mandataires examinées au cours de la 22ème session de la commission permanente des mandats tenue a Genève du 3 novembre au 6 décembre 1932, c.p.m. 1298.

3. United States National Archives and Records, Washington, DC

General Records of the Department of State, General Political Developments in Iraq, 787.00, Internal Affairs, 1960–January 1963; Records of the Department of State Relating to Internal Affairs of Iraq, 1930–1944; Records of the Department of State; Central Files 1967–69
Record Group 59: National Archives at College Park – Archives II (College Park, MD); US Department of State Online Archive
Record Group 263: Records of the Central Intelligence Agency 1894–2002, Series: Intelligence Publication Files 1946–1950

4. United Nations Reports

Convention on Prevention and Punishment of the Crime of Genocide, 9 December 1948, https://treaties.un.org/doc/Publication/UNTS/Volume%2078/volume-78-I-1021-English.pdf
'Convention on the Prevention and Punishment of the Crime of Genocide: Declarations and Reservations', United Nations Treaty Collection https://treaties.un.org/Pages/ViewDetails.aspx?mtdsg_no=IV-1&chapter=4&lang=en#EndDec

Summary Record of the Fourteenth Meeting of the Ad Hoc Committee on Genocide, UN ESCOR, E/AC.25/SR.14, 1948

'Unesco and the Struggle against Ethnocide', Declaration of San José, December 1981, http://unesdoc.unesco.org/images/0004/000499/049951eo. pdf

United Nations Declaration on the Rights of Indigenous Peoples, 13 September 2007, http://www.un.org/esa/socdev/unpfii/documents/DRIPS_ en.pdf

United Nations Document A/C.6/SR.83

United Nations Economic and Social Council Report, A/5429, 36th session, 11 July 1963

5. Presbyterian Historical Society, Philadelphia, Board of Foreign Missions

6. Woodrow Wilson Presidential Library, Staunton, Virginia

Cary T. Grayson Papers

7. Library of Congress

The Iraq Times
Alwaqai Aliraqiya: The Official Gazette of the Republic of Iraq

8. Modern Assyrian Research Archive, Stockholm

Action assyro-chaldéenne, Beirut
Al-Fikr al-Masihi, Baghdad
Athra, Beirut
Khuyada Umtanaya, Beirut
Mordinna Atouraya, Baghdad

9. Assyrian Universal Alliance Foundation Library (Ashurbanipal Library), Chicago

Nineveh, Berkeley, CA
Qala Suryaya, Baghdad

10. Afram Rayis, Assyrian Universal Alliance Secretary General, private archive, Michigan

Assyrian Sentinel, Hartford, CT

11. Iraq Memory Foundation Archives, Hoover Institution, Stanford University

Ba'th Regional Command Collection
North Iraq Data Set (NIDS)

12. WikiLeaks

US Department of State Documents

13. Superior Court of the State of California

14. Center for Jewish History, New York

Raphael Lemkin Collection, Genocide as a Crime under International Law (Box 6, Folder 2)

Unpublished Material/ Private Collections

Assyrian Academic Society, 'Field Mission Iraq 2004', report and database
Assyrian Democratic Movement Archives, Ba'th Secret Files and Correspondence

Select Oral Interviews and Correspondence

B.A. (Komāne), interview with author, 26 July 2008, Toronto
Banipal Babella (Baghdad), interview with author, 12 July 2013, San Jose, California
B.B. (Harīr), interview with author, 17 February 2008, Toronto
C.C. (Darbandoke), interview with author, 17 February 2008, Toronto
D.I. (Inishke), interview and email correspondence, 1–10 January 2008
D.T. (Blejanke), interview with author, 24 February 2008, Toronto
D.Y. (Komāne), interview with author, 26 July 2008, Toronto
Elias Haroon Bazi (Hejerke-Simele), interview with author, 24 February 2008, Toronto
Firas Jatou (Baghdad), interview with author, 5 July 2012, San Jose, California
Hirmis Aboona PhD (Alqosh), interview with author, 11 October 2007, Mississauga, Ontario
I.Y. (Diyana), interview with author, 17 February 2008, Toronto, Canada
K.D. (Komāne), interview with author, 26 July 2008, Toronto, Canada
K.S. (Dūre), interview with author, 24 February 2008, Toronto, Canada
Mikhael Benjamin, Nineveh Center for Research and Development, Qaraqosh, Iraq, email correspondence, February–October 2007
M.S. (Tel Keppe), interview with author, 13 August 2007, Detroit

P.D. (Dūre, Hayyis), interview with author, 26 July 2008, Toronto

Prof. Peter Gran, personal correspondence, 11 November 2013

P.W. (Diyana), interview with author, 17 February 2008, Toronto

R.B. (Kirkuk), interview with author, 16 January 2008, Toronto

S.A. (Dūre), interview with author, 2 July 2007, Toronto

Dr Shorsh Haji Resool, personal correspondence, 3 July 2008

T.S. (Dūre), interview with author, 19 July 2008, Toronto

Y.C. (Darbandoke-Baghdad), interview with author, 1 September 2006, Chicago

Y.D. (Annūnē), interview with author, 24 February 2008, Toronto

Y.G. (Bebede), interview with author, 24 February 2008, Toronto

Z.Y. (Annūnē), interview with author, 24 February 2008, Toronto

Reports and Compilations

American Sunday-School Union, Committee of Publication, *The Nestorians of Persia: A History of the Origin and Progress of the People, and of the Missionary Labours amongst Them* (Philadelphia: American Sunday-School Union, 1848)

Amnesty International Report 1979 (London: Amnesty International, 1979).

Amnesty International Report 1985 (London: Amnesty International, 1985).

Amnesty International Report 1989 (London: Amnesty International, 1989).

Amnesty International Report 1991 (London, Amnesty International, 1991).

Assyrian Academic Society in conjunction with Human Rights without Frontiers, *The ChaldoAssyrians of Iraq: The Indigenous Christian Minority at Risk*, February 2004.

A Catalogue of Paris Peace Conference Delegation Propaganda in the Hoover War Library (Stanford, CA: Stanford University Press, 1926)

'The Chaldoassyrian Community in Today's Iraq: Opportunities and Challenges', Human Rights without Frontiers Mission Report, November 2003, http://www.aina.org/reports/hrwf.htm (accessed 17 July 2014)

The Claims of the Assyrians before the Conference of the Preliminaries of Peace at Paris (Paris: Rosen, 1919)

A Committee of Officials, *An Introduction of the Past and Present of the Kingdom of Iraq* (Baltimore, MD: Lord Baltimore Press, 1946).

Al-Dalīl al-ʿIrāqī ['The Official Directory of Iraq'] (Baghdad, 1936)

'Guide to the Raphael Lemkin (1900–1959) Collection, 1763–2002 (Bulk 1941–1951)', American Jewish Historical Society, http://digifindingaids.cjh.org/?pID=109202

A Handbook of Mesopotamia, vol. IV: Northern Mesopotamia and Central Kurdistan, Admiralty War Staff, Intelligence Division, CB 296, April 1917.

A Handbook of Mesopotamia, vol. IV: Northern Mesopotamia and Central Kurdistan, Corrections and Additions, Admiralty War Staff, Intelligence Division, CB 296A, December 1918.

International Committee of the Red Cross, Geneva Convention Relative to the Protection of Civilian Persons in Time of War, 12 August 1949, http://www.unhcr.org/refworld/pdfid/3ae6b36d2.pdf

Iraq: Continuous and Silent Ethnic Cleansing – Displaced Persons in Iraqi Kurdistan and Iraqi Refugees in Iran (Paris: FIDH/International Alliance for Justice, 2003).

Iraq: Human Rights Abuses in Iraqi Kurdistan since 1991, Amnesty International, February 1995.

Iraq Ministry of Information, 'Granting the Cultural Rights to the Turkman and Syriac-speaking Nationals', Information Series 58 (Baghdad: Al-Hurriya, 1974).

Iraq Sustainable Democracy Project, *ChaldoAssyrians of Iraq & the Iraqi Interim Constitution* (Chicago: Assyrian Academic Society, 2004)

Iraq Sustainable Democracy Project, 'Northern Iraq Human Rights Field Mission', 2006, http://www.iraqdemocracyproject.org/pdf/Northern%20Iraq%20Human%20Rights%20Field%20Mission.pdf

'Nazi Occupied Europe 1941–1945: Genocide of Roma-Sinti (Parajmos)', Prevent Genocide International website, http://www.preventgenocide.org/edu/pastgenocides/nazi/parajmos/resources/

Report of the American Section of the International Commission on Mandates in Turkey (the King–Crane Commission Report), Paris, 28 August 1919

Reports by Her Majesty's Diplomatic and Consular Agents in Turkey Respecting the Condition of the Christian Subjects of the Porte 1868–75 (London, 1877)

Rome Statute of the International Criminal Court, July 1998, http://www.icc-cpi.int/NR/rdonlyres/ADD16852-AEE9-4757-ABE7-9CDC7CF02886/283503/RomeStatutEngl.pdf

Royal Government of Iraq, *Correspondence Relating to Assyrian Settlement from 13th July, 1932 to 5th August, 1933* (Baghdad: Government Press, 1933).

United States Department of State, Bureau of Democracy, Human Rights, and Labor, 'International Religious Freedom Report 2005: Iraq', http://www.state.gov/j/drl/rls/irf/2005/51600.htm

Updated Statute of the International Criminal Tribunal for the Former Yugoslavia, September 2009, http://www.icty.org/x/file/Legal%20Library/Statute/statute_sept09_en.pdf

Accessible Magazines and Newspapers

Archaeology
Assyrian International News Agency
Assyrian Star
Bahra
Brisbane Courier-Mail
Canberra Times
The Guardian
Huffington Post
Kurdistan Tribune
Lowell Sun
Al-Monitor
New York Times
San Antonio Light
Al-Thawra

Books and Articles

Abdullah, Thabit A. J., *A Short History of Iraq: From 636 to the Present* (London: Pearson Longman, 2003)

Aboona, Hirmis, *Assyrians, Kurds, and Ottomans: Intercommunal Relations on the Periphery of the Ottoman Empire* (Amherst, NY: Cambria Press, 2008)

Ainsworth, W. Francis, 'The Assyrian Origin of the Izedis or Yezidis – the So-called "Devil Worshippers",' *Transactions of the Ethnological Society of London*, vol. 1 (1861), 11–44

Allison, Christine, *The Yezidi Oral Tradition in Iraqi Kurdistan* (Richmond: Curzon Press, 2001)

Anderson, Benedict, *Imagined Communities: Reflections on the Origin and Spread of Nationalism*, 2nd ed. (London: Verso, 1991)

Anderson, Betty S., *The American University of Beirut: Arab Nationalism and Liberal Education* (Austin: University of Texas Press, 2011)

Andrade, Nathanael John, '"Imitation Greeks": Being Syrian in the Greco-Roman World (175 BCE–275 CE)', PhD dissertation, University of Michigan, 2009

Antonius, George, *The Arab Awakening: The Story of the Arab National Movement* (Philadelphia: J. B. Lippincott, 1939)

Appadurai, Arjun, *Fear of Small Numbers: An Essay on the Geography of Anger* (Durham, NC: Duke University Press, 2006).

Aprim, Fred, 'Assyrians in the World War I Treaties: Paris, Sèvres, and Lausanne', *Assyrian Star* 58.1 (2006)

Aprim, Frederick, *Assyrians: From Bedr Khan to Saddam Hussein – Driving into Extinction the Last Aramaic Speakers* (Frederick A. Aprim, 2006).

Aprim, Frederick, *Indigenous People in Distress* (Chicago: Assyrian Academic Society Press, 2003)

Aprim, Frederick, 'El-Qosh (Alqosh), Yimma d'Athor (The Mother of Assyria)', August 2004, http://www.fredaprim.com/pdfs/2004/Alqosh.pdf

Al-Arif, Ismail, *Iraq Reborn: A Firsthand Account of the July 1958 Revolution and After* (New York: Vantage Press, 1982)

Atto, Naures, *Hostages in the Homeland, Orphans in the Diaspora: Identity Discourses among the Assyrian/Syriac Elites in the European Diaspora* (Leiden: Leiden University Press, 2011)

Auron, Yair, *The Banality of Indifference: Zionism and the Armenian Genocide* (New Brunswick, NJ: Transaction, 2000).

Austin, H. H., *The Baqubah Refugee Camp: An Account of Work on Behalf of the Persecuted Assyrian Christians* (London: Faith House Press, 1920)

Baaba, Youel, *The Assyrian Homeland before World War I* (Alamo, CA: Youel A. Baaba Library, 2009)

Badger, George Percy, *The Nestorians and Their Rituals*, 2 vols (London: Darf, [1852] 1987)

Banerjee, Pompa, *Burning Women: Widows, Witches, and Early Modern European Travelers in India* (New York: Palgrave, 2003)

Baram, Amatzia, *Culture, History, and Ideology in the Formation of Ba'thist Iraq 1968–89* (Basingstoke: Macmillan, 1991)

Bartov, Omer and Eric Weitz (eds), *Shatterzone of Empires: Coexistence and Violence in the German, Hapsburg, Russian, and Ottoman Borderlands* (Bloomington: Indiana University Press, 2013)

Barzana, 'Abdyešu', *Dašna d-Saybūtī* ['The Gift of My Elder Years'] (Chicago: Assyrian Academic Society Press, 2003)

Barzana, 'Abdyešu', *Sinnē d-'Asqūtā: Qrābā d-Dayrabūn w-Ggunḥā d-Simele* ['Years of Hardship: The Battle of Dayrabun and Massacre of Simele'] (Chicago: Assyrian Academic Society Press, 2003)

Bashkin, Orit, *The Other Iraq: Pluralism and Culture in Hashemite Iraq* (Stanford, CA: Stanford University Press, 2009)

Batatu, Hanna, *The Old Social Classes and the Revolutionary Movements in Iraq* (London: Saqi, [1978] 2004).

Baumer, Christoph, *The Church of the East: An Illustrated History of Assyrian Christianity* (London: I. B. Tauris, 2006)

Bengio, Ofra, 'Faysal's Vision of Iraq: A Retrospect', in Asher Susser and Aryeh Shmuelevitz (eds), *The Hashemites in the Modern Arab World: Essays in Honour of the Late Professor Uriel Dann* (London: Frank Cass, 1995)

Betts, Robert Brenton, *Christians in the Arab East: A Political Study* (Athens: Lycabettus Press, 1975)

Bieńczyk-Missala, Agnieszka (ed.), *Rafał Lemkin: A Hero of Humankind* (Warsaw: Polski Instytut Spraw Międzynarodowych, 2010)

Black, George, *Genocide in Iraq: the Anfal Campaign against the Kurds* (New York: Human Rights Watch, 1993)

Black, Ian and Benny Morris, *Israel's Secret Wars: The Untold History of Israeli Intelligence* (London: Hamish Hamilton, 1991)

Bloxham, Donald, *The Great Game of Genocide, Imperialism, Nationalism, and the Destruction of the Ottoman Armenians* (Oxford: Oxford University Press, 2005)

Bou-Nackie, N. E., 'Les Troupes Speciales: Religious and Ethnic Recruitment 1916–46', *International Journal of Middle East Studies* 25.4 (1993), 645–60.

Brentjes, Burchard, *The Armenians, Assyrians and Kurds: Three Nations, One Fate?* (Campbell, CA: Rishi, 1997)

Brock, S. P., 'Christians in the Sasanian Empire: A Case of Divided Loyalties', in Stuart Mews (ed.), *Religion and National Identity: Papers Read at the 19th Summer Meeting and the 20th Winter Meeting of the Ecclesiastical History Society* (Oxford: Basil Blackwell, 1982), 1–19

Browne, Brigadier-General J. G. 'The Assyrians: A Debt of Honour', *Geographical Magazine* 4.6 (1936)

Browne, J. Gilbert, *The Iraq Levies 1915–1932* (London: Royal United Service Institution, 1932)

Bryce, James and Arnold Toynbee, *The Treatment of Armenians in the Ottoman Empire, 1915–16: Documents Presented to Viscount Grey of Fallodon by Viscount Bryce (Uncensored Edition)*, ed. Ara Sarafian, 2nd ed. (London: Gomidas Institute, 2005).

Budge, E. A. Wallis, *The Book of Governors: The Historia Monastica of Thomas Bishop of Marga AD 840*, 2 vols (London: Kegan Paul, Trench, Trübner, 1893)

Busch, Briton Cooper, *Britain, India, and the Arabs 1914–1921* (Berkeley, CA: University of California Press, 1971).

Canon, Yousip Nimrud, 'Tashʿītā', *Mordinna Atouraya* 1.1 (1973).

Castellino, Joshua and Kathleen A. Cavanaugh, *Minority Rights in the Middle East* (Oxford: Oxford University Press, 2013)

'The ChaldoAssyrian Community in Today's Iraq: Opportunities and Challenges', Human Rights without Frontiers Mission Report, November 2003

Charny, Israel, 'The Psychological Satisfaction of Denials of the Holocaust or Other Genocides by Non-extremists or Bigots, and Even by Known Scholars', *IDEA: A Journal of Social Issues* 6.1 (2001)

Chatty, Dawn, *Displacement and Dispossession in the Modern Middle East* (Cambridge: Cambridge University Press, 2010)

Chevalier, Michel, Montagnards chrétiens du Hakkâri et du Kurdistan septentrional (Paris: Université de Paris-Sorbonne, 1985)

Chiarello, Barbara, 'Deflected Missives: Zitkala-Ša's Resistance and Its (Un)Containment', *Studies in American Indian Literatures* 17.3 (2005), 1–26

Choueiri, Youssef M., *Arab Nationalism: A History – Nation and State in the Arab World* (Oxford: Blackwell, 2000)

Churchill, Ward, *A Little Matter of Genocide: Holocaust and Denial in the Americas, 1492 to the Present* (Winnipeg: Arbeiter Ring, 1998).

Clastres, Pierre, *Society against the State: Essays in Political Anthropology*, tr. Robert Hurley (New York: Zone, 1988)

Cleveland, William L., *The Making of an Arab Nationalist: Ottomanism and Arabism in the Life and Thought of Sati' al-Husri* (Princeton, NJ: Princeton University Press 1971)

Clyne, Meghan, 'Kana's Iraq', National Review Online, 19 May 2004, http://www.nationalreview.com/articles/210717/kanas-iraq/meghan-clyne

Coakley, J. F., *The Church of the East and the Church of England: A History of the Archbishop of Canterbury's Assyrian Mission.* Oxford: Clarendon Press, 1992.

Cole, Juan, 'The difficulty writing Iraqi history in the United States'. History News Network, 20 January 2003, http://hnn.us/articles/1207.html

Cooper, John, *Raphael Lemkin and the Struggle for the Genocide Convention* (Basingstoke: Palgrave Macmillan, 2008)

Cordesman, Anthony H. and Ahmed S. Hashim, *Iraq: Sanctions and Beyond* (Boulder, CO: Westview Press, 1997)

Crone, Patricia and Michael Cook, *Hagarism: The Making of the Islamic World* (Cambridge: Cambridge University Press, 1977)

Cuinet, Vital, *La Turquie d'Asie: géographie administrative, statistique, descriptive et raisonée de chaque province de l'Asie-Mineure*, 4 vols (Paris: Leroux, 1890–5)

Cunliffe-Owen, Betty, *Thro' the Gates of Memory: From the Bosphorus to Baghdad* (London: Hutchinson, 1924)

Curry, Patrick, *Defending Middle-Earth: Tolkien, Myth and Modernity* (New York: Houghton Mifflin, 2004)

Curtis, John, 'The Achaemenid Period in Northern Iraq', presented at the Archéologie de l'empire achéménide colloquium, Collège de France, Paris, 21–22 November 2003, http://www.aina.org/articles/curtis.pdf

Cutts, Edward Lewes, *Christians under the Crescent in Asia* (London: Society for Promoting Christian Knowledge; New York, Pott, Young, 1877)

Dann, Uriel, *Iraq under Qassem: A Political History 1958–1963* (New York: Praeger, 1969).

Davidson, Lawrence, *Cultural Genocide* (New Brunswick, NJ: Rutgers University Press, 2012)

Davis, Eric, *Memories of State: Politics, History, and Collective Identity in Modern Iraq* (Berkeley: University of California Press, 2005)

Davison, Roderic H., *Nineteenth-century Ottoman Diplomacy and Reforms* (Istanbul: Isis Press, 1999)

Dawisha, Adeed, *Arab Nationalism in the Twentieth Century: From Triumph to Despair* (Princeton, NJ: Princeton University Press, 2002)

Dawisha, Adeed, *Iraq: A Political History from Independence to Occupation* (Princeton, NJ: Princeton University Press, 2009)

Dawood, Fadi, 'Minorities and Makings of the Modern Iraqi State: Refugees and Warriors – The Case of Assyrians 1920–1933', thesis, University of London, 2014

Dere, Eliyo and Thomas Isik, *Tash'ito d-Ḥāyē d-Yuḥanon Dolabani* ['Biography of Yuhanon Dolabani'] (Södertälje, Sweden: Assyriska Riksförbundet Sverige, 2007)

Dinno, Khalid and Amir Harrak, 'Six Letters from Paul Bedjan to Aphram Barsoum the Syriac Orthodox Patriarch of Syria and Lebanon', *Journal of the Canadian Society for Syriac Studies* 9 (2009), 55–73.

Donabed, Ninos and Sargon Donabed, *Assyrians of Eastern Massachusetts* (Charleston, SC: Arcadia, 2006)

Donabed, Sargon, 'The Assyrian Heroic Epic of Qaṭīne Gabbara: A Modern Poem in the Ancient Bardic Tradition', *Folklore* 118.3 (2007), 342–55

Donabed, Sargon, 'Neither Syriac-speaking nor Syrian Orthodox Christians: (K) Harputli Assyrians in the United States as a Model for Ethnic Self-Categorization and Expression', in H. G. B. Teule, E. Keser-Kayaalp, K. Akalin, N. Doru and M. S. Toprak (eds), *Syriac in its Multi-cultural Context* (Leuven: Peeters, 2014)

Donabed, Sargon, *Remnants of Heroes: The Assyrian Experience* (Chicago: Assyrian Academic Society Press, 2003)

Donabed, Sargon, 'Rethinking Nationalism and an Appellative Conundrum: Historiography and Politics in Iraq', *National Identities* 14.4 (2012), 407–31.

Donabed, Sargon and Shamiran Mako, 'Ethno-cultural and Religious Identity of Syrian Orthodox Christians', *Chronos* 19 (2009), 69–111

Donef, Racho, *Massacres and Deportation of Assyrians in Northern Mesopotamia: Ethnic Cleansing by Turkey 1924–1925* (Stockholm: Nsibin, 2009)

Duara, Prasenjit, 'Historicizing National Identity, or Who Imagines What and When', in Geoff Eley and Ronald Grigor Suny (eds), *Becoming National: A Reader* (New York: Oxford University Press, 1996), 150–77

Duff, Douglas V., *Poor Knight's Saddle* (London: Herbert Jenkins, 1938)

Duval, Rubens, *Išoyahb Patriarchae III: Liber Epistularum* (Leuven: CSCO, 1962)

Eastman, Elaine, 'The Ghost Dance War', in Stephen Duncombe (ed.), *Cultural Resistance: A Reader* (London: Verso, 2002), 193–200

Edmonds, Cecil, *Kurds, Turks, and Arabs: Politics, Travel, and Research in Northeastern Iraq, 1919–1925* (New York: AMS Press, [1957] 1988)

Eickelman, Dale F., *The Middle East: An Anthropological Approach*, 2nd ed. (Englewood Cliffs, NJ: Prentice Hall, 1989)

Elder, Tanya, 'What You See before Your Eyes: Documenting Raphael Lemkin's Life by Exploring His Archival Papers 1900–1959', in Dominik J. Schaller and Jürgen Zimmerer (eds), *The Origins of Genocide: Raphael Lemkin as a Historian of Mass Violence* (Abingdon: Routledge, 2009)

Ellis, Deborah, *Children of War: Voices of Iraqi Refugees* (Toronto: Groundwood, 2009)

Encyclopedia Judaica, 2nd ed. (Farmington Hills, MI: Macmillan Reference USA, 2007)

Eppel, Michael, 'The Elite, the *Effendiyya*, and the Growth of Nationalism and Pan-Arabism in Hashemite Iraq, 1921–1958', *International Journal of Middle East Studies* 30.2 (1998), 227–50.

Eshoo, Majed, 'The Fate of Assyrian Villages Annexed to Today's Dohuk Governorate in Iraq and the Conditions in These Villages Following the Establishment of the Iraqi State in 1921', tr. Mary Challita, Assyrian General Conference website, 2004, http://www.assyriangc.com/magazine/eng1.pdf

Farouk-Sluglett, Marion and Peter Sluglett, 'The Historiography of Modern Iraq', *American Historical Review* 96.5 (1991), 1408–21

Farrokh, Kaveh, *Shadows in the Desert: Ancient Persia at War* (Oxford: Osprey, 2007)

Field, Henry, *The Anthropology of Iraq* (Millwood, NY: Kraus Reprint, [1940] 1968)

Field, Henry, 'Reconnaissance in Southwestern Asia', *Southwestern Journal of Anthropology* 7.1 (1951), 86–102

Fieldhouse, D. K., *Kurds, Arabs and Britons: The Memoir of Wallace Lyon in Iraq 1918–44* (London: I. B. Tauris, 2002)

Fiey, J. M., *Assyrie Chrétienne*, 3 vols (Beirut: Imprimerie Catholique, 1963)

Fiey, J. M., '"Assyriens" ou "Araméens"?', *L'Orient syrien* 10 (1965), 141–60

Fiey, J. M., 'Pour un Oriens Christianus Novus: répertoire des diocèses syriaques orientaux et occidentaux', *Beiruter Texte und Studien* 49 (1993)

Fischer, Eric, *Minorities and Minority Problems* (Takoma Park, MD: Erasmus House, 1980)

Fisher, John, *Curzon and British Imperialism in the Middle East 1916–19* (London: Frank Cass, 1999)

Fisk, Robert, *The Great War for Civilisation: The Conquest of the Middle East* (London: Fourth Estate, 2005)

Gaunt, David, 'Failed Identity and the Assyrian Genocide', in Omer Bartov and Eric D. Weitz (eds), *Shatterzone of Empires: Coexistence and Violence in the German, Habsburg, Russian, and Ottoman Borderlands* (Bloomington: Indiana University Press, 2013)

Gaunt, David, *Massacres, Resistance, Protectors: Muslim–Christian Relations in Eastern Anatolia during World War I* (Piscataway, NJ: Gorgias Press, 2006)

Gaury, Gerald de, *Three Kings in Baghdad: The Tragedy of Iraq's Monarchy* (London: I. B. Tauris, [1961] 2008)

Ghareeb, Edmund, *The Kurdish Question in Iraq* (New York: Syracuse University Press, 1981)

Ghareeb, Edmund A., *Historical Dictionary of Iraq* (Lanham, MD: Scarecrow Press, 2004)

Giwargis, Ashor, 'Until when? The Assyrian ethnicity persecuted and marginalized in its own homeland', tr. Mary C., *Zinda Magazine*, 30 September 2002

Habbi, Yūsuf, 'Christians in Iraq', in Andrea Pacini (ed.), *Christian Communities in the Arab Middle East: The Challenge of the Future* (Oxford: Clarendon Press, 1998)

Hamilton, A. M., *Road through Kurdistan: The Narrative of an Engineer in Iraq*, new ed. (London: Faber & Faber, 1958)

Hancock, Ian, 'Downplaying the Porrajmos: The Trend to Minimize the Romani Holocaust', review of Guenter Lewy, *The Nazi Persecution of the Gypsies, Journal of Genocide Research* 3.1 (2001), 79–85.

Hanoosh, Yasmeen, 'The Politics of Minority: Chaldeans between Iraq and America', PhD dissertation, University of Michigan, 2008

Harrak, Amir, 'Middle Assyrian bīt ḫašīmi', *Zeitschrift für Assyriologie und Vorderasiatische Archäologie* 79.1 (1989), 61–72

Harrak, Amir, 'Northern Mesopotamia in a 19th Century Syriac Annalistic Source', *Le Muséon: revue d'études orientales* 119.3–4 (2006), 293–305.

Hay, Sir William Rupert KCIE, *Two Years in Kurdistan: Experiences of a Political Officer 1918–1920* (London: Sidgwick & Jackson, 1921)

Heazell, Rev. F. N., Mrs Margoliouth and Jessie Payne, *Kurds and Christians* (London: Wells Gardner, Darton, 1913)

Hewitt, William, *Defining the Horrific: Readings on Genocide and Holocaust in the 20th Century* (Upper Saddle River, NJ: Pearson Education, 2004)

Hiltermann, Joost R., 'Case Study: The 1988 Anfal Campaign in Iraqi Kurdistan', Online Encyclopedia of Mass Violence, 3 February 2008, http://www.massviolence.org/Article?id_article=98&artpage=10

Hoffmann, Georg, *Auszüge aus syrischen Akten persischer Märtyrer* (Nendeln, Liechtenstein: Kraus, [1880] 1966)

Hourani, A. H., *Minorities in the Arab World* (London: Oxford University Press, 1947)

Human Rights Watch, *Iraq's Crime of Genocide: The Anfal Campaign against the Kurds* (New Haven, CT: Yale University Press, 1995)

Al-Ḥuṣrī, Sāṭiʿ, *Mudhakkirātī fī al-Iraq 1921–1941*, 2 vols (Beirut: Dar al-Taliah, 1967–8)

Husry, Khaldun, 'The Assyrian Affair of 1933 (I)', *International Journal of Middle East Studies* 5.2 (1974), 161–76

Husry, Khaldun, 'The Assyrian Affair of 1933 (II)', *International Journal of Middle East Studies* 5.3 (1974), 344–60

Iacovetta, Franca, Roberto Perin and Angelo Principe (eds), *Enemies Within: Italian and Other Internees in Canada and Abroad* (Toronto: University of Toronto Press, 2000)

Iadicola, Peter and Anson Shupe, *Violence, Inequality, and Human Freedom*, 2nd ed. (Lanham, MD: Rowman & Littlefield, 2003)

İnönü, İsmet, 'Hey'et-i Vekîle Riyâsetine', tr. Racho Donef, *Turkish Historical Society*, 15 January 1923

Isaac, Isaac, *Riyāḍiyah fī bilād mā bayn al-nahrayn* ['Sports in the Land of Mesopotamia'], 2 vols (Chicago: Alpha Graphic, 2000)

Isaac, Mardean, 'The desperate plight of Iraq's Assyrians and other minorities', *The Guardian*, 24 December 2011.

Isaac, Paul, 'The Urgent Reawakening of the Assyrian Question in an Emerging Iraqi Federalism: The Self-determination of the Assyrian People', *Northern Illinois University Law Review* 29.1 (2008), 209–43

Ishaya, Arianne, 'Settling into Diaspora: A History of Urmia Assyrians in the United States', *Journal of Assyrian Academic Studies* 20.1 (2006)

Ishow, Habib, *Les Structures sociales et politiques de l'Irak contemporain: pourquoi un état en crise?* (Paris: Harmattan, 2003)

Ishow, Habib, 'Un Village irakien, «Araden» en 1961', *Cahiers de l'Orient contemporain* (1966), 6–9

Ismael, Malik Yaqo (d'Malik), *Aturayé w-tre plashe tībilayé* ['Assyrians and the Two World Wars'] (Tehran: Assyrian Writers Board, 1964)

Ismael, Tareq and Jacqueline Ismael, *Government and Politics of the Contemporary Middle East: Continuity and Change* (Abingdon: Routledge, 2011)

Ismael, Tareq Y., *The Rise and Fall of the Communist Party of Iraq* (Cambridge: Cambridge University Press, 2008)

Israel, Khaziqaya, 'Freedom', *Mordinna Atouraya* 1.3–4 (1974)

Jacobson, Matthew Frye, *Whiteness of a Different Color: European Immigrants and the Alchemy of Race* (Cambridge, MA: Harvard University Press, 1998)

Jaulin, Robert, *La Paix blanche: introduction à l'ethnocide* (Paris: Seuil, 1970)

Al-Jeloo, Nicholas, 'Characteristics of Pre-19th Century Assyrian Christian Architecture East of the Tigris River: An Evaluation and Analysis Based on the Study of 114 Examples from Across the Region', MA thesis, Faculty of Theology, Leiden University, 2006

Jones, Adam, *Genocide: A Comprehensive Introduction* (London: Routledge, 2006)

Joseph, Isya, *Devil Worship: Sacred Books and Traditions of the Yezidiz* (Boston: Gorham Press, 1919)

Joseph, John, 'The Assyrian Affair: A Historical Perspective', *International Journal of Middle East Studies* 6.1 (1975), 115–17

Joseph, John, *The Modern Assyrians of the Middle East: Encounters with Western Christian Missions, Archaeologists, and Colonial Powers* (Leiden: Brill, 2000)

Joseph, John, *The Nestorians and Their Neighbors: A Study of Western Influence on Their Relations* (Princeton, NJ: Princeton University Press, 1961)

Joseph, John, 'The Turko-'Irāqi Frontier and the Assyrians', in James Kritzeck and R. Bayly Winder (eds), *The World of Islam: Studies in Honour of Philip K. Hitti* (London: Macmillan, 1959)

Al-Kan'ani, Na'aman Maher, *Ḍoh 'alla shimāl al 'Irāq* ['Light from the North of Iraq'] (Baghdad, 1965)

Karsh, Efraim and Inari Rautsi, *Saddam Hussein: A Political Biography* (London: Brassey's, 1991)

Kaşgarlı, Mehlika Aktok, *Mardin ve yöresi halkından Turko-Semitler* (Kayseri, Turkey: Erciyes Üniversitesi, 1991)

Kasim, Tony, 'An Interview with Sami Yako', *Nineveh* 30.1–2 (2007)

Kedourie, Elie, *The Chatham House Version, and Other Middle East Studies* (New York: Praeger, 1970)

Khan, Geoffrey, 'Remarks on the Historical Background of the Modern Assyrian Language', *Journal of Assyrian Academic Studies* 21.1 (2007), 1–6.

Khoobyarian, Milt, *Unraveling Iraq: Roots of Instability* (Kearney, NE: Morris, 2002)

Khoury, Dina Rizk, 'History and Historiography of Modern Iraq', *Middle East Studies Association Bulletin* 39.1 (2005), 64–79.

Khoury, Dina Rizk, *Iraq in Wartime: Soldiering, Martyrdom, and Remembrance* (New York: Cambridge University Press, 2013)

Khoury, Dina Rizk, *State and Provincial Society in the Ottoman Empire: Mosul 1540–1834* (Cambridge: Cambridge University Press, 1997)

King, Martin Luther Jr, *Stride toward Freedom: The Montgomery Story* (Boston: Beacon Press, [1958] 2010)

Klapper, Bradley S., '3,000 Christians Flee "Killing Campaign" in Mosul, Iraq', Huffington Post, 11 October 2008, http://www.huffingtonpost.com/2008/10/11/3000-christians-flee-kill_n_133912.html

Kleiner, Richard, 'Lemkin's 35-year crusade against genocide reaches successful end', *La Crosse Tribune*, 22 September 1949

Koivurova, Timo, 'Can Saami Transnational Indigenous Peoples Exercise Their Self-determination in a World of Sovereign States?', in Nigel Bankes and Timo Koivurova (eds), *The Proposed Nordic Saami Convention: National and International Dimensions of Indigenous Property Rights* (Oxford: Hart, 2013)

Korbani, Agnes, *The Political Dictionary of the Modern Middle East* (Lanham, MD: University Press of America, 1995)

Korn, David, *Human Rights in Iraq* (New Haven, CT: Yale University Press, 1990)

Kottak, Conrad, *Mirror for Humanity: A Concise Introduction to Cultural Anthropology*, 4th ed. (Boston: McGraw-Hill, 2006)

Krotkoff, Georg, *A Neo-Aramaic Dialect of Kurdistan: Texts, Grammar, and Vocabulary* (New Haven, CT: American Oriental Society, 1982)

Kubie, Nora Benjamin, *Road to Nineveh: The Adventures and Excavations of Sir Austen Henry Layard* (Garden City, NY: Doubleday, 1964)

Kukis, Mark, *Voices from Iraq: A People's History 2003–2009* (New York: Columbia University Press, 2011)

Kyriakos, Fr M. and Dr V. Yonann, 'Devant la Conference de la paix', *Action assyro-chaldéenne* 1 (1920)

Laing-Marshall, Andrea, 'Modern Assyrian Identity and the Church of the East: An Exploration of Their Relationship and the Rise of Assyrian Nationalism from the World Wars to 1980', MA thesis, University of Toronto, 2001

Lamassu, Nineb, 'Gilgamesh's Plant of Rejuvenation and Qatine's Sisisambar', paper presented at Melammu Symposium: Globalisation in the First Millennium, Sofia, September 2008.

Laqueur, Walter, *Communism and Nationalism in the Middle East* (London: Routledge & Kegan Paul, 1956)

Layard, Austen Henry, *Nineveh and Its Remains: With an Account of a Visit to the Chaldaean Christians of Kurdistan, and the Yezidis, or Devil Worshippers; and an Enquiry into the Manners and Arts of the Ancient Assyrians* (London: John Murray, 1849)

LeBlanc, Lawrence J., *The United States and the Genocide Convention* (Durham, NC: Duke University Press, 1991)

Lemkin, Raphael, *Axis Rule in Occupied Europe: Laws of Occupation, Analysis of Government, Proposals for Redress* (Washington, DC: Carnegie Endowment for International Peace, 1944)

Levene, M., 'A Moving Target, the Usual Suspects and (Maybe) a Smoking Gun: The Problem of Pinning Blame in Modern Genocide', *Patterns of Prejudice* 33.4 (1999), 3–24.

Levene, Mark, 'Creating a Modern "Zone of Genocide": The Impact of Nation- and State-formation on Eastern Anatolia 1878–1923', *Holocaust and Genocide Studies* 12.3 (1998): 393–433.

Lewis, Jonathan Eric, 'Iraqi Assyrians: Barometer of Pluralism', *Middle East Quarterly*, Summer 2003

Lijphart, Arend, *Democracy in Plural Societies: A Comparative Exploration* (New Haven, CT: Yale University Press, 1977)

Longrigg, Stephen Hemsley, *Four Centuries of Modern Iraq* (Oxford: Clarendon Press, 1925)

Longrigg, Stephen Hemsley, *Iraq 1900–1950: A Political, Social and Economic History* (Beirut: Librairie du Liban, 1953)

Lorde, Audre, *Sister Outsider: Essays and Speeches* (New York: Random House, 2012)

Lorenz, Chris, 'Drawing the Line: "Scientific" History between Myth-making and Myth-breaking', in Stefan Berger, Linas Eriksonas and Andrew Mycock (eds), *Narrating the Nation: Representations in History, Media and the Arts* (New York: Berghahn, 2008, 35–55

Lorieux, Claude, *Chrétiens d'Orient en terres d'Islam* (Paris: Perrin, 2001)

Lyotard, Jean-François, *The Postmodern Condition: A Report on Knowledge*, tr. Geoff Bennington and Brian Massumi (Minneapolis: University of Minnesota Press, [1984] 1997)

McDowall, David, *A Modern History of the Kurds*, 3rd ed. (London: I. B. Tauris, 2004)

Mackey, Sandra, *The Reckoning: Iraq and the Legacy of Saddam Hussein* (New York: W. W. Norton, 2002)

Main, Ernest, *Iraq: From Mandate to Independence* (London: George Allen & Unwin, 1935)

Makdisi, Ussama, *Artillery of Heaven: American Missionaries and the Failed Conversion of the Middle East* (Ithaca, NY: Cornell University Press, 2009)

Makiya, Kanan, *Cruelty and Silence: War, Tyranny, Uprising, and the Arab World* (New York: W. W. Norton, 1993)

Makiya, Kanan, *Republic of Fear: The Politics of Modern Iraq*, rev. ed. (Berkeley: University of California Press, 1998)

Makko, Aryo, 'The Historical Roots of Contemporary Controversies: National Revival and the Assyrian 'Concept of Unity', *Journal of Assyrian Academic Studies* 24.1 (2010), 1–29

Malek, Yusuf, *The Assyrian Tragedy* (Annemasse, Switzerland: Granchamp, 1934)

Malek, Yusuf, *The British Betrayal of the Assyrians* (Chicago: Assyrian National Federation /Assyrian National League of America, 1935)

Malek, Yusuf, *Simeil: The Cemetery of Betrayed Giants* (Beirut, 1938)

Mamouri, Ali, 'Assyrians discuss possible state in Iraq', Al-Monitor, 20 August 2013, http://www.al-monitor.com/pulse/originals/2013/08/assyrians-iraq-autonom ous-state-dreams.html

Mann, Michael, *The Dark Side of Democracy: Explaining Ethnic Cleansing* (Cambridge: Cambridge University Press, 2005)

Marquis, Albert Nelson, *Who's Who in New England*, 2nd ed. (Chicago: A. W. Marquis, 1916)

Marr, Phebe, 'The Development of a Nationalist Ideology in Iraq 1920–1941', *Muslim World* 75.2 (1985), 85–101

Marr, Phebe, *A Modern History of Iraq* (Boulder, CO: Westview, 1985).

Martin, James J., *The Man Who Invented 'Genocide': The Public Career and Consequences of Raphael Lemkin* (Torrance, CA: Institute for Historical Review, 1984)

Martin, Pauline, *La Chaldée, esquisse historique, suivie de quelques réflexions sur l'Orient* (Rome, 1867)

Maṭar, Fu'ād, *Saddam Hussein: A Biographical and Ideological Account of His Leadership Style and Crisis Management* (London: Highlight, 1990)

Metz, Helen Chapin (ed.), *Iraq: A Country Study*, 4th ed. (Washington, DC: Library of Congress, 1990)

Middle East Watch, *Endless Torment: The 1991 Uprising in Iraq and Its Aftermath* (New York: Middle East Watch, 1992)

Middle East Watch, *Human Rights in Iraq* (New Haven, CT: Yale University Press, 1990)

Midlarsky, Manus I., *The Killing Trap: Genocide in the Twentieth Century* (Cambridge: Cambridge University Press, 2005)

Mohan, Giles and Gordon Wilson, 'The Antagonistic Relevance of Development Studies', *Progress in Development Studies* 5.4 (2005), 261–78.

Mouawad, Ray, 'Syria and Iraq – Repression: Disappearing Christians of the Middle East', *Middle East Quarterly*, Winter 2001

Mufti, Malik, 'Pan-Arabism and State Formation in Syria and Iraq 1920–1992', PhD dissertation, Harvard University, 1993

Mushe, Akhtiyar Benyamin, 'Leshanā d-Yimmā', *Mordinna Atouraya* 3.11 (1977)

Naayem, Joseph, *Shall This Nation Die?* (New York: Chaldean Rescue, 1921).

Naby, Eden, 'The Assyrians of Iran: Reunification of a "Millat" 1906–1914', *International Journal of Middle East Studies* 8 (1977), 237–49

Namik, Saïd and Rustom Nedjib, *La Question assyro-chaldéenne devant la Conférence de la paix* (Paris, 1919)

Natali, Denise, *The Kurds and the State: Evolving National Identity in Iraq, Turkey, and Iran* (Syracuse, NY: Syracuse University Press, 2005)

Nerburn, Kent (ed.), *The Soul of an Indian and Other Writings from Ohiyesa (Charles Alexander Eastman)* (Novato, CA: New World Library, 2001)

Niebuhr, Reinhold, *Moral Man and Immoral Society: A Study in Ethics and Politics* (New York: Scribner, 1960)

Niezen, Ronald, *The Origins of Indigenism: Human Rights and the Politics of Identity* (Berkeley: University of California Press, 2003)

Nisan, Mordechai, *Minorities in the Middle East*, 2nd ed. (Jefferson, NC: McFarland, 2002)

Nuro, Abrohom, *My Tour in the Parishes of the Syrian Church in Syria & Lebanon* (Beirut: Pioneer, 1967)

O'Ballance, Edgar, *The Kurdish Revolt 1961–1970* (Hamden, CT: Archon, 1973)

Odisho, Amir, 'Dūrī', *al-Fikr al-Masihi*, July–September 1996.

Olmstead, A. T., *History of the Persian Empire: Achaemenid Period* (Chicago: University of Chicago Press, 1948)

Olson, Robert W. and William F. Tucker, 'The Sheikh Sait Rebellion in Turkey (1925)', *Welt des Islams* 18.3–4 (1978), 195–211

O'Mahony, Anthony, 'The Chaldean Catholic Church: The Politics of Church–State Relations in Modern Iraq'. *Heythrop Journal* 45.4 (2004), 435–50

Omissi, David, 'Britain, the Assyrians and the Iraq Levies 1919–1932', *Journal of Imperial and Commonwealth History* 17.3 (1989), 301–22.

Osipov, Sergei G., 'Fraidon Atturaya in the Focus of the Soviet Press', *Melta* 10 (2000)

Ostler, Jeffrey, *The Plains Sioux and US Colonialism from Lewis and Clark to Wounded Knee* (Cambridge: Cambridge University Press, 2004)

Pappé, Ilan, *The Ethnic Cleansing of Palestine* (Oxford: Oneworld, 2007)

Parhad, Sam, *Beyond the Call of Duty: The Biography of Malik Kambar of Jeelu* (Chicago: Metropolitan Press, 1986)

Parpola, Simo, 'Assyrian Identity in Ancient Times and Today', Assyrian International News Agency, www.aina.org/articles/assyrianidentity.pdf

Parpola, Simo, 'Assyrians after Assyria', *Journal of Assyrian Academic Studies* 13.2 (1999)

Parpola, Simo, 'National and Ethnic Identity in the Neo-Assyrian Empire and Assyrian Identity in the Post-empire Times', *Journal of Assyrian Academic Studies* 18.2 (2004), 5–22

Parpola, Simo and Michael Porter, *The Helsinki Atlas of the Near East in the Neo-Assyrian Period* (Helsinki: Neo-Assyrian Corpus Text Project, 2001)

Perch, Harold. 'Biography of Abraham K. Yousef', in *Fiftieth Anniversary of St Mary's Assyrian Apostolic Church* (Worcester, MA: St Mary's Assyrian Apostolic Church, 1974

Perkins, Justin, *A Residence of Eight Years in Persia among the Nestorian Christians, with Notices of the Muhammedans* (Andover, MA: Allen, Morrill & Wardwell, 1843)

Perley, David Barsum JSD, *Whither Christian Missions? Reflections on the Works of a Missionary and on the Assyrian Case*, rev. ed. (Paterson, NJ: Kimball Press, 1946)

Peterson, Trudy Huskamp, 'Iraqi Records, US Involvement', 17 February 2008, http://www.trudypeterson.com/perspectives/

Petrosian, Vahram, 'Assyrians in Iraq', *Iran and the Caucasus* 10.1 (2006), 113–47

Petrovic, Drazen, 'Ethnic Cleansing: An Attempt at Methodology', *European Journal of International Law* 5.4 (1998), 1–19

Pierson, Paul, *Politics in Time: History, Institutions, and Social Analysis* (Princeton, NJ: Princeton University Press, 2004)

Pike, Kenneth Lee (ed.), *Language in Relation to a Unified Theory of Structure of Human Behavior*, 2nd ed. (The Hague: Mouton, 1967)

Pius, Michael K., 'Koubba Khouyada Aturaya was Born in Desert', *Nineveh* 22.3 (1999)

Polk, William R., *Understanding Iraq* (New York: HarperCollins, 2005)

Porterfield, Amanda, *Mary Lyon and the Mount Holyoke Missionaries* (New York: Oxford University Press, 1997)

Potros, Sargon Yousip, 'The Assyrian Rafidain Club in Basra City, Iraq', *Nineveh* 22.3 (1999)

Power, Samantha, *A Problem from Hell: America and the Age of Genocide* (New York: Basic, 2002)

Pratt, Scott L., 'Wounded Knee and the Prospect of Pluralism', *Journal of Speculative Philosophy* 19.2 (2005), 150–66

Preston, Zoë, *The Crystallization of the Iraqi State: Geopolitical Function and Form* (Bern: Peter Lang, 2003)

Prucha, Francis Paul, 'Wounded Knee through the Lens of Colonialism', *Diplomatic History* 29.4 (2005), 725–8

Prunhuber, Carol, *The Passion and Death of Rahman the Kurd: Dreaming Kurdistan* (Bloomington, IN: iUniverse, 2009)

Qarabashi, Abel Messiah Nu'man, *Dmo Zliho (Bloodshed/Vergossenes Blut): The Sorrowful Massacres and Tragedies of the Years 1915–1918* (Jönköping, Sweden: Ashurbanipals Bokförlag, 1997)

Al-Qaysī, Abd al-Majīd Hasīb, *al-Āthūriyūn fi al-ʿIrāq 1921–1999* ['The Assyrians in Iraq 1921–1999'] (Lebanon, 1999)

'La Question assyro-chaldéenne', *Action assyro-chaldéenne* 1 (1920)

Rae, Heather, *State Identities and the Homogenisation of Peoples* (Cambridge: Cambridge University Press, 2002)

Rassam, Hormizd, 'Biblical Nationalities Past and Present', in *Transactions of the Society of Biblical Archaeology*, vol. 8 (London: Society of Biblical Archaeology, 1885), 358–85

Rayis, Afram, 'Araden: A Living Village in Garbia', *Assyrian Star* 55.1 (2003), 32

Reneau, Reneau, *Misanthropology: A Florilegium of Bahumbuggery* (Inglewood, CA: Don Lazaro Translations, 2003)

'Residential schools apology too late, say survivors', CBC Online, 11 June 2008, http://www.cbc.ca/news/canada/prince-edward-island/residential-schools-apol ogy-too-late-say-survivors-1.719268

Rhétoré, Jacques, *Les chrétiens aux bêtes: souvenirs de la guerre sainte proclamée par les Turcs contre les chrétiens en 1915* (Paris: Cerf, 2005)

Rockwell, William Walker, *The Pitiful Plight of the Assyrian Christians in Persia and Kurdistan* (New York: American Committee for Armenian and Syrian Relief, 1916)

Rollinger, Robert, 'The Terms "Assyria" and "Syria" Again', *Journal of Near Eastern Studies* 65.4 (2006), 284–7

Romeny, Bas ter Haar, Naures Atto, Jan J. Van Ginkel, Mat Immerzeel and Bas Snelders, 'The Formation of a Communal Identity among West Syrian Christians: Results and Conclusions of the Leiden Project', in Bas ter Haar Romeny (ed.), *Religious Origins of Nations? The Christian Communities of the Middle East* (Leiden: Brill, 2010), 1–52

Rothfuss, Patrick, *The Name of the Wind* (New York: DAW, 2007)

Rubin, Avshalom H., 'Abd al-Karim Qasim and the Kurds of Iraq: Centralization, Resistance and Revolt 1958–63', *Middle Eastern Studies* 43.3 (2007), 353–82

Rudd, Jeffery A., 'Irak or Iraq? The Problem of Geographical Nomenclature in British Official Use', in Asher Susser and Aryeh Shmuelevitz (eds), *The Hashemites in the Modern World: Essays in Honour of the late Professor Uriel Dann* (London: Frank Cass, 1995), 111–38

'Saddam's Terrorizing of Christian Villages', WND, 4 August 2004, http://www. wnd.com/2004/08/25902/

Sáenz, Mario, *The Identity of Liberation in Latin American Thought: Latin American Historicism and the Phenomenology of Leopoldo Zea* (Lanham, MD: Lexington, 1999)

Said, Edward, *Representations of the Intellectual: The 1993 Reith Lectures* (London: Vintage, 1994)

Said, Edward W., *Orientalism* (New York: Pantheon, 1978)

Salibi, Kamal and Yusuf Khour, *The Missionary Herald: Reports from Northern Iraq 1833–1870* (Beirut: Royal Institute for Inter-Faith Studies, 1995)

Sanders, J. C. J., *Assyrian-Chaldean Christians in Eastern Turkey and Iran: Their Last Homeland Re-charted* (Hernen, Netherlands: AA Brediusstichting, 1997)

Sassoon, Joseph, *Saddam Hussein's Ba'th Party: Inside an Authoritarian Regime* (Cambridge: Cambridge University Press, 2012)

Schaller, Dominik J. and Jürgen Zimmerer (eds), *The Origins of Genocide: Raphael Lemkin as a Historian of Mass Violence* (Abingdon: Routledge, 2009)

Shedd, Mary Lewis, *The Measure of a Man: The Life of William Ambrose Shedd, Missionary to Persia* (New York: George H. Doran, 1922)

Shedd, William A., 'The Syrians of Persia and Eastern Turkey', *Bulletin of the American Geographical Society* 35.1 (1903), 1–7

Shimun, Theodore d'Mar, *The History of the Patriarchal Succession of the d'Mar Shimun Family*, 2nd ed. (Turlock, CA: Mar Shimun Memorial Foundation, 2008)

Shlimon d'Bit Badawi, Malik Loko, *Assyrian Struggle for National Survival in the 20th and 21st Centuries* (2012)

Silverfarb, Daniel, *Britain's Informal Empire in the Middle East: A Case Study of Iraq 1929–1941* (New York: Oxford University Press, 1986)

Simon, Reeva Spector, *Iraq between the Two World Wars: The Militarist Origins of Tyranny* (New York: Colombia University Press, 2004)

Sluglett, Peter, *Britain in Iraq: Contriving King and Country 1914–1932* (New York: Colombia University Press, 2007)

Sluglett, Peter and Marion Farouk-Sluglett, *Iraq since 1958: From Revolution to Dictatorship* (London: I. B. Tauris, 2001)

Smith, Anthony D., *The Antiquity of Nations* (Cambridge: Polity Press, 2004)

Smith, Linda Tuhiwai, *Decolonizing Methodologies: Research and Indigenous Peoples*, 2nd ed. (London: Zed, 2012)

Solecki, Ralph S., *Shanidar: The First Flower People* (New York: Knopf, 1971)

Southgate, Horatio, *Narrative of a Visit to the Syrian Church of Mesopotamia* (New York: Dana, 1844)

Stafford, R. S., 'Iraq and the Problem of the Assyrians', *International Affairs* 13.2 (1934), 159–85

Stafford, R. S., *The Tragedy of the Assyrians* (London: George Allen & Unwin, 1935)

Stansfield, Gareth R. V., *Iraqi Kurdistan: Political Development and Emergent Democracy* (London: RoutledgeCurzon, 2003)

Stern, Marcus, 'Worlds apart on Chaldean crisis', *San Diego Union Tribune*, 12 March 2003

Suermann, Harald, 'The History of Christianity in Iraq of the 20th and 21st Century', *The Harp: A Review of Syriac and Oriental Ecumenical Studies* 20.1 (2006), 171–94.

Sutton, Keith, 'Army Administration Tensions over Algeria's *Centres de regroupement* 1954–1962', *British Journal of Middle Eastern Studies* 26.2 (1999), 243–70

Mark Sykes, *The Caliphs' Last Heritage: A Short History of the Turkish Empire* (London: Macmillan, 1915)

Taneja, Preti, *Assimilation, Exodus, Eradication: Iraq's Minority Communities since 2003* (London: Minority Rights Group International, 2007)

Tashjian, James, *Turkey: Author of Genocide – The Centenary Record of Turkey 1822–1922* (Boston: Commemorative Committee on the 50th Anniversary of the Turkish Massacres of the Armenians, 1965)

Tejel, Jordi, Peter Sluglett, Riccardo Bocco and Hamit Bozarslan (eds), *Writing the Modern History of Iraq: Historiographical and Political Challenges* (Hackensack, NJ: World Scientific, 2012)

Tfinkdji, Joseph, 'L'Église chaldéenne catholique autrefois et aujourd'hui', *Annuaire Pontifical Catholique 1914* (Paris: Maison de la Bonne Presse, 1913), 449–525

Tomass, Mark K., 'Multiple Resource-sharing Groups as Basis for Identity Conflict', in Önver A. Cetrez, Sargon G. Donabed and Aryo Makko (eds), *The Assyrian Heritage: Threads of Continuity and Influence* (Uppsala: Acta Universitatis Upsaliensis, 2012)

Tomass, Mark K. 'Religious Identity, Informal Institutions, and the Nation-states of the Near East', *Journal of Economic Issues* 46.3 (2012), 705–28

Tomi, Habib Y., *Alqosh: Dirasa Anthropologiya, Ijtima'aiya, Thaqafiya* ['Alqosh: An Anthropological and Cultural Study'] (Baghdad: Sharikat al-Deewan li al-Tiba'aa, 2001)

Totten, Samuel and Paul R. Bartrop, *A Dictionary of Genocide, vol. I: A–L* (Westport, CT: Greenwood Press, 2008)

Travis, Hannibal, 'After Regime Change: United States Law and Policy Regarding Iraqi Refugees 2003–2008', *Wayne Law Review* 55.2 (2009), 1009–61

Travis, Hannibal, *Genocide in the Middle East: The Ottoman Empire, Iraq, and Sudan* (Durham, NC: Carolina Academic Press, 2010)

Travis, Hannibal, 'Native Christians Massacred: The Ottoman Genocide of the Assyrians during World War I', *Genocide Studies and Prevention* 1.3 (2006), 327–71

Tripp, Charles, *A History of Iraq*, 2nd ed. (Cambridge: Cambridge University Press, 2002)

Trouillot, Michel-Rolph, *Silencing the Past: Power and the Production of History* (Boston: Beacon Press, 1997)

Tucker, Michael, *Hell Is Over: Voices of the Kurds after Saddam* (Guilford, CT: Lyons Press, 2004).

Unrepresented Nations and Peoples Organization (UNPO), 'UN Calls for Return of Article 50', 13 October 2008, http://www.unpo.org/content/view/8775/81/

Valognes, Jean-Pierre, *Vie et mort des chrétiens d'Orient: des origines à nos jours* (Paris: Fayard, 1994)

Van Bruinessen, Martin, *Agha, Shaikh and State: The Social and Political Structures of Kurdistan* (London: Zed, 1992)

Van Dyke, Vernon, *Human Rights, Ethnicity, and Discrimination* (Newport, CT: Greenwood Press, 1985)

Vanly, Ismet Chériff, *The Revolution of Iraki Kurdistan: Part 1, September 1961 to December 1963* (Committee for the Defense of the Kurdish People's Rights, 1965)

Visser, Reidar, 'Historical Myths of a Divided Iraq', *Survival* 50.2 (2008), 95–106

Visser, Reidar, 'The Sectarian Master Narrative in Iraqi Historiography', in Jordi Tejel, Peter Sluglett, Riccardo Bocco and Hamit Bozarslan (eds), *Writing the Modern History of Iraq: Historiographical and Political Challenges* (Hackensack, NJ: World Scientific, 2012).

Wahby, Taufiq, 'The Rock Sculptures in Gunduk Cave', *Sumer* 4.2 (1948)

Weis, Margaret and Tracy Hickman, *Dragonlance Chronicles, vol. 3: Dragons of Spring Dawning* (Lake Geneva, WI: TSR, [1985] 1994)

Weitz, Eric, *A Century of Genocide: Utopias of Race and Nation* (Princeton, NJ: Princeton University Press, 2003)

Wendt, Alexander, *Social Theory of International Politics* (Cambridge: Cambridge University Press, 1999)

Werda, Joel E., *The Flickering Light of Asia or the Assyrian Nation and Church* (Joel E. Werda, 1924)

White, Benjamin Thomas, *The Emergence of Minorities in the Middle East: The Politics of Community in French Mandate Syria* (Edinburgh: Edinburgh University Press, 2011)

Wien, Peter, *Iraqi Arab Nationalism: Authoritarian, Totalitarian, and Pro-fascist Inclinations 1932–1941* (New York: Routledge, 2006)

Wigram, Rev. W. A. DD, *Our Smallest Ally: A Brief Account of the Assyrian Nation in the Great War* (London: Society for Promoting Christian Knowledge / New York: Macmillan, 1920)

Wigram, William A., *The Assyrians and Their Neighbours* (London: G. Bell, 1929)

Wilmshurst, David, *The Ecclesiastical Organization of the Church of the East 1318–1913* (Leuven: Peeters, 2000)

Wilson, Arnold T., 'The Middle East', *Journal of the British Institute of International Affairs* 5.2 (1926), 96–110

Wimmer, Andreas, 'Democracy and Ethno-religious Conflict in Iraq', paper presented at Center on Democracy, Development, and the Rule of Law, Stanford University, 5 May 2003, http://iis-db.stanford.edu/pubs/20214/wimmer.pdf

Wimmer, Andreas, *Nationalist Exclusion and Ethnic Conflict: Shadows of Modernity* (Cambridge: Cambridge University Press, 2002)

Yacoub, Claire Weibel, *Le rêve brisé des Assyro-Chaldéens: l'introuvable autonomie* (Paris: Cerf, 2011)

Yacoub, Joseph, *The Assyrian Question* (Chicago: Alpha Graphic, 1986)

Yacoub, Joseph, *Les Minorités: quelle protection?* (Paris: Desclée de Brouwer, 1995)

Yacoub, Joseph, *Les Minorités dans le monde: faits et analyses* (Paris: Desclée de Brouwer, 1998)

Yale, William, *The Near East: A Modern History* (Ann Arbor: University of Michigan Press, 1958)

Yildiz, Kerim, *The Kurds in Iraq: Past, Present and Future*, rev. ed. (London: Pluto Press, 2007)

Yohannan, Abraham, *The Death of a Nation; or, the Ever Persecuted Nestorians or Assyrian Christians* (New York: G. P. Putnam's Sons, 1916)

Yonan, Gabriele, *Assyrer heute* (Hamburg: Gesellschaft für bedrohte Völker, 1978)

Yonan, Gabriele, *Ein vergessener Holocaust: die Vernichtung der christlichen Assyrer in der Türkei* (Göttingen: Gesellschaft für Bedrohte Völker, 1989)

Yoosuf, A. K., *The Religion of Mohammed and Christian Sufferings* (Worcester, MA, 1905)

Youash, Michael, 'Iraq's Minority Crisis and US National Security: Protecting Minority Rights in Iraq', *American University International Law Review* 24.2 (2008)

Yousif, Basam, 'Development and Political Violence in Iraq 1950–1990', PhD dissertation, University of California Riverside, 2001

Yousif, Ephrem-Isa, *Parfums d'enfance a Sanate: un village chrétien au Kurdistan irakien* (Paris: Harmattan, 1993)

Zertal, Idith, *Israel's Holocaust and the Politics of Nationhood*, tr. Chaya Galai (Cambridge: Cambridge University Press, [2002] 2005)

Zubaida, Sami, 'Contested Nations: Iraq and the Assyrians', *Nations and Nationalism* 6.3 (2000), 363–82

Zubaida, Sami, 'The Fragments Imagine the Nation: The Case of Iraq', *International Journal of Middle East Studies* 34.2 (2002), 205–15

Zunes, Stephen, 'The US Obsession with Iraq and the Triumph of Militarism', in Tareq Y. Ismael and William W. Haddad (eds), *Iraq: The Human Cost of History* (London: Pluto Press, 2004)

Index